شرح الدروس المهمة لعامة الأمة

Explanation of
Important Lessons
(For Every Muslim)

2nd Edition: June 2003

© Maktaba Dar-us-Salam, 2002

King Fahd National Library Cataloging-in-Publication Data

Al-Arfaj, Muhammad bin Ali

Explanation of important lessons-Riyadh.

392p., 14x21 cm.

ISBN 9960-892-07-7

I-Islam, General Principles   I-Abdulaziz bin

Abdullah bin baz (author)   II- Title

210 dc.   1423/4716

Legal Deposit no. 1423/4716

ISBN 9960-892-07-7

شرح الدروس المهمة لعامة الأمة

Explanation of
Important Lessons
(For Every Muslim)

By
Abdul-Aziz bin Abdullah bin Baz

Compiled by
Muhammad bin Ali bin Ibrahim Al-Arfaj

Translated by
Darussalam

DARUSSALAM
Distributeur International de Livres Islamiques
Riyadh • Jeddah • Al-Khobar • Sharjah
Lahore • London • Houston • Newyork

2nd Edition: June 2003

Supervised by: **Abdul Malik Mujahid**

HEADOFFICE:

P.O. Box: 22743, Riyadh 11416 K.S.A.Tel: 00966-01-4033962/4043432 Fax: 4021659
E-mail: darussalam@awalnet.net.sa Website: www.dar-us-salam.com

K.S.A. Darussalam Showrooms:
  Riyadh
Olaya branch: Tel 00966-1-4614483 Fax: 4644945
Malaz branch: Tel 4735220 Fax: 4735221
- **Jeddah**
  Tel: 00966-2-6879254 Fax: 6336270
- **Al-Khobar**
  Tel: 00966-3-8692900 Fax: 00966-3-8691551
U.A.E
- Darussalam, Sharjah U.A.E
  Tel: 00971-6-5632623 Fax: 5632624
PAKISTAN
- Darussalam, 36 B Lower Mall, Lahore
  Tel: 0092-42-724 0024 Fax: 7354072
- Rahman Market, Ghazni Street
  Urdu Bazar Lahore
  Tel: 0092-42-7120054 Fax: 7320703
U.S.A
- Darussalam, Houston
  P.O Box: 79194 Tx 772779
  Tel: 001-713-722 0419 Fax: 001-713-722 0431
  E-mail: sales@dar-us-salam.com
- Darussalam, New York
  572 Atlantic Ave, Brooklyn
  New York-11217, Tel: 001-718-625 5925
U.K
- Darussalam International Publications Ltd.
  226 High Street, Walthamstow,
  London E17 7JH, Tel: 0044-208 520 2666
  Mobile: 0044-794 730 6706 Fax: 0044-208 521 7645
- Darussalam International Publications Limited
  Regent Park Mosque, 146 Park Road,
  London NW8 7RG Tel: 0044-207 724 3363
- Darussalam
  398-400 Coventry Road, Small Heath
  Birmingham, B10 0UF
  Tel: 0121 77204792 Fax: 0121 772 4345
  E-mail: info@darussalamuk.com
  Web: www.darussalamuk.com

FRANCE
- Editions & Librairie Essalam
  135, Bd de Ménilmontant- 75011 Paris
  Tél: 0033-01- 43 38 19 56/ 44 83
  Fax: 0033-01- 43 57 44 31
  E-mail: essalam@essalam.com
AUSTRALIA
- ICIS: Ground Floor 165-171, Haldon St.
  Lakemba NSW 2195, Australia
  Tel: 00612 9758 4040 Fax: 9758 4030
MALAYSIA
- E&D Books SDN. BHD.-321 B 3rd Floor,
  Suria Klcc
  Kuala Lumpur City Center 50088
  Tel: 00603-21663433 Fax: 459 72032
SINGAPORE
- Muslim Converts Association of Singapore
  32 Onan Road The Galaxy Singapore- 424484
  Tel: 0065-440 6924, 348 8344 Fax: 440 6724
SRI LANKA
- Darul Kitab 6, Nimal Road, Colombo-4
  Tel: 0094-1-589 038 Fax: 0094-74 722433
KUWAIT
- Islam Presentation Committee
  Enlightment Book Shop
  P.O. Box: 1613, Safat 13017 Kuwait
  Tel: 00965-244 7526, Fax: 240 0057
INDIA
- Islamic Dimensions
  56/58 Tandel Street (North)
  Dongri, Mumbai 4000 009,India
  Tel: 0091-22-3736875, Fax: 3730689
  E-mail:sales@IRF.net
SOUTH AFRICA
- Islamic Da'wah Movement (IDM)
  48009 Qualbert 4078 Durban,South Africa
  Tel: 0027-31-304-6883
  Fax: 0027-31-305-1292
  E-mail: idm@ion.co.za

Contents

In The Name Of Allâh, The Most Beneficent, The Most Merciful

Preface To The First Edition

Indeed, all praise is for Allâh, we praise Him, repent to Him, and seek His forgiveness and help. We seek refuge in Allâh from the evil of our own selves and our wicked deeds. Whomsoever Allâh guides, none can lead astray; and whomsoever Allâh leaves astray, none can guide. And I bear witness that none has the right to be worshipped except Allâh alone, and He has no partner; and I bear witness that our Prophet Muhammad is His servant and Messenger. May Allâh, send peace and blessings upon him, his family and his Companions until the Day of Judgement.

Indeed Allâh Almighty has protected this religion and raised its status among the nations, sending to the world the final Messenger, Muhammad ﷺ, and with him the final and most complete religion — as Allâh Almighty says:

﴿ٱلْيَوْمَ أَكْمَلْتُ لَكُمْ دِينَكُمْ وَأَتْمَمْتُ عَلَيْكُمْ نِعْمَتِى وَرَضِيتُ لَكُمُ ٱلْإِسْلَٰمَ دِينًا﴾

This day, I have perfected your religion for you, completed My Favor upon you, and have chosen for you Islam as your religion.[1]

Allâh Almighty has made the scholars inheritors of the Prophets; they explain to the people their religious duties and they enlighten them, so that their worship of Allâh Almighty is based on knowledge and insight. One such scholar, whom the Muslims recently lost, is the noble Shaikh and Imam, 'Abdul-'Aziz bin 'Abdullah bin Baz — may Allâh Almighty have mercy on him, for he spent his life in knowledge, in teaching, in passing scholarly judgements and rulings. But over and above his knowledge, he was a man who was righteous and pious; he sought little from this world, and his manners were truly noble. From the many works in which the Shaikh served the different branches of Islamic knowledge — *'Aqidah, Fiqh, Hadith, Da'wah*, and so on — is this very important work, *Important Lessons For Every Muslim*,[2] a book that is much needed at the present time

[1] (*Al-Ma'idah* 5:3)
[2] A translation of the text has been published by Darussalam.

because so many Muslims lack a grasp on the fundamentals of the religion, in terms of belief, worship, and manners.

Seeking reward, seeking to benefit others, and seeking to apply the *Hadith*:

«خَيْرُ النَّاسِ أَنْفَعُهُمْ لِلنَّاسِ»

The best of people is he who benefits others most.

I decided to explain this important book, expanding on the clear concepts and rules mentioned by the Shaikh. In explaining and expanding on the Shaikh's words, I relied heavily, first upon Allâh Almighty, and then upon the many other works of the Shaikh himself.

I chose to explain the copy printed by the Ministry of Islamic Affairs, Endowments, Preaching and Guidance; it is the last edition that was printed during the life of the Shaikh — may Allâh have mercy upon him. I chose it because it is the best copy in terms of organization and editing; moreover, it has an additional section on the topic of *Ihsan*.

To further help and encourage the reader — whether he is a student, teacher, caller to Islam, male, or female — I inserted questions for each lesson (at the end of the book), to help the student both understand and digest the material.

I ask Allâh Almighty by His Beautiful Names and Most High Attributes to rectify our intentions and to make our children righteous, and to grant us sincerity in speech and in deed; indeed, He is the One upon Whom we rely, and He is Most Capable of answering our prayers.

And the last of our supplications is that all praise is due to Allâh, the Lord of all that exists.

Muhammad bin 'Ali Al-'Arfaj

(May Allâh forgive him, his parents, and all Muslims)

Important Points To Consider
Before Reading The Book

1. We invite fathers and mothers who are in their old age, especially those who didn't have the opportunity to learn while they were young, to strive to correct their worship, so that by the Will of Allâh Almighty, they can have a good ending. When we say that they should correct their worship, we mean that they should worship Allâh Almighty based on correct knowledge. There are some Muslims, for example, who cannot properly recite *Al-Fatihah*, yet it is one of the pillars of prayer. The way to correct that problem is to seek guidance from those who are studying, whether it be from our own children or from students of knowledge, for Allâh Almighty says:

﴿فَسۡئَلُوٓاْ أَهۡلَ ٱلذِّكۡرِ إِن كُنتُمۡ لَا تَعۡلَمُونَ﴾

So, ask of those who know the Scripture (learned men of the Tawrah and the Injil), if you know not.[1]

Beware, brother Muslim, and do not allow *Iblis* to make you too proud to learn from those who are younger than you. The noble Companions, may Allâh be pleased with them, learned their religion from the Prophet ﷺ, and some of them were his elder relatives, and others though not relatives, were in their old age.

2. We invite the youth who have learned the precepts of their religion to correct the mistakes of their relatives, whether they are, for instance, their parents, grandfathers, or brothers. The youth should not be shy in this regard, nor should they disparage themselves, thinking they are too young to teach. If the youth have knowledge, they must teach their relatives, but with gentleness, manners, and wisdom, applying the saying of the Prophet ﷺ,

«إِنَّ اللهَ رَفِيقٌ يُحِبُّ الرِّفْقَ فِي الأَمْرِ كُلِّهِ وَيُعْطِي عَلَى الرِّفْقِ مَا لَا يُعْطِي عَلَى الْعُنْفِ»

Indeed Allâh is Most Gentle and He loves gentleness in all matters, and He gives for gentleness that which He doesn't

---

[1] (*An-Nahl* 16:43)

give for harshness.

Some historians related that once Al-Hasan and Al-Husain, may Allâh be pleased with them, saw an old man who was performing ablution incorrectly. They wanted to teach him in a gentle and kind way, so they approached him and said, "O uncle, we disagree about which of us performs ablution the best, and we want you to judge between us." Each of them took his turn in performing ablution before the man, and they said, "Rule between us." He said, "Indeed you have both done well, may Allâh bless the two of you (i.e. he realized that his own ablution was not done properly)." They said, "(We are) Al-Hasan and Al-Husain, the sons of 'Ali bin Abi Talib." He hugged them both and said admiringly, "Children, who take after their father."

Some historians related that on the day 'Umar bin 'Abdul-'Aziz, may Allâh be pleased with him, assumed the duties of the *Khilafah*, after burying Sulaiman bin 'Abdul-Malik (the previous *Khalifah*), he began to work immediately. He didn't sleep that night; instead, he stayed up to return important wealth to the Muslim treasury, to set free some slaves so that they could return to their families, and to take care of other important matters that related to the welfare of the Muslims. He continued working until *Zuhr* the following day. He prayed and then went out in search for a place to take a short afternoon nap. His son, 'Abdul-Malik, met him and said, "O leader of the believers, what are you intending to do?" He answered, "My son, I want to take a nap." "To take a nap without ruling between people, and returning the rights to their proper owners?" He said, "My son, I stayed up all night in the affairs of your uncle, Sulaiman. Even if I sleep, I will wake up and rule between people to return the rights to their proper owners." 'Abdul-Malik said, "O leader of the believers, who can guarantee for you that you will wake up and return them (i.e. the rights)." 'Umar said, "My son, come close." When he came close, his father took hold of him, kissed him between the eyes and said, "All praise is for Allâh, who has brought from my loins someone to help me in my religion." He went to work, without taking a nap or resting.

Notice — may Allâh have mercy on you — how 'Abdul-Malik was not shy to advise his father, and how 'Umar — may Allâh have mercy on him — was not too proud to take advice, even though he was, in this instance, both *Khalifah* and father.

3. Know that you must learn all that Allâh Almighty has made obligatory upon you in terms of your religious duties; give time to those duties just as you give time — perhaps a great portion of your time — to your worldly affairs.

May Allâh grant success to all, with that which He loves and is pleased with.

Foreword

1) Islam is the religion that Allâh Almighty created people upon, it is the religion that the Prophets and Messengers called to. Every Prophet invited his people to become Muslims, as Allâh Almighty said in His Magnificent Book regarding the father of Prophets and the *Khalil* of the Most Merciful, Ibrahim, peace be upon him:

﴿وَمَن يَرْغَبُ عَن مِّلَّةِ إِبْرَٰهِـۧمَ إِلَّا مَن سَفِهَ نَفْسَهُۥ وَلَقَدِ ٱصْطَفَيْنَٰهُ فِى ٱلدُّنْيَا وَإِنَّهُۥ فِى ٱلْءَاخِرَةِ لَمِنَ ٱلصَّٰلِحِينَ ﴿١٣٠﴾ إِذْ قَالَ لَهُۥ رَبُّهُۥٓ أَسْلِمْ قَالَ أَسْلَمْتُ لِرَبِّ ٱلْعَٰلَمِينَ ﴿١٣١﴾ وَوَصَّىٰ بِهَآ إِبْرَٰهِـۧمُ بَنِيهِ وَيَعْقُوبُ يَٰبَنِىَّ إِنَّ ٱللَّهَ ٱصْطَفَىٰ لَكُمُ ٱلدِّينَ فَلَا تَمُوتُنَّ إِلَّا وَأَنتُم مُّسْلِمُونَ ﴿١٣٢﴾﴾

And who turns away from the religion of Ibrahim (Islamic Monotheism) except him who fools himself? Truly, We chose him in this world and verily, in the Hereafter he will be among the righteous. When his Lord said to him, "Submit (i.e. be Muslim)." He said, "I have submitted myself (as a Muslim) to the Lord of all that exists." And this (submission to Allâh Almighty, Islam) was enjoined by Ibrahim upon his sons and by Ya'qub, (saying), "O my sons! Allâh Almighty has chosen for you the (true) religion, then die not except as Muslims"[1]

2) At the time when Allâh Almighty sent His Prophet Muhammad ﷺ, with this great religion, the Jews and the Christians were in a state of ignorance and misguidance after having distorted and corrupted the Tawrah and the Injil. Their desires led them to join the ranks of the disbelieving Quraish, and they too attacked Muhammad ﷺ and his mission, especially the Jews, even though they knew with certainty — from their own Scriptures — that they were supposed to believe in and follow the way of the Messenger of Allâh ﷺ:

﴿ٱلَّذِينَ ءَاتَيْنَٰهُمُ ٱلْكِتَٰبَ يَعْرِفُونَهُۥ كَمَا يَعْرِفُونَ أَبْنَآءَهُمْ وَإِنَّ فَرِيقًا مِّنْهُمْ لَيَكْتُمُونَ ٱلْحَقَّ وَهُمْ يَعْلَمُونَ ﴿١٤٦﴾﴾

Those to whom We gave the Scripture, recognize him as they recognize their sons. But verily a party of them conceal the

---
[1] (*Al-Baqarah* 2:130-132)

truth while they know it.[1]

3. As soon as our Prophet, Muhammad ﷺ, established himself in Al-Madinah, he sent messengers to the kings of the earth at that time, inviting them to the religion of Allâh Almighty, to remove them from the shadows of darkness to the light. When Rustum, the leader of Faris (Persia), asked one such messenger, Rab'i bin 'Amir, may Allâh be pleased with him, "What are you (people)?" Rab'i answered in a few words, "We are a people whom Allâh has sent, to take whom He wishes from people away from the worship of creatures to the worship of Allâh alone, from the narrowness of this world to the spaciousness (and comfort) of this world and the Hereafter, and from the injustice of religions to the justness of Islam."

4. This final message came to put matters in their rightful place and to direct people in the right direction; singling out Allâh, believing in His Prophets and Messengers, having faith in them, and inviting to their message of singling out Allâh and submitting oneself entirely to Him.

5. The merits of the religion of Islam are many and cannot be counted. It is the religion of Allâh Almighty, Who knows all things. His is the complete wisdom and irrefutable proofs. He is the All-Wise, the All-Knowing - in all that He willed and decreed, and in all that He legislated for His creatures. Therefore there is no matter that is good except that our Messenger ﷺ invited this nation to it, and there is no evil thing, except that he ﷺ has warned us against it. In his *Sahih*, Muslim recorded that 'Abdullah bin 'Amr bin Al-'Aas narrated from the Prophet ﷺ:

«مَا بَعَثَ اللهُ مِنْ نَبِيٍّ إِلَّا كَانَ حَقًّا عَلَيْهِ أَنْ يَدُلَّ أُمَّتَهُ عَلَى خَيْرِ مَا يَعْلَمُهُ لَهُمْ وَيُنْذِرَهُمْ شَرَّ مَا يَعْلَمُهُ لَهُمْ»

Allâh never sent a Prophet except that it was his duty to guide his nation to what he knew was good for them and to warn them against what he knew was evil for them.

In *Musnad Ahmad*, with an authentic chain of narration, it is recorded that Abu Hurairah, may Allâh be pleased with him, narrated that the Prophet ﷺ said.

---
[1] (*Al-Baqarah* 2:146)

«إِنَّمَا بُعِثْتُ لِأُتَمِّمَ صَالِحَ الأَخْلَاقِ»

Indeed I have been sent only to complete good manners.

Al-Hafiz Al-Khara'iti recorded it with a good [*Jayyid*] chain, but with the wording:

«إِنَّمَا بُعِثْتُ لِأُتَمِّمَ مَكَارِمَ الأَخْلَاقِ»

Indeed I have been sent only to complete the most noble of manners.

6. Indeed what we see today, that multitudes of people are entering the fold of Islam — people who were previously disbelievers, polytheists, People of the Book, both Jews and Christians — is a clear proof that other religions and philosophies have utterly failed to give peace, comfort, and happiness to people. Muslims then, and especially the callers, must be active among those nations in calling them to the religion of Allâh. But before we do that, we must not forget to exemplify Islam ourselves, in our knowledge and in our behavior, for human beings are in dire need of someone to remove them from the shadows of darkness to the light, by the Will of Allâh; Allâh Almighty says:

﴿وَمَنْ أَحْسَنُ قَوْلًا مِّمَّن دَعَآ إِلَى ٱللَّهِ وَعَمِلَ صَـٰلِحًا وَقَالَ إِنَّنِى مِنَ ٱلْمُسْلِمِينَ ٣٣﴾

And who is better in speech than he who invites men to Allâh, and does righteous deeds and says: "I am one of the Muslims."[1]

I ask Allâh to make us from those who call to good and to make us knowledgeable about our religion, just as I ask Him to grant us success when we are calling others to Him. Indeed He is able to grant that and He is All-Powerful over that. May Allâh send peace and blessings upon Muhammad, his family and his Companions.[2]

---

[1] (*Fussilat* 41:33)

[2] This is taken from the words of the venerated head *Mufti*, Shaikh 'Abdul-'Aziz bin 'Abdullah bin Baz entitled: *At-Ta'rif bil-Islam* from *Majmu' Al-Fatawa* 2:212-215 with minor editing.

Introduction

All praise is due to Allâh, Lord of all that exists; the successful ending is for those who have *Taqwa*. May Allâh send peace and blessings upon His servant and Messenger, our Prophet, Muhammad, upon his family and upon all of his Companions.

The following is a short work to explain what every Muslim needs to know about the religion of Islam. I called it, "Important Lessons For Every Muslim." I ask Allâh to cause the Muslims to benefit from it, and that He accept it from me. Indeed, He is Most Generous.

'Abdul-'Aziz bin 'Abdullah bin Baz

Lesson One

Surat Al-Fatihah And Other Short *Surahs*

One must learn *Surat Al-Fatihah* and whatever possible from the other short *Surahs*; from *Surat Az-Zalzalah* to *Surat An-Nas*, reciting them correctly; memorizing them, and their explanations which are required for one to understand.

❖ ❖ ❖

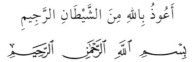

The Explanation of *Al-Isti'athah*

That is to say: (أَعُوذُ بِاللهِ مِنَ الشَّيْطَانِ الرَّجِيمِ) *A'oothu billahi minash-Shaitaanir-Rajeem* (I seek refuge in Allâh from the accursed *Shaitan*).

(أعوذ) *A'oothu*: I seek refuge, protection, and fortification in You, O Allâh.

(بالله) *Billahi*: The Lord of all things; the true God Who is worshipped alone, and He has no partner.

(الشيطان) *Ash-Shaitaan*: Otherwise known as *Iblis* or the Devil, may Allâh's curse be upon him.

(الرجيم) *Ar-Rajeem*: The one who is stoned, repelled, and banished - banished from all mercy and good; he has no power to harm us, neither in our worldly affairs nor in our religion.

The Meaning of *Al-Isti'athah*

I seek refuge and fortification from Allâh my Lord, against *Shaitan* (Satan) the accursed, that he confuse me while I recite, or that he should make me go astray, to destruction and misery.

When the Prophet ﷺ would stand up at night to pray, he would begin his prayer with the *Takbir*, then say:

«أَعُوذُ بِاللهِ السَّمِيعِ الْعَلِيمِ مِنَ الشَّيْطَانِ الرَّجِيمِ مِنْ هَمْزِهِ وَنَفْخِهِ وَنَفْثِهِ»

I take refuge with Allâh, the All-Hearing, the All-Knowing, from the accursed *Shaitan* — from his pride, his poetry, and his madness. (It was recorded by the *Sunan* Compilers)

The Ruling On *Al-Isti'athah*

Whenever one is about to recite the Qur'an — whether it is a chapter or more — it is Sunnah to first say, "I seek refuge in Allâh from the accursed *Shaitan*." It is also recommended to say this phrase when one is angry or when one has evil thoughts.

The Explanation of *Al-Basmalah*

That is to say:

بِنِـــمِ اللَّهِ الرَّحْمَنِ الرَّحِيـــمِ

Bismillaahir Rahmaanir Raheem (In the Name of Allâh, the Most Beneficent, the Most Merciful).

The Meaning of *Al-Basmalah*

Before doing anything, I begin by naming and remembering Allâh Almighty, seeking His help in everything, asking Him alone for support in all of my affairs. Indeed, He is the Lord, the One worshipped, His favors are many and great, His generosity is vast, and His mercy encompasses all creatures.

The Exalted Word (الله) *Allâh*: The Possessor of divinity and the right to be worshipped over all creatures. It is the Name known and recognized to refer to the Lord, Glorious and Most High.

(الرحمن) *Ar-Rahmaan* (The Most Beneficent): This is one of Allâh's Names; it is derived from *Ar-Rahmah*, or mercy, and it signifies its vastness. This name signifies a mercy that embraces all of creation, for Allâh Almighty creates them and provides for them; that is from the completeness of His favors, which is why it is said, "O *Rahmaan* over this world."

(الرحيم) *Ar-Raheem* (The Most Merciful): This is also one of Allâh's Names, and it too is derived from *Ar-Rahmah* (mercy), signifying the greatness of His mercy, but this time specifically for the believers in the Hereafter. Allâh Almighty says:

$$\text{﴿وَكَانَ بِٱلۡمُؤۡمِنِينَ رَحِيمًا ٤٣﴾}$$

And He is Ever Most Merciful to the believers.[1]

And that is why it is said, "O *Raheem* of the Hereafter."

The Ruling On *Al-Basmalah*

It is legislated for the worshipper, or one asking, to say, "In the Name of Allâh, the Most Beneficent, the Most Merciful," with his recitation of every *Surah* from the Book of Allâh Almighty except for *Surat At-Tawbah*, in which case it is not recited. In the obligatory *Salat* one says it silently, even during the audible prayers. It is Sunnah for the worshipper to say *Bismillah* when eating and drinking, wearing clothing, entering and exiting the *Masjid*, sitting on a mount, and for every important matter. Just as it is obligatory for him to say *Bismillah* and *Allâhu Akbar* when slaughtering (a sheep) or sacrificing a camel.

Methodology In Explaining The Selected *Surahs*

The following shall be the methodology in explaining the short *Surahs* that were chosen:

- The name of the *Surah*
- The subject of the *Surah*
- Its relation to what is before it
- Vocabulary
- To summarize the meaning
- The lessons from the *Surah*

---

[1] (*Al-Ahzab* 33:43)

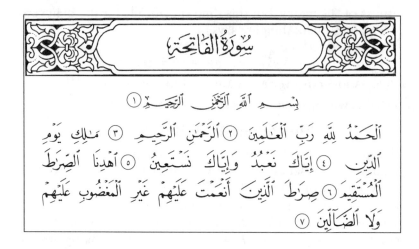

Surat Al-Fatihah

1. *In the Name of Allâh, the Most Beneficent, the Most Merciful.* **2.** *All the praise is due to Allâh, the Lord of Al-'Alamin.* **3.** *The Most Beneficent and the Most Merciful.* **4.** *The only Owner (and the Only Ruling Judge) of the Day of Recompense (i.e. the Day of Resurrection).* **5.** *You (alone) we worship and You (alone) we ask for help (for each and everything).* **6.** *Guide us to the straight path,* **7.** *The way of those on whom You have bestowed Your grace, not (the way) of those who earned Your anger nor of those who went astray.*

The Names Of This *Surah*

1) The Opening Chapter (*Fatihatul-Kitab*)
2) The Mother of the Book (*Ummul-Kitab*)
3) The Mother of the Qur'an (*Ummul-Qur'an*)
4) The Seven Oft-Recited and the Magnificent Qur'an (*As-Sab'ul-Mathani wal-Qur'anul-'Azim*)
5) The Praise (*Al-Hamd*), because it begins with the mention of praise.
6) The Prayer (*As-Salat*), because (the Prophet ﷺ mentioned that Allâh Almighty said):

«قَسَمْتُ الصَّلَاةَ بَيْنِي وَبَيْنَ عَبْدِي نِصْفَيْنِ» [رواه مسلم]

"I have divided the *Salat* into two halves between Me and My servant." (Reported by Muslim)

7) The Cure (*Ash-Shifa*)

8) The Incantation (*Ar-Ruqyah*)

9) The Protection *Al-Waqiyah*

The Virtues Of *Surat Al-Fatihah*

1) *Surat Al-Fatihah* is the greatest *Surah* of the Qur'an. The Prophet ﷺ said to Abu Sa'id bin Al-Mu'alla:

«لَأُعَلِّمَنَّكَ أَعْظَمَ سُورَةٍ فِي الْقُرْآنِ قَبْلَ أَنْ تَخْرُجَ مِنَ الْمَسْجِدِ»

I will teach you the greatest Surah of the Qur'an before you leave the *Masjid*.

He then said to him:

﴿ٱلْحَمْدُ لِلَّهِ رَبِّ ٱلْعَٰلَمِينَ﴾

All praise is for Allâh, Lord of all that exists.

2) In the story of the scorpion sting, which was recorded by Al-Bukhari, it implies that it is a sufficient cure, and that it may be used for *Ruqyah*.

3) To recite this chapter is one of the pillars of prayer: for both the *Imam* and the one who prays alone; therefore one's prayer is incomplete without it. As for the one who prays behind the *Imam*, reciting it is obligatory. Abu Hurairah narrated that the Prophet ﷺ said:

«مَنْ صَلَّى صَلَاةً لَمْ يَقْرَأْ فِيهَا بِأُمِّ الْقُرْآنِ فَهِيَ خِدَاجٌ – ثَلَاثًا – غَيْرُ تَمَامٍ»
[رواه مسلم]

Whoever performs *Salat*, without reciting *Ummul-Qur'an* in it, then it is insufficient (he said it three times:), it is not complete. (It was recorded by Muslim)

The Meanings Of Its Words

(ٱلْحَمْدُ لِلَّهِ) *Al-Hamdulillah*: *Al-Hamd* is praising Allâh with His perfect Attributes, loving Him, glorifying Him, and exalting Him.

(رَبِّ ٱلْعَٰلَمِينَ) *Rabbil-'Aalameen*: *Ar-Rabb* is the worshipped King, the Disposer of affairs. He is the Educator of all the worlds with all types of education. He is the One Who created them, provides for them, and blesses them with blessings that are apparent as well as hidden.

(ٱلْعَٰلَمِينَ) *Al-'Aalameen*: All that exists other than Allâh Almighty.

(ٱلرَّحْمَٰنِ ٱلرَّحِيمِ) *Ar-Rahmaanir-Raheem*: Two of Allâh's Names that indicate that He is the Possessor of the vast magnificent mercy that reaches everything, and embraces every creature. He is *Ar-Rahmaan*, with a mercy that is for all of His creation in this world, *Ar-Raheem*, with a special mercy for the believers. Allâh Almighty says:

$$﴿وَكَانَ بِٱلْمُؤْمِنِينَ رَحِيمًا ٤٣﴾$$

And He is Ever Most Merciful to the believers.[1]

And He said:

$$﴿قُلِ ٱدْعُواْ ٱللَّهَ أَوِ ٱدْعُواْ ٱلرَّحْمَٰنَ أَيًّا مَّا تَدْعُواْ فَلَهُ ٱلْأَسْمَآءُ ٱلْحُسْنَىٰ﴾$$

Say: "Invoke Allâh or invoke the Most Beneficent (Allâh), by whatever name you invoke Him (it is the same), for to Him belong the Best Names."[2]

(مَٰلِكِ يَوْمِ ٱلدِّينِ) *Maaliki Yawmid-Deen*: The One Who alone has control on the Day of Recompense and Reward, the Day when everyone is rewarded for his deeds - if good, then the recompense is good, and if evil, then the recompense is the same, except for he whom Allâh Almighty pardons. He said:

$$﴿وَمَآ أَدْرَىٰكَ مَا يَوْمُ ٱلدِّينِ ١٧ ثُمَّ مَآ أَدْرَىٰكَ مَا يَوْمُ ٱلدِّينِ ١٨ يَوْمَ لَا تَمْلِكُ نَفْسٌ لِنَفْسٍ شَيْـًٔا وَٱلْأَمْرُ يَوْمَئِذٍ لِلَّهِ ١٩﴾$$

And what will make you know what the Day of Recompense is? Again, what will make you know what the Day of Recompense is? (It will be) the Day when no person shall have power (to do) anything for another, and the Decision, that Day, will be

---

[1] (*Al-Ahzab* 33:43)

[2] (*Al-Isra'* 17:110)

(wholly) with Allâh.[1]

(المالك) *Al-Maalik*: He is the One Who is attributed the most perfect attributes of majesty by which the title King is deserved. It indicates that He orders and forbids, rewards and punishes, dispensing with all matters in the higher and lower worlds with complete control, with the rulings of Preordainment, of legislation, and of reward. This is why He mentioned His Sovereignty over the Day of Recompense, which is the Day of Resurrection, for on that Day, Allâh Almighty will recompense the creatures according to their deeds and Will give them a just recompense.

(إِيَّاكَ نَعْبُدُ وَإِيَّاكَ نَسْتَعِينُ) *Iyyaaka Na'budu wa Iyyaaka Nasta'een*: "You (alone) we worship, and You (alone) we ask for help. We worship none other than You, we seek help from none other than You when asking, and we rely upon none other than You." This phrase signifies a covenant between the worshipper and his Lord - that the worshipper will worship Him alone and seek help from Him alone.

(العبادة) *Al-'Ibaadah* (worship) is a comprehensive term for all that Allâh loves and is pleased with; it includes sayings and deeds that are both apparent and hidden.

(اهْدِنَا الصِّرَاطَ الْمُسْتَقِيمَ) *Ihdinas-Siraatal-Mustaqeem*: Guide us, lead us, and keep us on the straight path, the path in which there is no crookedness, that is knowledge and application of the truth, both of which lead to Allâh, His Paradise, and His Generosity.

(صِرَاطَ الَّذِينَ أَنْعَمْتَ عَلَيْهِمْ) *Siraatal-Latheena An'amta 'Alaihim*: i.e., that path of those You have blessed with guidance and facilitation to faith and righteousness. These are the Prophets, the truthful believers, the martyrs, and the righteous.

(غَيْرِ الْمَغْضُوبِ عَلَيْهِمْ وَلَا الضَّالِّينَ) *Ghairil-Maghdhoobi 'Alaihim waladh-Dhaaleen*: They are the ones who recognized the truth but abandoned it: the Jews and those like them.

Following other than the path of the misguided ones, refers to those who have strayed from the truth, such as the Christians and those who are like them that have forsaken knowledge: they wander in

---

[1] (*Al-Infitar* 82:17-19)

their misguidance without being guided to the truth.

Both in and outside of the prayer, when you finish reciting *Surah*, it is recommended for you to say, "*Aameen*," which means: "O Allâh, answer us." The Prophet ﷺ would say, "*Aameen*," after reciting this *Surah*, and he ordered us to do so as well. It is confirmed from the Prophet ﷺ that *Surat Al-Fatihah* is the greatest chapter of the Qur'an and that there is no prayer for the one who doesn't recite it.

Some Benefits That Can Be Derived From *Surat Al-Fatihah*

1) The recitation of *Al-Fatihah* is one of the pillars of prayer, for the Prophet ﷺ said:

«لَا صَلَاةَ لِمَنْ لَمْ يَقْرَأْ بِفَاتِحَةِ الْكِتَابِ»

There is no prayer for he who doesn't recite the Opening of the Book.

This applies to both the *Imam* and the one who prays alone.

2) As for the one who follows an *Imam* during prayer, it is obligatory according to the correct opinion, in both the quiet and audible prayers.

3) This chapter embraces those principles that necessitate faith in Allâh's perfect Names and exalted Attributes, principles that the Imams and the early generations of Islam upheld. They would affirm for Allâh a quality that He affirmed for Himself or that His Messenger ﷺ affirmed - without distorting the meaning of that Name, without comparing any of Allâh's Qualities with those of creation, without likening them to those of His creation, and without trying to explain the reality of those qualities. They believed, for example, that Allâh is Rahman and Raheem, the Possessor of mercy that these Names describe; that He is the All-Knowing, the Possessor of knowledge, Who knows all things; that He is All-Capable, the Possessor of ability Who is able to do all things.

4) It includes the meaning of worship, which is comprehensive. It signifies all that Allâh loves and is pleased with, from sayings and deeds, both apparent and hidden.

5) The Muslim must remember the Day of Recompense, the Day of

accountability and reward. When one remembers that Day, one will be better able to perform the obligatory deeds and avoid unlawful deeds.

6) When *Shirk* is mixed with worship, the act of worship becomes nullified.

7) It includes the three categories of *Tawhid*:

   i) *Tawhid Ar-Rububiyyah* (Lordship), which is taken from Allâh's saying, "the Lord of all that exists."

   ii) *Tawhid Al-Ilahiyyah*, which means to single out Allâh for worship; and it is inferred from the word "Allâh" and from, "You alone do we worship and from You alone do we ask for help."

   iii) *Tawhid Al-Asma' was-Sifat*, which means to affirm those perfect Qualities of Allâh that He affirmed for Himself, or that the Prophet ﷺ affirmed for Him. And this is indicated by the statement, "All praise is for Allâh."

8) "Guide us to the straight path," affirms Prophethood.

9) "Owner of the Day of Recompense," affirms that we will be punished or rewarded according to our deeds.

10) And "Guide us to the straight path," includes an affirmation of the Divine Will and a refutation of the people of innovation and misguidance, since it is a recognition of the truth and acting upon it.

11) "You (alone) we worship and (from) You (alone) we ask for help," clearly shows that worship must be dedicated purely and sincerely for Allâh alone.[1]

---

[1] This was taken from *Al-Ahkamul-Mulimmah 'Alad-Durusul-Muhimmah* by 'Abdul-'Aziz Al-Fayiz.

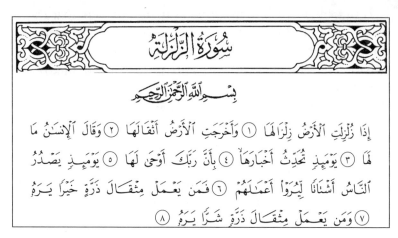

Surat Az-Zalzalah

In the Name of Allâh, the Most Beneficent, the Most Merciful

1. *When the earth is shaken with its (final) earthquake.* **2.** *And when the earth throws out its burdens.* **3.** *And man will say: "What is the matter with it?"* **4.** *That Day it will declare its information (about all what happened over it of good or of evil).* **5.** *Because your Lord has inspired it.* **6.** *That day mankind will proceed in scattered groups that they may be shown their deeds.* **7.** *So whosoever does good equal to the weight of an atom (or a small ant) shall see it.* **8.** *And whosoever does evil equal to the weight of an atom (or a small ant), shall see it.*

Its Name

It is called *Az-Zalzalah*, or *Az-Zilzal* (The Earthquake) because it begins by informing us about the fierce earthquake that will take place just prior to the Day of Judgement.

The Subject Matter Of This *Surah*

A description of the Day of Judgement and the recompense for good and evil.

Its Relation to What is Before It

Allâh Almighty described in the previous *Surah - Al-Baiyyinah* - the warning to the disbeliever and the promise for the believer, the fire of Hell for the former and Paradise for the latter. Here Allâh Almighty clarifies the time for giving those rewards and mentions what will happen just prior to that time: that there will be an earthquake and the earth will throw out its burdens. And Allâh Almighty informs us that we will be rewarded for a deed even if it is the size of the smallest thing.

The Virtues Of This *Surah*

At-Tirmithi recorded a *Hadith* - and he said it was *Hasan* - from Anas bin Malik, that the Messenger of Allâh ﷺ said that this *Surah* is equivalent to one-fourth of the Qur'an.

In What Context Was This *Surah* Revealed

Since the disbelievers would frequently ask about the time of the Hour and the Day of Reckoning, Allâh Almighty here mentions not the exact time, but some of the signs of its coming, letting them know that the knowledge of when that time will arrive is with Allâh Almighty alone. Therefore there is no way for us to specify when that time will come.

The Meanings Of Its Words

Ibn 'Abbas, may Allâh be pleased with them, said:

(إِذَا زُلْزِلَتِ ٱلْأَرْضُ زِلْزَالَهَا) *Itha Zulzilatil-Ardhu-Zilzaalahaa*: The shaking of the bottom of the earth. Allâh Almighty informs us, about the Day of Judgement, and that the earth will shake and give a violent jolt, causing all buildings and structures to fall; the mountains will be crushed and hills will be levelled; the earth become like a level floor, with no crookedness in it.

(وَأَخْرَجَتِ ٱلْأَرْضُ أَثْقَالَهَا) *Wa Akhrajitil-Ardhu Athqaalahaa*: meaning the earth will throw out its treasures and the dead.

(وَقَالَ ٱلْإِنسَٰنُ) *Wa Qaalal-Insaanu:* (When he sees the enormous matters that are happening.)

(مَا لَهَا) *Ma lahaa*: Man will say: "What is happening to it?"

(يَوْمَئِذٍ تُحَدِّثُ أَخْبَارَهَا) *Yawma'ithin Tuhaddithu Akhbaarahaa*: The earth will bear witness to what mankind perpetrated over it, both the good and bad of it. The earth is one of the many witnesses that will give testimony regarding the deeds of Allâh's creatures. Abu Hurairah, may Allâh be pleased with him, related that the Prophet ﷺ recited:

$$﴿يَوْمَئِذٍ تُحَدِّثُ أَخْبَارَهَا﴾$$

That Day it will declare its information.[1]

He ﷺ said:

$$«أَتَدْرُونَ مَا أَخْبَارُهَا؟»$$

Do you know what its information is?

The Companions said, "Allâh and His Messenger know best." He ﷺ said:

$$«فَإِنَّ أَخْبَارَهَا أَنْ تَشْهَدَ عَلَى كُلِّ عَبْدٍ أَوْ أَمَةٍ بِمَا عَمِلَ عَلَى ظَهْرِهَا، تَقُولُ$$
$$عَمِلَ كَذَا وَ كَذَا يَوْمَ كَذَا وَكَذَا، فَهَٰذِهِ أَخْبَارُهَا»$$

Its news is that it will give testimony about the deeds performed over it by every male and female slave (of Allâh). It will say, 'Such and such person performed such and such deeds on such and such day': that will be its information.

And about Allâh's saying:

(بِأَنَّ رَبَّكَ أَوْحَى لَهَا) *Bianna Rabbaka Awha Lahaa:* Because your Lord has inspired it.[2]

Ibn 'Abbas, may Allâh be pleased with them, said, "Its Lord will say, 'Speak,' and it will speak." Mujahid, may Allâh have mercy upon him, said, "It means that He orders it to speak of those deeds that were performed over it, and it will not disobey His Order."

(يَوْمَئِذٍ يَصْدُرُ النَّاسُ أَشْتَاتًا) *Yawma'ithin Yasdurun-Naasu Ashtaatan*: It is about the Resurrection, *Ashtaat* means divided groups, some miserable and some happy, some ordered to go to Paradise and others ordered to go to the Fire.

(لِيُرَوْا أَعْمَالَهُمْ) *Li Yuraw A'maalahum*: So that Allâh Almighty may

---

[1] (*Az-Zalzalah* 99:4)

[2] (*Az-Zalzalah* 99:5)

show them their good and bad deeds, and the rewards they receive for them.

(فَمَن يَعْمَلْ مِثْقَالَ ذَرَّةٍ خَيْرًا يَرَهُ ○ وَمَن يَعْمَلْ مِثْقَالَ ذَرَّةٍ شَرًّا يَرَهُ) *Faman Ya'mal Mithqaala Tharratin Khairan Yarah. Wa Man Ya'mal Mithqaala Tharratin Sharran Yarah*: *Tharrah* means the weight of the smallest ant. So when one sees a good deed equal to that weight in his book (of deeds), he will be pleased by it. The principle is the same for both the righteous and wicked persons: for each bad deed performed one has one sin held against him, and for each good deed performed, one has ten good deeds written for him. And on the Day of Judgement, Allâh Almighty further multiplies the good deeds of the believers. Here, it is important to understand that since the smallest of deeds is judged, any deed that is greater than that will also be judged. Allâh Almighty says:

$$﴿يَوْمَ تَجِدُ كُلُّ نَفْسٍ مَّا عَمِلَتْ مِنْ خَيْرٍ مُّحْضَرًا وَمَا عَمِلَتْ مِن سُوَءٍ تَوَدُّ لَوْ أَنَّ بَيْنَهَا وَبَيْنَهُ أَمَدًا بَعِيدًا (٣٠)﴾$$

On the Day when every person will be confronted with all the good he has done, and all the evils he has done, he will wish that there were a great distance between him and his evil.[1]

$$﴿وَوَجَدُواْ مَا عَمِلُواْ حَاضِرًا وَلَا يَظْلِمُ رَبُّكَ أَحَدًا (٤٩)﴾$$

And they will find all that they did, placed before them.[2]

Allâh Almighty encourages us to do good deeds — even if they are small — and warns us against performing evil deeds — even if they are small, which is why the Prophet ﷺ used to say:

«اتَّقُوا النَّارَ وَلَوْ بِشِقِّ تَمْرَةٍ فَمَنْ لَمْ يَجِدْ فَبِكَلِمَةٍ طَيِّبَةٍ»

Protect yourselves from the Fire, even if you do so with a part of a date (by giving it in charity); when one doesn't find (anything), then with a good word.

He ﷺ also said:

«كَانَ صَلَّى الله عَلَيْهِ وَسَلَّمَ يَقُولُ يَا عَائِشَةُ إِيَّاكِ وَمُحَقَّرَاتِ الذُّنُوبِ فَإِنَّ

---

[1] (*Aal 'Imran* 3:30)
[2] (*Al-Kahf* 18:49)

لَهَا مِنَ اللهِ طَالِباً»

O 'Aishah! Stay away from those sins that are belittled, for indeed they will be taken account of by Allâh.

Muslim and At-Tirmithi recorded from Abu Hurairah, may Allâh be pleased with him, that Allâh's Messenger ﷺ said:

«تَقِيءُ الْأَرْضُ أَفْلَاذَ كَبِدِهَا أَمْثَالَ الْأُسْطُوَانِ مِنَ الذَّهَبِ وَالْفِضَّةِ فَيَجِيءُ الْقَاتِلُ فَيَقُولُ: فِي هَذَا قَتَلْتُ، وَيَجِيءُ الْقَاطِعُ فَيَقُولُ: فِي هَذَا قَطَعْتُ وَيَجِيءُ السَّارِقُ فَيَقُولُ: فِي هَذَا قُطِعَتْ يَدِي ثُمَّ يَدَعُونَهُ فَلَا يَأْخُذُونَ مِنْهُ شَيْئًا»

The earth will spew forth its treasures, such as pillars of gold and silver. The murderer will come and say, "For this I have killed." The one who breaks ties with relatives will come and say, "For this I have broken ties (with relatives)." And the thief will come and say, "For this my hand was cut off." Then all of them will leave (the treasures), taking nothing from it.

The Meaning in Summary

When Allâh wills for the end of this world to occur and the time of the Hour to begin, He will order the earth to shake, and it will quake with unprecedented violence. It will throw up its burdens and those things buried inside; when man sees this epic occurrence, he will say, "What is the matter with it!" Meaning, what is happening to the earth, for neither has its like occurred nor is its cause known. At that time, the earth will speak its information to you, and it will articulate with the language of events not with the language of speech, as was said by the great scholar, At-Tabari in his *Tafsir*. For these are events occurring in the earth without a precedence or apparent reason, but by Allâh's inspiration to it. Even though some things occur in the universe by an obvious cause and others by a hidden cause, all that takes place in the universe happens by Allâh's Will and Command.

People will come out of their graves in scattered groups, and each person will be shown his deeds. Whoever does a good deed equal to the weight of the smallest ant, he will be rewarded for it; whoever does an evil deed equal to the weight of the smallest ant, he will be recompensed according to the deed. Allâh Almighty says:

﴿وَنَضَعُ ٱلْمَوَٰزِينَ ٱلْقِسْطَ لِيَوْمِ ٱلْقِيَٰمَةِ فَلَا تُظْلَمُ نَفْسٌ شَيْـًٔا وَإِن كَانَ مِثْقَالَ حَبَّةٍ مِّنْ خَرْدَلٍ أَتَيْنَا بِهَا وَكَفَىٰ بِنَا حَٰسِبِينَ ٤٧﴾

And We shall set up Balance for justice on the Day of Resurrection, then none will be dealt with unjustly in any thing. And if there be the weight of a mustard seed, We will bring it. And Sufficient are We as Reckoners.[1]

In this *Surah*, we are equally encouraged to do good deeds and warned against perpetrating evil ones.

What Can Be Derived From These Verses

1) The belief in the Resurrection and recompense are acknowledged.

2) We are informed of an epic transformation, the transformation of the earth and the heavens into another earth and other heavens.

3) Inanimate objects speaking is from Allâh's signs that indicates His perfect Ability, Knowledge, and Wisdom; moreover, it indicates His divine and complete power, which necessitates from us that we worship Him alone, without associating partners with Him.

4) It supports the authentic *Hadith*:

«اتَّقُوا النَّارَ وَلَوْ بِشِقِّ تَمْرَةٍ»

Protect yourselves from the Fire, even if you do so with a part of a date (by giving it in charity).

5) The disbeliever reaps the rewards of his good deeds in this world, but not in the Hereafter.

6) The believer is recompensed for evil in this world, and his good deeds are saved to help him in the Hereafter.

---

[1] (*Al-Anbiya'* 21:47)

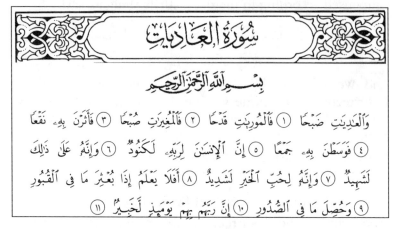

Surat Al-'Adiyat

In the Name of Allâh, the Most Beneficent, the Most Merciful.

1. *By the (steeds) that run, with panting (breath),* **2.** *Striking sparks of fire (by their hooves),* **3.** *And scouring to the raid at dawn.* **4.** *And raise the dust in clouds the while.* **5.** *And penetrating forthwith as one into the midst (of the foe);* **6.** *Verily! Man is ungrateful to his Lord;* **7.** *And to that he bears witness (by his deeds);* **8.** *And verily, he is violent in the love of wealth.* **9.** *Knows he not that when the contents of the graves are brought and poured forth (all mankind is resurrected).* **10.** *And that which is in the breasts (of man) shall be made known.* **11.** *Verily, that day (i.e. the Day of Resurrection) their Lord will be Well-Acquainted with them (as to their deeds), (and will reward them for their deeds).*

Its Name

It is called *Surat Al-'Adiyat* (Those That Run) because Allâh Almighty begins it swearing by "those that run," referring to the horses of those who fight in *Jihad*, those who are riding quickly to meet their enemy.

Its Relation to What is Before it

Both *Surahs* discuss the time when the earth will spew forth the dead: In *Surat Az-Zalzalah*:

$$﴿ وَأَخْرَجَتِ ٱلْأَرْضُ أَثْقَالَهَا ﴾$$

And when the earth throws out its burdens

And in this *Surah*:

$$﴿ إِذَا بُعْثِرَ مَا فِى ٱلْقُبُورِ ﴾$$

When the contents of the graves are brought out and poured forth.

Az-Zalzalah ends by mentioning that we will be recompensed for both good and evil deeds. *Al-'Adiyat* ends with the same:

$$﴿ إِنَّ رَبَّهُم بِهِمْ يَوْمَئِذٍ لَّخَبِيرٌ ﴾$$

Verily, that Day their Lord will be Well-Acquainted with them (as to their deeds), (and will reward them for their deeds).

The Meanings of Its Words

(وَٱلْعَٰدِيَٰتِ ضَبْحًا) *Wal-'Aadiyaati Dhabha*: The horse that races at an amazingly strong and fast pace, which causes it to make the sound of the "*Dhabh*." The "*Dhabh*," is the breathing sound that emanates from the chest of a horse when it races at top speeds.

(فَٱلْمُورِيَٰتِ) *Al-Mooriyaati*: The striking of their hooves on the rocks on the ground.

(قَدْحًا) *Qadha*: meaning the fire that sparks from the hardness of their hooves and the strength of their racing.

(فَٱلْمُغِيرَٰتِ) *Fal-Mugheeraati*: Those that attack their enemy by making a raid.

(صُبْحًا) *Subha*: Morning time. For the most part, raids took place in the morning, for when the Prophet ﷺ wanted to attack, he waited until the morning; if he heard the call to prayer, he would stop, and if he didn't, he would attack. He advised those who went on group missions to follow the same strategy.

(فَأَثَرْنَ بِهِ) *Fa-Atharna Bihi*: By their racing and raids they stir up:

(نَقْعًا) *Naq'a*: dust from the intensity of their moving.

(فَوَسَطْنَ بِهِ) *Fawasatna Bihi*: meaning on their mounts

(جَمّاً) *Jam'a*: they would surround the enemy they were raiding.

(إِنَّ الْإِنْسَانَ لِرَبِّهِ لَكَنُودٌ) *Innal Insaana Li-Rabbihi Lakanood*: Man as a species hates to share with others the good he has, good that Allâh Almighty has blessed him with, and he refuses to acknowledge the good that Allâh Almighty bestows upon him.

(وَإِنَّهُ عَلَى ذَلِكَ لَشَهِيدٌ) *Wa Innahu 'Ala Thalika Lashaheed*: Man bears witness, through his ingratitude and refusal, that he is averse to doing good and that he is greedy.

(وَإِنَّهُ لِحُبِّ الْخَيْرِ لَشَدِيدٌ) *Wa Innahu Lihubbil Khairi Lashadeed*: Man loves wealth with such a violent passion that he is stingy with it.

(أَفَلَا يَعْلَمُ إِذَا) *Afala Ya'lamu Ithaa*: Knows he not that.

(بُعْثِرَ مَا فِي الْقُبُورِ) *Bu'thira Maa Fil Quboor*: Corpses are taken out of their graves, and this is referring to the time when Allâh Almighty resurrects man.

(وَحُصِّلَ مَا فِي الصُّدُورِ) *Wa Hussila Ma Fis-Sudoor*: What people hide in their hearts will become clear and apparent, whether it is good or evil.

(إِنَّ رَبَّهُم بِهِم يَوْمَئِذٍ لَخَبِيرٌ) *Inna Rabbahum Bihim Yawma'ithin La-Khabeer*: Indeed, Allâh Almighty knows all of man's deeds, both apparent and hidden, and He Almighty will reward man for those deeds.

The Meaning in Summary

Because the horse has certain good qualities that are non-existent in other animals, and as it has been authentically established, there is good in the forelocks of the horse until the Day of Judgement, so Allâh Almighty swore by them. For among the Arabs, the horse has always been a means of waging war, and as an animal, it has always had a high status with the believers. Therefore we should take care of horses and train on them for fighting in the way of Allâh Almighty and we should take possession of horses for noble aims, just as we should strive and work hard in all important and significant matters.

After making the oath, Allâh Almighty clarifies the nature of man: that he is ungrateful, that he forgets Allâh's many favors — a nature that might lead him to rejecting Allâh's religion and commands. Here, the believers should take pause to understand the realities of this world and the Hereafter; they must strive against the desires of their own selves, doing good deeds, and avoiding evil ones. Also, Allâh Almighty clarifies man's ardent love for wealth, a love that promotes the characteristic of miserliness. But there is a further consequence: man strives so eagerly after wealth that he forgets the Hereafter, forgets Allâh's rights upon him and upon what He gave him, which is why Allâh Almighty warns man against possessing those abominable qualities.

Does not the one who refuses — who feigns to forget Allâh's order and prohibitions — know that he will be taken out of his grave, that even his innermost intentions will become clear, that Allâh Almighty knows all that he does including the deeds he does privately, and finally, that Allâh Almighty will give him just recompense for all of his actions. Therefore, one should never allow the love of wealth to deviate him from gratefulness to his Lord, from worshipping Him, and from striving for the Hereafter.

What Can Be Derived From These Verses

1) We are encouraged to *Jihad* and to make preparations for war.

2) The nature of man is explained: he forgets the many favours of His Lord while he only remembers a misfortune that may have befallen him — except he who believes and does good deeds.

3) Man's eager love for wealth is made known; here, as Muslims, we are implicitly invited to improve ourselves — by having faith, by performing good deeds, and by spending in the way of Allâh Almighty.

4) The belief in Resurrection and Recompense is established.

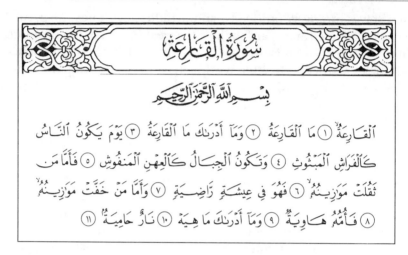

Surat Al-Qari'ah

In the Name of Allâh, the Most Beneficent, the Most Merciful

1. *Al-Qari'ah (the striking Hour, i.e., the Day of Resurrection).*
2. *What is the striking (Hour)?* **3.** *And what will make you know what the striking (Hour) is?* **4.** *It is a Day whereon mankind will be like moth scattered about.* **5.** *And the mountains will be like carded wool.* **6.** *Then as for those whose Balance (of good deeds) will be heavy.* **7.** *He will live a pleasant life (in Paradise).* **8.** *But as for them whose Balance (of good deeds) will be light.* **9.** *He will have his home in Hawiyah (pit, i.e., Hell).* **10.** *And what will make you know what it is?* **11.** *(It is) a hot blazing Fire!*

Its Name

It is called *Surat Al-Qari'ah* (The Striking Hour) because it begins by mentioning it, to send fear into the hearts of man, just like *Surat Al-Haqqah* (The Inevitable) and *Surat Al-Ghashiyah* (The Overwhelming). *Al-Qari'ah* is one of the names of the Day of Judgement, because it strikes horror into hearts.

The Subject Matter Of This *Surah*

This *Surah* is a Makkan *Surah* (i.e., it was revealed before the

Prophet ﷺ emigrated to Al-Madinah), it outlines some of the awesome and frightening events that will take place on the Day of Judgement, a time when mankind will be divided into two groups: those that are happy and those that are miserable.

Its Relation To What is Before It

As the previous *Surah* ended by mentioning certain aspects of the Day of Judgement — "Knows he not that when the contents of the graves are brought out and poured forth, And that which is in the breasts (of men) shall be made known. Verily, that Day their Lord will be Well-Acquainted with them," — this *Surah* continues by describing some of the awesome events that will take place at that time.

The Meanings Of Its Words

(اَلْقَارِعَةُ) *Al-Qaari'ah*: This is one of the names of the Day of Judgement, and it is thus called because it strikes hearts and ears with its frightening events, and *Qari'ah* is taken from the word *Qar'a*, which means to strike violently.

(وَمَا أَدْرَاكَ مَا ٱلْقَارِعَةُ) *Wa Maa Adraaka Mal-Qaari'ah*: What will make you know what the *Qaari'ah* is, a question that is used to instill fear, for such terrifying are the events of the Day of Judgement, that no man can perceive its reality. The question is repeated, adding intensity to the description of that day.

(كَٱلْفَرَاشِ) *Kal-Farash*: *Al-Farash* is a flying insect, known for its foolish habit of crowding over fire.

(ٱلْمَبْثُوثِ) *Al-Mabthooth*: Scattered in great numbers over a large area, many people will be confused and humiliated, crowding some over the other, waiting in panic to be called for the settlement of their accounts.

(وَتَكُونُ ٱلْجِبَالُ كَٱلْعِهْنِ ٱلْمَنفُوشِ) *Wa-Takoonul-Jibaalu Kal-'Ihnil-Manfoosh*: In other words, like carded wool, so light will the mountains be in their movement and in the way they disperse until finally, they will be level with the earth.

(ثَقُلَتْ مَوَازِينُهُ) *Thaqulat Mawaazeenuhu*: Meaning, that his good deeds outweigh his bad ones.

(فَهُوَ فِي عِيشَةٍ رَّاضِيَةٍ) *Fahuwa Fee 'Eeshatir-Raadhiyah*: A life pleasing to him, in Paradise.

(حَفَّتْ مَوَازِينُهُ) *Khaffat Mawaazeenuhu*: One whose bad deeds outweigh his good ones.

(فَأُمُّهُ هَاوِيَةٌ) *Fa Ummuhu Haawiyah*: i.e., his home and place to reside in will be the Fire of Hell.

(وَمَا أَدْرَنكَ) *Wa Maa Adraaka*: What will make you know? This is a question that instills fear.

(مَا هِيَهْ) *Maa Hiyah*: And what will make you know what the *Hawiyah* is! *Hawiyah* is one of the names of the Hellfire.

(نَارٌ حَامِيَةٌ) *Naarun Haamiyah*: It is a blazing hot fire.

There are some *Ahadith* that describe the Hellfire. Al-Bukhari, Muslim, Malik and others recorded from Abu Hurairah, may Allâh be pleased with him, that the Prophet ﷺ said:

«إِنَّ نَارَ بَنِي آدَمَ الَّتِي تُوقِدُونَ جُزْءًا مِنْ سَبْعِينَ جُزْءًا مِنْ نَارِ جَهَنَّمَ»

Indeed the fire of the children of Adam that you ignite is one part out of seventy parts of the fire of Hell.

They asked, "O Messenger of Allâh, isn't it (i.e. the fire of this world) sufficient (in punishment)!" He ﷺ said:

«إِنَّهَا فُضِّلَتْ عَلَيْهَا بِتِسْعٍ وَسِتِّينَ جُزْءًا»

The fire of Hell is more intense by sixty-nine parts.

Ahmad recorded from Abu Hurairah that the Prophet ﷺ said:

«إِنَّ أَهْوَنَ أَهْلِ النَّارِ عَذَاباً مَنْ لَهُ نَعْلَانِ يَغْلِي مِنْهُمَا دِمَاغُهُ»

The least-punished of the people of the Fire will be he who will have two shoes: from them (from the intensity of their heat), his brain will boil.

At-Tirmithi and Ibn Majah recorded that Abu Hurairah, may Allâh be pleased with him, said, "The Messenger of Allâh ﷺ said:

«أُوقِدَ عَلَى النَّارِ أَلْفَ سَنَةٍ حَتَّى احْمَرَّتْ، ثُمَّ أُوقِدَ عَلَيْهَا أَلْفَ سَنَةٍ حَتَّى ابْيَضَّتْ، ثُمَّ أُوقِدَ عَلَيْهَا أَلْفَ سَنَةٍ حَتَّى اسْوَدَّتْ فَهِيَ سَوْدَاءُ مُظْلِمَةٌ.»

The Fire was ignited for one thousand years until it became red; it was then ignited for one thousand years until it became white; and then it was ignited for one thousand years until it became black; it is black and dark."

The Meaning in Summary

This *Surah* highlights some of our beliefs regarding the Resurrection and recompense, beliefs that the polytheists and disbelievers vehemently reject. Allâh Almighty informs us that on the Day of Judgement — the Day that will strike terror into the hearts of people — people, who are the noblest of species on the earth, will be like scattered moths, frightened, alarmed, and in a state of panic. Humans are likened to moths that, in their large numbers, crowd on top of one another, not guided to any specific course.

The mountains, despite their size and height, will be like carded wool, flying here and there, breaking apart. When man will be brought before His Lord, whoever's good deeds outweigh his bad ones will be saved from the Fire, and he will have a most pleasant and pleasing life: Paradise, the abode of eternal bliss. Whoever's bad deeds outweigh his good ones, or whoever has only bad deeds (such as the disbelievers and polytheists), then his mother, who holds him close and keeps him at her side, will be the fire of Hell, a blazing fire that has no counterpart in terms of the punishment felt by those who touch it (may Allâh protect us from it). The life of the dwellers of the Fire is one of eternal loss (we seek protection in Allâh Almighty from it). The *Qari'ah* is described by some of the things that will take place during it, and not its reality, because our human mind cannot perceive its reality, so awesome is that reality.

What Can be Derived From These Verses

1) It supports the belief in Resurrection and recompense since it mentions some events related to that.

2) It warns of the terrors of the Day of Judgement and Allâh's punishment that will take place at that time.

3) It supports the belief that deeds — both good and evil — will be weighed and assigned recompense accordingly.

4) It acknowledges that people will be in two groups on the Day of Judgement: A group in Paradise and a group in Hell, in accordance with their deeds.

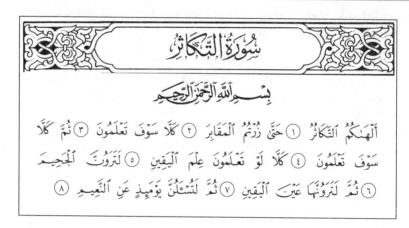

Surat At-Takathur

In the Name of Allâh, the Most Beneficent, the Most Merciful

1. *The mutual rivalry for piling up of worldly things diverts you.* **2.** *Until you visit the graves (i.e. till you die).* **3.** *Nay! You shall come to know!* **4.** *Again, nay! You shall come to know!* **5.** *Nay! If you knew with a sure knowledge (the end result of piling up, you would not have occupied yourself in worldly things).* **6.** *Verily, you shall see the blazing Fire (Hell)!* **7.** *And again, you shall see it with certainty of sight!* **8.** *Then, on that Day you shall be asked about the delight (you indulged in, in this world).*[1]

Its Name

It is called *Surat At-Takathur* because of the mention of the mutual rivalry for piling up. It means: "You busy yourselves with boasting, by deeds, children, and servants.''

The Subject Matter of This Makkan *Surah*

Deeds done purely for this world are condemned; we are warned not to avoid preparing for the Hereafter, which is why this *Surah* includes three major points:

---

[1] (*At-Takathur* 102:1-8)

1) It explains that some people become so occupied with the pleasures and temptations of this world that they will remain in such a state until death overtakes them:

$$﴿أَلْهَىٰكُمُ ٱلتَّكَاثُرُ ۝ حَتَّىٰ زُرْتُمُ ٱلْمَقَابِرَ ۝﴾$$

The mutual rivalry for piling up of worldly things diverts you, until you visit the graves (i.e. until you die)

2) We are given notice that we will be asked about all of our deeds on the Day of Judgement:

$$﴿كَلَّا سَوْفَ تَعْلَمُونَ﴾$$

Nay! You shall come to know! Again, nay! You shall come to know!

3) We are informed that we will see the Hellfire with certainty of sight; at that time, when we witness the horrors of the Fire, we will be asked about the pleasures of this world.

$$﴿ثُمَّ كَلَّا سَوْفَ تَعْلَمُونَ﴾$$

Nay! If you knew with a sure knowledge (the end result of piling up, you would not have occupied yourselves in worldly things).

Its Relation To What is Before it

Surat Al-Qari'ah deals with some of the awesome events that will take place on the Day of Judgement; then it discusses the rewards awaiting those who will be eternally happy and those who will be eternally miserable. In this *Surah*, one of the reasons why some people deserve eternal misery and the Fire is given - the perpetration of sins and preoccupation with worldly matters rather than with the religion. This *Surah*, in very clear terms, warns us that we will be held responsible in the Hereafter for our actions in this world.

In What Context Was This *Surah* Revealed

In *Sahih Muslim* it is recorded that Mutarraf related that his father said, "As I approached the Prophet ﷺ, he was reciting *Al-Haakumut-Takaathur*. He then said:

$$«يَقُولُ ابْنُ آدَمَ مَالِي مَالِي، وَهَلْ لَكَ يَا ابْنَ آدَمَ مِنْ مَالِكَ إِلَّا مَا أَكَلْتَ$$

فَأَفْنَيْتَ، أَوْ لَبِسْتَ فَأَبْلَيْتَ، أَوْ تَصَدَّقْتَ فَأَمْضَيْتَ، وَمَا سِوَى ذَلِكَ فَذَاهِبٌ وَتَارِكُهُ لِلنَّاسِ»

The son of Adam says; "My wealth, my wealth!" O, son of Adam! Do you have other than that which you ate and depleted, that which you wore and worn out, and that which you gave in charity and preserved. Everything else is fleeting, and being left for the people (i.e., heirs).

The Meaning Of Its Words

(أَلْهَىكُمُ) *Al-Haakum*: It keeps you so busy and occupied that you turn away from obedience to Allâh Almighty.

(التَّكَاثُرُ) *At-Takaathur*: i.e., flaunting and showing-off because one has a lot of wealth.

(حَتَّى زُرْتُمُ الْمَقَابِرَ) *Hatta-Zurtumul-Maqaabir*: You will continue to be preoccupied in accumulating and flaunting wealth until you die and are transported to your grave.

(كَلَّا) *Kalla*: You must not do that, so leave your preoccupation of amassing wealth.

(سَوْفَ تَعْلَمُونَ) *Sawfa Ta'lamoon*: When you enter your graves, you will know that you made a huge mistake by boasting about your wealth and your children.

(كَلَّا) *Kalla*: here it means: "Truly!"

(لَوْ تَعْلَمُونَ عِلْمَ الْيَقِينِ) *Law Ta'lamoona 'Ilmal-Yaqeen*: If you knew results of amassing wealth with certainty, then you would not boast of the wealth you possess.

(لَتَرَوُنَّ الْجَحِيمَ) *Latarawunnal-Jaheem*: You will indeed see the Hellfire.

(يَوْمَئِذٍ) *Yawma'ithin*: On the day that you will see the Hellfire with certainty of sight.

(عَنِ النَّعِيمِ) *'Anin-Na'eem*: (You will be asked) about the blessings you enjoyed, such as health, free time, safety, food, and drink.

The Meaning in Summary

Allâh Almighty begins the *Surah* by mentioning those who are so busy in amassing wealth to compete and boast that they turn away from obedience to Allâh Almighty and His Messenger ﷺ. These are people who will die without producing any good deeds for themselves, deeds that would have served them in the Hereafter.

Allâh Almighty mentions that such people will continue on their evil path until they die; then they are transported to their graves and will stay therein until the Day of Judgement, the time of recompense. He warns us that we should avoid this path, a path that leads to our destruction and ultimate loss.

"You shall come to know": i.e., we shall come to know the evil results of turning away from the obedience of Allâh Almighty and His Messenger ﷺ. And then in the next verse, Allâh Almighty repeats the warning.

"Truly! If you knew with a sure knowledge": Meaning, truly, if we knew what is awaiting us in the grave and in the Hereafter, we would not occupy ourselves with accumulating wealth.

Next, we are informed that we will see the Hellfire with our very eyes on the Day of Judgement: the disbeliever will see it and then roast in it; the believer will see it and then Allâh Almighty will save him from it. Here, Allâh Almighty says that without a doubt, we will all see the Hellfire.

And finally, we are told that on that Day, the Day we will see the Hellfire, the Day of Judgement, we will be asked about the pleasures we enjoyed in this world, such as health, free time, safety, food, and drink. Whoever is grateful for those pleasures will be saved; whoever is not grateful will be held responsible. Some of the people of knowledge say that he will not be pardoned (for his ungratefulness) except for the garment that covers his private areas, for the piece of bread that saves him from hunger, and for the room that protects him from heat and cold.

In *Sahih Muslim* it is recorded that Abu Hurairah ؓ said, "Allâh's Messenger ﷺ went out one day, or night. He met up with Abu Bakr and 'Umar, may Allâh be pleased with them. He ﷺ said to them:

«مَا أَخْرَجَكُمَا مِنْ بُيُوتِكُمَا هَذِهِ السَّاعَةَ؟»

"What has made you come out of your homes at this time?"

They said, "Hunger, O Messenger of Allâh." He said:

«وَالَّذِي نَفْسِي بِيَدِهِ لَأَخْرَجَنِي الَّذِي أَخْرَجَكُمَا، قُومَا»

"And I, by the One Who has my soul in His hand, what has made me to come out is the same reason that has caused you to come out."

They continued with him until he approached the house of a man from the Ansar, who was not at home. When the man's wife saw them, she said, "Welcome." The Prophet ﷺ said:

«أَيْنَ فُلَانٌ؟»

"Where is so and so.?"

She said, "He is gone to get some water for us." At that point the man returned, and when he saw the Messenger of Allâh ﷺ and his two Companions, he said, "All praise belongs to Allâh, for no one has more honored guests with him today than I." The man went and returned with a cluster of ripe dates, unripe dates, and dried dates. He said, "Eat from this." The man took a knife, intending to slaughter an animal, and the Prophet ﷺ said:

«إِيَّاكَ وَالْحَلُوبَ»

"Do not slaughter the one that gives milk."

He slaughtered a sheep for them, and they ate from the slaughter and from the dates and they drank as well — until they became full. The Prophet ﷺ said to Abu Bakr and 'Umar:

«وَالَّذِي نَفْسِي بِيَدِهِ لَتُسْأَلُنَّ عَنْ نَعِيمِ هَذَا الْيَوْمِ يَوْمَ الْقِيَامَةِ أَخْرَجَكُمْ مِنْ بُيُوتِكُمُ الْجُوعُ ثُمَّ لَمْ تَرْجِعُوا حَتَّى أَصَابَكُمْ هَذَا النَّعِيمُ»

"By the One Who has my soul in His hand, you will indeed be asked about the pleasures of today on the Day of Judgement. Hunger caused you to leave your homes and you would not have returned to your homes until you had been given these delights."

The name of the man from the Ansar is Malik bin At-Tayyihan, and is also known as Abul-Haitham, may Allâh be pleased with him.

In another authentic narration, he ﷺ said:

«لَا تَزُولُ قَدَمَا عَبْدٍ يَوْمَ الْقِيَامَةِ حَتَّى يُسْأَلَ عَنْ عُمُرِهِ فِيمَ أَفْنَاهُ، وَعَنْ شَبَابِهِ فِيمَ أَبْلَاهُ، وَعَنْ عِلْمِهِ مَاذَا عَمِلَ بِهِ، وَعَنْ مَالِهِ مِنْ أَيْنَ اكْتَسَبَهُ وَفِيمَ أَنْفَقَهُ»

"The servant will not cease being questioned on the Day of Judgement until he is asked about his life and how he spent it; his youth and how he spent it; his knowledge and what he did because of it; and his wealth, and where he acquired it from and in what he spent it."

What Can Be Derived From These Verses

1) We are warned not to do two things at once: 1) gathering wealth, 2) not being thankful for it and not obeying Allâh Almighty and His Messenger ﷺ for its sake.

2) Here, our belief in the punishment of the grave is affirmed and emphasized: "Until you visit the grave. Nay! You shall come to know!" Meaning, you shall come to know when you are in your grave.

3) Our belief in Resurrection and recompense is affirmed; we will be justly recompensed after we will be questioned for our deeds.

4) The worshipper of Allâh will be asked regarding the blessings that Allâh Almighty poured upon him in this world; if he was grateful here, he will be successful there; if he denied those favors here, he will be taken to account there. And we seek protection in Allâh Almighty.

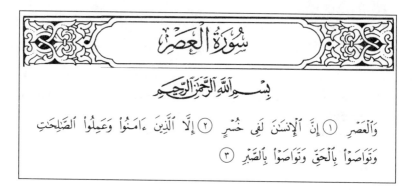

Surat Al-'Asr

In the Name of Allâh, the Most Beneficent, the Most Merciful

1. *By Al-Asr (the time).* **2.** *Verily! man is in loss.* **3.** *Except those who believe in and do righteous good deeds, and recommend each other to the truth, and recommend one another to patience.*[1]

Its Name

Because Allâh Almighty swears by *Al-'Asr* (the time) in the beginning of the *Surah*, it is given that name.

Its Relationship to What is Before It

In the previous *Surah*, we are told that a preoccupation with worldly pursuits is a most objectionable way to live; in this *Surah*, we are informed about those pursuits that we must preoccupy ourselves with: faith in Allâh, good deeds, advising one another to follow the truth, and advising one another to be patient upon the truth, for these pursuits reap good for both individual and society.

The Virtues Of This *Surah*

At-Tabarani mentioned that 'Ubaidullah bin Hafs said, "When two men from the Companions of the Messenger of Allâh ﷺ would meet, they wouldn't part from one another until one of them recited *Surat*

---

[1] (*Al-'Asr* 103:1-3)

Al-'Asr, until its end; then they would give greetings of peace to one another after it." It was also recorded by Al-Bayhaqi from Abu Huthaifah. Ash-Shafi'i said, "If Allâh had revealed only this *Surah* to His creatures, it would have been enough for them." He said that because in this *Surah* stages are mentioned, that if one completes all of those stages, he achieves his completion. The stages are as follows:

1) To know the truth.

2) To apply it in practice.

3) To teach it to one who doesn't know it or who is weak in his knowledge of it.

4) To be patient regarding the preceding stages: patient when you are learning the truth, patient when you are applying the truth, and patient when you are teaching the truth.

To strengthen your knowledge you must have faith, and to strengthen your application you must perform good deeds. Then you should be patient in your knowledge, your actions, and in your teaching.

This *Surah*, despite its brevity, is one of the most comprehensive *Surahs* of the Qur'an, and all praise is due to Allâh.

The Meanings Of Its Words

(وَٱلۡعَصۡرِ) *Wal-'Asr*: *'Asr* means time; there are many lessons to be learnt through the passing of time - the continual succession of day and night, night and day - because that consistent pattern clearly indicates the Creator, Glorious is He and Most High, and that He should be singled out for worship.

They say that *Al-'Asr* means the time in which the good and evil actions of man take place.

(إِنَّ ٱلۡإِنسَٰنَ) *Innal-Insaana*: Man as a species.

(لَفِى خُسۡرٍ) *Lafee Khusr*: Man is in a state of loss since his life is his most valuable wealth: if he dies without believing and performing good deeds, he will have suffered the ultimate loss. This is the reason for the oath

(إِلَّا ٱلَّذِينَ ءَامَنُوا۟ وَعَمِلُوا۟ ٱلصَّٰلِحَٰتِ) *Illallatheena Aamanu wa 'Amilus-Saalihaat*:

This refers to those who have faith and do good deeds, for they are in profit, not loss. This is because they worked for the Hereafter, and were not preoccupied with worldly pursuits. Every male and female believer falls under this exception: the wording is general, and embraces all who have faith and do good deeds.

(وَتَوَاصَوْا بِالْحَقِّ) *Watawaasaw Bil-Haqq*: They advise one another to believe in the truth, to speak it, and to apply it. That is faith in Allâh alone, and upholding what Allâh legislated and staying away from what He forbade.

(وَتَوَاصَوْا بِالصَّبْرِ) *Watawaasaw Bis-Sabr*: Those who advise one another to be patient upon their belief of the truth, upon their true speech, and upon their application of the truth. Patience is strength in the soul that calls one to bear hardship, yet to continue to work. There are many forms of patience. One must be patient in staying away from sins; patient in performing obligatory deeds; patient when one is faced with the vicissitudes of life, those decrees that we find it painful to bear. That we are supposed to advise one another to patience after having been ordered to advise one another to the truth indicates the superiority of patience and the great rewards waiting for those who are patient:

$$﴿ إِنَّ ٱللَّهَ مَعَ ٱلصَّٰبِرِينَ ﴾$$

Truly! Allâh is with the patient ones.[1]

The Meaning in Summary

Allâh Almighty swears in this chapter by "the time," and Allâh Almighty may swear by anything from his creation, according to His Will; all others, however, may swear only by Allâh alone. Here, Allâh Almighty swears by "the time" that every human being is in a state of loss, except for those who believe and do good deeds. The first stage includes those who know the truth and believe in it; the second stage those who do good deeds because of the truth they have believed in; the third stage includes those who advise one another to do good and teach one another about the truth. The final stage includes those who advise one another to be patient and steadfast upon the truth. At the end of this last stage, one achieves

---

[1] (*Al-Baqarah* 2:153)

completeness, for completeness means for one to not only be complete alone, but also to help make others complete. One can achieve that by strengthening his knowledge and ability of application, by having faith and by performing good deeds. Then he completes others by teaching them and by advising them to have patience upon knowledge and good deeds. This *Surah*, despite its brevity, is one of the most comprehensive *Surahs* of the Qur'an, and all praise is due to Allâh.

What Can Be Derived From These Verses

1) In only three verses, *Surat Al-'Asr* explains the way to salvation. Imam Ash-Shafi'i said, "If Allâh had revealed only this *Surah* to His creatures, it would have been enough for them."

2) We are informed of the end for the disbeliever: complete and utter loss.

3) We are informed of the ultimate success awaiting those who believe and do good deeds, those who stay away from *Shirk* and disobedience.

4) It is compulsory to advise one another to follow the truth and to be patient.

5) Here, Allâh Almighty swore by "the time," for in the passing of time, things change constantly, a reality from which we can learn many lessons.

Other General Benefits

1) When we are informed that we must advise one another and cooperate with one another to promote truth, good deeds, and patience, we learn what the life of the believer should be, a life in which one patiently establishes the truth despite the hardships he may suffer while working for the benefit of Islam and his nation.

2) One of the best of deeds is to repent from sins.

3) "And recommend one another to the truth and recommend one another to patience": In regards to this verse, Ar-Razi said, "This verse indicates that the truth is heavy and that hardships necessarily accompany it, that is why recommending one another about patience is mentioned directly after it."

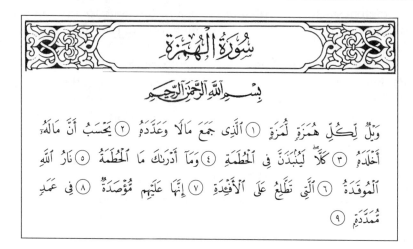

Surat Al-Humazah

In the Name of Allâh, the Most Beneficent, the Most Merciful

1. *Woe to every slanderer and backbiter.* **2.** *Who has gathered wealth and counted it.* **3.** *He thinks that his wealth will make him last forever!* **4.** *Nay! Verily, he will be thrown into the crushing Fire.* **5.** *And what will make you know what the crushing Fire is?* **6.** *The Fire of Allâh Almighty kindled.* **7.** *Which leaps up over the hearts.* **8.** *Verily, it shall be closed in on them.* **9.** *In pillars stretched forth.* [1]

Its Name

It is called *Surat Al-Humazah* because Allâh said in the beginning of it:

﴿وَيْلٌ لِّكُلِّ هُمَزَةٍ لُّمَزَةٍ﴾

Woe to every *Humazah Lumazah.*

Its Relation To What is Before It

After Allâh Almighty mentioned in the last *Surah* that man as a species is in a state of loss and destruction, He Almighty clarifies what the state will be of he who loses; here, Allâh Almighty also gives

---

[1] (*Al-Humazah* 104:1-9)

an example of those who will suffer the ultimate loss.

In What Context Was This *Surah* Revealed

Abu Haiyan said, "This was revealed about Al-Akhnas bin Shuraiq, Al-'Aas bin Wa'il, Jamil bin Ma'mar, Al-Walid bin Al-Mughirah, or Umayyah bin Khalaf. These are the different opinions, and it is possible that it was revealed with regard to all of them. At any rate, it is general in that this chapter applies to anyone who has the characteristics described herein."

The Meanings Of Its Words

(وَيْلٌ) *Wail*: Ignominy and a painful punishment; it has been said that it is a valley in the Hellfire.

(لِكُلِّ هُمَزَةٍ لُمَزَةٍ) *Likulli Humazatin Lumazah*: *Humazah* means a backbiter, but more extreme: one who always attacks the honor and dignity of others. *Lumazah*: One who finds fault with others, and is expressive in doing so, usually with the movements of his eyebrows, eyes, hand, or head; he always puts on airs of superiority over others.

(جَمَعَ مَالًا وَعَدَّدَهُ) *Jama'a Maala wa 'Addadah*: Who gathers wealth and then counts it.

(يَحْسَبُ) *Yahsabu*: He thinks;

(أَنَّ مَالَهُ أَخْلَدَهُ) *Anna Maalahu Akhladah*: He thinks that his wealth makes him immortal in this world.

(كَلَّا) *Kalla*: A word that has a meaning of deterrence. No, the situation isn't as he supposes it to be (his wealth will not prevent him from dying).

(لَيُنْبَذَنَّ) *Layunbathanna*: He will be thrown in a most humiliating fashion...

(فِي الْحُطَمَةِ) *Fil-Hutamah*: (Into) the fire of Hell; *Hatm* means to crush or smash, so the Hellfire crushes all that is thrown into it.

(الْمُوقَدَةُ) *Al-Muwqadah*: That is ablaze or aflame.

(تَطَّلِعُ عَلَى الْأَفْئِدَةِ) *Tattali'u 'Alal-Af'idah*: Goes over the center of hearts, surrounding them. The heart is specifically mentioned here because it is the place where false and evil beliefs reside and it is the starting point or source of evil and wicked deeds.

(مُؤْصَدَةٌ) *Mu'sadah*: (The Fire) will be closed in and covering them.

(فِي عَمَدٍ مُمَدَّدَةٍ) *Fee 'Amadin Mumaddadah*: In long pillars, so the Fire will be inside the pillars.

The Meaning in Summary

Allâh Almighty warns us of a valley in the Hellfire that flows with the pus (liquid that issues forth from a wound) of its inhabitants. Allâh Almighty describes people who backbite and slander, people who constantly find faults in others, and a person who has no care other than to amass wealth and count it, without having the slightest desire to spend it in the way of good, such as spending it to join ties with relatives. In his ignorance, he thinks that his wealth makes him immortal in this life; he works and strives to gather even more wealth, thinking that the more he has, the longer he will live. He doesn't realize that in reality, miserliness causes one's life to shorten, and homes to be destroyed. Meanwhile, righteousness and generosity cause one's life span to increase. Then Allâh Almighty says:

﴿ كَلَّا لَيُنۢبَذَنَّ فِي ٱلۡحُطَمَةِ ۝ وَمَآ أَدۡرَىٰكَ مَا ٱلۡحُطَمَةُ ۝ ﴾

Nay! Verily, he will be thrown into the crushing Fire. And what will make you know what the crushing Fire is?

This repetition affirms the terror and awesome destructive power of the Fire.

﴿ نَارُ ٱللَّهِ ٱلۡمُوقَدَةُ ۝ ﴾

The Fire of Allâh, kindled.

The fuel of that Fire is men and stones, and from its violence, it

﴿ ٱلَّتِي تَطَّلِعُ عَلَى ٱلۡأَفۡـِٔدَةِ ۝ ﴾

leaps up over the hearts

penetrating bodies and reaching their hearts. Living in the intensity of that heat, the inhabitants of the Fire are stuck therein, having no hope of coming out, which is why Allâh Almighty says:

﴿ إِنَّهَا عَلَيۡهِم مُّؤۡصَدَةٌ ۝ فِي عَمَدٍ ... ﴾

It shall be closed in on them, in pillars...

These long pillars will be behind doors, and the inhabitants of the Fire will not be able to come out. Allâh Almighty says:

﴿كُلَّمَآ أَرَادُوٓاْ أَن يَخْرُجُواْ مِنْهَا مِنْ غَمٍّ أُعِيدُواْ فِيهَا ﴾ ﴿٢٢﴾

Every time they seek to get away therefrom, from anguish, they will be driven back therein.[1]

We ask Allâh Almighty to protect us from that.

What Can Be Derived From These Verses

1) Our belief in Resurrection and recompense is affirmed.

2) It warns against backbiting and slander.

3) Those who are enamoured with wealth are censured.

4) It describes the intensity and the horror of the Hellfire.

5) Ignominy, punishment and destruction — these await the one who backbites, the one who slanders, the one who always finds faults in others, and the one who is miserly with his wealth.

---

[1] (*Al-Hajj* 22:22)

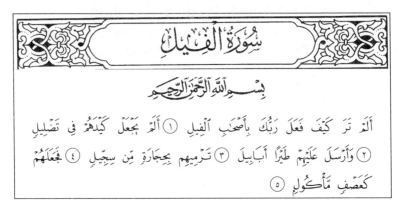

Surat Al-Fil

In the Name of Allâh, the Most Beneficent, the Most Merciful

1. *Have you not seen how your Lord dealt with the owners of the Elephant?* **2.** *Did He not make their plot go astray?* **3.** *And sent against them birds, in flocks.* **4.** *Striking them with stones of Sijjil.* **5.** *And made them like an empty field of stalks.*[1]

Its Name

This chapter is called *Al-Fil* (The Elephant) because it begins by introducing the story about the People of the Elephant.

Its Relation To What is Before It

In the last *Surah*, Allâh Almighty described people who backbite, who slander, who sow dissension among people, who gather wealth and are boastful of what they have amassed; and Allâh Almighty clarified that wealth will not benefit its boastful owner when he faces Allâh Almighty. In this *Surah*, Allâh Almighty relates a story that proves the futility of wealth, a story about the People of the Elephant. They were a people who were much more powerful than the Quraish; they were also wealthier and more arrogant. Despite that, Allâh Almighty destroyed them with tiny, weak birds; their wealth, numbers, and strength were all of no avail to them.

---

[1] (*Al-Fil* 105:1-5)

The Meanings Of Its Words

(أَلَمۡ تَرَ كَيۡفَ فَعَلَ رَبُّكَ) *Alam Tara Kaifa Fa'ala Rabbuka*: Did you not know - Allâh's Messenger ﷺ is being addressed, and though he was not alive at the time this story took place, he was alive to see its effects.

(بِأَصۡحَٰبِ ٱلۡفِيلِ) *Ashaabil-Feel*: There were 13 elephants, the largest of which was called Mahmud. Their owner was Abrahah, the ruler of Ethiopia.

(أَلَمۡ يَجۡعَلۡ كَيۡدَهُمۡ) *Alam Yaj'al Kaidahum*: *Kaid* means plot; they were plotting to destroy the Ka'bah.

(فِى تَضۡلِيلٍ) *Fee Tadhleel*: Allâh Almighty caused their plan to fail and He destroyed them.

(طَيۡرًا) *At-Tayr*: It is used to refer to anything that flies in the air, be it big or small.

(أَبَابِيلَ) *Abaabeel*: In many groups: in flocks.

Sijjeel: Baked clay.

(كَعَصۡفٍ مَّأۡكُولٍ) *Ka'asfim-Ma'kool*: Like the leaves of crops that have been eaten by animals and trampled under their feet.

The Meaning in Summary

This *Surah* relates the story of a momentous occurrence, which took place before the birth of the Prophet ﷺ. Abrahah Al-Ashram, the governor of Yemen at the time, served under the rule of the King of Habashah. Abrahah had an idea to build a house in San'a, Yemen, hoping that the Arabs would make pilgrimage to it instead of to Makkah. By doing that, he wanted to shift the center of trade and profits from Makkah to Yemen, and when he mentioned his idea to the Ethiopian King, the latter agreed and was most pleased by the plan.

When the house — Church — was built, he called it Al-Qullais; no structure comparable to it was built before. One day, a man from the Quraish was so angry at this house being built that he defecated inside of it and then soiled the walls with his own excrement. When Abrahah saw what happened, he grew furious and prepared an army to attack Makkah and to destroy the Ka'bah. He had thirteen elephants with him, the largest of which was called Mahmud. As they were going to Makkah, they destroyed any Arab or tribal resistance that came in their way, until finally, they reached a place close to Makkah. Negotiations took place between them and the chief of Makkah, 'Abdul-Muttalib bin Hashim, the grandfather of the Prophet ﷺ. An agreement was made: Abrahah returned camels that he usurped from 'Abdul-Muttalib; in return, he was free to approach the Ka'bah. The men, women, and children of Makkah were ordered to leave and to seek safety in the peaks of the neighboring mountains, for the fear that the tyrannical army approaching would harm them.

As they reached a nearby valley, many flocks of birds sent down stones from above; each stone ranged between the size of a chickpea and a lentil. As soon as a stone fell on a man, he would melt and his flesh would scatter; thus the army was destroyed. As Abrahah was fleeing, his flesh was falling off and he died on the way. This was a great blessing from Allâh Almighty for the dwellers of His inviolable city and for the keepers of His House. Until this day, the Arabs venerate the Ka'bah and honor the residents of Makkah.

What Can Be Derived From These Verses

1) Allâh's Messenger ﷺ is consoled in this *Surah* for the harm inflicted on him by the Quraish.

2) Allâh Almighty reminds the Quraish of what He Almighty did with Abrahah and his army, to instill fear into them.

3) We should appreciate Allâh's All-Powerful Abilities, and we should learn a lesson after learning of how Allâh Almighty destroys His enemies.

4) Allâh Almighty protects His House from the enemies of His religion.

5) This occurrence had serious effects on events to take place afterwards; the year it took place, 580, is called the year of the Elephant, and it is the year in which the Prophet ﷺ was born.

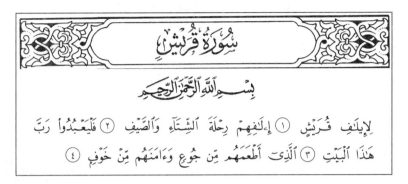

Surah Quraish

In the Name of Allâh, the Most Beneficent, the Most Merciful

1. *For the protection of the Quraish.* **2.** *The caravans to set forth safe in winter, and in summer.* **3.** *So let them worship the Lord of this House.* **4.** *Who has fed them against hunger, and has made them safe from fear.*[1]

Its Name

The *Surah* is named Quraish to remind the tribe of Quraish of Allâh's favors upon them, favors that are mentioned at the beginning of the *Surah*.

Its Relation To What is Before It

Both of these *Surahs* mention Allâh's favors on the people of Makkah. The first relates the destruction of their enemies, enemies who came to destroy their inviolable House; the second relates that because Allâh united them, they were able to pursue a life of trade with two expeditions, one in the summer and one in the winter. Through those excursions, they were able to bring back stores of supplies. So strong is the relation between both *Surahs* that Ubai bin Ka'b considered them to be one *Surah*; it has been related that he wouldn't separate the two chapters by *Basmalah* (reciting *Bismillah*).

---

[1] (*Al-Quraish* 106:1-4)

The Virtues Of This *Surah*

It was recorded by Al-Hakim, and Al-Bayhaqi in *Al-Khilafiyat*, that Umm Hani bint Abu Talib said that Allâh's Messenger ﷺ said:

«فَضَّلَ اللهُ قُرَيْشًا بِسَبْعِ خِلَالٍ: إِنِّي مِنْهُمْ، وَإِنَّ النُّبُوَّةَ فِيهِمْ، وَالْحِجَابَةَ وَالسِّقَايَةَ مِنْهُمْ، وَإِنَّ اللهَ نَصَرَهُمْ عَلَى الْفِيلِ، وَإِنَّهُمْ عَبَدُوا اللهَ عَزَّ وَجَلَّ عَشْرَ سِنِينَ لَا يَعْبُدُهُ غَيْرُهُمْ، وَإِنَّ اللهَ أَنْزَلَ فِيهِمْ سُورَةً مِنَ الْقُرْآنِ»

Allâh has blessed the Quraish with seven qualities; I am one of them; the Prophethood is in them; they are responsible for the curtain of the Ka'bah; providing water for the pilgrims is theirs; Allâh has made them victorious over the Elephant; indeed, they worshipped Allâh for ten years during a period that no one else worshipped Him; and Allâh revealed about them a chapter of the Qur'an.

After having said that, the Prophet ﷺ began to recite,

﴿لِإِيلَافِ قُرَيْشٍ﴾

For the protection of the Quraish.[1]

[Indicating that it is not an authentic narration], Ibn Kathir said, "It is *Gharib*."

In What Context Was This *Surah* Revealed

It was recorded by Al-Hakim, and Al-Bayhaqi in *Al-Khilafiyat*, that Umm Hani bint Abu Talib said that Allâh's Messenger ﷺ said:

«فَضَّلَ اللهُ قُرَيْشًا بِسَبْعِ خِصَالٍ وَذَكَرَ الْحَدِيثَ، وَفِيهِ»

Allâh has blessed the Quraish with seven qualities.

One of the qualities he enumerated is as follows:

«وَ نَزَلَتْ سُورَةٌ لَمْ يُذْكَرْ فِيهَا أَحَدٌ غَيْرُهُمْ»

...And He revealed a chapter that contained a mention of none except them.

The Meanings Of Its Words

(لِإِيلَافِ قُرَيْشٍ) *Li-Eelaafi Quraish*: *Eelaaf* comes from the verb *Alifa*,

---
[1] (*Quraish* 106:1)

which means to stick to something and to be devoted to it - each with a sense of familiarity, not aversion.

(قُرَيْشٍ) *Quraish*: The name of Arab tribes that descended from An-Nadhr bin Kinanah.

(رِحْلَةَ) *Rihlah*: A people's journey or their setting off to travel.

(أَطْعَمَهُمْ) *At'amahum*: i.e., given them a comfortable amount of sustenance, and the way to acquiring that sustenance made easy for them.

(ءَامَنَهُم) *Aamanahum*: Kept them safe from external transgression and from those who desire to wrongfully take their wealth and lives.

The Meaning in Summary

Many of the scholars of *Tafsir* said that the beginning of this *Surah* is grammatically connected to the end of the *Surah* preceding it, meaning: We dealt in the way We did with the companions of the Elephant for the sake of the Quraish, for their safety, for their welfare, for their trade and profits, so that they could make the winter journey to Yemen and the summer journey to Sham.

Allâh destroyed those who intended to do evil to the Quraish while He raised the status of the inviolable city of Makkah and its inhabitants. So venerated became the Quraish in the hearts of the Arabs that the latter would not stand in the way of the former whenever they wanted to travel anywhere.

That is why Allâh ordered them to be grateful: He said:

$$ ﴿فَلْيَعْبُدُواْ رَبَّ هَٰذَا ٱلْبَيْتِ﴾ $$

So let them worship (Allâh) the Lord of this House.
So let them worship Him, making that worship pure for Him alone.

$$ ﴿ٱلَّذِىٓ أَطْعَمَهُم مِّن جُوعٍ وَءَامَنَهُم مِّنْ خَوْفِۭ﴾ $$

Who has fed them against hunger, and has made them safe from fear.

Bountiful provisions and safety are some of the greatest of worldly blessings, blessings that require gratefulness to Allâh. For You, O Allâh, is praise and gratitude - for Your apparent favors and for Your favors that we do not perceive. The Prophet ﷺ said:

«مَنْ أَصْبَحَ آمِنًا فِي سِرْبِهِ مُعَافًى فِي بَدَنِهِ عِنْدَهُ قُوتُ يَوْمِهِ وَلَيْلِهِ فَكَأَنَّمَا حَازَ الدُّنْيَا بِحَذَافِيرِهَا»

Whosoever dawns safe in his bed, healthy in his body, while he has enough to sustain him for his day and night, then it is as if he has gained the entire world.

Allâh has specified His Lordship over the House, even though He is the Lord of all that exists; He singled out the mention of the House to honor it.

﴿وَءَامَنَهُم مِّنْ خَوْفٍ﴾

And made them safe from fear.

Because He has given them the favors of safety and stability, they should worship Him alone without associating partners with Him, and without worshipping anyone other than Him, such as a statue, a rival, or a child.

Ibn Kathir said, "Whoever answers this command, Allâh will give him both safety in this world and in the Hereafter. Whoever disobeys Him, He Almighty will take it away from him in both worlds. Allâh Almighty says:

﴿وَضَرَبَ ٱللَّهُ مَثَلًا قَرْيَةً كَانَتْ ءَامِنَةً مُّطْمَئِنَّةً يَأْتِيهَا رِزْقُهَا رَغَدًا مِّن كُلِّ مَكَانٍ فَكَفَرَتْ بِأَنْعُمِ ٱللَّهِ فَأَذَاقَهَا ٱللَّهُ لِبَاسَ ٱلْجُوعِ وَٱلْخَوْفِ بِمَا كَانُوا۟ يَصْنَعُونَ ﴿١١٢﴾ وَلَقَدْ جَآءَهُمْ رَسُولٌ مِّنْهُمْ فَكَذَّبُوهُ فَأَخَذَهُمُ ٱلْعَذَابُ وَهُمْ ظَٰلِمُونَ ﴿١١٣﴾﴾

And Allâh puts forward the example of a township (Makkah), that dwelt secure and well content; its provision coming to it in abundance from every place, but it (its people) denied the favors of Allâh (with ungratefulness). So Allâh made it taste the extreme hunger (famine) and fear, because of that which they used to do. And verily, there had come to them a Messenger from among themselves, but they denied him, so the torment overtook them while they were wrongdoers.[1]

---

[1] (*An-Nahl* 16:112,113)

What Can Be Derived From These Verses

1) When one reflects on this *Surah*, one appreciates Allâh's wisdom, mercy, and planning. How perfect He is! The All-Wise, Most Merciful.

2) Allâh Almighty relates His favors on the Quraish: the destruction of their enemies, preventing those enemies from entering Makkah, providing them with safety, giving them abundant provisions - all of which require gratitude.

3) It is compulsory to worship Allâh Almighty alone and to leave the worship of anyone other than Him.

4) We must be thankful for Allâh's blessings by praising Him and by using His favors in a way that pleases Him.

5) Life revolves around two: food to protect one from hunger and safety from fear.

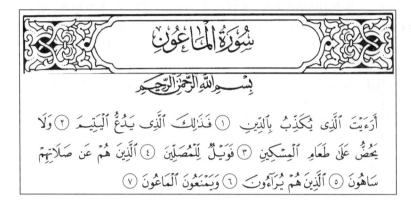

Surat Al-Ma'un

In the Name of Allâh, the Most Beneficent, the Most Merciful

1. *Have you seen him who denies the Recompense?* **2.** *That is he who repulses the orphan.* **3.** *And urges not the feeding of the poor.* **4.** *So woe unto those performers of Salat,* **5.** *Who delay their Salat from their stated fixed times.* **6.** *Those who do good deeds only to be seen.* **7.** *And refuse Al-Ma'un.*[1]

Its Name

It is called *Surat Al-Ma'un* because at the end of it Allâh Almighty condemned those who withhold *Al-Ma'un*. It is also called *Surat Ad-Deen* because at the beginning Allâh reproaches those who disbelieve in the *Deen*, meaning recompense in the Hereafter.

Its Relation To What is Before It

1) In the last *Surah* Allâh reminds the Quraish of one of His many favors: that it is He Who has fed them against hunger. Here, Allâh reproaches those who do not encourage the feeding of the poor.

2) Ordering us to worship Him alone, Allâh previously ordered them to worship the Lord of this House (the Ka'bah in Makkah). In this *Surah*, Allâh censures those who delay the prayers from their stated fixed times.

---

[1] (*Al-Ma'un* 107:1-7)

3) In the previous *Surah*, Allâh mentioned that despite His many favors on the Quraish, they still disbelieved in both resurrection and recompense. Here, Allâh Almighty follows up by warning and threatening them of His punishment.

The Meanings Of Its Words

(أَرَءَيْتَ) *Ara'aita*: Did you know? This is asked in a way to attract the attention of the listener.

(بِٱلدِّينِ) *Ad-Deen*: Accountability and recompense (in the Hereafter).

(ٱلَّذِى يَدُعُّ ٱلْيَتِيمَ) *Allathee Yadu'ul-Yateem*: One who violently pushes away an orphan, viciously repelling him, and taking away his rights.

(وَلَا يَحُضُّ عَلَىٰ طَعَامِ ٱلْمِسْكِينِ) *Wa laa Yahudhdhu 'Ala Ta'aamil-Miskeen*: i.e., he neither encourages himself nor others to feed the poor.

(فَوَيْلٌ لِّلْمُصَلِّينَ) *Fawailullil-Musalleen*: Ultimate ignominy and punishment for those who delay their prayers from their stated fixed times.

(عَن صَلَاتِهِمْ سَاهُونَ) *'An Salaatihim Saahoon*: They delay their prayers from the fixed times.

(يُرَآءُونَ) *Yuraa'oon*: They pray and do good deeds to show them off to others, not to perform them sincerely and purely for Allâh Almighty.

(وَيَمْنَعُونَ ٱلْمَاعُونَ) *Wa Yamna'oonal-Ma'oon*: *Ma'un* means all small things that are helpful in life, such as a needle, an axe, or a cooking pot. So Allâh Almighty is referring to people who refuse to give simple things to help others, things that can be used and returned without damage, such as kitchen utensils.

The Meaning in Summary

This *Surah* discusses two kinds of people:

1) The disbeliever who refuses to even acknowledge Allâh's favors and who disbelieves in the Day of Judgement, when deeds will be judged and just recompense will be given.

2) The hypocrite who does deeds not for the sake of Allâh Almighty; rather, he does them to show off to others.

As for the first group, Allâh Almighty mentions some of their contemptible deeds: they humiliate the orphan, repelling him viciously, and they do not perform good deeds; they do not even encourage others to help the poor. They do not fulfill the rights of their Lord, nor do they show the least bit of kindness to His creatures.

The second group, the hypocrites, delay their prayers, and when they do perform the prayer, they perform it in form, but not in spirit. In fact, they do deeds simply so others can watch and appreciate them. Both groups are threatened with ignominy and destruction; Allâh Almighty highlights their villainy by using a style that shows wonder at their contemptible deeds.

What Can Be Derived From These Verses

1) The emphasis on feeding orphans and the poor, and encouraging others to do so as well.

2) Belief in recompense and accountability are affirmed.

3) Being cautious about prayer, maintaining it in its time, being sincere while praying as well as when performing all other deeds.

4) We are encouraged to do good deeds, to help others in large and small matters, even if it is by lending, for instance, a pot or a book. This is because Allâh Almighty strongly reproached those who do not do even the small acts of kindness.

5) We must be careful and avoid adopting any of the characteristics of the hypocrites.

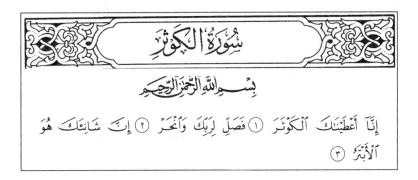

Surat Al-Kawthar

In the Name of Allâh, the Most Beneficent, the Most Merciful

1. Verily, We have granted you Al-Kawthar. 2. Therefore turn in prayer to your Lord and sacrifice (to Him only). 3. For he who hates you, he will be cut off.[1]

Its Name

The name of this *Surah*, *Al-Kawthar* is mentioned in the first verse:

Verily, We have granted you *Al-Kawthar*.

Al-Kawthar means much and perpetual good in this world and in the Hereafter. It is also said to mean a river in Paradise.

The Subject Matter Of This *Surah*

It discusses the blessed favors given to the Prophet ﷺ.

In What Context Was This *Surah* Revealed

It was revealed to refute one of the disbelievers, Al-'Aas bin Wa'il. When the Prophet's son from Khadijah, 'Abdullah, died, Al-'Aas said that the Prophet ﷺ was *Abtar*, or a man who has no son. This was said by Ibn 'Abbas, Muqatil, Al-Kalbi, and most scholars of *Tafsir*. It is also reported that Ibn 'Abbas said, "It was revealed about Abu Jahl." Nonetheless, its meaning embraces all those who show enmity to the

---

[1] (*Al-Kawthar* 108:1-3)

Prophet ﷺ, those who are mentioned above, and others as well.

The Meanings Of Its Words

(إِنَّآ أَعْطَيْنَاكَ) *Inna A'tainaaka*: We (Allâh Almighty) have bestowed upon you, O Muhammad.

(ٱلْكَوْثَرَ) *Al-Kawthar*: i.e., a river in Paradise, or much and perpetual good in this life and in the Hereafter.

(فَصَلِّ لِرَبِّكَ) *Fa-Salli Li-Rabbika*: So consistently perform the prayer, purely and sincerely for Allâh Almighty, showing gratefulness for His blessings.

(وَٱنْحَرْ) *Wanhar*: The sacrifice, or the *Hadi* (the *Hajj* sacrifice), or *Udhhiyyah* (sacrificed on 'Eid Al-Adhha).

(شَانِئَكَ) *Shaani'aka*: The one who detests you.

(ٱلْأَبْتَرُ) *Al-Abtar*: (The one who detests you) is the one who is cut off, cut off from all good, or cut off from having offspring.

The Meaning in Summary

Allâh Almighty says to His Prophet, Muhammad ﷺ, "Verily, We have granted you *Al-Kawthar*," much good and blessings, which also includes a river in Paradise called *Al-Kawthar*. The Prophet ﷺ is also granted the *Hawdh* (on the Day of Judgement), which in size is one month (the time it takes to cross it) in length and one month in width. The water of the *Hawdh* is whiter than milk and sweeter than honey. Its containers are like the stars in the sky, in terms of their numbers and brightness. Whoever takes a drink from the *Hawdh* will never feel thirst afterwards, for eternity.

After mentioning His favors upon the Prophet ﷺ, He ordered him: "turn in prayer to your Lord and sacrifice." Allâh Almighty mentions these two forms of worship because they are the best forms of worship and the best means of getting closer to Allâh Almighty. During the prayer, one submits both his heart and limbs to Allâh Almighty. And when one makes the sacrifice, he gives up the most valuable thing he has, which is his wealth, and the hearts of men innately love wealth and love to keep it to themselves. Then Allâh Almighty continues by mentioning the situation of the one who hates the Prophet ﷺ, and who belittles him; such a person, Allâh

Almighty says, is cut off from all good, cut off from being remembered.

As for the Prophet ﷺ, he is truly complete, the most complete a human being can possibly be. His name is remembered and his helpers and followers are many. The *Surah* ends by giving glad tidings to the Prophet ﷺ - that his enemies will be humiliated and cut off from all good, both in this life and in the Hereafter. On the other hand, the Prophet's name is mentioned on the pulpit and in other places; the tongues of men will continue to mention his noble name until the end of this world.

What Can Be Derived From These Verses

1) Allâh clarified His honor for His Messenger Muhammad ﷺ.

2) The *Ahadith* about *Al-Kawthar* emphasize this, and that it is a river in Paradise.

3) The prayer, the sacrifice, and all other acts of worship - must be performed purely and sincerely for the sake of Allâh Almighty only.

4) Supplicating against the oppressor is legislated.

5) Allâh Almighty granted victory to His servant and Messenger, Muhammad ﷺ. He consoled the Prophet ﷺ and refuted his enemies.

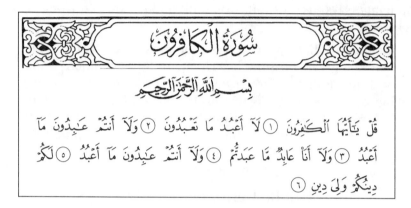

Surat Al-Kafirun

In the Name of Allâh, the Most Beneficent, the Most Merciful

1. *Say: "O you disbelievers!* **2.** *I worship not that which you worship.* **3.** *Nor will you worship that which I worship.* **4.** *And I shall not worship that which you are worshipping.* **5.** *Nor will you worship that which I worship.* **6.** *To you be your religion, and to me my religion."*[1]

Its Name

It is called *Surat Al-Kafirun* because Allâh Almighty ordered His Prophet Muhammad ﷺ to address the disbelievers, telling them that he will not worship the idols and statues that they worship: "Say: 'O you disbelievers! I do not worship what you worship...'" It is also called *Surat Al-Ikhlas* and *Surat Al-Munabatha* (the rejection) and *Al-Bara'ah* (the innocence) from *Shirk*.

The Subject Matter Of This *Surah*

It is a *Surah* about *Tawhid* and declaring one's innocence from *Shirk* and misguidance. The idolators of Makkah invited Allâh's Messenger ﷺ to a truce, requesting him to worship their gods for one year in return for them worshipping his God for one year. This *Surah* was revealed to put a stop to the ambitions of the disbelievers, making a distinction between the people of faith and the worshippers of idols,

---

[1] (*Al-Kafirun* 109:1-6)

and it rejects the base offer that was presented by the disbelievers for the present and future.

Its Relation to What is Before It

In the previous *Surah*, Allâh Almighty ordered us to sincerely worship Him Almighty alone, without associating any partners with Him. In this *Surah*, the *Surah* of *Tawhid* and innocence from *Shirk*, Allâh makes it clear that our worship is different, independent, and autonomous from the worship of the disbelievers, for the Prophet ﷺ and his followers worship Allâh Almighty alone: they worship neither the statues nor the idols of the disbelievers. This point is emphasized through repetition, and it ends by clearly stating that the Prophet ﷺ has his religion, while they have theirs.

The Virtues Of This *Surah*

It is established that Allâh's Messenger ﷺ read this *Surah* along with *Qul Huwallâhu Ahad* (*Surah* 112) on the following occasions:

1) In the two units of prayer made after *Tawaf*.

2) In the two units of the *Fajr* (*Sunnah*) prayer.

3) In the two units (*Sunnah*) that follow the *Maghrib* prayer.

4) And he ﷺ would perform the *Witr* prayer by reciting, *Sabbih*, *Qul Yaa-Ayuhal-Kaafiroon*, and *Qul Huwallahu Ahad*.

In What Context Was This *Surah* Revealed

'Abdur-Razzaaq reported that Wahb said, "The disbelievers of Quraish said to the Messenger of Allâh ﷺ, 'If it would please you to follow us for a year and then for us to return to your religion for a year.' And so Allâh Almighty revealed:

$$﴿قُل يَـٰٓأَيُّهَا ٱلۡكَـٰفِرُونَ﴾$$

Say: O you disbelievers ...''

There are other narrations as well, and though they are slightly different, they impart a similar meaning.

The Meanings Of Its Words

(قُل) *Qul*: Say (O Muhammad ﷺ).

(يَـٰٓأَيُّهَا ٱلۡكَـٰفِرُونَ) *Yaa-Ayuhal-Kaafiroon*: The leaders of *Shirk* in Makkah.

(لَا أَعْبُدُ مَا تَعْبُدُونَ) *Laa A'budu Maa Ta'budoon*: I worship not that which you worship — in the future.

(وَلَا أَنتُمْ عَبِدُونَ مَا أَعْبُدُ) *Wa laa Antum 'Aabidoona Maa A'bud*: Nor will you worship that which I worship — in the future and the present. It has been said that the previous two phrases are meant to emphasize the same point. It has also been said that verses 2 and 3 point to the different objects of worship, for the Prophet ﷺ worships Allâh alone, while the disbelievers worship statues and idols. Meanwhile, verses 4 and 5 point to the difference in worship itself, for the worship of the Prophet ﷺ is pure for Allâh Almighty alone — it is not corrupted by *Shirk* or by forgetfulness; their worship, however, is *Shirk* in its entirety, so the two different kinds of worship can never meet.

(لَكُمْ دِينُكُمْ) *Lakum Deenukum*: To you be your religion — the *Shirk* that you follow.

(وَلِيَ دِينِ) *Wa Liya Deen*: And to me my religion — *Tawhid* and Islam, which I follow, and which I do not reject.

What Can Be Derived From These Verses

1) The belief in divine Preordainment and Decree is established here for both the disbeliever and the believer.

2) Allâh Almighty protected the Prophet ﷺ from accepting the evil proposal of the disbelievers.

3) A clear distinction must be made between the people of faith and the people of disbelief and *Shirk*.

Important Note

Ar-Razi said, "When people disagree with one another these days, they say the phrase, 'To you be your religion, and to me my religion.' This practice is forbidden; the Qur'an was not revealed to be quoted in such a way; rather, it was revealed to be reflected upon and to be applied." (*Tafsir Ar-Razi* 22:148)

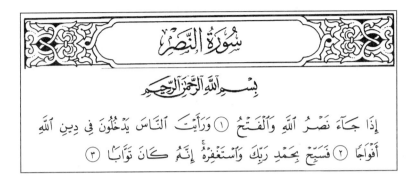

Surat An-Nasr

In the Name of Allâh, the Most Beneficent, the Most Merciful

1. *When there comes the help of Allâh and the Conquest.* **2.** *And you see that the people enter in Allâh's religion in crowds.* **3.** *So, glorify the Praises of your Lord, and ask for His forgiveness. Verily, He is the One Who accepts the repentance and Who forgives.* [1]

Its Name

It is called *Surat An-Nasr* because it is a word that appears in the first verse. It literally means "help" and it is referring to Allâh's help that caused the conquest of Makkah. It is also called *Surat At-Tawdi'* (farewell, because it suggests the parting of the Prophet ﷺ from this world).

The Subject Matter Of This *Surah*

This *Surah* discusses the conquest of Makkah, through which Allâh Almighty granted victory and honor to the Muslims. Islam then spread throughout the Arabian Peninsula, and ever so quickly, *Shirk* and misguidance were rooted out. With this conquest people entered into Allâh's religion in crowds: the banner of Islam was raised and the religion of statues faded away. That the Prophet ﷺ was informed about this conquest before it occurred is one of the clear signs that indicate the validity of his Prophethood.

---

[1] (*An-Nasr* 110:1-3)

Its Relation To What is Before It

In the previous *Surah*, Allâh Almighty said that the religion that Muhammad ﷺ was calling to was diametrically opposed to the religion of the disbelievers; here, Allâh Almighty informs the disbelievers of Makkah that their religion will die away and that the religion called to by the Prophet ﷺ will overcome it, and become the religion of the vast majority in their populated areas.

The Virtues Of This *Surah*

At-Tirmithi recorded a *Hadith* from Anas, may Allâh be pleased with him, and he said that it was *Hasan*. In it the Prophet ﷺ said:

«أَنَّهَا تَعْدِلُ رُبْعَ الْقُرْآنِ»

It (*An-Nasr*) is equivalent to one quarter of the Qur'an.

In What Context Was This *Surah* Revealed

Al-Bukhari and others recorded that Ibn 'Abbas, may Allâh be pleased with them, said, "Umar bin Al-Khattab used to make me sit with the elderly men who fought in the Battle of Badr. Some of them were uncomfortable with that and said to 'Umar, 'Why do you bring this boy to sit with us while we have sons like him?' One day, 'Umar called me and made me sit in the gathering of those people; and I think that he called me just to show them. 'Umar then asked them, 'What do you say about the interpretation of the saying of Allâh:

﴿إِذَا جَآءَ نَصْرُ اللَّهِ وَالْفَتْحُ﴾

When there comes the help of Allâh and the Conquest'[1]

Some of them said, 'We are ordered to praise Allâh and ask His forgiveness when Allâh's help and Conquest comes to us.' Some others kept quiet and did not say anything. On that, 'Umar asked me, 'Do you say the same, O Ibn 'Abbas?' I replied, 'No.' He asked, 'What do you say then?' I replied, 'That is the sign of the death of Allâh's Messenger ﷺ which Allâh informed him of. Allâh said:

﴿إِذَا جَآءَ نَصْرُ اللَّهِ وَالْفَتْحُ ۝ وَرَأَيْتَ النَّاسَ يَدْخُلُونَ فِي دِينِ اللَّهِ أَفْوَاجًا ۝ فَسَبِّحْ بِحَمْدِ رَبِّكَ وَاسْتَغْفِرْهُ إِنَّهُ كَانَ تَوَّابًا ۝﴾

---

[1] (*An-Nasr* 110:1)

When there comes the Help of Allâh and the Conquest. So
glorify the praises of your Lord and ask His forgiveness. He is
the One Who accepts the repentance and forgives.'[1]

With that, 'Umar said, 'I do not know anything about it other than
what you have said.'"

The Meanings Of Its Words

(إِذَا جَآءَ نَصْرُ اللَّهِ) *Itha Jaa'a Nasrullahi*: i.e., when Allâh makes His
Prophet Muhammad ﷺ victorious over his enemies — the
polytheists.

(وَٱلْفَتْحُ) *Al-Fath*: i.e., the conquest of Makkah.

(فِى دِينِ اللَّهِ) *Fee Deenillahi*: Allah's religion, i.e., Islam.

(أَفْوَاجًا) *Afwaaja*: In many packed crowds.

(فَسَبِّحْ بِحَمْدِ رَبِّكَ) *Fasabbih Bihamdi Rabbika*: Glorify Allâh Almighty,
considering Him far above having a partner, and at the same time,
praise Him.

(وَٱسْتَغْفِرْهُ) *Wastaghfirhu*: Repent to Allâh Almighty and ask Him to
forgive you.

(تَوَّابًا) *Tawwaaba*: i.e., Allâh Almighty often accepts the repentance
of His worshippers.

The Meaning in Summary

This *Surah* first gives glad tidings of a great event with far reaching
implications and then gives the Prophet ﷺ certain commands to
follow when that event takes place. At the same time, Allâh Almighty
alludes to some of the results of that event.

The glad tidings are for Allâh's help to the Messenger of Allâh ﷺ, the
conquest of Makkah, and the mass acceptance of Islam, when
throngs upon throngs of people will enter the religion, many of
whom were previously its enemies. All of those blessed events took
place.

Upon the realization of the conquest, Allâh Almighty ordered the
Prophet ﷺ to thank Him, glorify Him, praise Him, and ask His
forgiveness. Then there are two matters that Allâh Almighty alludes to:

[1] (*An-Nasr* 110:1-3)

1) That the victory of the religion will continue and increase with the Prophet's glorification and praising of Allâh Almighty; and with his asking for Allâh's forgiveness. Allâh Almighty says:

$$﴿ لَئِن شَكَرْتُمْ لَأَزِيدَنَّكُمْ ﴾$$

If you give thanks, I will give you more.[1]

This was seen during and after the period of the rightly-guided caliphs, which is why Allâh's help continued, so that the boundaries of Islam expanded to a size unsurpassed by any other religion in history. And there were peoples who entered the fold of Islam, who had previously resisted entering any other religion. But only when Muslims abandoned Allâh's commands and divided into groups did well-known events take place that signified something of a decline for Muslims. Nonetheless, Allâh's favors and mercy for this nation and religion have reached high levels that surpassed anyone's expectations and dreams.

2) That the Prophet's death is near. His life was a most superior one, and in Islam, all superior matters end with asking forgiveness from Allâh ﷻ, such as in the prayer and Hajj. By ordering the Prophet ﷺ to praise Him and seek forgiveness from Him, Allâh Almighty hints to his death, and suggests that he should prepare to meet his Lord. So the Prophet ﷺ ended his life on the highest of notes - may Allâh's blessings and peace be upon him. When bowing and prostrating, he ﷺ would say, "How perfect You are, O Allâh, our Lord, and I praise you. O Allâh, forgive me."

What Can Be Derived From These Verses

1) It is legislated to inform others of someone's death, but not in the way of an announcement and not in a loud voice.

2) When a blessing is realized for us, we must be thankful to Allâh Almighty; one way of doing so is to make the prostration for thankfulness.

3) When bowing or prostrating in the prayer, it is legislated to say, "How perfect You are, O Allâh, our Lord, and I praise you. O Allâh, forgive me."

---

[1] (*Ibrahim* 14:7)

4) Allâh's religion is Islam, for He said:

﴿إِنَّ ٱلدِّينَ عِنـدَ ٱللَّهِ ٱلْإِسْلَـٰمُ﴾

Truly, the religion with Allâh Almighty is Islam.[1]

And, He said:

﴿وَمَن يَبْتَغِ غَيْرَ ٱلْإِسْلَـٰمِ دِينًا فَلَن يُقْبَلَ مِنْهُ﴾

And whoever seeks the religion other than Islam, it will never be accepted of him.[2]

5) We appreciate the virtues of saying "*Subhaanallah* (How perfect Allâh is!)" and "*Alhamdulillah* (All praise is for Allâh)" when we consider this: To glorify and praise Allâh Almighty was enough for the Prophet ﷺ and his nation to fulfill what was incumbent upon them in terms of showing thankfulness for the blessings of the victory and conquest.

---

[1] (*Aal 'Imran* 3:19)
[2] (*Aal 'Imran* 3:85)

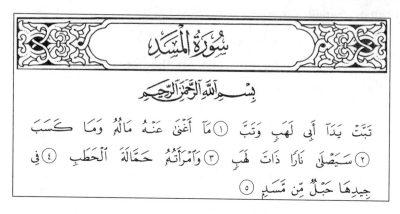

Surat Al-Masad

In the Name of Allâh, the Most Beneficent, the Most Merciful
1. *Perish the two hands of Abu Lahab, and perish he.* **2.** *His wealth and his children will not benefit him!* **3.** *He will be burnt in a Fire of blazing flames!* **4.** *And his wife too, who carries wood.* **5.** *In her neck is a twisted rope of Masad (palm fiber).* [1]

Its Name

It is called *Surat Al-Masad* because it mentions that Umm Jamil, the wife of Abu Lahab, will have a twisted rope of palm fiber tied around her neck in the Hellfire.

It is also called *Surat Tabbat*, a name that is taken from the first word of the first verse, which means, perish the two hands of Abu Lahab. It is also called *Abu Lahab* and *Lahab*.

The Subject Matter Of This *Surah*

This *Surah* deals with the punishment and destruction of Abu Lahab and his wife. Abu Lahab was an enemy of Allâh Almighty and His Messenger ﷺ; so bitter was his enmity that he abandoned his living in order to follow the Prophet ﷺ wherever he would go and discourage people from believing in him. This *Surah* promises him that the Hellfire will surround him from all directions and that he will roast therein. His wife accompanies him because she was his

[1] (Al-Masad 111:1-5)

partner, helping him to harm the Prophet ﷺ.

Its Relation To What is Before It

In *Surat An-Nasr*, Allâh Almighty informs us that the recompense for the obedient worshipper is victory in this world and a great reward in the Hereafter; meanwhile, in *Surat Al-Masad* Allâh Almighty shows us the end awaiting the disobedient: loss in this world and punishment in the Hereafter.

In What Context Was This *Surah* Revealed

In their *Sahihs*, Al-Bukhari and Muslim recorded that Sa'id bin Jubair narrated that Ibn 'Abbas, said, "When

$$﴿وَأَنذِرْ عَشِيرَتَكَ ٱلْأَقْرَبِينَ ٢١٤﴾$$

And warn your tribe of near kindred.

was revealed, Allâh's Messenger ﷺ climbed As-Safa and said:

«يَا صَبَاحَاهُ»

'*Yaa Sabaahaa* (A loud call for help, one that is usually made during the morning time).'

The people of Quraish gathered around him and said, 'What is the matter with you?' He said:

«أَرَأَيْتُمْ إِنْ أَخْبَرْتُكُم أَنَّ الْعَدُوَّ مُصَبِّحُكُم أَوْ مُمَسِّيكُمْ أَمَا كُنْتُمْ تُصَدِّقُونِي»

'If I were to tell you that the enemy was coming in the morning or evening, would you believe me.'

They said, 'Yes, indeed!' He ﷺ said,

«فَإِنِّي نَذِيرٌ لَكُمْ بَيْنَ يَدَيْ عَذَابٍ شَدِيدٍ»

'Then I am a warner to you of an imminent punishment that is severe.'

Abu Lahab said, 'Perish and loss to you, is this why you called us.' And then Allâh Almighty revealed:

$$﴿تَبَّتْ يَدَا أَبِي لَهَبٍ﴾$$

Perish the two hands of Abu Lahab and perish he!"

The Meaning Of Its Words

(تَبَّتْ يَدَا أَبِي لَهَبٍ) *Tabbat Yadaa Abee Lahab*: Literally, may his hands be perished and lost; but here, it is referring to his deeds.

(وَتَبَّ) *Wa Tabb*: The word for perished is used again, but this time it means, may he perish himself in the Hellfire.

(مَا أَغْنَى عَنْهُ مَالُهُ وَمَا كَسَبَ) *Maa Aghnaa Anhu Maaluhoo wa Maa Kasab*: What will his wealth serve him in the face of Allâh's anger and punishment, in this world and in the Hereafter!

(وَمَا كَسَبَ) *Wa Maa Kasab*: i.e., his wealth, children, and so on.

(سَيَصْلَى نَارًا ذَاتَ لَهَبٍ) *Sayasla Naaran Thaata Lahab*: He will be burnt in a Fire of blazing flames.

(ذَاتَ لَهَبٍ) *Thaata Lahab*: Blazing and burning.

(وَامْرَأَتُهُ) *Wamraa'tuhu*: i.e., Umm Jamil, his wife.

(حَمَّالَةَ الْحَطَبِ) *Hammalatal-Hatab*: i.e., she will carry the thorns of *Sa'dan*, which she used to scatter on paths she expected the Prophet ﷺ to take.

(فِي جِيدِهَا) *Fee Jeedihaa*: i.e., on her neck.

(حَبْلٌ مِن مَسَدٍ) *Hablum-mim-Masad*: i.e., made from palm fiber.

The Meaning in Summary

This *Surah* discusses the destruction of Abu Lahab, an uncle of the Prophet ﷺ. He was a bitter enemy and would inflict severe harm on the Prophet ﷺ. He had no religion, no scruples, and not even a sense of loyalty to relatives — may Allâh punish him severely. Allâh Almighty condemned Abu Lahab in this *Surah*, which is to serve as a humiliation for him until the Day of Judgement. So He said:

﴿تَبَّتْ يَدَآ أَبِى لَهَبٍ﴾

Perish the two hands of Abu Lahab.

Meaning, he will be lost and humiliated in his works.

﴿وَتَبَّ﴾

And perish he!

He will never escape.

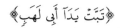

﴿مَآ أَغْنَىٰ عَنْهُ مَالُهُ﴾

His wealth and children will not benefit him...
The wealth he has that causes him to transgress.

﴿وَمَا كَسَبَ﴾

...and children.

None of this will avert Allâh's punishment from him when he suffers it.

﴿سَيَصْلَىٰ نَارًا ذَاتَ لَهَبٍ﴾

He will be burnt in a Fire of blazing flames!

Meaning, he will be surrounded by the Fire from every side, he and his wife who carried the wood. She was severe in her atrocities against Allâh's Messenger ﷺ, she and her husband cooperating in sin and transgression, rushing and hastening to evil in any way they could to harm the Messenger ﷺ. She would even scatter *Sa'dan* (a tree) thorns in the path where the Prophet ﷺ would walk.

﴿فِي جِيدِهَا حَبْلٌ مِّن مَّسَدٍ﴾

In her neck is a twisted rope of *Masad.*

Meaning around her neck will be a rope of palm fiber, as a judgement from Allâh for their enmity against Allâh and His Messenger ﷺ.

What Can Be Derived From These Verses

1) Allâh Almighty destroyed not only Abu Lahab's wicked plans to hurt the Prophet ﷺ, but destroyed him as well.

2) Neither money nor children can avail a person when he deserves the Hellfire for perpetrating deeds that anger Allâh Almighty.

3) It is categorically forbidden to harm a believer.

4) That being related to a righteous person will be of no help if one is following *Shirk* and disbelief, for was not Abu Lahab the uncle of the Prophet ﷺ, and is not his abode the blazing Hellfire.

5) There is an amazing miracle in this chapter. It was revealed while Abu Lahab and his wife were still alive and it informed them that they would be punished in the Hellfire, which meant that they would not accept Islam before they died. And indeed, things turned out exactly as Allâh Almighty informed, and He Almighty is the All-Knower of both the seen and the unseen.

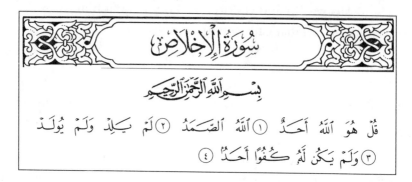

Surat Al-Ikhlas

In the Name of Allâh, the Most Beneficent, the Most Merciful

1. *Say: "He is Allâh Almighty, (the) One.* **2.** *Allâhus-Samad (Allâh — the Self-Sufficient Master, Whom all creatures need, He neither eats nor drinks).* **3.** *He begets not, nor was He begotten.* **4.** *And there is none coequal or comparable to Him.*"[1]

Its Name

It has many names, the most famous of which is *Surat Al-Ikhlas*, because it speaks about the pure *Tawhid* of Allâh Almighty, Who is free from all faults, and Who has no partner.

The Subject Matter of This *Surah*

It discusses the perfect Qualities of Allâh, the Exalted, the One, qualities that are eternal. He Almighty doesn't need anyone, but all turn to Him with their needs. Far above is He from having any faults and from anyone being similar to, or like Him. This chapter refutes the Christians, who believe in the trinity, and it refutes the polytheists, who believe that He Almighty has children — far, far is Allâh Almighty above the evil they attribute to Him.

Its Relation To What is Before It

Surat Al-Kafirun frees one from having any ties with all forms of

---

[1] (*Al-Ikhlas* 112:1-4)

disbelief and *Shirk*, while this *Surah* establishes the opposite of *Shirk* and disbelief — *Tawhid*, for indeed Allâh Almighty has all perfect qualities that are eternal in their perfection, while He Almighty is free from having a partner or one who is similar to Him. That is why these two *Surahs* are often recited together in prayer — such as the two units of (the *Sunnah* prayer for) *Fajr* and after *Tawaf*, the *Sunnah* prayer after *Maghrib*, the *Istikharah* prayer, and the traveller's prayer.

The Virtues Of This Surah

There are many *Ahadith* that have been related mentioning the virtues of this *Surah*, some of which signify that when one recites it, his reward is equal to that for reciting one-third of the Qur'an. Muslim and At-Tirmithi recorded that Abu Hurairah, may Allâh be pleased with him, related that Allâh's Messenger ﷺ said:

«احْتَشِدُوا فَإِنِّي سَأَقْرَأُ عَلَيْكُمْ ثُلُثَ الْقُرْآنِ»

Gather together, for I will recite to you one-third of the Qur'an.

When some people gathered, the Prophet ﷺ came out to them and recited:

﴿قُلْ هُوَ اللَّهُ أَحَدٌ﴾

Say: "He is Allâh, (the) One."

Then he entered, and the Companions said to one another, "The Messenger of Allâh ﷺ said, 'I will recite to you one-third of the Qur'an?" Then the Prophet ﷺ came out and said:

«إِنِّي قُلْتُ: سَأَقْرَأُ عَلَيْكُمْ ثُلُثَ الْقُرْآنِ، أَلَا وَإِنَّهَا تَعْدِلُ ثُلُثَ الْقُرْآنِ»

Indeed, I said that I would recite one-third of the Qur'an to you; indeed, it is equal to one-third of the Qur'an.

In What Context Was This *Surah* Revealed

Imam Ahmad, At-Tirmithi, and Ibn Jarir (At-Tabari) recorded that Ubai bin Ka'b said that the polytheists said to the Prophet ﷺ, "O Muhammad, tell us of your Lord's lineage." And Allâh Almighty revealed:

﴿قُلْ هُوَ ٱللَّهُ أَحَدٌ ۝ ٱللَّهُ ٱلصَّمَدُ ۝ لَمْ يَلِدْ وَلَمْ يُولَدْ ۝ وَلَمْ يَكُن لَّهُۥ كُفُوًا أَحَدٌ ۝﴾

Say: "He is Allâh, (the) One. *Allâhus-Samad* (Allâh — the Self-Sufficient Master, Whom all creatures need, He neither eats nor drinks). He begets not, nor was He begotten. And there is none coequal or comparable to Him."

The Meanings Of Its Words

(قُلْ هُوَ ٱللَّهُ أَحَدٌ) *Qul Huwallahu Ahad*: Say, O Muhammad, to the one who asks you about your Lord, "He is Allâh, the One."

(ٱللَّهُ ٱلصَّمَدُ) *Allâhus-Samad*: Allâh is the only One Who deserves to be worshipped.

(ٱلصَّمَدُ) *As-Samad*: The Self-Sufficient Master, Whom all creatures perpetually ask to have their needs fulfilled.

(لَمْ يَلِدْ) *Lam Yalid*: He Almighty will never perish, for nothing is born except that it dies.

(وَلَمْ يُولَدْ) *Wa Lam Yoolad*: There was never a time that He Almighty didn't exist and then was brought into being; rather, He Almighty always was and always will be.

(وَلَمْ يَكُن لَّهُۥ كُفُوًا أَحَدٌ) *Wa Lam Yakullahu Kufuwan Ahad*: There is none that is similar or equal to Him.

The Meaning in Summary

Allâh Almighty orders us to say the following with certainty and conviction and understanding: "He is Allâh, the One." For He Almighty alone is perfect; He Almighty has the Most Beautiful Names and the Most Perfect and Exalted Attributes, and His Actions are most divine — there is nothing similar or equal to Him. Everyone in the heavens and earth turns to Him Almighty to fulfill their needs, for they are most needy of Him. Indeed Allâh Almighty is perfect and complete — His Knowledge is perfect and complete, His mercy is perfect and complete, and so are His other Qualities. From His perfection and completeness is that He begets not, nor was He begotten: He Almighty indeed doesn't need anyone. "And there is none equal or comparable to Him": Not in His Names, not in His

Attributes, and not in His Actions, Exalted is He, Most High. This chapter deals with that category of *Tawhid* that relates to His Names and Attributes.

What Can Be Derived From These Verses

1) In this *Surah*, we learn about Allâh Almighty by learning some of His Names and Attributes.

2) *Tawhid* and prophethood are affirmed in this *Surah*.

3) It is from the greatest of falsehood to ascribe a child to Allâh Almighty.

4) We must worship Allâh Almighty alone, without associating any partner with Him, for He Almighty alone has the right to be worshipped by His creation.

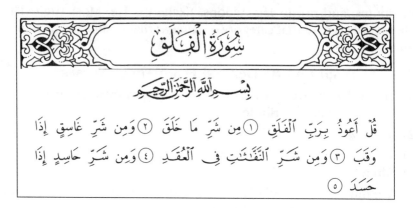

Surat Al-Falaq

In the Name of Allâh, the Most Beneficent, the Most Merciful

1. Say: "I seek refuge with (Allâh) the Lord of the Falaq
(daybreak). **2.** From the evil of what He has created; **3.** And
from the evil of the darkening (night) as it comes with its
darkness; (or the moon as it sets or goes away). **4.** And from
the evils of those who practice witchcraft when they blow in
the knots. **5.** And from the evil of the envier when he
envies."[1]

Its Name

It is called *Surat Al-Falaq* because that word appears in the first
verse: "I seek refuge with (Allâh) the Lord of the *Falaq*."

The Subject Matter Of This *Surah*

Here, the reciter seeks refuge from the evil found in the creation. We
are taught in this *Surah* to take refuge in the sanctuary of the Most
Merciful. So we seek refuge in Allâh from the evil of the night when it
becomes dark, a time when souls feel uncomfortable and when evil
and the people of evil spread throughout the land. We also seek
refuge here from the envious and the magician. This is one of the
two chapters that the Prophet ﷺ would read to take protection with
Allâh Almighty.

---

[1] (*Al-Falaq* 113:1-5)

Its Relation To What is Before It

In *Surat Al-Ikhlas*, Allâh Almighty explained something of His Divinity, teaching us not to ascribe to Him that which is not suitable to Him, His Names, or His Attributes. Here, we learn what we should take refuge in Allâh Almighty from, regarding this world; we also learn of some of those from creation who try to prevent people from worshipping Allâh Almighty alone, such as the polytheists and the rest of the devils from mankind and the jinn.

The Virtues Of the *Mu'awwithatain*

Muslim in his *Sahih*, Ahmad, At-Tirmithi and An-Nasa'i, all recorded that 'Uqbah bin 'Amir said, "Allâh's Messenger ﷺ said:

«أَلَمْ تَرَ آيَاتٍ أُنْزِلَتْ هَذِهِ اللَّيْلَةَ لَمْ يُرَ مِثْلُهُنَّ قَطُّ»

Did you not see that there have been verses revealed tonight the like of which has not been seen before? (They are:)

﴿قُلْ أَعُوذُ بِرَبِّ ٱلْفَلَقِ﴾

Say: "I seek refuge with the Lord of the *Falaq*."

﴿قُلْ أَعُوذُ بِرَبِّ ٱلنَّاسِ﴾

Say: "I seek refuge with the Lord of mankind."

Al-Bukhari and the *Sunan* Compilers recorded the usage of these three *Surahs* related to seeking refuge as a means of cure. 'Aishah, may Allâh be pleased with her, said that when Allâh's Messenger ﷺ would take rest in his bed every night, he would gather his hands, blow a mist of saliva into them, and recite into them:

﴿قُلْ هُوَ ٱللَّهُ أَحَدٌ﴾

Say: "He is Allâh, (the) One."

﴿قُلْ أَعُوذُ بِرَبِّ ٱلْفَلَقِ﴾

Say: "I seek refuge in (Allâh) the Lord of the *Falaq*."

and:

﴿قُلْ أَعُوذُ بِرَبِّ ٱلنَّاسِ﴾

Say: "I seek refuge in (Allâh) the Lord of mankind."

Then he would wipe his hands over those areas of his body that he was able to reach, beginning with his head, his face, and then the front part of his body, doing all of the above three times.

In What Context Were The *Mu'awwithatain* Revealed

The circumstances surrounding the revelation of this *Surah* relate to the story of the spell cast by Lubayd bin Al-A'sam the Jew upon Allâh's Messenger ﷺ as recorded in the Two *Sahihs* from 'Aishah, may Allâh be pleased with her. He cast a spell by taking the remains of the Prophet's hair after he combed it and by taking the teeth of the comb. He then took a string, put eleven knots in it that were pricked by needles. On that occasion, the *Mu'awwithatain* (the last two *Surahs* of the Qur'an) were revealed. Each time the Prophet ﷺ recited a verse, one of the knots would untie. The Prophet ﷺ felt a sense of liveliness as the last knot became untied; he stood as if he was freed from a rope being tied around him. Jibril began to read invocations upon him, saying, "In the Name of Allâh, I read invocations that, by the Will of Allâh, are meant to cure) from all things that harm you, from the evil of the jealous one and the one with the evil eye. And may Allâh cure you.''

The Meanings Of Its Words

(أَعُوذُ) *A'oothu*: I take refuge and protection in...

(ٱلْفَلَقِ) *Al-Falaq*: A splitting in something until one part of it separates from another. It is said that it refers to the morning.

(ٱلرَّبِّ) *Ar-Rabb*: The sole Owner and Controller of the universe: Allâh Almighty.

(وَٱلرَّبِّ) *War-Rabb*: Ar-Rabb is more suitable in this context than all of Allâh's other Names, because protecting from harm is one of the Qualities of the Lord.

(مِن شَرِّ مَا خَلَقَ) *Min Sharri Maa Khalaq*: From animals and inanimate objects.

(غَاسِقٍ) *Ghaasiqin*: The night when its darkness is most intense.

(وَقَبَ) *Waqab*: When the darkness enters it, because it is a time when evil permeates.

(ٱلنَّفَّٰثَٰتِ) *An-Naffaathaati*: Magicians who blow in knots.

(فِى ٱلْعُقَدِ) *Feel-'Uqad*: The plural of *'Uqdah*, which means knot.

Magicians make knots from rope, thread and the like.

(النَّفْث) *An-Nafth*: Blowing, with spit coming out from the mouth.

(حَاسِد) *Haasid*: The one who desires for the blessings of others to be taken away from them.

The Meaning in Summary

Allâh Almighty orders us to say:

﴿أَعُوذُ﴾

I seek protection

meaning, we should say it, seeking protection in Him.

﴿بِرَبِّ ٱلْفَلَقِ﴾

with the Lord of *Al-Falaq*

The splitter of the seed and the pit, and the splitting of the dawn.

﴿مِن شَرِّ مَا خَلَقَ﴾

from the evil of what He has created.

— including men, jinn and animals. So we seek protection from them with their Creator.

Then Allâh Almighty, after saying that in general, mentions a specific example:

﴿وَمِن شَرِّ غَاسِقٍ إِذَا وَقَبَ﴾

From the evil of the darkening (night) as it comes with its darkness.

At night, evil spirits and harmful animals roam in the open.

﴿وَمِن شَرِّ ٱلنَّفَّثَٰتِ فِى ٱلْعُقَدِ﴾

And from the evils of those who practice witchcraft when they blow in the knots.

i.e., from the evil of magicians who practice their nefarious activities by blowing into knots.

﴿وَمِن شَرِّ حَاسِدٍ إِذَا حَسَدَ﴾

And from the evil of the envier when he envies.

The envious is one who wishes for the blessings to be removed from the one that he is envious of. He strives to the best of his ability to have that blessing removed; to foil his plans, we need to seek refuge in Allâh Almighty from his evil. One category of the envious one is that of the evil eye, for the evil eye only results from an envious person who has a wicked nature and evil soul.

In this *Surah*, we seek refuge in Allâh Almighty from evil in general and in specific; in it, we learn that magic is a reality, the harms of which we should beware of, and so we seek refuge in Allâh Almighty from magic and from its practitioners.

What Can Be Derived From These Verses

1) We must seek protection in Allâh Almighty from every frightful thing and from anything we cannot defend ourselves from, either because that thing is hidden or because we are not able (to defend ourselves from it).

2) It is forbidden to blow in knots, for it is a form of magic. Performing magic is disbelief; the punishment for the magician is execution by sword.

3) Envy is categorically forbidden, for it is a most dangerous disease: it made the son of Adam kill his brother and it led the brothers of Yusuf to plot against him. And because of envy, Adam was taken out of Paradise.

4) *Al-Ghibtah* (desire) is not a form of envy. The difference is that the envious person wishes for a blessing to be removed from his brother, while desire means that one wants what his brother has without wishing for that blessing to be taken away from his brother.

5) Magic is real; one should be wary of its harm by seeking refuge in Allâh Almighty from it and from its practitioners.

6) The one who is responsible for the evil eye is in the same category as the envious one, for they have the same evil and wicked nature.

7) There are three things that Allâh Almighty specifically mentioned as things that we should seek refuge from, such as the night when it becomes most dark; during the night, as Ar-Razi mentioned, predators come out of their lairs, harmful rodents and insects come out of their dark hideouts, the thief attacks, fires occur; little help can be found at that time, when the people of evil and corruption are in their greatest numbers.

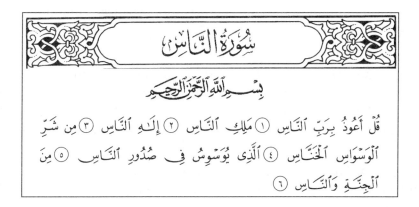

Surat An-Nas

In the Name of Allâh, the Most Beneficent, the Most Merciful

1. *Say: "I seek refuge with (Allâh) the Lord of mankind,* **2.** *The King of mankind,* **3.** *The Illah (God) of mankind,* **4.** *From the evil of the whisperer (devil who whispers in the hearts of men) who withdraws (from his whispering in one's heart after one remembers Allâh),* **5.** *Who whispers in the breasts of mankind,* **6.** *Of jinn and mankind"*[1]

Its Name

It is called *Surat An-Nas* not only because it is a word that appears in its first verse, but also because it is a word that appears five times in this short *Surah*.

The Subject Matter Of This *Surah*

In it, we seek protection with Allâh Almighty from the most evil and wicked of our enemies, *Iblis* (Satan, i.e., the Devil), and from his helpers, some of whom are from the jinn and some of whom are from mankind. The Devil and his helpers strive to lead man astray by whispering evil ideas into his heart and by any other means available.

The Meanings Of Its Words

(أَعُوذُ) *A' oothu*. I seek refuge, protection, and aid in...

---

[1] (*An-Nas* 114:1-6)

(بِرَبِّ ٱلنَّاسِ) *Bi-Rabbin-Naas*: The Creator, Owner, and Lord of mankind.

(مَلِكِ ٱلنَّاسِ) *Malikin-Naas*: The Master, King and Ruler of mankind.

(إِلَهِ ٱلنَّاسِ) *Ilahin-Naas*: The God of mankind, because no one deserves to be worshipped save Him.

(مِن شَرِّ ٱلْوَسْوَاسِ) *Min Sharril-Waswaas*: From the evil of the whisperer (Shaitaan), the noun is used because he whispers much evil into the hearts of men.

(ٱلْخَنَّاسِ) *Al-Khannaas*: The one who recoils and draws back from the heart when Allâh Almighty is remembered.

(فِى صُدُورِ ٱلنَّاسِ) *Fee Sudoorin-Naas*: (The *Shaitan* whispers) in their hearts when they are neglectful in remembering Allâh Almighty.

(مِنَ ٱلْجِنَّةِ وَٱلنَّاسِ) *Minal-Jinnati wan-Naas*: From the devils of the jinn and from the devils of mankind.

The Meaning in Summary

In this *Surah* we seek refuge in the Lord, King and God of mankind from the *Shaitan* (Satan), who is the source and material of all evil. He whispers in the hearts of men, beautifying evil deeds to them, making those deeds take on a good form. He invigorates them to do evil and enervates them from doing good, always twisting and distorting reality. But when one remembers His Lord and seeks His aid, the *Shaitan* recoils and draws back. Therefore, man should always seek refuge and protection in Allâh Almighty, the Lord of all that exists. The *Shaitan* strives to take man away from his main purpose, the worship of Allâh Almighty alone, which is why we must repel his evil by remembering Allâh Almighty; indeed, the *Shaitan* desires to make men join him and desires to make them become some of the inhabitants of the Hellfire. Whisperings and enticements to doing evil can issue from both jinn and men, which is why Allâh Almighty says, "Of jinn and mankind."

Explaining this chapter, Ibn Kathir said that three of Allâh's Attributes are mentioned: Lordship (*Rububiyyah*), Kingship (*Mulk*), and Godhood (*Uluhiyyah*).

He Almighty is the Lord, King, and God of all things. Because Allâh

Almighty has those perfect qualities, we seek refuge and protection in Him from the evil whisperings of the *Khannas* (i.e., the *Shaitan*, who recoils when Allâh Almighty is remembered). To every man is appointed a devil companion, who beautifies evil deeds in his eyes. In his *Sahih*, Muslim recorded that 'Abdullah bin Mas'ud, may Allâh be pleased with him, said Allâh's Messenger ﷺ said:

«مَا مِنْكُمْ مِنْ أَحَدٍ إِلَّا وَقَدْ وُكِّلَ بِهِ قَرِينُهُ مِنَ الْجِنِّ»

"There is none from you except that he is entrusted with a companion from the jinn."

The Companions asked, "And you as well, O Messenger of Allâh." He said:

«وَإِيَّايَ إِلَّا أَنَّ الله أَعَانَنِي عَلَيْهِ فَأَسْلَمَ فَلَا يَأْمُرُنِي إِلَّا بِخَيْرٍ»

"And me as well, except that Allâh has helped me overcome him, and he has become a Muslim. He doesn't order me except to do good."

There are two narrations: the first one, as mentioned above, indicates that the jinn companion of the Prophet ﷺ accepted Islam and became a believer; the second narration indicates that no, his jinn companion didn't accept Islam, but that Allâh Almighty kept the Prophet ﷺ safe from his evil and temptation.

What Can Be Derived From These Verses

1) We must seek refuge and protection in Allâh Almighty from the *Shaitan* (the Devil).

2) We seek refuge in Allâh Almighty, with His Lordship, with His being the Possessor and Owner of all things, with His being the One true God Who is worshipped alone, with His Beautiful Names and Exalted Attributes.

3) Mankind is honored here as Allâh Almighty specifically mentions that He Almighty is their Lord, even though He Almighty is the Lord of all that exists.

4) The *Shaitan* is man's most bitter foe; he tries to lead man astray by whispering evil thoughts to him.

5) We must be wary of the *Shaitan*, his whispers, and we should

never be neglectful in remembering Allâh Almighty.

6) When we mention Allâh Almighty, the *Shaitan* is repelled, and he withdraws in a state of grief.

7) When we seek refuge and protection in Allâh Almighty, we are worshipping Him; so to dedicate this kind of worship to anyone else is *Shirk*.

8) We must seek refuge and protection in Allâh from both the devils from among the jinn and from the devils among man.

9) Allâh Almighty alone deserves to be worshipped. He is the Owner and Possessor and King of all that exists, and He Almighty alone deserves to be worshipped by creation.

10) Just as the *Shaitan* whispers in the hearts of man, he also whispers in the hearts of jinn.

Important Benefit

The Qur'an ends on the *Mu'awwithatain* and begins with *Al-Fatihah*, so it has both a good beginning and end. That is the epitome and pinnacle of beauty because the worshipper seeks protection with his Lord at the beginning of his affairs and at the end of them.

Important Note

Ibn 'Abbas, may Allâh be pleased with them, said, "The *Shaitan* crouches on the heart of the son of Adam; when he (i.e. the son of Adam) forgets and is heedless (of the remembrance of Allâh), he whispers. But when the son of Adam remembers Allâh, he recoils and draws back."

The Prophet ﷺ said:

«إِنَّ الشَّيْطَانَ وَاضِعٌ خَطِمَهُ عَلَى قَلْبِ ابْنِ آدَمَ فَإِنْ هُوَ ذَكَرَ اللهَ خَنَسَ وَإِنْ نَسِيَهُ الْتَقَمَ قَلْبَهُ، فَذَلِكَ الْوَسْوَاسُ الْخَنَّاسُ»

Indeed, *Shaitan* puts his snout on the heart of the son of Adam. If he (the son of Adam) remembers Allâh, he recoils, and if he forgets, he devours his heart: and that is the whispering one who recoils and draws back.

Lesson Two
The Pillars Of Islam

Clarifying the five pillars of Islam, the first and greatest of which is to bear witness that *Laa Ilaha Illallâh wa Anna Muhammadan Rasoolullah* (none has the right to be worshipped except Allâh and Muhammad is Allâh's Messenger), with explanation of their meanings, and the conditions of *Laa Ilaha Illallâh* and its meaning: *Laa Ilaha* negates all that is worshipped other than Allâh; *Illa Allâh* affirms that worship must be for Allâh alone, Who has no partner.

As for the conditions of *Laa Ilaha Illallâh*, they are as follows:

1) Knowledge that negates ignorance
2) Certainty which negates doubt
3) Sincerity which negates *Shirk*
4) Truth which negates denial
5) Love which negates hate
6) Submission which negates abandoning
7) Acceptance which negates rejection
8) Disbelief in all that is worshipped other than Allâh

Clarifying the testimony *Muhammadan Rasoolullah* and what it includes: to believe what he informs, to obey what he commands, and to leave what he forbids. And we must worship Allâh only in a way that He Almighty and His Messenger ﷺ legislated.

Next, a student should learn about the remainder the five pillars of Islam: *Salat, Zakat*, fasting the month of Ramadhan, and *Hajj* to the Sacred House of Allâh for those who are able to perform it.

Defining Islam

Islam means for you to submit yourself to Allâh, by making your worship sincere and pure for Him alone, by obeying Him, and by absolving yourself of *Shirk* and its people. *Shirk* (to associate partners with Allâh in worship) was the creed of the Arabs before the advent of Muhammad ﷺ. Al-Bukhari related that Abu Raja' Al-'Utaridi said, "We used to worship stones, and when we would find a stone that was better than the one we were worshipping, we would throw the former away and start worshipping the latter. If we couldn't find a stone, we would gather a heap of dirt, then we would bring a sheep and milk it over that pile, and then we would walk around it (as a ritual worship)."

In many different verses, the Qur'an clarified for us the state of nations in general before the advent of the Prophet's message; Allâh Almighty says:

$$﴿ وَيَعْبُدُونَ مِن دُونِ ٱللَّهِ مَا لَا يَضُرُّهُمْ وَلَا يَنفَعُهُمْ وَيَقُولُونَ هَٰؤُلَاءِ شُفَعَٰؤُنَا عِندَ ٱللَّهِ ﴿١٨﴾ ﴾$$

And they worship besides Allâh things that hurt them not, nor profit them, and they say: "These are our intercessors with Allâh."[1]

$$﴿ وَٱلَّذِينَ ٱتَّخَذُوا۟ مِن دُونِهِۦٓ أَوْلِيَآءَ مَا نَعْبُدُهُمْ إِلَّا لِيُقَرِّبُونَآ إِلَى ٱللَّهِ زُلْفَىٰٓ ﴿٣﴾ ﴾$$

And those who take protectors and helpers besides Him (say): "We worship them only that they may bring us near to Allâh."[2]

$$﴿ إِنَّا جَعَلْنَا ٱلشَّيَٰطِينَ أَوْلِيَآءَ لِلَّذِينَ لَا يُؤْمِنُونَ ﴿٢٧﴾ وَإِذَا فَعَلُوا۟ فَٰحِشَةً قَالُوا۟ وَجَدْنَا عَلَيْهَآ ءَابَآءَنَا وَٱللَّهُ أَمَرَنَا بِهَاۗ قُلْ إِنَّ ٱللَّهَ لَا يَأْمُرُ بِٱلْفَحْشَآءِۖ أَتَقُولُونَ عَلَى ٱللَّهِ مَا لَا تَعْلَمُونَ ﴿٢٨﴾ ﴾$$

Verily, We made the *Shayatin* (devils) protectors and helpers for those who believe not. And when they commit a *Fahishah* (evil deed, going around the Ka'bah in naked state, every kind

---

[1] (*Yunus* 10:18)

[2] (*Az-Zumar* 39:3)

of unlawful sexual intercourse etc.), they say: "We found our fathers doing it, and Allâh has commanded us of it." Say: "Nay, Allâh never commands of *Fahishah*. Do you say of Allâh what you know not?"[1]

﴿ إِنَّهُمُ ٱتَّخَذُواْ ٱلشَّيَـٰطِينَ أَوْلِيَآءَ مِن دُونِ ٱللَّهِ وَيَحْسَبُونَ أَنَّهُم مُّهْتَدُونَ ۝ ﴾

Surely they took the *Shayatin* (devils) as protectors and helper instead of Allâh, and consider that they are guided.[2]

﴿ وَجَعَلُواْ لِلَّهِ مِمَّا ذَرَأَ مِنَ ٱلْحَرْثِ وَٱلْأَنْعَـٰمِ نَصِيبًا فَقَالُواْ هَـٰذَا لِلَّهِ بِزَعْمِهِمْ وَهَـٰذَا لِشُرَكَآئِنَا فَمَا كَانَ لِشُرَكَآئِهِمْ فَلَا يَصِلُ إِلَى ٱللَّهِ وَمَا كَانَ لِلَّهِ فَهُوَ يَصِلُ إِلَىٰ شُرَكَآئِهِمْ سَآءَ مَا يَحْكُمُونَ ۝ ﴾

And they assign to Allâh a share of the tilth and cattle which He has created, and they say: "This is for Allâh," according to their pretending, "and this is for our (Allâh's so called) partners." But the share of of their (Allâh's so called) "partners" reaches not Allâh, while the share of Allâh reaches their (Allâh's so called) "partners"! Evil is the way they judge![3]

There are many other verses that impart a similar meaning. Other than the Qur'an, the sayings of the Prophet ﷺ and of trustworthy historians give us a good glimpse of the state of the previous nations: before the advent of the Prophet's message, people were practicing many different kinds of *Shirk* - some worshipped statues and idols, others worshipped the dwellers of graves, others worshipped the sun, moon, and planets, while yet others worshipped other things. The Messenger of Allâh ﷺ invited them all to worship Allâh alone and to leave the falsehood that they and their fathers were upon. Allâh Almighty says:

﴿ قُلْ يَـٰٓأَيُّهَا ٱلنَّاسُ إِنِّى رَسُولُ ٱللَّهِ إِلَيْكُمْ جَمِيعًا ٱلَّذِى لَهُۥ مُلْكُ ٱلسَّمَـٰوَٰتِ وَٱلْأَرْضِ لَآ إِلَـٰهَ إِلَّا هُوَ يُحْىِۦ وَيُمِيتُ فَـَٔامِنُواْ بِٱللَّهِ وَرَسُولِهِ ٱلنَّبِىِّ ٱلْأُمِّىِّ ٱلَّذِى يُؤْمِنُ بِٱللَّهِ وَكَلِمَـٰتِهِۦ وَٱتَّبِعُوهُ لَعَلَّكُمْ تَهْتَدُونَ ۝ ﴾

---

[1] *(Al-A'raf* 7:27,28)

[2] *(Al-A'raf* 7:30)

[3] *(Al-An'am* 6:136)

Say (O Muhammad ﷺ): "O mankind! Verily, I am sent to you all as the Messenger of Allâh — to whom belongs the dominion of the heavens and the earth. None has the right to be worshiped but He. It is He who gives life and causes death. So believe in Allâh and His Messenger, the Prophet who can neither read nor write, who believes in Allâh and His Words, and follow Him so that you may be guided."[1]

﴿الٓرۚ كِتَٰبٌ أَنزَلْنَٰهُ إِلَيْكَ لِتُخْرِجَ ٱلنَّاسَ مِنَ ٱلظُّلُمَٰتِ إِلَى ٱلنُّورِ بِإِذْنِ رَبِّهِمْ إِلَىٰ صِرَٰطِ ٱلْعَزِيزِ ٱلْحَمِيدِ ١﴾

Alif-Lam-Ra. (This is) a Book which We have revealed to you in order that you might lead mankind out of darkness into light by their Lord's Leave to the path of Almighty, the Owner of all praise.[2]

﴿يَٰٓأَيُّهَا ٱلنَّبِيُّ إِنَّآ أَرْسَلْنَٰكَ شَٰهِدًا وَمُبَشِّرًا وَنَذِيرًا ٤٥ وَدَاعِيًا إِلَى ٱللَّهِ بِإِذْنِهِۦ وَسِرَاجًا مُّنِيرًا ٤٦﴾

O Prophet! Verily, We have sent you as a witness, and a bearer of glad tidings, and a warner. And as one who invites to Allâh by His Leave, and as a lamp spreading light.[3]

﴿وَمَآ أُمِرُوٓاْ إِلَّا لِيَعْبُدُواْ ٱللَّهَ مُخْلِصِينَ لَهُ ٱلدِّينَ حُنَفَآءَ ٥﴾

And they were commanded not, but that they should worship Allâh, and worship none but Him Alone.[4]

﴿يَٰٓأَيُّهَا ٱلنَّاسُ ٱعْبُدُواْ رَبَّكُمُ ٱلَّذِى خَلَقَكُمْ وَٱلَّذِينَ مِن قَبْلِكُمْ لَعَلَّكُمْ تَتَّقُونَ ٢١﴾

O mankind! Worship your Lord who created you and those who were before you so that you may become pious.[5]

﴿وَقَضَىٰ رَبُّكَ أَلَّا تَعْبُدُوٓاْ إِلَّآ إِيَّاهُ . . . ﴾

And your Lord has decreed that you worship none but Him.[6]

---

[1] (*Al-A'raf* 7:158)

[2] (*Ibrahim* 14:1)

[3] (*Al-Ahzab* 33:45,46)

[4] (*Al-Bayyinah* 98:5)

[5] (*Al-Baqarah* 2:21)

[6] (*Al-Isra'* 17:23)

And the verses that impart a similar meaning are many.

In many verses of the Qur'an, Allâh informs us that though they were polytheists, they admitted that Allâh was their Creator and Provider; they only worshipped other than Him as intermediaries between them and Allâh. He says:

$$﴿وَيَعْبُدُونَ مِن دُونِ ٱللَّهِ مَا لَا يَضُرُّهُمْ وَلَا يَنفَعُهُمْ وَيَقُولُونَ هَٰٓؤُلَآءِ شُفَعَٰٓؤُنَا عِندَ ٱللَّهِ﴾$$

And they worship besides Allâh things that hurt them not, nor profit them, and they say: "These are our intercessors with Allâh."[1]

Here are only some of the many verses that give a similar meaning:

$$﴿قُلْ مَن يَرْزُقُكُم مِّنَ ٱلسَّمَآءِ وَٱلْأَرْضِ أَمَّن يَمْلِكُ ٱلسَّمْعَ وَٱلْأَبْصَٰرَ وَمَن يُخْرِجُ ٱلْحَيَّ مِنَ ٱلْمَيِّتِ وَيُخْرِجُ ٱلْمَيِّتَ مِنَ ٱلْحَيِّ وَمَن يُدَبِّرُ ٱلْأَمْرَ فَسَيَقُولُونَ ٱللَّهُ فَقُلْ أَفَلَا تَتَّقُونَ ۝﴾$$

Say: "Who provides for you from the sky and from the earth? Or who owns hearing and sight? And who brings out the living from the dead and brings out dead from living? And who disposes the affairs?" They will say: "Allâh." Say: "Will you not be then afraid of Allâh's punishment?"[2]

$$﴿وَلَئِن سَأَلْتَهُم مَّنْ خَلَقَهُمْ لَيَقُولُنَّ ٱللَّهُ فَأَنَّىٰ يُؤْفَكُونَ ۝﴾$$

And if you ask them who created them, they will surely say: "Allâh." How then are they turned away?[3]

The Pillars Of Islam:

This Great Religion — Islam — stands on five pillars; as recorded in the Two *Sahihs*, that Ibn 'Umar, may Allâh be pleased with them, related that the Prophet ﷺ said:

«بُنِيَ الإِسْلَامُ عَلَى خَمْسٍ: شَهَادَةِ أَنْ لَا إِلَهَ إِلَّا اللهُ، وَأَنَّ مُحَمَّدًا رَسُولُ اللهِ، وَإِقَامِ الصَّلَاةِ، وَإِيتَاءِ الزَّكَاةِ، وَصَوْمِ رَمَضَانَ، وَحَجِّ الْبَيْتِ»

[1] (*Yunus* 10:18)
[2] (*Yunus* 10:31)
[3] (*Az-Zukhruf* 43:87)

Islam is built on five: The testimony that none has the right to be worshipped but Allâh and that Muhammad is the Messenger of Allâh, the establishment of the prayer, the giving of *Zakat*, the fasting of Ramadhan, and *Al-Hajj* (pilgrimage) to the House (the Ka'bah).

The two testimonies comprise the first and most important pillar of Islam. Those testimonies are not meant for one to only utter them on his tongue - even though, by doing so, one outwardly enters the fold of Islam; rather, one must apply its meanings and implications as well. One must sincerely worship Allâh alone, believing that He truly deserves his worship, and believing that worship to all else is the greatest of falsehood.

One of the implications of those testimonies is that one must love Allâh and His Messenger ﷺ, which consequently requires one to worship Allâh alone, glorify Him, and follow the way of His Prophet ﷺ. Allâh Almighty says:

$$﴿قُلْ إِن كُنتُمْ تُحِبُّونَ ٱللَّهَ فَٱتَّبِعُونِي يُحْبِبْكُمُ ٱللَّهُ وَيَغْفِرْ لَكُمْ ذُنُوبَكُمْ﴾$$

Say: "If you (really) love Allâh then follow me, Allâh will love you and forgive you of your sins..."[1]

Another one of its implications is that we should obey the Messenger of Allâh ﷺ in all that he has commanded us:

$$﴿وَمَآ ءَاتَىٰكُمُ ٱلرَّسُولُ فَخُذُوهُ وَمَا نَهَىٰكُمْ عَنْهُ فَٱنتَهُوا۟﴾$$

And whatsoever the Messenger gives you, take it, and whatsoever he forbids you, abstain (from it).[2]

In a *Hadith* whose authenticity is agreed upon, the Prophet ﷺ said:

«ثَلَاثٌ مَنْ كُنَّ فِيهِ وَجَدَ بِهِنَّ حَلَاوَةَ الإِيمَانِ: أَنْ يَكُونَ اللهُ وَرَسُولُهُ أَحَبَّ إِلَيْهِ مِمَّا سِوَاهُمَا .. الحديث»

When one has in him the following three, he will have found with them the sweetness of faith: That Allâh and His Messenger are more beloved to him than all else...

---

[1] (*Aal 'Imran* 3:31)
[2] (*Al-Hashr* 59:7)

He ﷺ also said:

«لَا يُؤْمِنُ أَحَدُكُمْ حَتَّى أَكُونَ أَحَبَّ إِلَيْهِ مِنْ وَالِدِهِ وَوَلَدِهِ وَالنَّاسِ أَجْمَعِينَ»

Not one of you believes until I become more beloved to him than his father, child, and all other people.

The First Pillar Of Islam:

Ash-Shahadah (The Testimony)

"To bear witness that none has the right to be worshipped except Allâh and that Muhammad is the Messenger of Allâh."

Here is an outline of our discussion regarding the first pillar of Islam:

1) A discussion about *Laa Ilaha Illallâh* (None has the right to be worshipped except Allâh):
   i) The meaning of *Laa Ilaha Illallah*
   ii) What it means to bear witness to *Laa Ilaha Illallâh*.
   iii) Its status
   iv) Its virtues
   v) The pillars of the two testimonies
   vi) The conditions of *Laa Ilaha Illallâh*
   vii) Its effects

The Meaning of *Laa Ilaha Illallâh*

This phrase of *Tawhid* (Islamic Monotheism) contains many lofty meanings and implications; and we must first understand those meanings if we are to apply them; that way our application of the phrase will be based on knowledge. The phrase *Laa Ilaha Illallâh* has been mentioned in the Qur'an more than thirty times.

What It Means To Bear Witness To *Laa Ilaha Illallah*

Ash-Shahadah, or to bear witness, means to inform about something that you know of and that you believe to be true and established. That is the meaning of *Shahadah* in the Arabic language; in the *Shari'ah* it has this meaning: To admit and to believe that none deserves worship except Allâh alone, and He has no partners. So by saying *Laa Ilaha Illallâh*, we believe and affirm that none deserves worship except Allâh; we must stay steadfast upon this phrase and apply it. Therefore we must worship Allâh alone without associating any partner with Him. Allâh Almighty says:

﴾فَٱعْلَمْ أَنَّهُ لَا إِلَٰهَ إِلَّا ٱللَّهُ وَٱسْتَغْفِرْ لِذَنۢبِكَ﴿

So know that *Laa Ilaha Illallâh (none has the right to be worshiped but Allâh), and ask forgiveness for your sins.*[1]

Other *Ahadith* give a similar meaning and the Islamic nation agreed that the two testimonies, "I bear witness that none has the right to be worshipped except Allâh and that Muhammad is the Messenger of Allâh," are the first pillar of Islam, and upon them actions are based, meaning that no deed is accepted without them. The Imams of *Hadith* relate that the Prophet ﷺ said:

«بُنِيَ الإِسْلَامُ عَلَى خَمْسٍ: شَهَادَةِ أَنْ لَا إِلَهَ إِلَّا اللهُ وَأَنَّ مُحَمَّدًا رَسُولُ اللهِ وَإِقَامِ الصَّلَاةِ وَإِيتَاءِ الزَّكَاةِ وَصَوْمِ رَمَضَانَ وَالْحَجِّ لِمَنِ اسْتَطَاعَ إِلَيْهِ سَبِيلًا»

Islam is built on five: To bear witness that none has the right to be worshipped except Allâh and that Muhammad is the Messenger of Allâh, the establishment of the prayer, giving the *Zakat*, fasting the month of Ramadhan, and *Al-Hajj* (pilgrimage to Makkah) for whoever is able to bear the journey.

When we reflect on these five pillars, we should appreciate that each one of them deals with an important aspect related to man, and that each one makes up a strong and firm pillar in the house of Islam, a house that no one stays in except for the believer. The phrase of *Tawhid* (*Laa Ilaha Illallâh*) therefore wholly engages the heart while its effects surface on the limbs. The prayer uses all limbs, it is the strong and firm link between the creature and his Creator. A Muslim's relation to other Muslims is solidified through the rich giving the *Zakat* to the poor. A person is comprised of a soul and a body, of purity and desire; if man were left to himself, he would stray far away from Allâh, which is why Allâh legislated fasting for us. When we fast, our soul is cleansed and polished. After the heart has been filled with faith and after wealth is distributed as Allâh wishes, time comes for the societal ties to be strengthened in the Islamic world, and that occurs during their huge national conference during *Hajj*, when Muslims come from all places and gather.

We can also view the pillars from another perspective: the *Shahadah*

---

[1] (*Muhammad* 47:19)

is a test for the heart; prayer is a test for the limbs and for a Muslim's ability to organize himself and his time; *Zakat* is a test for man in his wealth; the fast is a test to see how much one is able to leave his desires for the sake of his Creator and Lord; and the *Hajj* is a test to see how much one is able to bear hardship and the difficulties of travelling in the way of Allâh.[1]

The Status of *Laa Ilaha Illallâh*

When they call to prayer, when they straighten the rows for prayer, during their sermons and conversations — Muslims announce the phrase of *Tawhid* on all of those occasions; it is the phrase by which the earth and the heavens are raised; all of creation is created for this phrase, and with it Allâh sent His Messengers, revealed His Books, and legislated His Laws. The Scale and Book of deeds have been set up for it. By this phrase we distinguish between the believers and the disbelievers. And concerning the phrase of *Tawhid*, all will be asked and held accountable for their deeds, some being rewarded and some punished.

The *Qiblah* and the swords of *Jihad* are both founded on this phrase, the phrase that is Allâh's right upon all of His creatures. It is the phrase of Islam and the key to Paradise. On the Day of Judgement everyone will be asked regarding two matters:

1) Whom did you worship?
2) How did you answer the Messengers?

The first is answered by the realization of one knowing, affirming, and applying *Laa Ilaha Illallâh*. The second is answered by knowing, following, and obeying the Messenger of Allâh ﷺ.[2]

It is the phrase that distinguishes between disbelief and Islam; it is the phrase of piety; it is the firm rope, and it is the phrase that Ibrahim made lasting among his offspring:

$$﴿وَجَعَلَهَا كَلِمَةً بَاقِيَةً فِي عَقِبِهِ لَعَلَّهُمْ يَرْجِعُونَ ۝﴾$$

And He made it a word lasting among his offspring, that they

---

[1] Taken from *"Ma'ni Laa Ilaha Illallâh"* by Badrud-Din Muhammad bin 'Abdullah Az-Zarkashi, who died in the year 794 after *Hijrah*.

[2] *Zaadul-Ma'aad*

may turn back (to repent to Allâh).[1]

Allâh testified to this phrase Himself, and so did the angels and those who have knowledge from His creation:

﴿شَهِدَ ٱللَّهُ أَنَّهُۥ لَآ إِلَٰهَ إِلَّا هُوَ وَٱلْمَلَٰٓئِكَةُ وَأُوْلُوا۟ ٱلْعِلْمِ قَآئِمًۢا بِٱلْقِسْطِ لَآ إِلَٰهَ إِلَّا هُوَ ٱلْعَزِيزُ ٱلْحَكِيمُ ١٨﴾

Allâh bears witness that *Laa Ilaha Illa Huwa* (none has the right to be worshiped but He), and the angels, and those having knowledge (also give this witness); (He is always) maintaining His creation in justice. *Laa Ilaha Illa Huwa* (none has the right to be worshiped but He), the All-Mighty, the All-Wise.[2]

The Virtues Of *Laa Ilaha Illallâh*

It has many virtues and superior merits that give it a high status; whoever says it sincerely, Allâh makes him enter Paradise; whoever says it without believing in it, his blood is spilled and his wealth is taken, in this world and the Hereafter — and his account is with Allâh. Al-Hafiz Ibn Rajab mentioned some of the many virtues of this phrase in his book, *Kalimatul-Ikhlaas*. One of its virtues is that it is the price for entering Paradise; when one's last words are *Laa Ilaha Illallâh*, he enters Paradise. It also protects one from the Hellfire.

Laa Ilaha Illallâh necessitates forgiveness, wipes away sins, and it is the best of good deeds. It breaks through all barriers until it reaches Allâh. It is the best phrase ever spoken by the Prophets, it is the best form of remembrance, and it is the best deed, and the deed most multiplied. Saying it is equivalent to freeing slaves and it protects one from the *Shaitan*. It is safety from the terrors of the Day of Gathering and it is the slogan of the believers when they will be raised from their graves. For whoever speaks it, the eight doors of Paradise are opened for him: he enters whichever one he pleases.

Another one of its virtues is that those who say it but also do evil deeds might enter the Hellfire, but they will necessarily exit from it.

---

[1] (*Az-Zukhruf* 43:28)

[2] (*Aal 'Imran* 3:18) Taken from *Muhaadharaat Feel-'Aqeedah* by Dr. Salih Al-Fawzan, p 61.

What is mentioned above consists of the titles written by Ibn Rajab to enumerate the virtues of *Laa Ilaha Illallâh*; he then went on to clarify and expand on each one of them in his book *Kalimatul-Ikhlaas,* pp 54-66.

There Are Two Pillars Of *Laa Ilaha Illallâh*

1) The first involves a negation by *Laa Ilaha*, a statement that does away with all forms of *Shirk* and that necessitates disbelief in all that is worshipped other than Allâh Almighty.

2) The second involves an affirmation by *Illallâh*, wherein we affirm that only Allâh deserves to be worshipped.

Both of these pillars are present in the following verse:

﴿فَمَن يَكْفُرْ بِٱلطَّٰغُوتِ وَيُؤْمِنۢ بِٱللَّهِ فَقَدِ ٱسْتَمْسَكَ بِٱلْعُرْوَةِ ٱلْوُثْقَىٰ﴾

Whoever disbelieves in *Taghut* (false deities) and believes in Allâh, then he has grasped the most trustworthy handhold that will never break.[1]

The first pillar is:

﴿فَمَن يَكْفُرْ بِٱلطَّٰغُوتِ﴾

Whosoever disbelieves in *Taghut.*

And the second pillar:

﴿وَيُؤْمِنۢ بِٱللَّهِ﴾

And believes in Allâh.

In another verse Allâh Almighty says:

﴿إِنَّنِى بَرَآءٌ مِّمَّا تَعْبُدُونَ ۝ إِلَّا ٱلَّذِى فَطَرَنِى فَإِنَّهُۥ سَيَهْدِينِ ۝﴾

Verily, I am innocent of what you worship, except Him Who did create me, and verily, He will guide me.[2]

The first pillar:

﴿إِنَّنِى بَرَآءٌ﴾

Verily, I am innocent of what you worship...

---

[1] (*Al-Baqarah* 2:256)
[2] (*Az-Zukhruf* 43:26,27)

The second pillar:

$$﴿ إِلَّا ٱلَّذِى فَطَرَنِى ﴾$$

...except Him Who did create me...

As Shaikh Muhammad bin 'Abdul-Wahhab said, "To bear witness that Muhammad is the Messenger of Allâh ﷺ means to obey him in what he orders, to believe him in what he informs, to stay away from that which he forbids, and to worship Allâh only in ways that are legislated in Islam."

When we obey the Messenger of Allâh ﷺ, we are in fact obeying Allâh, for Allâh ﷺ says:

$$﴿ قُلْ إِن كُنتُمْ تُحِبُّونَ ٱللَّهَ فَٱتَّبِعُونِى يُحْبِبْكُمُ ٱللَّهُ ﴾$$

Say: "If you really love Allâh then follow me, Allâh will love you.[1]

$$﴿ قُلْ أَطِيعُوا۟ ٱللَّهَ وَٱلرَّسُولَ ﴾$$

Say: "Obey Allâh and the Messenger..."[2]

We must believe what the Messenger of Allâh ﷺ informed us about regarding the past and the future, and regarding the unseen. And we should obey and follow him when he orders us, staying away from that which he forbids:

$$﴿ وَمَآ ءَاتَىٰكُمُ ٱلرَّسُولُ فَخُذُوهُ وَمَا نَهَىٰكُمْ عَنْهُ فَٱنتَهُوا۟ ﴾$$

And whatsoever the Messenger gives you, take it, and whatsoever he forbids you, abstain (from it).[3]

The Prophet ﷺ said:

«مَا أَمَرْتُكُمْ مِنْ أَمْرٍ فَأْتُوا مِنْهُ مَا اسْتَطَعْتُمْ، وَمَا نَهَيْتُكُمْ عَنْهُ فَاجْتَنِبُوهُ»

Whatever matters I have commanded you in, perform from them what you are able; and any matter that I have forbidden you from, stay away from it.

Also, we are limited in our worship of Allâh to only that which the Prophet ﷺ legislated, which is why the second condition for our

---

[1] (*Aal 'Imran* 3:31)

[2] (*Aal 'Imran* 3:32)

[3] (*Al-Hashr* 59:7)

deeds to be accepted is following the Messenger of Allâh ﷺ, who said:

«مَنْ عَمِلَ عَمَلاً لَيْسَ عَلَيْهِ أَمْرُنَا فَهُوَ رَدٌّ»

When one does an action that is not upon our matter, then it is rejected.

There are two pillars to the Testimony *Muhammadur-Rasoolullah* (Muhammad is the Messenger of Allâh):

1) To believe in and accept his message.
2) To believe that he is a slave of Allâh.

He himself said:

«إِنَّمَا أَنَا عَبْدٌ فَقُولُوا عَبْدُاللهِ وَرَسُولُهُ»

Indeed I am only a slave, so say: The slave of Allâh and His Messenger.

Therefore he is not to be raised above his status, nor are we to attribute to him any of the qualities that solely belong to Allâh, such as knowledge of the unseen, the ability to harm or benefit, the ability to remove hardship from the afflicted. In the most important occasions and contexts, Allâh described him as being His slave:

i) In regard to the revelation of the Qur'an:

﴿تَبَارَكَ ٱلَّذِى نَزَّلَ ٱلْفُرْقَانَ عَلَىٰ عَبْدِهِۦ﴾

Blessed is He Who sent down the Criterion (of right and wrong, i.e., this Qur'an) to His slave (Muhammad).[1]

ii) In relation to the Night Journey:

﴿سُبْحَٰنَ ٱلَّذِىٓ أَسْرَىٰ بِعَبْدِهِۦ﴾

Glorified (and Exalted) is He (Allâh) Who took His slave (Muhammad) for a journey by night.[2]

iii) In relation to prayer and supplication:

﴿وَأَنَّهُۥ لَمَّا قَامَ عَبْدُ ٱللَّهِ يَدْعُوهُ﴾

And when the slave of Allâh (Muhammad ﷺ) stood up

---

[1] (*Al-Furqan* 25:1)

[2] (*Al-Isra'* 17:1)

invoking in prayer to Him...[1]

iv) In the context of Allâh being sufficient for him as his Protector and Guardian:

$$﴿أَلَيْسَ اللَّهُ بِكَافٍ عَبْدَهُ﴾$$

Is not Allâh sufficient for His slave?[2]

Indeed Allâh honored the Prophet ﷺ, and He granted him many noble and wonderful characteristics, characteristics through which Allâh raised him in status and significance in relation to the rest of creation. Some of the ways in which Allâh distinguished him are listed as follows:

1) Allâh mentioned him among the elite group of Prophets, Prophets who were inspired by Allâh Almighty:

$$﴿إِنَّا أَوْحَيْنَا إِلَيْكَ كَمَا أَوْحَيْنَا إِلَى نُوحٍ وَالنَّبِيِّنَ مِنْ بَعْدِهِ وَأَوْحَيْنَا إِلَى إِبْرَاهِيمَ وَإِسْمَاعِيلَ وَإِسْحَاقَ وَيَعْقُوبَ وَالْأَسْبَاطِ وَعِيسَى وَأَيُّوبَ وَيُونُسَ وَهَارُونَ وَسُلَيْمَانَ وَآتَيْنَا دَاوُدَ زَبُورًا ﴿١٦٣﴾﴾$$

Verily, We have inspired you as We inspired Nuh and the Prophets after him; We (also) inspired Ibrahim, Isma'il, Ishaq, Yaqub, and *Al-Asbat* [the twelve sons of Ya'qub], 'Iesa, Ayub, Yunus, Harun, and Sulaiman, and to Dawud We gave the Zabur[3]

2) He is the last of the Prophets:

$$﴿مَا كَانَ مُحَمَّدٌ أَبَا أَحَدٍ مِّن رِّجَالِكُمْ وَلَكِن رَّسُولَ اللَّهِ وَخَاتَمَ النَّبِيِّنَ﴾$$

Muhammad is not the father of any man among you, but he is the Messenger of Allâh and the last (end) of the Prophets.[4]

3) He is the first of the Muslims, those who submit themselves to Allâh:

$$﴿إِنِّي أُمِرْتُ أَنْ أَكُونَ أَوَّلَ مَنْ أَسْلَمَ﴾$$

---

[1] (*Al-Jinn* 72:19)

[2] (*Az-Zumar* 39:36)

[3] (*An-Nisa'* 4:163)

[4] (*Al-Ahzab* 33:40)

Verily, I am commanded to be the first of those who submit themselves to Allâh (as Muslims).[1]

4) We should appreciate his high ranking when we learn that he is closer to the believers than their own selves are and that his wives are their mothers:

﴿ٱلنَّبِىُّ أَوْلَىٰ بِٱلْمُؤْمِنِينَ مِنْ أَنفُسِهِمْ وَأَزْوَٰجُهُۥٓ أُمَّهَٰتُهُمْ وَأُوْلُوا۟ ٱلْأَرْحَامِ بَعْضُهُمْ أَوْلَىٰ بِبَعْضٍ فِى كِتَٰبِ ٱللَّهِ﴾

The Prophet is closer to the believers than their own selves are, and his wives are their (believers') mothers (as regards respect and marriage). And blood relations among each other have closer personal ties in the Decree of Allâh (regarding inheritance).[2]

5) On the Day of Gathering, he will have special rights from Allâh to intercede for Muslims; he is the Prophet of mercy, the best of creation. The general nature of his message is meant for both mankind and jinn. He is the chief of the children of Adam and he is the Prophet of Islam.

The Conditions Of *Laa Ilaha Illallâh* Are Seven

While some scholars believe that there are seven conditions to the Phrase of *Ikhlaas* (purity, i.e., the phrase, *Laa Ilaha Illallâh*), others hold that there are eight:

1. Knowledge: When one knows that Allâh is the only One Who deserves to be worshipped and that to worship other than Him is falsehood, and when he adheres to the implications of that knowledge, he truly knows its meanings. Allâh Almighty says:

﴿فَٱعْلَمْ أَنَّهُۥ لَآ إِلَٰهَ إِلَّا ٱللَّهُ﴾

So know that *Laa Ilaha Illallâh* (none has the right to be worshipped but Allâh).[3]

﴿إِلَّا مَن شَهِدَ بِٱلْحَقِّ وَهُمْ يَعْلَمُونَ﴾

Except those who bear witness to the truth, and they

---

[1] (*Al-An'am* 6:14)

[2] (*Al-Ahzab* 33:6)

[3] (*Muhammad* 47:19)

know.[1]

The Prophet ﷺ said:

«مَنْ مَاتَ وَهُوَ يَعْلَمُ أَنَّهُ لَا إِلَهَ إِلَّا الله دَخَلَ الْجَنَّةَ»

When one dies, knowing that indeed none has the right to be
worshipped except Allâh, he enters Paradise.

2. **Certainty:** One must not only say this phrase, but he must also
believe with certainty and conviction in his heart that what he is
saying is true: That Allâh truly deserves to be worshipped and
that all others taken as gods are false:

﴿وَالَّذِينَ يُؤْمِنُونَ بِمَا أُنزِلَ إِلَيْكَ وَمَا أُنزِلَ مِن قَبْلِكَ وَبِالْآخِرَةِ هُمْ يُوقِنُونَ﴾

And who believe in that which has been sent down (revealed)
to you, and in what was sent down before you, and they
believe with certainty in the Hereafter.[2]

Abu Hurairah, may Allâh be pleased with him, related that the
Prophet ﷺ said:

«أَشْهَدُ أَنْ لَا إِلَهَ إِلَّا الله وَأَنِّي رَسُولُ الله لَا يَلْقَى اللهَ بِهَا عَبْدٌ غَيْرَ شَاكٍّ
فِيهَا إِلَّا دَخَلَ الْجَنَّةَ»

I bear witness that none has the right to be worshipped
except Allâh and that indeed I am the Messenger of Allâh. No
slave meets Allâh with this, having no doubt thereof, except
that he enters Paradise. (Recorded by Muslim)

In another *Hadith*, Abu Hurairah, may Allâh be pleased with him,
related that the Prophet ﷺ said to him:

«مَنْ لَقِيتَ وَرَاءَ هَذَا الْحَائِطِ يَشْهَدُ أَنَّهُ لَا إِلَهَ إِلَّا الله مُسْتَيْقِنًا بِهَا قَلْبُهُ
فَبَشِّرْهُ بِالْجَنَّةِ»

Whoever you meet behind this wall who testifies that indeed
none has the right to be worshipped except Allâh, with his
heart believing in it with certainty, then give him glad tidings
of Paradise. (Recorded by Muslim)

---

[1] (*Az-Zukhruf* 43:86)
[2] (*Al-Baqarah* 2:4)

Allâh Almighty described the believers:

﴿إِنَّمَا ٱلْمُؤْمِنُونَ ٱلَّذِينَ ءَامَنُوا۟ بِٱللَّهِ وَرَسُولِهِ ثُمَّ لَمْ يَرْتَابُوا۟﴾

Only those are the believers who believe in Allâh and His Messenger, and afterward doubt not.[1]

Meaning, they have a complete level of certainty and conviction. Those who have doubts are the hypocrites:

﴿إِنَّمَا يَسْتَـْٔذِنُكَ ٱلَّذِينَ لَا يُؤْمِنُونَ بِٱللَّهِ وَٱلْيَوْمِ ٱلْأَخِرِ وَٱرْتَابَتْ قُلُوبُهُمْ فَهُمْ فِى رَيْبِهِمْ يَتَرَدَّدُونَ﴾

It is only those who believe not in Allâh and the Last Day and whose hearts are in doubt that ask your leave (to be exempted from *Jihad*). So in their doubts they waver.[2]

3. Sincerity that negates *Shirk*: one must perform all deeds and actions, sincerely and purely for Allâh, seeking His pleasure. That intention must not be corrupted or polluted in the least:

﴿وَمَآ أُمِرُوٓا۟ إِلَّا لِيَعْبُدُوا۟ ٱللَّهَ مُخْلِصِينَ لَهُ ٱلدِّينَ﴾

And they were commanded not, but that they should worship Allâh and worship none but Him Alone.[3]

Abu Hurairah, may Allâh be pleased with him, related that the Prophet ﷺ said:

«أَسْعَدُ النَّاسِ بِشَفَاعَتِي مَنْ قَالَ لَا إِلَهَ إِلَّا اللهُ خَالِصًا مِنْ قَلْبِهِ»

The happiest of people with my intercession is he who says, 'None has the right to be worshipped but Allâh,' sincerely from his heart. (Recorded by Al-Bukhari)

'Uthman, may Allâh be pleased with him, related that the Prophet ﷺ said:

«إِنَّ الله حَرَّمَ عَلَى النَّارِ مَنْ قَالَ لَا إِلَهَ إِلَّا اللهُ إِلَهَ يَبْتَغِي بِذَلِكَ وَجْهَ اللهِ»

Verily, Allâh has made forbidden the Fire from the one who says, 'None has the right to be worshipped except Allâh,'

---

[1] (*Al-Hujurat* 49:15)

[2] (*At-Tawbah* 9:45)

[3] (*Al-Bayinah* 98:5)

seeking from that Allâh's Face. (Recorded by Al-Bukhari)

4. Truth which negates denial: One must be truthful with Allâh in his faith, truthful in his belief, truthful in his sayings, and truthful in the way he carries the message of Islam. Allâh Almighty says:

﴿يَـٰٓأَيُّهَا ٱلَّذِينَ ءَامَنُواْ ٱتَّقُواْ ٱللَّهَ وَكُونُواْ مَعَ ٱلصَّـٰدِقِينَ ۝﴾

O you who believe! Be afraid of Allâh, and be with those who are true (in words and deeds).[1]

Mu'ath bin Jabal, may Allâh be pleased with him, related that the Prophet ﷺ said:

«مَا مِنْ أَحَدٍ يَشْهَدُ أَنْ لَا إِلَهَ إِلَّا اللهُ وَأَنَّ مُحَمَّدًا عَبْدُهُ وَرَسُولُهُ صَادِقًا مِنْ قَلْبِهِ إِلَّا حَرَّمَهُ اللهُ عَلَى النَّارِ»

There is none that truthfully from his heart bears witness that none has the right to be worshipped except Allâh and that Muhammad is His slave and Messenger, except that Allâh will forbid upon him the Hellfire. (Recorded by Al-Bukhari)

5. Love which negates hate: One must love this phrase, its implications, and its adherents who act according to its meanings. Also, one must love Allâh and His Messenger ﷺ, giving preference to loving them over all objects of love:

﴿وَمِنَ ٱلنَّاسِ مَن يَتَّخِذُ مِن دُونِ ٱللَّهِ أَندَادًا يُحِبُّونَهُمْ كَحُبِّ ٱللَّهِ وَٱلَّذِينَ ءَامَنُوٓاْ أَشَدُّ حُبًّا لِّلَّهِ﴾

And of mankind are some who take others besides Allâh as rivals (to Allâh). They love them as they love Allâh. But those who believe, love Allâh more.[2]

6. Submission which negates *Shirk*: One must submit himself to all that this magnificent phrase requires of him - Allâh Almighty says:

﴿وَأَنِيبُوٓاْ إِلَىٰ رَبِّكُمْ وَأَسْلِمُواْ لَهُ﴾

And turn in repentance to your Lord and submit to Him (in Islam).[3]

---

[1] (*At-Tawbah* 9:119)

[2] (*Al-Baqarah* 2:165)

[3] (*Az-Zumar* 39:54)

Submission means compliance to Allâh's Commands. Allâh Almighty says:

﴿وَمَن يُسْلِمْ وَجْهَهُ إِلَى اللَّهِ وَهُوَ مُحْسِنٌ فَقَدِ اسْتَمْسَكَ بِالْعُرْوَةِ الْوُثْقَى﴾

And whosoever submits his face (himself) to Allâh, while he is a *Muhsin* (good-doer) then he has grasped the most trustworthy handhold.[1]

And Allâh said:

﴿وَمَنْ أَحْسَنُ دِينًا مِّمَّنْ أَسْلَمَ وَجْهَهُ لِلَّهِ وَهُوَ مُحْسِنٌ﴾

And who can be better in religion than one who submits his face (himself) to Allâh and he is a *Muhsin* (a good doer).[2]

And:

﴿فَلَا وَرَبِّكَ لَا يُؤْمِنُونَ حَتَّى يُحَكِّمُوكَ فِيمَا شَجَرَ بَيْنَهُمْ ثُمَّ لَا يَجِدُوا فِي أَنفُسِهِمْ حَرَجًا مِّمَّا قَضَيْتَ وَيُسَلِّمُوا تَسْلِيمًا ۝﴾

But no, by your Lord, they can have no faith, until they make you (Muhammad ﷺ) judge in all disputes between them, and find in themselves no resistance against your decisions, and accept (them) with full submission.[3]

7. Acceptance which negates rejection: One must accept all of the implications of this phrase, both with his heart and tongue, for Allâh Almighty says:

﴿قُولُوا ءَامَنَّا بِاللَّهِ وَمَا أُنزِلَ إِلَيْنَا﴾

Say, "We believe in Allâh and that which has been sent down to us..."[4]

As for those who say it without accepting it, they are those about whom Allâh Almighty says:

﴿إِنَّهُمْ كَانُوا إِذَا قِيلَ لَهُمْ لَا إِلَهَ إِلَّا اللَّهُ يَسْتَكْبِرُونَ ۝ وَيَقُولُونَ أَئِنَّا لَتَارِكُوا ءَالِهَتِنَا لِشَاعِرٍ مَّجْنُونٍ ۝﴾

---

[1] (*Luqman* 31:22)
[2] (*An-Nisa'* 4:125)
[3] (*An-Nisa'* 4:65)
[4] (*Al-Baqarah* 2:136)

Truly, when it was said to them: "*La Ilaha Illallâh* (none has the right to be worshiped but Allâh)," they puffed themselves up with pride. And (they) said: "Are we going to abandon our *Alihah* (gods) for the sake of a mad poet?"[1]

8. **Disbelief in all that is worshipped other than Allâh:** Allâh Almighty says:

$$﴿فَمَن يَكْفُرْ بِالطَّاغُوتِ وَيُؤْمِنۢ بِاللَّهِ فَقَدِ ٱسْتَمْسَكَ بِالْعُرْوَةِ ٱلْوُثْقَىٰ﴾$$

Whoever disbelieves in *Taghut* and believes in Allâh, then he has grasped the most trustworthy handhold.[2]

The Prophet ﷺ said:

«مَنْ قَالَ لَا إِلَهَ إِلَّا اللهُ وَكَفَرَ بِمَا يُعْبَدُ مِنْ دُونِ اللهِ حُرِّمَ مَالُهُ وَدَمُهُ وَحِسَابُهُ عَلَى اللهِ»

Whoever says, "*Laa Ilaha Illallâh*," disbelieving in all that is worshipped other than Allâh, his wealth and blood become inviolable, and his account is with Allâh. (Recorded by Muslim)

Some Of The Effects Of *Laa Ilaha Illallâh*

When one says this phrase truthfully and sincerely, applying its implications both outwardly and inwardly, there will be many blessed effects on him as an individual and on society; here are a few of those effects:

1. The Muslims will be united on one basis, which results in strength for the Muslims and victory over their enemies:

$$﴿وَٱعْتَصِمُواْ بِحَبْلِ ٱللَّهِ جَمِيعًا وَلَا تَفَرَّقُواْ﴾$$

And hold fast, all of you together, to the Rope of Allâh, and be not divided among yourselves.[3]

And He Almighty says:

$$﴿هُوَ ٱلَّذِىٓ أَيَّدَكَ بِنَصْرِهِۦ وَبِٱلْمُؤْمِنِينَ ۝ وَأَلَّفَ بَيْنَ قُلُوبِهِمْ لَوْ أَنفَقْتَ مَا فِى$$

---

[1] (*As-Saffat* 37:35,36)

[2] (*Al-Baqarah* 2:256)

[3] (*Aal 'Imran* 3:103)

الْأَرْضِ جَمِيعًا مَّا أَلَّفْتَ بَيْنَ قُلُوبِهِمْ وَلَٰكِنَّ اللَّهَ أَلَّفَ بَيْنَهُمْ إِنَّهُ عَزِيزٌ حَكِيمٌ ۝

He it is Who has supported you with His help and with the believers. And He has united their hearts. If you had spent all that is in the earth, you could not have united their hearts, but Allâh has united them. Certainly He is All-Mighty, All-Wise.[1]

Different views regarding beliefs leads only to disunity and strife, for Allâh Almighty says:

﴿ إِنَّ الَّذِينَ فَرَّقُوا دِينَهُمْ وَكَانُوا شِيَعًا لَّسْتَ مِنْهُمْ فِى شَىْءٍ ﴾

Verily, those who divide their religion and break up into sects, you have no concern in them in the least.[2]

And:

﴿ فَتَقَطَّعُوا أَمْرَهُم بَيْنَهُمْ زُبُرًا كُلُّ حِزْبٍ بِمَا لَدَيْهِمْ فَرِحُونَ ۝ ﴾

But they have broken their religion among them into sects, each group rejoicing in its belief.[3]

What is mentioned in this last verse occurred among the Arabs before the advent of Islam and after it.

2. Because unity results when all members of society accept and apply *Laa Ilaha Illallâh*, safety and peace will be widespread:

﴿ إِنَّمَا الْمُؤْمِنُونَ إِخْوَةٌ ﴾

The believers are nothing other than brothers.[4]

﴿ مُّحَمَّدٌ رَّسُولُ اللَّهِ وَالَّذِينَ مَعَهُ أَشِدَّاءُ عَلَى الْكُفَّارِ رُحَمَاءُ بَيْنَهُمْ ﴾

Muhammad is the Messenger of Allâh, and those who are with him are severe against disbelievers, and merciful among themselves.[5]

﴿ وَاذْكُرُوا نِعْمَتَ اللَّهِ عَلَيْكُمْ إِذْ كُنتُمْ أَعْدَاءً فَأَلَّفَ بَيْنَ قُلُوبِكُمْ فَأَصْبَحْتُم بِنِعْمَتِهِ

---

[1] (*Al-Anfal* 8:62,63)
[2] (*Al-An'am* 6:159)
[3] (*Al-Mu'minun* 23:53)
[4] (*Al-Hujurat* 49:10)
[5] (*Al-Fath* 48:29)

﴿إِخْوَانًا﴾

And remember Allâh's favor on you, for you were enemies one to another but He joined your hearts together, so that, by His grace, you became brethren.[1]

3. Happiness and purity of religion will not only be achieved for the believers, but it will be perpetuated for them:

﴿وَعَدَ اللَّهُ الَّذِينَ ءَامَنُوا۟ مِنكُمْ وَعَمِلُوا۟ الصَّـٰلِحَـٰتِ لَيَسْتَخْلِفَنَّهُمْ فِى الْأَرْضِ كَمَا اسْتَخْلَفَ الَّذِينَ مِن قَبْلِهِمْ وَلَيُمَكِّنَنَّ لَهُمْ دِينَهُمُ الَّذِى ارْتَضَىٰ لَهُمْ وَلَيُبَدِّلَنَّهُم مِّنۢ بَعْدِ خَوْفِهِمْ أَمْنًا يَعْبُدُونَنِى لَا يُشْرِكُونَ بِى شَيْـًٔا﴾

Allâh has promised those among you who believe, and do righteous good deeds, that He will certainly grant them succession in the earth, as He granted it to those before them, and that He will grant them the authority to practice their religion, that which He has chosen for them. And He will surely give them in exchange a safe security after their fear (provided) they (believers) worship Me and do not associate anything (in worship) with Me.[2]

We must understand, however, that the benefits mentioned in this verse hinge upon our worship of Allâh alone, without associating partners with Him.

4. The one who says *Laa Ilaha Illallâh* and applies its meanings, achieves inner peace and mental stability:

﴿ءَأَرْبَابٌ مُّتَفَرِّقُونَ خَيْرٌ أَمِ اللَّهُ الْوَٰحِدُ الْقَهَّارُ﴾

Are many different lords (gods) better or Allâh, the One, the Irresistible?[3]

5. The adherents of *Laa Ilaha Illallâh* are treated gently and are raised in status, as opposed to the disbelievers and polytheists:

﴿حُنَفَآءَ لِلَّهِ غَيْرَ مُشْرِكِينَ بِهِۦ وَمَن يُشْرِكْ بِاللَّهِ فَكَأَنَّمَا خَرَّ مِنَ السَّمَآءِ فَتَخْطَفُهُ الطَّيْرُ أَوْ تَهْوِى بِهِ الرِّيحُ فِى مَكَانٍ سَحِيقٍ ٣١﴾

---

[1] (*Aal 'Imran* 3:103)

[2] (*An-Nur* 24:55)

[3] (*Yusuf* 12:39)

Hunafa Lillah (i.e., to worship none but Allâh), not
associating partners (in worship, etc.) to Him; and whoever
assigns partners to Allâh, it is as if he had fallen from the sky,
and the birds had snatched him, or the wind had thrown him
to a far off place.[1]

This verse indicates that *Tawhid* is highness and exaltedness,
while *Shirk* represents a downfall and decline.

6. Inviolability of blood, wealth, and honor, for the Prophet ﷺ said:

«أُمِرْتُ أَنْ أُقَاتِلَ النَّاسَ حَتَّى يَقُولُوا لَا إِلَهَ إِلَّا اللهُ، فَإِذَا قَالُوهَا عَصَمُوا
مِنِّي دِمَاءَهُمْ وَأَمْوَالَهُمْ إِلَّا بِحَقِّهَا»

I have been ordered to fight people until they say, "None has
the right to be worshipped but Allâh." And when they say it,
they have protected their blood and their wealth, except by
its right.

What does the last sentence, "by its right" mean? It means that if
one does not fulfill the rights of *Tawhid* and has not truly
distanced himself from *Shirk*; then it doesn't benefit him to say
Laa Ilaha Illallâh."

This phrase has far-reaching implications on both individuals
and society — in their worship, dealings, characteristics, and
manners.

The last of the Prophets, Muhammad ﷺ, was sent not only to the
Arabs, but to the rest of mankind as well; he ﷺ came at a time
when mankind was in dire need to be taken out of darkness and
brought into the light.

---

[1] (*Al-Hajj* 22:31)

The Second Pillar Of Islam:
Establishing The Prayer (As-*Salat*)

The prayer (As-*Salat*), as a pillar of Islam, is second only to the two testimonies in importance and ranking: it is the first deed for which one will be held accountable on the Day of Judgement - if one's prayer is good and acceptable, then he will have achieved success; but if it is incorrect and corrupted in some way, then one has achieved failure. The prayer is a form of worship that must be performed on time:

$$﴿ إِنَّ ٱلصَّلَوٰةَ كَانَتْ عَلَى ٱلْمُؤْمِنِينَ كِتَٰبًا مَّوْقُوتًا ﴾$$

Verily, the prayer is enjoined on the believers at fixed hours.[1]

In the following verse, Allâh orders us to strictly guard the five obligatory prayers, meaning that we should be diligent in performing all of them on time. Since Allâh orders us to perform them on time, we necessarily conclude that there are known times for each prayer.

$$﴿ حَٰفِظُوا۟ عَلَى ٱلصَّلَوَٰتِ وَٱلصَّلَوٰةِ ٱلْوُسْطَىٰ وَقُومُوا۟ لِلَّهِ قَٰنِتِينَ ﴾$$

Guard strictly (five obligatory) As-*Salawat* (the prayers) especially the middle *Salat* (i.e., the best prayer '*Asr*). And stand before Allâh with obedience [and do not speak to others during the *Salat* (prayers)].[2]

Allâh gives a stern warning to those who are neglectful regarding the prayer and those who delay the prayer until its time passes:

$$﴿ فَخَلَفَ مِنۢ بَعْدِهِمْ خَلْفٌ أَضَاعُوا۟ ٱلصَّلَوٰةَ وَٱتَّبَعُوا۟ ٱلشَّهَوَٰتِ فَسَوْفَ يَلْقَوْنَ غَيًّا ٥٩ ﴾$$

Then, there has succeeded them a posterity who have neglected As-*Salat* (the prayers) and have followed lusts. So, they will be thrown in Hell.[3]

And Allâh Almighty said:

$$﴿ فَوَيْلٌ لِّلْمُصَلِّينَ ٤ ٱلَّذِينَ هُمْ عَن صَلَاتِهِمْ سَاهُونَ ٥ ﴾$$

---

[1] (*An-Nisa'* 4:103)

[2] (*Al-Baqarah* 2:238)

[3] (*Maryam* 19:59)

So woe to those performers of *Salat* (prayers) (hypocrites), who delay their *Salat* (prayer) from their stated fixed times.[1]

So, the meaning of neglected (above) is that they delayed the prayer from its proper time. It does not mean that they abandoned it, since abandoning it is disbelief, and we seek refuge in Allâh Almighty from that.

The prayer is a sign that distinguishes between Islam and disbelief. In his *Sahib*, Muslim recorded that Jabir, may Allâh be pleased with him, said he heard the Messenger of Allâh ﷺ say:

«بَيْنَ الرَّجُلِ وَبَيْنَ الشِّرْكِ وَالْكُفْرِ تَرْكُ الصَّلَاةِ»

Between man and between *Shirk* and disbelief is abandoning the *Salat*.

And in a *Hadith* narrated by Buraidah, may Allâh be pleased with him, the Prophet ﷺ said:

«الْعَهْدُ الَّذِي بَيْنَنَا وَبَيْنَهُمُ الصَّلَاةُ، فَمَنْ تَرَكَهَا فَقَدْ كَفَرَ»

The covenant between us and them is the *Salat*; whoever leaves it has indeed disbelieved. (It was recorded by Imam Ahmad and the *Sunan* Compilers with an authentic chain of narration.)

And what — in significance — is the prayer?

It is the link between a worshipper and his Lord. The Prophet ﷺ said:

«إِنَّ أَحَدَكُمْ إِذَا صَلَّى يُنَاجِي رَبَّهُ»

When one of you prays, he speaks confidentially to his Lord. (Recorded by Al-Bukhari)

In a *Hadith Qudsi* Allâh Almighty said:

«قَسَمْتُ الصَّلَاةَ بَيْنِي وَبَيْنَ عَبْدِي نِصْفَيْنِ وَلِعَبْدِي مَا سَأَلَ فَإِذَا قَالَ الْعَبْدُ: الْحَمْدُ لله رَبِّ الْعَالَمِينَ قَالَ تَعَالَى: حَمِدَنِي عَبْدِي. وَإِذَا قَالَ: الرَّحْمٰنِ الرَّحِيمِ، قَالَ الله تَعَالَى: أَثْنَى عَلَيَّ عَبْدِي. وَإِذَا قَالَ: مَالِكِ يَوْمِ الدِّينِ

---

[1] (*Al-Ma'un* 107:4,5.)

قَالَ: مَجَّدَنِي عَبْدِي، فَإِذَا قَالَ: إِيَّاكَ نَعْبُدُ وَإِيَّاكَ نَسْتَعِينُ، قَالَ: هَذَا بَيْنِي
وَبَيْنَ عَبْدِي وَلِعَبْدِي مَا سَأَلَ، فَإِذَا قَالَ: اهْدِنَا الصِّرَاطَ الْمُسْتَقِيمَ.
صِرَاطَ الَّذِينَ أَنْعَمْتَ عَلَيْهِمْ غَيْرِ الْمَغْضُوبِ عَلَيْهِمْ وَلَا الضَّالِينَ، قَالَ:
هَذَا لِعَبْدِي وَلِعَبْدِي مَا سَأَلَ»

I have divided the prayer between Me and My slave into two halves, and for my slave is what he asks. When my slave says, "All the praises and thanks are to Allâh, the Lord of all that exists," Allâh Almighty says, "My slave has praised me." When he says, "The Most Beneficent, the Most Merciful," Allâh Almighty says, "My slave has extolled me." When he says, "The Only Owner of the Day of Recompense," Allâh Almighty says, "My slave has glorified me." Then when he says, "You alone we worship and You alone we ask for help," Allâh Almighty says, "This is between Me and My slave, and for My slave is what he asks." And then when he says, "Guide us to the straight way, the way of those on whom You have bestowed Your grace, not (the way) of those who earned Your anger, nor of those who went astray," Allâh Almighty says, "This is for My slave, and for My slave is what he asks." (Recorded by Muslim)

The prayer consists of a number of different kinds of worship — saying: *"Allâhu Akbar"* (Allâh is the Most Great) to begin the prayer; standing to recite Allâh's Speech; bowing, and in that position, glorifying the Lord; standing from the bowing position, filling the time while one is standing with praises for Allâh; prostrating to glorify Allâh for His Greatness, and to supplicate to Him; sitting to supplicate, to say the *Tashahhud*, and then finally, to say the *Taslim*, which signifies the end of prayer.

The prayer not only helps us in our important affairs, it also prevents us from committing wicked and evil deeds, for Allâh Almighty says:

$$﴿وَٱسْتَعِينُوا۟ بِٱلصَّبْرِ وَٱلصَّلَوٰةِ﴾$$

And seek help in patience and *As-Salat*[1]

And He says:

---

[1] (*Al-Baqarah* 2:45)

﴿ٱتْلُ مَآ أُوحِىَ إِلَيْكَ مِنَ ٱلْكِتَٰبِ وَأَقِمِ ٱلصَّلَوٰةَ إِنَّ ٱلصَّلَوٰةَ تَنْهَىٰ عَنِ ٱلْفَحْشَآءِ وَٱلْمُنكَرِ ﴾

Recite what has been revealed to you of the Book, and perform
As-Salat. Verily, *As-Salat* prevents from *Al-Fahsha'* (great sins
of every kind, unlawful sexual intercourse, etc.) and *Al-
Munkar* (disbelief, polytheism, and every kind of evil wicked
deed, etc.)[1]

The prayer is illumination in the hearts of the believers, for the
Prophet ﷺ said:

«الصَّلَاةُ نُورٌ»

The prayer is light. (Recorded by Muslim)

He ﷺ also said:

«مَنْ حَافَظَ عَلَيْهَا كَانَتْ لَهُ نُورًا وَبُرْهَانًا وَنَجَاةً يَوْمَ الْقِيَامَةِ»

Whoever commits it to memory, he will have, on the Day of
Judgement, a light, a proof, and a deliverance. (Ahmad, Ibn
Hibban, and At-Tabarani)

The prayer is happiness and contentment in the hearts and souls of
the believers; the Prophet ﷺ said:

«جُعِلَتْ قُرَّةُ عَيْنِي فِي الصَّلَاةِ»

My joy has been made in the prayer. (Ahmad and An-Nasa'i)

When one prays, his sins are erased and atoned for. The Prophet ﷺ
said:

«أَرَأَيْتُمْ لَوْ أَنَّ نَهْرًا بِبَابِ أَحَدِكُمْ يَغْتَسِلُ فِيهِ كُلَّ يَوْمٍ خَمْسَ مَرَّاتٍ هَلْ يَبْقَى مِنْ دَرَنِهِ (وَسْخِهِ) شَيْءٌ؟»

"If there was a river by the door of one of you, in which he
bathed five times every day, do you think that any of his filth
would remain?"

They said, "None of his filth would remain."

---

[1] (*Al-'Ankabut* 29:45)

He ﷺ said:

«فَكَذَلِكَ مَثَلُ الصَّلَوَاتِ الْخَمْسِ يَمْحُو اللهُ بِهِنَّ الْخَطَايَا»

"The same is the case with the five prayers: through them Allâh wipes the sins away." (Al-Bukhari and Muslim)

In another *Hadith*, he ﷺ said:

«الصَّلَوَاتُ الْخَمْسُ وَالْجُمُعَةُ إِلَى الْجُمُعَةِ كَفَّارَةٌ لِمَا بَيْنَهُنَّ مَا لَمْ تُغْشَ الْكَبَائِرُ»

The five prayers and *Jumu'ah* (Friday Prayer) to *Jumu'ah* are expiations for what occurs between them (i.e., sins), as long as the major sins are not perpetrated. (Recorded by Muslim)

Ibn Mas'ud, may Allâh be pleased with him, said: "Whoever wishes to meet Allâh tomorrow as a Muslim, then let him carefully guard these five prayers when they are called for. Indeed Allâh has legislated for your Prophet ways of guidance, and the prayers are from the ways of guidance. Were you to pray in your homes as this person does who remains behind in his home, then you would have left the way of your Prophet, and if you were to leave the way of your Prophet, you would have gone astray. There is not a man who purifies himself, and purifies himself well, and then heads to a *Masjid* among these *Masjids*, except that for each step he takes, Allâh writes for him a good deed, raises him one rank, and removes a sin from him. I remember (that during previous times) that no one would remain behind from the congregational prayer except for the one who was known to be a hypocrite. (Even the sick) man was brought to the prayer; he was helped from in between two men, until he was made to stand in the row." (Recorded by Muslim)

Al-Khushu' which is to have a heart that is present and reflective and to be steadfast in the prayer is one of the means of achieving Paradise. Allâh Almighty says:

﴿قَدْ أَفْلَحَ ٱلْمُؤْمِنُونَ ۝ ٱلَّذِينَ هُمْ فِى صَلَاتِهِمْ خَٰشِعُونَ ۝ وَٱلَّذِينَ هُمْ عَنِ ٱللَّغْوِ مُعْرِضُونَ ۝ وَٱلَّذِينَ هُمْ لِلزَّكَوٰةِ فَٰعِلُونَ ۝ وَٱلَّذِينَ هُمْ لِفُرُوجِهِمْ حَٰفِظُونَ ۝ إِلَّا عَلَىٰ أَزْوَٰجِهِمْ أَوْ مَا مَلَكَتْ أَيْمَٰنُهُمْ فَإِنَّهُمْ غَيْرُ مَلُومِينَ ۝ فَمَنِ ٱبْتَغَىٰ وَرَآءَ ذَٰلِكَ

فَأُوْلَٰٓئِكَ هُمُ ٱلْعَادُونَ ۝ وَٱلَّذِينَ هُمْ لِأَمَٰنَٰتِهِمْ وَعَهْدِهِمْ رَٰعُونَ ۝ وَٱلَّذِينَ هُمْ عَلَىٰ صَلَوَٰتِهِمْ يُحَافِظُونَ ۝ أُوْلَٰٓئِكَ هُمُ ٱلْوَٰرِثُونَ ۝ ٱلَّذِينَ يَرِثُونَ ٱلْفِرْدَوْسَ هُمْ فِيهَا خَٰلِدُونَ ۝

Successful indeed are the believers. Those who have *Khushu'* in their *Salat*. And those who turn away from *Al-Laghw* (dirty, false, evil vain talk, falsehood, and all that Allâh has forbidden). And those who pay the *Zakat*, and those who guard their chastity (i.e., private parts, from illegal sexual acts) except from their wives or (the captives and slaves) that their right hands possess, for then, they are free from blame. But whoever seeks beyond that, then those are the transgressors. Those who are faithfully true to their trusts and to their covenants; And those who strictly guard their *Salawat* (prayers). These are indeed the inheritors; who shall inherit the *Firdaws* (Paradise). They shall dwell therein forever.[1]

Sincerity to Allâh in prayer, and performing it according to the way it came to us in the Sunnah — these are the two fundamental conditions for one's prayer to be accepted. The Prophet ﷺ said:

«إِنَّمَا الْأَعْمَالُ بِالنِّيَّاتِ وَإِنَّمَا لِكُلِّ امْرِئٍ مَا نَوَى»

Indeed deeds are by intentions, and for each one is that which he intended. (Al-Bukhari and Muslim)

And he said:

«صَلُّوا كَمَا رَأَيْتُمُونِي أُصَلِّي»

Pray as you have seen me praying.[2]

There are many great virtues of performing prayer in congregation in the mosque; furthermore, doing so is compulsory. Ibn 'Umar, may Allâh be pleased with them, related that the Prophet ﷺ said:

«الصَّلَاةُ جَمَاعَةً أَفْضَلُ مِنْ صَلَاةِ الْفَذِّ بِسَبْعٍ وَعِشْرِينَ دَرَجَةً»

The congregational prayer is superior to the individual prayer

---

[1] (*Al-Mu'minun* 23:1-11)

[2] This section was taken from *Risalaat As-Salah* by Shaikh Muhammad bin Salih Al-'Uthaimin.

by twenty-seven degrees. (Agreed upon)

On one occasion, according to the agreed upon *Hadith*, the Prophet ﷺ intended to burn the houses of men who remained behind instead of going to pray in congregation. The Prophet ﷺ said:

«مَنْ سَمِعَ النِّدَاءَ فَلَمْ يَأْتِ فَلَا صَلَاةَ لَهُ إِلَّا مِنْ عُذْرٍ»

Whoever hears the call (to prayer) but doesn't come, then there is no prayer for him, unless he has an excuse. (It was recorded by Ibn Majah, Ad-Daraqutni, Ibn Hibban, and Al-Hakim with an authentic chain of narration.)

This *Hadith* indicates the elevated status of congregational prayer in Islam.

The Prophet ﷺ ordered the one who did not have tranquillity in his prayer to repeat it.

The congregational prayer is a manifestation of equality, brotherhood, and organization: All Muslims turn toward the direction of the Sacred Ka'bah when they pray.

Whenever the Prophet ﷺ faced a difficult matter, he would hasten to prayer. Allâh Almighty says:

﴿ٱسْتَعِينُواْ بِٱلصَّبْرِ وَٱلصَّلَوٰةِ﴾

Seek help in patience and *As-Salat* (the prayer).[1]

The Prophet ﷺ used to say to Bilal:

«يَا بِلَالُ أَرِحْنَا بِهَا»

O Bilal, give us comfort by it.[2]

When praying, one is sure to find comfort and peace in his heart, body, and soul, for He is standing before His Lord, Protector, and Guardian.

---

[1] (*Al-Baqarah* 2:153)

[2] That is because he was the one who called the call to prayer.

The Ruling Regarding Those Who Abandon The Prayer

A great evil is perpetrated by many of those who claim to be Muslims when they abandon the prayer, for abandoning the prayer is disbelief. In an authentic *Hadith*, the Prophet ﷺ said:

«بَيْنَ الرَّجُلِ وَالْكُفْرِ أَوِ الشِّرْكِ تَرْكُ الصَّلَاةِ»

Between the man and disbelief or *Shirk* is abandoning the prayer.

He ﷺ also said:

«الْعَهْدُ الَّذِي بَيْنَنَا وَبَيْنَهُمُ الصَّلَاةُ، فَمَنْ تَرَكَهَا فَقَدْ كَفَرَ»

The covenant between us and them is the prayer; whoever leaves it has indeed disbelieved.

Because the prayer is the support for Islam, and because there is no religion of Islam for the person who abandons it, the one who abandons the prayer most likely has abandoned all other religious duties as well. Abandoning the prayer is one of the actions that lead to entering the Hellfire; Allâh Almighty says about the wrongdoers:

﴿مَا سَلَكَكُمْ فِى سَقَرَ ۞ قَالُوا۟ لَمْ نَكُ مِنَ ٱلْمُصَلِّينَ ۞﴾

"What has caused you to enter Hell?" They will say: "We were not of those who used to offer their *Salat*."[1]

Allâh says:

﴿وَأَقِيمُوا۟ ٱلصَّلَوٰةَ وَلَا تَكُونُوا۟ مِنَ ٱلْمُشْرِكِينَ﴾

And perform *As-Salat* and be not of the polytheists.[2]

And Allâh Almighty says:

﴿وَأَنْ أَقِيمُوا۟ ٱلصَّلَوٰةَ وَٱتَّقُوهُ وَهُوَ ٱلَّذِىٓ إِلَيْهِ تُحْشَرُونَ ۞﴾

And to perform *As-Salat*, and to be obedient to Allâh, and fear Him, and it is He to Whom you shall be gathered.[3]

And:

---

[1] (*Al-Muddaththir* 74:42,43)

[2] (*Ar-Rum* 30:31)

[3] (*Al-An'am* 6:72)

﴿فَإِن تَابُوا۟ وَأَقَامُوا۟ ٱلصَّلَوٰةَ وَءَاتَوُا۟ ٱلزَّكَوٰةَ فَإِخْوَٰنُكُمْ فِى ٱلدِّينِ﴾

But if they repent, perform *As-Salat* and give *Zakat*, then they are your brethren in religion.[1]

Establishing the prayer, then, is made as a condition for repentance to be accepted and for entering Islam. Allâh Almighty says:

﴿وَيْلٌ يَوْمَئِذٍ لِّلْمُكَذِّبِينَ ۝ وَإِذَا قِيلَ لَهُمُ ٱرْكَعُوا۟ لَا يَرْكَعُونَ ۝﴾

Woe that Day to the deniers (of the Day of Resurrection)! And when it is said to them: "Bow down yourself (in prayer)!" They bow not down.[2]

The scholars from both early and later generations agree that the punishment for the one who persists in not praying is death; the verses and *Hadiths* that indicate the disbelief of one who abandons the prayer are indeed many.

In our time, it has become very common for one to pray the *Fajr* prayer after the sun has risen — and we seek protection with Allâh. One way to forsake the prayer is to not pray in congregation, even though one is able to do so. The Prophet ﷺ said:

«مَنْ سَمِعَ النِّدَاءَ فَلَمْ يُجِبْ فَلَا صَلَاةَ لَهُ»

Whoever hears the call to prayer but does not answer it, then there is no prayer for him.

He ﷺ also said:

«لَا صَلَاةَ لِجَارِ الْمَسْجِدِ إِلَّا فِي الْمَسْجِدِ»

There is no prayer for the neighbor of the *Masjid* except in the *Masjid*.

The neighbor of the *Msajid* is one who hears the call to prayer. In yet another *Hadith*, the Prophet ﷺ said:

«مَنْ سَمِعَ النِّدَاءَ فَلَمْ يُجِبْ صُبَّ فِي أُذُنَيْهِ الْآنُكُ يَوْمَ الْقِيَامَةِ»

Whoever hears the call (to prayer), but doesn't answer it, on the Day of Judgement, molten lead will be poured into his ears.

---

[1] (*At-Tawbah* 9:11)

[2] (*Al-Mursalat* 77:47,48)

The only person who remains behind, not performing prayer in congregation is the hypocrite, just as Ibn Mas'ud said.

Another way to be neglectful in prayer is to pray in a hasty manner — praying quickly, preceding the *Imam* from one part of the prayer to the next, or bowing and prostrating for such a short period of time that calmness is not achieved. This is the state of the one who tries to precede the *Imam*: he is neither praying alone nor following his *Imam*, and his forelocks are in the hands of the *Shaitan*. This hastiness prevents one from having a wakeful heart during prayer, and having a wakeful heart is the fruit and soul of prayer without which the prayer is not accepted. Rather it (i.e., the prayer) is coiled like an old garment, and with it the face of the one who prayed without a wakeful heart is struck. It says, "May Allâh ruin you as you have ruined me." Such has been narrated in authentic *Ahadith*.

As for the conditions and pillars of prayer, we will discuss them in detail in ensuing chapters.

The Third Pillar Of Islam: *Zakat*

Zakat is quite often juxtaposed with the prayer in verses of the Qur'an and sayings of the Prophet ﷺ. It is a social obligation through which the believer appreciates many of the higher aims of Islam — such as love, kindness, generosity, and cooperation among Muslims. But here is an important point: by paying *Zakat*, no one is doing a favor for another, because it is a compulsory duty. In reality it is Allâh's wealth that He has bestowed upon us:

﴿وَءَاتُوهُم مِّن مَّالِ اللَّهِ الَّذِىٓ ءَاتَىٰكُمْ﴾

And give them something yourselves out of the wealth of Allâh which He has bestowed upon you.[1]

And Allâh Almighty says:

﴿ءَامِنُوا بِاللَّهِ وَرَسُولِهِ وَأَنفِقُوا مِمَّا جَعَلَكُم مُّسْتَخْلَفِينَ فِيهِ فَٱلَّذِينَ ءَامَنُوا مِنكُمْ وَأَنفَقُوا لَهُمْ أَجْرٌ كَبِيرٌ ۝⑦﴾

Believe in Allâh and His Messenger, and spend of that whereof He has made you trustees. And such of you as believe and

---

[1] (*An-Nur* 24:33)

spend, theirs will be a great reward.[1]

Because of the importance of *Zakat*, Abu Bakr, may Allâh be pleased with him, fought certain Arab tribes when they refused to pay it. He said, "By Allâh, I will indeed fight those who differentiate between prayer and *Zakat*." The Companions followed him in that judgement.

Allâh gives a severe warning to those who are miserly with their wealth:

$$﴿وَٱلَّذِينَ يَكْنِزُونَ ٱلذَّهَبَ وَٱلْفِضَّةَ وَلَا يُنفِقُونَهَا فِى سَبِيلِ ٱللَّهِ فَبَشِّرْهُم بِعَذَابٍ أَلِيمٍ ٣٤﴾$$

And those who hoard up gold and silver, and spend it not in the way of Allâh — announce to them a painful torment.[2]

For each of the different kinds of wealth, there is a minimum amount, that if one possesses that amount, he must give *Zakat* when the year ends. The exception is for grains and fruits, because *Zakat* for those items is due when they grow completely and become ripe, even if a year has not passed. The *Zakat* wealth is given to the deserving, and the categories of people who deserve *Zakat* are listed in the following verse:

$$﴿إِنَّمَا ٱلصَّدَقَٰتُ لِلْفُقَرَآءِ وَٱلْمَسَٰكِينِ وَٱلْعَٰمِلِينَ عَلَيْهَا وَٱلْمُؤَلَّفَةِ قُلُوبُهُمْ وَفِى ٱلرِّقَابِ وَٱلْغَٰرِمِينَ وَفِى سَبِيلِ ٱللَّهِ وَٱبْنِ ٱلسَّبِيلِ فَرِيضَةً مِّنَ ٱللَّهِ﴾$$

As-Sadaqat are only for the *Fuqara* (poor), and *Al-Masakin* (the needy) and those employed to collect (the funds); and to attract the hearts of those who have been inclined (towards Islam); and to free the captives; and for those in debt; and for Allâh's cause (for *Jihad*), and for the wayfarer (a traveller who is cut off from everything); a duty imposed by Allâh.[3]

Speaking about the duty of giving *Zakat*, Shaikh 'Abdul-'Aziz bin Baz said:

"I remind you of the obligation of giving *Zakat*, an obligation that

---

[1] (*Al-Hadid* 57:7)

[2] (*At-Tawbah* 9:34)

[3] (*At-Tawbah* 9:60)

many Muslims neglect. Though many may give, some do not give in a way that is legislated. The *Zakat* has a great significance, for it is one of the five pillars upon which one's Islam stands. The Prophet ﷺ said:

«بُنِيَ الإِسْلَامُ عَلَى خَمْسٍ: شَهَادَةِ أَنْ لَا إِلَهَ إِلَّا اللهُ، وَأَنَّ مُحَمَّدًا رَسُولُ اللهِ، وَإِقَامِ الصَّلَاةِ، وَإِيتَاءِ الزَّكَاةِ، وَصَوْمِ رَمَضَانَ، وَحَجِّ الْبَيْتِ»

Islam is built on five: to bear witness that none has the right to be worshipped but Allâh and that Muhammad is the Messenger of Allâh, to establish the prayer, to give *Zakat*, to fast Ramadhan, and *Al-Hajj* to the House (the Ka'bah). (Its authenticity is agreed upon)

The Benefits Of *Zakat*

1) Making *Zakat* obligatory for Muslims is one of the most obvious merits of Islam, demonstrating its care for those who adopt it as a way of life.

2) The ties of love and brotherhood are strengthened between the rich and the poor — people innately love those who are good to them.

3) By paying *Zakat*, one purifies his own self, training it to stay away from the evil quality of miserliness; the Qur'an refers to this meaning in the following verse:

﴿خُذْ مِنْ أَمْوَٰلِهِمْ صَدَقَةً تُطَهِّرُهُمْ وَتُزَكِّيهِم بِهَا﴾

Take *Sadaqah* (alms) from their wealth in order to purify them and sanctify them with it.[1]

4) By always giving *Zakat* on time, one makes it his habit to be generous and to help the needy.

5) One who pays *Zakat* is blessed in his wealth, and is himself given more, for Allâh Almighty says:

﴿وَمَآ أَنفَقْتُم مِّن شَىْءٍ فَهُوَ يُخْلِفُهُۥ وَهُوَ خَيْرُ الرَّٰزِقِينَ ٣٩﴾

And (also) restricts (it) for him, and whatsoever you spend of anything (in Allâh's cause), He will replace it. And He is the

---

[1] (*At-Tawbah* 9:103)

Best of providers.[1]

In *Hadith Qudsi*, the Prophet ﷺ related that Allâh said:

«يَا ابْنَ آدَمَ أَنْفِقْ نُنْفِقْ عَلَيْكَ»

O son of Adam, spend (in charity) and We will spend on you.
There are many other virtues regarding it.

Allâh's Threat To Those Who Are Negligent In Paying *Zakat*

Allâh Almighty says:

﴿يَٰٓأَيُّهَا ٱلَّذِينَ ءَامَنُوٓاْ إِنَّ كَثِيرًا مِّنَ ٱلْأَحْبَارِ وَٱلرُّهْبَانِ لَيَأْكُلُونَ أَمْوَٰلَ ٱلنَّاسِ بِٱلْبَٰطِلِ وَيَصُدُّونَ عَن سَبِيلِ ٱللَّهِ وَٱلَّذِينَ يَكْنِزُونَ ٱلذَّهَبَ وَٱلْفِضَّةَ وَلَا يُنفِقُونَهَا فِى سَبِيلِ ٱللَّهِ فَبَشِّرْهُم بِعَذَابٍ أَلِيمٍ ۝ يَوْمَ يُحْمَىٰ عَلَيْهَا فِى نَارِ جَهَنَّمَ فَتُكْوَىٰ بِهَا جِبَاهُهُمْ وَجُنُوبُهُمْ وَظُهُورُهُمْ هَٰذَا مَا كَنَزْتُمْ لِأَنفُسِكُمْ فَذُوقُواْ مَا كُنتُمْ تَكْنِزُونَ ۝﴾

O you who believe! Verily, many of the (Jewish) rabbis and the (Christian) monks who devour the wealth of mankind in falsehood, and hinder (them) from the way of Allâh. And those who hoard up gold and silver, and spend it not in the way of Allâh — announce to them a painful torment. On the Day when that (wealth) will be heated in the fire of Hell, and with it will be branded their foreheads, their flanks, and their backs, (and it will be said unto them): "This is the treasure which you hoarded for yourselves. Now taste of what you used to hoard."[2]

One will be punished on the Day of Judgement for hoarding what is called *Kanz*: any wealth, the *Zakat* of which has not been paid. In an authentic *Hadith*, the Prophet ﷺ said:

«مَا مِنْ صَاحِبِ ذَهَبٍ وَلَا فِضَّةٍ لَا يُؤَدِّي حَقَّهَا إِلَّا إِذَا كَانَ يَوْمُ الْقِيَامَةِ صُفِّحَتْ لَهُ صَفَائِحُ مِنْ نَارٍ فَأُحْمِيَ عَلَيْهَا فِي نَارِ جَهَنَّمَ فَيُكْوَى بِهَا جَنْبُهُ وَجَبِينُهُ وَظَهْرُهُ، كُلَّمَا بَرَدَتْ أُعِيدَتْ لَهُ فِي يَوْمٍ كَانَ مِقْدَارُهُ خَمْسِينَ أَلْفَ

[1] (Saba' 34:39)
[2] (At-Tawbah 9:34,35)

سَنَةٍ حَتَّى يُقْضَى بَيْنَ الْعِبَادِ فَيَرَى سَبِيلَهُ إِمَّا إِلَى الْجَنَّةِ، وَإِمَّا إِلَى النَّارِ»

Any owner of gold or silver who does not pay their due will have plates of fire prepared for him on the Day of Judgement. They will be heated in the Hellfire, and then his side, his forehead, and his back will be ironed (by those plates). Each time they become cool again, the process is repeated on him in a day whose measure is equal to fifty thousand years, until finally judgements will have been passed among (Allâh's) creatures, and each one sees his course: either to Paradise or to Hell.

Then the Prophet ﷺ mentioned the owner of camels, cows, and sheep: if he too doesn't pay *Zakat* for them, he will be punished on the Day of Judgement.

In another authentic *Hadith*, the Prophet ﷺ said:

«مَنْ آتَاهُ اللهُ مَالًا فَلَمْ يُؤَدِّ زَكَاتَهُ مُثِّلَ لَهُ يَوْمَ الْقِيَامَةِ شُجَاعًا أَقْرَعَ لَهُ زَبِيبَتَانِ يُطَوَّقُهُ يَوْمَ الْقِيَامَةِ، ثُمَّ يَأْخُذُ بِلِهْزِمَتَيْهِ - يَعْنِي شِدْقَيْهِ - ثُمَّ يَقُولُ: أَنَا مَالُكَ أَنَا كَنْزُكَ»

Whomsoever Allâh gives wealth to but doesn't pay *Zakat* for it, a large snake with two black dots above its eyes will take form for him and squeeze him on the Day of Judgement. Then the snake will take him by the corners of his mouth and say, "I am your wealth, I am your *Kanz*."

Then the Prophet ﷺ recited this verse:

﴿وَلَا يَحْسَبَنَّ ٱلَّذِينَ يَبْخَلُونَ بِمَآ ءَاتَىٰهُمُ ٱللَّهُ مِن فَضْلِهِۦ هُوَ خَيْرًا لَّهُمۖ بَلْ هُوَ شَرٌّ لَّهُمۖ سَيُطَوَّقُونَ مَا بَخِلُوا۟ بِهِۦ يَوْمَ ٱلْقِيَٰمَةِ﴾

And let not those who covetously withhold of that which Allâh has bestowed on them of His bounty (wealth) think that it is good for them. Nay, it will be worse for them; the things which they covetously withheld shall be tied to their necks like a collar on the Day of Resurrection.[1]

---

[1] (Aal 'Imran 3:180)

Zakat Is Obligatory On Four Types Of Wealth

1) What comes out of the earth, such as grains and fruits.
2) (Grazing) livestock.
3) Gold and silver.
4) Merchandise that is meant for sale.

Each one of the above-mentioned categories has what is called a *Nisab*, or a minimum amount: one only has to pay *Zakat* in each respective category if he owns that minimum amount.

The *Nisab* for grains and fruits is measured in what is known as a *Sa'*; one *Sa'* is equal to four scoops of the average sized man, with both of his hands together.

The *Nisab*, or minimum amount required for *Zakat* to be obligatory on dates, raisins, wheat, rice, barley, and so on is three-hundred *Sa'*.

The *Nisab* for grazing livestock — camels, cows, and sheep — is mentioned in detail in certain authentic *Ahadith*; if one has questions regarding those details, one should ask the people of knowledge. Were not brevity intended here, we would have explained the details of this issue.

The Fourth Pillar: Fasting The Month Of Ramadan

Allâh Almighty says:

$$﴿يَٰٓأَيُّهَا ٱلَّذِينَ ءَامَنُوا۟ كُتِبَ عَلَيْكُمُ ٱلصِّيَامُ كَمَا كُتِبَ عَلَى ٱلَّذِينَ مِن قَبْلِكُمْ لَعَلَّكُمْ تَتَّقُونَ ١٨٣ ﴾$$

O you who believe! Observing *As-Sawm* (the fasting) is prescribed for you as it was prescribed for those before you, that you may attain piety.[1]

For certain periods at a time, the Muslim trains himself to curb his desires, desires that are even lawful. By fasting one not only benefits spiritually, but physically as well. One of the spiritual benefits of fasting is that one feels for those from among his Muslim brothers who are poor, and who spend long periods of time without food or drink, such as is happening to many of our brothers around the globe.

---

[1] (*Al-Baqarah* 2:183)

Ramadhan is the best month of the year, the month in which Allâh revealed the Qur'an:

﴿شَهْرُ رَمَضَانَ ٱلَّذِىٓ أُنزِلَ فِيهِ ٱلْقُرْءَانُ هُدًى لِّلنَّاسِ وَبَيِّنَتٍ مِّنَ ٱلْهُدَىٰ وَٱلْفُرْقَانِ﴾

The month of Ramadhan in which was revealed the Qur'an, a guidance for mankind and clear proofs for the guidance and the Criterion (between right and wrong).[1]

In it is a night that is better than one thousand months. Allâh Almighty says:

﴿إِنَّآ أَنزَلْنَٰهُ فِى لَيْلَةِ ٱلْقَدْرِ ① وَمَآ أَدْرَىٰكَ مَا لَيْلَةُ ٱلْقَدْرِ ② لَيْلَةُ ٱلْقَدْرِ خَيْرٌ مِّنْ أَلْفِ شَهْرٍ﴾

Verily! We have sent it (this Qur'an) down in the night of *Al-Qadr* (Decree). And what will make you know what the night of *Al-Qadr* (Decree) is? The night of *Al-Qadr* (Decree) is better than a thousand months.[2]

If one fasts Ramadhan with faith, seeking his reward from Allâh, then his previous sins are forgiven.

In an authentic *Hadith* related by Abu Hurairah, may Allâh be pleased with him, the Prophet ﷺ said:

«مَنْ صَامَ رَمَضَانَ إِيمَانًا وَاحْتِسَابًا غُفِرَ لَهُ مَا تَقَدَّمَ مِنْ ذَنْبِهِ، وَمَنْ قَامَ رَمَضَانَ إِيمَانًا وَاحْتِسَابًا غُفِرَ لَهُ مَا تَقَدَّمَ مِنْ ذَنْبِهِ وَمَنْ قَامَ لَيْلَةَ الْقَدْرِ إِيمَانًا وَاحْتِسَابًا غُفِرَ لَهُ مَا تَقَدَّمَ مِنْ ذَنْبِهِ»

Whosoever fasts the month of Ramadhan, having faith and seeking his reward from Allâh, then he will be forgiven for his previous sins. Whosoever stands (to perform the voluntary night prayer) in Ramadhan, having faith and seeking his reward from Allâh, he will be forgiven his previous sins. And whosoever stands (to pray at night) on the night of *Qadr*, having faith and seeking his reward from Allâh, he will be

---

[1] (*Al-Baqarah* 2:185)
[2] (*Al-Qadr* 97:1-3)

forgiven his previous sins. (Agreed upon)

When one is fasting, one must also especially avoid backbiting, spreading false tales, lying, or listening to music or false speech; moreover, one should especially stay away from all forbidden deeds. The one who is fasting should, based on the Sunnah, recite the Qur'an more often, remember Allâh, give charity, and strive more to worship Allâh, especially during the last ten days of the month.

Shaikh Muhammad bin Salih Al-'Uthaimin said:

Indeed fasting is one of the pillars of Islam and one of its great foundations. Allâh Almighty says:

﴿يَٰٓأَيُّهَا ٱلَّذِينَ ءَامَنُوا۟ كُتِبَ عَلَيْكُمُ ٱلصِّيَامُ كَمَا كُتِبَ عَلَى ٱلَّذِينَ مِن قَبْلِكُمْ لَعَلَّكُمْ تَتَّقُونَ ۝ أَيَّامًا مَّعْدُودَٰتٍ فَمَن كَانَ مِنكُم مَّرِيضًا أَوْ عَلَىٰ سَفَرٍ فَعِدَّةٌ مِّنْ أَيَّامٍ أُخَرَ وَعَلَى ٱلَّذِينَ يُطِيقُونَهُۥ فِدْيَةٌ طَعَامُ مِسْكِينٍ فَمَن تَطَوَّعَ خَيْرًا فَهُوَ خَيْرٌ لَّهُۥ وَأَن تَصُومُوا۟ خَيْرٌ لَّكُمْ إِن كُنتُمْ تَعْلَمُونَ ۝ شَهْرُ رَمَضَانَ ٱلَّذِىٓ أُنزِلَ فِيهِ ٱلْقُرْءَانُ هُدًى لِّلنَّاسِ وَبَيِّنَٰتٍ مِّنَ ٱلْهُدَىٰ وَٱلْفُرْقَانِ فَمَن شَهِدَ مِنكُمُ ٱلشَّهْرَ فَلْيَصُمْهُ وَمَن كَانَ مَرِيضًا أَوْ عَلَىٰ سَفَرٍ فَعِدَّةٌ مِّنْ أَيَّامٍ أُخَرَ يُرِيدُ ٱللَّهُ بِكُمُ ٱلْيُسْرَ وَلَا يُرِيدُ بِكُمُ ٱلْعُسْرَ وَلِتُكْمِلُوا۟ ٱلْعِدَّةَ وَلِتُكَبِّرُوا۟ ٱللَّهَ عَلَىٰ مَا هَدَىٰكُمْ وَلَعَلَّكُمْ تَشْكُرُونَ ۝﴾

O you who believe! Observing *As-Sawm* (the fasting) is prescribed for you as it was prescribed for those before you, that you may attain piety. [Fasting] for a fixed number of days, but if any of you is ill or on a journey, the same number (should be made up for) from other days. And as for those who can fast with difficulty, (the elderly, etc.), they have (a choice either to fast or) to feed a *Miskin* (poor person) (for every day). But whoever does good of his own accord; it is better for him. And that you fast, is better for you if only you know. The month of Ramadhan in which was revealed the Qur'an, a guidance for mankind and clear proofs for the guidance and the Criterion (between right and wrong). So whoever of you sights (the crescent on the first night of) the month (of Ramadhan, i.e., is present at his home), he must observe

Sawm (fasts) that month, and whoever is ill or on a journey, the same number [of days which one did not observe *Sawm* (fasts) must be made up for] from other days. Allâh intends for you ease, and He does not want to make things difficult for you. (He wants that you) must complete the same number (of days), and that you must exalt Allâh [to say *"Allâhu Akbar"* (Allâh is the Most Great) on seeing the crescent of the months of Ramadhan and Shawwal] for having guided you so that you may be grateful to Him.[1]

The Prophet ﷺ said:

«بُنِيَ الإِسْلَامُ عَلَى خَمْسٍ، شَهَادَةِ أَنْ لَا إِلَهَ إِلَّا اللهُ وَأَنَّ مُحَمَّداً رَسُولُ الله وَإِقَامِ الصَّلَاةِ وَإِيتَاءِ الزَّكَاةِ وَحَجِّ الْبَيْتِ وَصَوْمِ رَمَضَانَ»

Islam is built on five: to bear witness that none has the right to be worshipped but Allâh and that Muhammad is the Messenger of Allâh, to establish the prayer, to give *Zakat*, *Al-Hajj* to the House (the Ka'bah), and to fast the month of Ramadhan. (Agreed upon)

And in the narration of Muslim, the order is different:

«وَصَوْمِ رَمَضَانَ وَحَجِّ الْبَيْتِ»

To fast the month of Ramadhan, *Al-Hajj* to the House (the Ka'bah).

There is a consensus among the Muslims that it is obligatory to fast the month of Ramadhan; the knowledge thereof is one of those matters that are necessary to know as a Muslim. Whoever denies its being compulsory has disbelieved and must be asked to repent. If he repents and admits that it is compulsory, then all is well; otherwise, he is killed as a disbelieving apostate: he is neither washed, nor enshrouded; he is not prayed for, nor do others supplicate to Allâh for having mercy on him. He is to be buried quickly so that people are not harmed by his awful smell and so that his family is not harmed by having to look at him.

Fasting was prescribed two years after the *Hijrah* (migration to Al-Madinah), and so the Prophet ﷺ fasted Ramadhan for nine years.

[1] (*Al-Baqarah* 2:183-185)

Fasting was prescribed in two stages:

1) Muslims were given a choice between fasting and feeding a poor person, yet fasting was made preferable.

2) Without being given a choice, Muslims were ordered to fast. Salamah bin Akwa', may Allâh be pleased with him, said, 'When this verse was revealed:

﴿وَعَلَى ٱلَّذِينَ يُطِيقُونَهُۥ فِدۡيَةٌ طَعَامُ مِسۡكِينٖ﴾

And as for those who can fast with difficulty (the elderly, etc.), they have (a choice either to fast or) to feed a *Miskin* (poor person) (for every day).[1]

Whoever wished to break their fast did so (by feeding a poor person) until the following verse was revealed, abrogating the previous one.''

By the following verse, he meant:

﴿فَمَن شَهِدَ مِنكُمُ ٱلشَّهۡرَ فَلۡيَصُمۡهُۖ وَمَن كَانَ مَرِيضًا أَوۡ عَلَىٰ سَفَرٖ فَعِدَّةٌ مِّنۡ أَيَّامٍ أُخَرَ﴾

So, whoever of you sights (the crescent on the first night of) the month (of Ramadhan, i.e., is present at his home), he must observe *Sawm* (fasts) that month, and whoever is ill or on a journey, the same number [of days which one did not observe *Sawm* (fasts) must be made up for] from other days.[2]

So, Allâh made fasting obligatory on each individual, without a choice. The fast is not compulsory until the month of Ramadhan begins, which also means that one should not fast the days before Ramadhan begins, for the Prophet ﷺ said:

«لَا يَتَقَدَّمَنَّ أَحَدُكُمْ بِصَوْمِ يَوْمٍ أَوْ يَوْمَيْنِ إِلَّا أَنْ يَكُونَ رَجُلٌ كَانَ يَصُومُ صَوْمَهُ فَلۡيَصُمْ ذَلِكَ الْيَوْمَ»

Let not one of you precede by fasting one or two days (before Ramadhan begins) except for a man who habitually fasts that

---

[1] (*Al-Baqarah* 2:184)
[2] (*Al-Baqarah* 2:185)

day, then let him fast on that day. (Recorded by Al-Bukhari)[1]

The Fifth Pillar:
Making Pilgrimage (*Hajj*) To The Sacred House

Allâh Almighty says:

﴿وَلِلَّهِ عَلَى ٱلنَّاسِ حِجُّ ٱلْبَيْتِ مَنِ ٱسْتَطَاعَ إِلَيْهِ سَبِيلًا﴾

And *Hajj* to the House (Ka'bah) is a duty that mankind owes to Allâh, those who can afford the expenses (for one's conveyance, provision and residence).[2]

It is obligatory for a Muslim to perform *Hajj* at least once in his lifetime, and the same ruling applies to the *'Umrah* (the lesser pilgrimage). They are both obligatory upon the Muslim who fulfills the following:

1) He is sane
2) He has reached the age of puberty
3) He is free as opposed to being a slave, in which case it is not obligatory
4) He is able — financially, physically, etc. — to perform the *Hajj*.

When a child performs one of the two, though his pilgrimage is correct, he must still perform the obligatory pilgrimages when he becomes an adult and is able to make the journey. The *Hajj* and *'Umrah* are not obligatory upon a woman who does not have a *Mahram* (a male relative to whom she can never marry and with whom she may be in seclusion with) to accompany her, for there are authentic *Ahadith* in which the Prophet ﷺ forbade a woman from travelling without a *Mahram*.

Hajj is a kind of Islamic convention. Muslims come to it from all corners of the globe, representing all nationalities, colors, languages — yet they wear one clothing, they stand on one level, and they are all performing one worship; no distinction is made between old and young, between rich and poor, or between black and white. Allâh Almighty says:

---

[1] From *Majaalis Shahar Ramadhan*, pp. 15, 16.
[2] (*Aal 'Imran* 3:97)

﴿يَٰٓأَيُّهَا ٱلنَّاسُ إِنَّا خَلَقْنَٰكُم مِّن ذَكَرٍ وَأُنثَىٰ وَجَعَلْنَٰكُمْ شُعُوبًا وَقَبَآئِلَ لِتَعَارَفُوٓاْ إِنَّ أَكْرَمَكُمْ عِندَ ٱللَّهِ أَتْقَىٰكُمْ﴾

O mankind! We have created you from a male and a female, and made you into nations and tribes, that you may know one another. Verily, the most honorable of you with Allâh is the one who has the most *At-Taqwa*.[1]

The reward for the *Hajj* that is accepted is Paradise. In the Two *Sahihs* it is recorded from Abu Hurairah, may Allâh be pleased with him, that the Prophet ﷺ said:

«الْعُمْرَةُ إِلَى الْعُمْرَةِ كَفَّارَةٌ لِمَا بَيْنَهُمَا، وَالْحَجُّ الْمَبْرُورُ لَيْسَ لَهُ جَزَاءٌ إِلَّا الْجَنَّةُ»

From one '*Umrah* to the next is an expiation for what takes place (i.e., sins) between the two. And the accepted *Hajj* has no reward other than Paradise.

Also in the *Sahih*, the Prophet ﷺ said:

«مَنْ حَجَّ فَلَمْ يَرْفُثْ وَلَمْ يَفْسُقْ رَجَعَ كَيَوْمَ وَلَدَتْهُ أُمُّهُ»

Whoever makes *Hajj* without having intercourse (or without speaking evil speech during *Hajj*) and without doing evil deeds, then he returns as the day his mother gave birth to him.

Indeed Allâh has prescribed *Hajj* upon His worshippers and made it one of the pillars of Islam. Allâh Almighty says:

Explaining this, Shaikh Ibn Baz said:

﴿وَلِلَّهِ عَلَى ٱلنَّاسِ حِجُّ ٱلْبَيْتِ مَنِ ٱسْتَطَاعَ إِلَيْهِ سَبِيلًا وَمَن كَفَرَ فَإِنَّ ٱللَّهَ غَنِيٌّ عَنِ ٱلْعَٰلَمِينَ ۝٩٧﴾

And *Hajj* to the House (Ka'bah) is a duty that mankind owes to Allâh, those who can afford the expenses (for one's conveyance, provision and residence); and whoever disbelieves, then Allâh stands not in need of any of the creatures.[2]

---

[1] (*Al-Hujurat* 49:13)

[2] (*Aal 'Imran* 3:97)

In the Two *Sahihs*, Ibn 'Umar related that the Prophet ﷺ said:

«بُنِيَ الإِسْلَامُ عَلَى خَمْسٍ: شَهَادَةِ أَنْ لَا إِلَهَ إِلَّا اللهُ، وَأَنَّ مُحَمَّداً رَسُولُ اللهِ، وَإِقَامِ الصَّلَاةِ، وَإِيتَاءِ الزَّكَاةِ، وَصَوْمِ رَمَضَانَ، وَحَجِّ بَيْتِ اللهِ الْحَرَامِ»

Islam is built on five: to bear witness that none has the right to be worshipped except Allâh and that Muhammad is the Messenger of Allâh, to establish the prayer, to give *Zakat*, to fast Ramadhan, and *Al-Hajj* to Allâh's Sacred House (the Ka'bah).

In his *Sunan*, Sa'id (bin Mansur) related the following saying of 'Umar bin Al-Khattab: "I intended to send men to these regions to see who had sufficient wealth yet had not made *Hajj*, so that I could levy the *Jizyah*[1] on them: They are not Muslims, they are not Muslims."

It has been related that 'Ali, may Allâh be pleased with him, said, "Whoever was able to perform *Hajj* but did not perform it, then it is no difference whether he dies a Jew or a Christian."

If one is able to perform *Hajj* but has not performed it, then he must hasten to it, for Ibn 'Abbas, may Allâh be pleased with them, related that the Prophet ﷺ said:

«تَعَجَّلُوا إِلَى الْحَجِّ - يَعْنِي: الْفَرِيضَةَ - فَإِنَّ أَحَدَكُمْ لَا يَدْرِي مَا يَعْرِضُ لَهُ»

Hurry to perform *Hajj* — the *Hajj* that is compulsory (i.e., the first one) — for one of you doesn't know what will occur to him. (Recorded by Ahmad)

Based on the following saying of Allâh, *Hajj* becomes compulsory immediately, meaning as soon as one is able to perform it:

﴿وَلِلَّهِ عَلَى ٱلنَّاسِ حِجُّ ٱلْبَيْتِ مَنِ ٱسْتَطَاعَ إِلَيْهِ سَبِيلاً وَمَن كَفَرَ فَإِنَّ ٱللَّهَ غَنِيٌّ عَنِ ٱلْعَٰلَمِينَ ٩٧﴾

And *Hujj* to the House (Ka'bah) is a duty that mankind owes to

---

[1] A tax that is paid by Jews and Christians who live in Muslim lands.

Allâh, those who can afford the expenses (for one's conveyance, provision and residence); and whoever disbelieves, then Allâh stands not in need of any of the creatures.[1]

In his *Khutbah* (sermon), the Prophet ﷺ said:

«أَيُّهَا النَّاسُ، إِنَّ اللهَ فَرَضَ عَلَيْكُمُ الْحَجَّ فَحُجُّوا»

O people, indeed Allâh has made *Hajj* obligatory upon you, so make *Hajj*. (Recorded by Muslim).

That '*Umrah* (the lesser pilgrimage) is also obligatory is proven by certain *Ahadith*, one of them being the following:

«الإِسْلَامُ: أَنْ تَشْهَدَ أَنْ لَا إِلَهَ إِلَّا اللهُ وَأَنَّ مُحَمَّدًا رَسُولُ اللهِ، وَتُقِيمَ الصَّلَاةَ وَتُؤْتِي الزَّكَاةَ، وَتَحُجَّ الْبَيْتَ وَتَعْتَمِرَ، وَتَغْتَسِلَ مِنَ الْجَنَابَةِ، وَتُتِمَّ الْوُضُوءَ، وَتَصُومَ رَمَضَانَ»

Islam is to bear witness that none has the right to be worshipped but Allâh, to establish the prayer, to pay the *Zakat*, to make *Hajj* to the House (Ka'bah), to make '*Umrah*, to take a shower from *Janabah* (i.e., after performing sexual intercourse or after having a wet dream), to make a complete ablution, and to fast Ramadhan. (Ibn Khuzaimah and Ad-Daraqutni from a *Hadith* related by 'Umar bin Al-Khattab, may Allâh be pleased with him; Ad-Daraqutni said, "This chain is established and authentic.")

In a *Hadith* related by 'Aishah, she asked the Prophet ﷺ, "O Messenger of Allâh, is there *Jihad* upon women?" He ﷺ answered:

«عَلَيْهِنَّ جِهَادٌ لَا قِتَالَ فِيهِ: الْحَجُّ وَالْعُمْرَةُ»

"Upon them is a *Jihad* in which there is no fighting: *Hajj* and '*Umrah*." (Recorded by Ahmad and Ibn Majah, with an authentic chain.)

Neither *Hajj* nor '*Umrah* are obligatory upon a Muslim except once in his life, for the Prophet ﷺ said in an authentic *Hadith*:

«الْحَجُّ مَرَّةً، فَمَنْ زَادَ فَهُوَ تَطَوُّعٌ»

---

[1] (*Aal 'Imran* 3:97)

Hajj is once; whosoever does more, then it is voluntary.

Nonetheless it is legislated in Islam to perform both *Hajj* and *'Umrah* often, a ruling that is based on the following *Hadith* related by Abu Hurairah, may Allâh be pleased with him:

«الْعُمْرَةُ إِلَى الْعُمْرَةِ كَفَّارَةٌ لِمَا بَيْنَهُمَا، وَالْحَجُّ الْمَبْرُورُ لَيْسَ لَهُ جَزَاءٌ إِلَّا الْجَنَّةُ»

From one *'Umrah* to the next is expiation for what occurs between them (i.e., sins), and the reward for an accepted *Hajj* is none other than Paradise.

Shaikh Ibn Baz - may Allâh have mercy upon him - said:

Though they are not pillars in the religion, Islam has many other deeds that are of paramount importance, such as ordering others to do good deeds and forbidding them from evil. In fact, Allâh described this nation as being the best nation because it orders to do good and forbids evil:

﴿كُنتُمْ خَيْرَ أُمَّةٍ أُخْرِجَتْ لِلنَّاسِ تَأْمُرُونَ بِالْمَعْرُوفِ وَتَنْهَوْنَ عَنِ ٱلْمُنكَرِ وَتُؤْمِنُونَ بِٱللَّهِ﴾

You are the best of peoples ever raised up for mankind; you enjoin *Al-Ma'ruf* (all that Islam has ordained) and forbid *Al-Munkar* (all that Islam has forbidden), and you believe in Allâh.[1]

One of our pious predecessors said, "If one wishes to be from the best of this nation, let him fulfill a condition: ordering others to do good and forbidding them from perpetrating evil."

Another important aspect of Islam that Muslims should be serious about is *Jihad* in the way of Allâh, for through it, Allâh's Word is raised, Muslims achieve honor, and Muslim lands are protected from their disbelieving enemies. Ibn 'Umar, may Allâh be pleased with them, related that the Prophet ﷺ said:

«أُمِرْتُ أَنْ أُقَاتِلَ النَّاسَ حَتَّى يَشْهَدُوا أَنْ لَا إِلَهَ إِلَّا اللهُ، وَأَنَّ مُحَمَّداً

---

[1] (Aal 'Imran 3:110)

رَسُولُ اللهِ، وَيُقِيمُوا الصَّلَاةَ وَيُؤْتُوا الزَّكَاةَ، فَإِذَا فَعَلُوا ذَلِكَ عَصَمُوا مِنِّي دِمَاءَهُمْ وَأَمْوَالَهُمْ إِلَّا بِحَقِّ الإِسْلَام وَ حِسَابُهُمْ عَلَى اللهِ»

I have been ordered to fight the people until they bear witness that none has the right to be worshipped except Allâh and that Muhammad is the Messenger of Allâh, they establish the prayer, and they pay the *Zakat* — when they will have done all of that, they will have protected from me their blood and wealth, unless it is by a right, and their account (judgement) is with Allâh. (Agreed upon)

Mu'ath, may Allâh be pleased with him, related that the Prophet ﷺ said:

«رَأْسُ الأَمْرِ الإِسلَامُ وَعَمُودُهُ الصَّلَاةُ وَذِرْوَةُ سَنَامِهِ الْجِهَادُ فِي سَبِيلِ اللهِ»

The head of the matter is Islam, its pillar is the prayer, and its peak is *Jihad* in the way of Allâh. (Ahmad and At-Tirmithi with an authentic chain).

Right after the Muslims pledged allegiance to him as *Khalifah*, Abu Bakr, may Allâh be pleased with him, gave a sermon, and in it he said, "No people leave *Jihad* in the way of Allâh except that Allâh strikes them into ignominy." In *Jihad*, truth is enforced and falsehood is crushed, Allâh's *Shari'ah* is applied, and the Muslims are protected in their lands from the plots of their enemies.[1]

This is the end of the intended explanation of the five pillars.

---

[1] For what has preceded, refer to the sections entitled *At-Tahqiq wal-Iedhah* and *Mahaasin Ash-Shari'ah* in *Majmu'ah Fatawa wa Maqalat*, volume 2, by Shayikh 'Abdul-'Aziz bin Baz, may Allâh have mercy upon him.

Lesson Three

The Pillars Of Faith

There are six pillars of Faith: To believe in:

1) Allâh.
2) His Angels.
3) His Books.
4) His Messengers.
5) The Last Day.
6) Divine Preordainment, and that the good and bad of it are from Allâh Almighty.

❖ ❖ ❖

Before discussing the different pillars of faith, we begin with the following introduction:

1) The Difference Between Islam and *Iman* (Faith)

Islam and *Iman* are terms that include the entire religion. When they are mentioned together in one place — then Islam means the outwardly performed deeds, while *Iman* refers to the affairs of the inside, such as belief. Allâh Almighty says:

﴿قَالَتِ ٱلْأَعْرَابُ ءَامَنَّا ۖ قُل لَّمْ تُؤْمِنُوا۟ وَلَٰكِن قُولُوٓا۟ أَسْلَمْنَا﴾

The bedouins say: "We believe." Say: "You believe not but you only say, 'We have surrendered (in Islam)."'[1]

In the famous *Hadith* of Jibril, peace be upon him, 'Umar, may Allâh be pleased with him, said, "One day, as we were sitting with the Messenger of Allâh ﷺ, a man appeared before us: he had on him a garment that was pure white and his hair was pure black; though no sign of travel was upon him, not one of us knew him. He sat directly in front of the Prophet ﷺ, making his knees touch those of the Prophet ﷺ, and placing his hands on the Prophet's thighs. He said,

---

[1] (*Al-Hujurat* 49:14)

'O Muhammad! Inform me about Islam.' The Messenger of Allâh ﷺ said,

«الإِسْلَامُ أَنْ تَشْهَدَ أَنْ لَا إِلَهَ إِلَّا اللهُ وَأَنَّ مُحَمَّداً رَسُولُ اللهِ وَتُقِيمَ الصَّلَاةَ وَتُؤْتِي الزَّكَاةَ وَتَصُومَ رَمَضَانَ وَتَحُجَّ الْبَيْتَ إِنِ اسْتَطَعْتَ إِلَيْهِ سَبِيلًا»

'Islam is to bear witness that none has the right to be worshipped but Allâh and that Muhammad is the Messenger of Allâh; to establish the prayer; to give *Zakat*; to fast Ramadhan; to perform *Al-Hajj* to the House (Ka'bah), for whoever is able to do so.'

The man said, 'You have spoken the truth.' We were amazed at him because he first asked a question and then affirmed the truthfulness of the answer. He then said, 'Inform me about *Iman*.' The Prophet ﷺ said,

«أَنْ تُؤْمِنَ بِاللهِ وَمَلَائِكَتِهِ وَكُتُبِهِ وَرُسُلِهِ وَالْيَوْمِ الآخِرِ وَتُؤْمِنَ بِالْقَدَرِ خَيْرِهِ وَشَرِّهِ»

'To believe in Allâh, His Angels, His Books, His Messengers, the Last Day, and to believe in Divine Preordainment, the good of it and the bad of it.'

The man said, 'You have spoken the truth.' He then said, 'And inform me about *Ihsan*.' He ﷺ answered,

«أَنْ تَعْبُدَ اللهَ كَأَنَّكَ تَرَاهُ فَإِنْ لَمْ تَكُنْ تَرَاهُ فَإِنَّهُ يَرَاكَ»

'To worship Allâh as if you see Him, although you don't see Him, yet He indeed sees you.'

He said, 'And inform me about the Hour.' The Prophet ﷺ answered,

«مَا الْمَسْؤُولُ عَنْهَا بِأَعْلَمَ مِنَ السَّائِلِ»

'The one who is asked knows not more about it than the questioner.'

He said, 'Then inform me of its signs.' He ﷺ said,

«أَنْ تَلِدَ الْأَمَةُ رَبَّتَهَا وَأَنْ تَرَى الْحُفَاةَ الْعُرَاةَ الْعَالَةَ رُعَاةَ الشَّاءِ يَتَطَاوَلُونَ فِي الْبُنْيَانِ»

'That a slave woman will give birth to her female master and you will see the barefooted, naked, poor, guardians of sheep competing in constructing buildings'

The man then left, and I stayed for a long period of time, after which the Prophet ﷺ said to me,

«يَا عُمَرُ! أَتَدْرِي مَنِ السَّائِلُ»

'O 'Umar! Do you know who the questioner was?'

I said, 'Allâh and His Messenger know best.' He ﷺ said,

«فَإِنَّهُ جِبْرِيلُ أَتَاكُمْ يُعَلِّمُكُمْ دِينَكُمْ»

'Indeed he was Jibril, coming to teach you your religion'."
(Recorded by Muslim)

If the two words — Islam and *Iman* — appear separately, then each of them carries the meaning of the other. Allâh Almighty says:

﴿إِنَّ ٱلدِّينَ عِندَ ٱللَّهِ ٱلْإِسْلَٰمُ﴾

Truly, the religion with Allâh is Islam.[1]

Here, Allâh Almighty described Islam as being the religion, with both its outward and inward legislation. And the Messenger of Allâh ﷺ explained *Iman* to the delegation of 'Abdul-Qais with the same meaning that Islam is given in the above-mentioned *Hadith* of Jibril عليه السلام. Ibn 'Abbas, may Allâh be pleased with them, narrated that the Prophet ﷺ ordered them to have faith in Allâh alone, after which he said,

«أَتَدْرُونَ مَا الإِيمَانُ بِاللهِ وَحْدَهُ؟»

"Do you know what *Iman* in Allâh alone is?"

They answered, "Allâh and His Messenger know best." He ﷺ said,

شَهَادَةُ أَنْ لَا إِلَهَ إِلَّا اللهُ وَأَنَّ مُحَمَّداً رَسُولُ اللهِ وَإِقَامِ الصَّلَاةِ وَإِيتَاءِ الزَّكَاةِ وَصِيَامِ رَمَضَانَ . . . »

"To bear witness that none has the right to be worshipped but Allâh and that Muhammad is the Messenger of Allâh, to establish the prayer, to give *Zakat*, to fast Ramadhan..."

---

[1] (*Aal 'Imran* 3:19)

We also can appreciate the fact that they have the same meaning when mentioned alone from the *Hadith* that discusses the branches of faith; in it, the Prophet ﷺ said:

«أَعْلَاهَا قَوْلُ لَا إِلَهَ إِلَّا الله، وَأَدْنَاهَا إِمَاطَةُ الأَذَى عَنِ الطَّرِيقِ»

The highest of them is the saying, 'none has the right to be worshipped but Allâh', and the lowest of them is to remove something harmful from the road.

The different branches of faith that are between the highest and lowest one necessarily include both outward and inward deeds.

It should also be known that outward deeds are not called Islam unless basic belief and faith are first present. If the basic faith is not first present in someone, then even with his deeds, he becomes a hypocrite. Both outwardly manifest deeds, and belief with conviction in the heart are obligatory — one cannot be separated from the other.

One cannot complete the Islam and faith that are obligatory unless he obeys Allâh's commands and avoids His prohibitions; if one truly wishes completeness — which implies that there are degrees to deeds and belief — then he must increase his faith and perform many voluntary deeds.

2) The Definition Of *Iman*

First, its meaning in the Arabic Language: Belief that necessitates both acceptance and submission.

The meaning of *Iman* in the *Shari'ah*: Belief in the heart, acknowledgement with the tongue, and action with the limbs - it increases through obedience and decreases with sin.

Actions Are Included in the Term *Iman*?

Actions are included in the term *Iman*, a fact that is supported by the Qur'an, the Sunnah, and the consensus of the earlier generations of Muslims. Allâh Almighty says:

﴿وَمَا كَانَ اللَّهُ لِيُضِيعَ إِيمَنَكُمْ﴾

And Allâh would never make your *Iman* (prayers) to be lost

(i.e., your prayers offered towards Jerusalem).[1]

Here, the term *Iman* is referring to prayer, so Allâh is in effect saying to them: Your prayers that you prayed while you faced Jerusalem before you were ordered to turn toward the Ka'bah are not lost.

The Prophet ﷺ said:

«الإِيمَانُ بِضْعٌ وَسَبْعُونَ (أَوْ بِضْعٌ وَسِتُّونَ) شُعْبَةً فَأَفْضَلُهَا قَوْلُ لَا إِلَهَ إِلَّا اللهُ وَأَدْنَاهَا إِمَاطَةُ الأَذَى عَنِ الطَّرِيقِ وَالْحَيَاءُ شُعْبَةٌ مِنَ الْإِيمَانِ»

Iman consists of more then seventy (or more then sixty) branches, the best of them is the saying, "None has the right to be worshipped but Allâh," and the lowest of them is removing something harmful from the road (or path); and modesty (shyness) is one of the branches of *Iman*. (Recorded by Muslim)

Imam Ash-Shafi'i related that there was a consensus among the Companions and their followers regarding this issue.

3) Faith Increases And Decreases

Faith increases and decreases. It increases with obedience and decreases with sin. There are many proofs which show that faith increases and decreases, and among them are the following:

1) Allâh Almighty says:

﴿وَمَا جَعَلْنَا أَصْحَابَ ٱلنَّارِ إِلَّا مَلَٰئِكَةً وَمَا جَعَلْنَا عِدَّتَهُمْ إِلَّا فِتْنَةً لِّلَّذِينَ كَفَرُوا لِيَسْتَيْقِنَ ٱلَّذِينَ أُوتُوا ٱلْكِتَٰبَ وَيَزْدَادَ ٱلَّذِينَ ءَامَنُوا إِيمَٰنًا﴾

And We have set none but angels as guardians of the Fire, and We have fixed their number only as a trial for the disbelievers, in order that the People of the Scripture may arrive at a certainty and the believers may increase in faith.[2]

2) Allâh Almighty says:

﴿إِنَّمَا ٱلْمُؤْمِنُونَ ٱلَّذِينَ إِذَا ذُكِرَ ٱللَّهُ وَجِلَتْ قُلُوبُهُمْ وَإِذَا تُلِيَتْ عَلَيْهِمْ ءَايَٰتُهُ زَادَتْهُمْ إِيمَٰنًا وَعَلَىٰ رَبِّهِمْ يَتَوَكَّلُونَ ٢ ٱلَّذِينَ يُقِيمُونَ ٱلصَّلَوٰةَ وَمِمَّا رَزَقْنَٰهُمْ يُنفِقُونَ﴾

---

[1] (*Al-Baqarah* 2:143)

[2] (*Al-Muddaththir* 74:31)

﴿(٣) أُولَٰئِكَ هُمُ ٱلْمُؤْمِنُونَ حَقًّا ۚ لَّهُمْ دَرَجَٰتٌ عِندَ رَبِّهِمْ وَمَغْفِرَةٌ وَرِزْقٌ كَرِيمٌ (٤)﴾

The believers are only those who, when Allâh is mentioned, feel a fear in their hearts and when His verses (this Qur'an) are recited to them, they (i.e., the verses) increase their faith; and they put their trust in their Lord (alone); Who perform *As-Salat* and spend out of that We have provided them. It is they who are the believers in truth. For them are grades of dignity with their Lord, and forgiveness and a generous provision (Paradise).[1]

3) Abu Sa'id Al-Khudri, may Allâh be pleased with him, related that he heard the Prophet ﷺ say:

«مَنْ رَأَى مِنْكُمْ مُنْكَرًا فَلْيُغَيِّرْهُ بِيَدِهِ، فَإِنْ لَمْ يَسْتَطِعْ فَبِلِسَانِهِ، فَإِنْ لَمْ يَسْتَطِعْ فَبِقَلْبِهِ، وَذَلِكَ أَضْعَفُ الإِيمَانِ»

Whosoever from you sees an evil, let him change it with his hand; if he is not able, then with his tongue; and if he is not able, then with his heart; and that is the weakest level of faith.

This *Hadith* not only indicates the different levels of changing evil, but it also indicates that changing evil is part of faith. The weakest level of faith is to change evil with one's heart; the other two ways of changing evil indicate a stronger level of faith. And Allâh knows best.

4) In early *Hadith* regarding the branches of faith, we learn that faith includes a number of branches — each is distinguished in status. Regarding some of those actions, faith disappears when they disappear, such as the two testimonies of faith. With other actions faith doesn't disappear when they disappear, such as removing something harmful from the road. The more branches of faith one follows and applies, the higher will be the level of his faith.

After establishing the reality that faith increases and decreases, we must consequently appreciate that the people of faith are at different levels: some have a complete faith while others are at lower levels; one may even be a believer because of his faith and at the same time an evil-doer because of a great sin he perpetrated — therefore his

---

[1] (*Al-Anfal* 8:2-4)

faith is deficient due to his sin.

Because some wrongfully take deeds outside of the category of faith, they consequently believe that faith neither increases nor decreases and that people are equal in the level of their faith. They equate the most wicked person's faith with that of one of the Prophet's Companions, may Allâh be pleased with them. This notion is categorically false, for it goes against the Qur'an, the Sunnah, and sound reasoning — there are so many contradictions within the idea that deeds are not a part of faith, that the idea itself becomes invalid.

As for faith in Allâh, it is a certainty of belief that Allâh is the Lord and Sovereign of all that exists, that He is the Creator and Planner and Sustainer of the entire universe, that He alone — and without a partner — deserves to be worshipped, that all that is worshipped other than Him is worshipped in vain, that Allâh has the most exalted and perfect attributes, and that He is far above from having any fault or defect.

4) The Effects Of Disobedience On Faith

Disobedience is the opposite of obedience to Allâh, and the term embraces both leaving a command and perpetrating that which is prohibited. We have already learned that faith is slightly more than seventy branches, the highest of which is the saying, "None has the right to be worshipped but Allâh," and the lowest of which is removing something harmful from the path. So the branches of faith are not of one level in terms of size and significance, and the same can be said for disobedience. Some sins nullify faith itself, as in the following verse:

But [Fir'awn (Pharaoh)] belied and disobeyed;[1]

Some sins are at a lower level: the perpetrator does not exit from a state of faith, but his faith is definitely diminished by committing those sins. When one commits a major sin, such as fornication, drinking alcohol, or stealing, and when he at the same time doesn't believe that those actions are permissible, piety, righteousness, and illumination leave his heart, even though the basic level of

---

[1] (*An-Nazi'at* 79:21)

acceptance or belief in Allâh may remain in his heart. If he repents to Allâh and does good deeds, light and piety return to his heart. But if he persists in perpetrating sins, the covering on his heart will increase and grow, until it will completely cover his heart — we seek protection in Allâh — at which time he will not know good from evil.

In a *Hadith* recorded by Imam Ahmad, Abu Hurairah, may Allâh be pleased with him, narrated that the Messenger of Allâh ﷺ said:

«إِنَّ الْمُؤْمِنَ إِذَا أَذْنَبَ كَانَتْ نُكْتَةٌ سَوْدَاءُ فِي قَلْبِهِ، فَإِنْ تَابَ وَنَزَعَ وَاسْتَغْفَرَ صَقِلَ قَلْبُهُ، وَإِنْ زَادَ زَادَتْ حَتَّى يَعْلُو قَلْبُهُ ذَاكَ الرَّيْنُ الَّذِي ذَكَرَ اللهُ – عَزَّوَجَلَّ – فِي الْقُرْآنِ:»

Verily, when a believer sins, a black dot appears on his heart; if he repents, desists, and asks (Allâh) forgiveness, then his heart will be polished. But if he increases (in his sins) then the spot increases and grows until his heart will be covered by the *Ran* (covering of sins and evil deeds) that Allâh mentioned in the Qur'an:

﴿كَلَّا بَلْ رَانَ عَلَىٰ قُلُوبِهِم مَّا كَانُوا يَكْسِبُونَ ۝﴾

Nay! But on their hearts is the *Ran* (covering of sins and evil deeds) which they used to earn.[1]

5) Actions That Nullify One's Faith And Islam

Here we are referring to those actions that nullify one's faith after one has already entered into a state of faith; here are some of those actions:

1) If one rejects the belief in Allâh's Lordship, or anything that comes under that belief, one's faith becomes void:

﴿وَقَالُوا مَا هِيَ إِلَّا حَيَاتُنَا الدُّنْيَا نَمُوتُ وَنَحْيَا وَمَا يُهْلِكُنَا إِلَّا الدَّهْرُ وَمَا لَهُم بِذَٰلِكَ مِنْ عِلْمٍ إِنْ هُمْ إِلَّا يَظُنُّونَ ۝﴾

And they say: "There is nothing but our life of this world, we die and we live and nothing destroys us except *Ad-Dahr* (the time)." And they have no knowledge of it, they only

[1] (*Al-Mutaffifin* 83:14)

conjecture. [1]

2) Being too proud and haughty to worship Allâh. Allâh Almighty says:

$$﴿لَّن يَسْتَنكِفَ ٱلْمَسِيحُ أَن يَكُونَ عَبْدًا لِّلَّهِ وَلَا ٱلْمَلَٰٓئِكَةُ ٱلْمُقَرَّبُونَ وَمَن يَسْتَنكِفْ عَنْ عِبَادَتِهِۦ وَيَسْتَكْبِرْ فَسَيَحْشُرُهُمْ إِلَيْهِ جَمِيعًا ١٧٢ فَأَمَّا ٱلَّذِينَ ءَامَنُوا۟ وَعَمِلُوا۟ ٱلصَّٰلِحَٰتِ فَيُوَفِّيهِمْ أُجُورَهُمْ وَيَزِيدُهُم مِّن فَضْلِهِۦ وَأَمَّا ٱلَّذِينَ ٱسْتَنكَفُوا۟ وَٱسْتَكْبَرُوا۟ فَيُعَذِّبُهُمْ عَذَابًا أَلِيمًا وَلَا يَجِدُونَ لَهُم مِّن دُونِ ٱللَّهِ وَلِيًّا وَلَا نَصِيرًا ١٧٣ ﴾$$

The Messiah will never be proud to reject to be a slave to Allâh, nor the angels who are near. And whosoever rejects His worship and is proud, then He will gather them all together unto Himself. So, as for those who believed and did deeds of righteousness, He will give their (due) rewards, and more out of His bounty. but as for those who refuse His worship and were proud, He will punish them with a painful torment. And they will not find for themselves besides Allâh any protector or helper.[2]

3) Associating partners with Allâh in worship, either by dedicating some acts of worship to other than Allâh or by taking intercessors or intermediaries, asking them instead of Allâh, relying on them, or asking them for intercession. Allâh Almighty says:

$$﴿وَيَعْبُدُونَ مِن دُونِ ٱللَّهِ مَا لَا يَضُرُّهُمْ وَلَا يَنفَعُهُمْ وَيَقُولُونَ هَٰٓؤُلَاءِ شُفَعَٰٓؤُنَا عِندَ ٱللَّهِ قُلْ أَتُنَبِّئُونَ ٱللَّهَ بِمَا لَا يَعْلَمُ فِي ٱلسَّمَٰوَٰتِ وَلَا فِي ٱلْأَرْضِ سُبْحَٰنَهُۥ وَتَعَٰلَىٰ عَمَّا يُشْرِكُونَ ١٨ ﴾$$

And they worship besides Allâh things that hurt them not, nor profit them, and they say: "These are our intercessors with Allâh." Say: "Do you inform Allâh of that which He knows not in the heavens and on the earth?" Glorified and Exalted is He above all that which they associate as partners with Him! [3]

---

[1] (*Al-Jathiyah* 45:24)

[2] (*An-Nisa'* 4:172,173)

[3] (*Yunus* 10:18)

In another verse, Allâh Almighty says:

﴿لَهُ دَعْوَةُ ٱلْحَقِّ وَٱلَّذِينَ يَدْعُونَ مِن دُونِهِۦ لَا يَسْتَجِيبُونَ لَهُم بِشَيْءٍ إِلَّا كَبَٰسِطِ كَفَّيْهِ إِلَى ٱلْمَآءِ لِيَبْلُغَ فَاهُ وَمَا هُوَ بِبَٰلِغِهِۦ وَمَا دُعَآءُ ٱلْكَٰفِرِينَ إِلَّا فِى ضَلَٰلٍ ١٤﴾

For Him is the Word of Truth. And those whom they invoke, answer them no more than one who stretches forth his hand (at the edge of a deep well) for water to reach his mouth, but it reaches him not, and the invocation of the disbelievers is nothing but an error.[1]

4) Rejecting anything that Allâh has affirmed for Himself or that the Prophet ﷺ has affirmed for Him. Also, ascribing to someone from creation some of those qualities that are specific to Allâh, such as knowledge of the unseen. And finally, affirming something that Allâh has negated about Himself or that the Prophet ﷺ has negated about Him. Addressing the Messenger of Allâh ﷺ, Allâh Almighty says:

﴿قُلْ هُوَ ٱللَّهُ أَحَدٌ ١ ٱللَّهُ ٱلصَّمَدُ ٢ لَمْ يَلِدْ وَلَمْ يُولَدْ ٣ وَلَمْ يَكُن لَّهُۥ كُفُوًا أَحَدُۢ ٤﴾

Say: "He is Allâh, (the) One *Allâhus-Samad* (Allâh —the Self-Sufficient Master, Whom all creatures need, He neither eats nor drinks). He begets not, nor was He begotten; And there is none co-equal or comparable unto Him. [2]

And Allâh Almighty says:

﴿وَلِلَّهِ ٱلْأَسْمَآءُ ٱلْحُسْنَىٰ فَٱدْعُوهُ بِهَا وَذَرُوا۟ ٱلَّذِينَ يُلْحِدُونَ فِىٓ أَسْمَٰٓئِهِۦ سَيُجْزَوْنَ مَا كَانُوا۟ يَعْمَلُونَ ١٨٠﴾

And (all) the Most Beautiful Names belong to Allâh, so call on Him by them, and leave the company of those who belie or deny (or utter impious speech against) His Names. They will be requited for what they used to do.[3]

---

[1] (*Ar-Ra'd* 13:14)

[2] (*Al-Ikhlas* 112:1-4)

[3] (*Al-A'raf* 7:180)

﴿رَبُّ السَّمَوَاتِ وَالْأَرْضِ وَمَا بَيْنَهُمَا فَاعْبُدْهُ وَاصْطَبِرْ لِعِبَادَتِهِ هَلْ تَعْلَمُ لَهُ سَمِيًّا ٦٥﴾

Lord of the heavens and the earth, and all that is between them, so worship Him (Alone) and be constant and patient in His worship. Do you know of any who is similar to Him?[1]

5) Disbelieving in anything that the Messenger of Allâh ﷺ came with; Allâh Almighty says:

﴿وَإِن يُكَذِّبُوكَ فَقَدْ كَذَّبَ الَّذِينَ مِن قَبْلِهِمْ جَاءَتْهُمْ رُسُلُهُم بِالْبَيِّنَاتِ وَبِالزُّبُرِ وَبِالْكِتَابِ الْمُنِيرِ ٢٥ ثُمَّ أَخَذْتُ الَّذِينَ كَفَرُوا فَكَيْفَ كَانَ نَكِيرِ ٢٦﴾

And if they deny you, those before them also denied. Their Messengers came to them with clear signs, and with the Scriptures, and the Book giving light. Then I took hold of those who disbelieved, and how terrible was My denial (punishment)! [2]

6) Believing that the Prophet's guidance is incomplete, disbelieving some of Allâh's Commands that were revealed to him, believing that another system of laws is better and more suitable to mankind, believing that any other law or system of laws is equal to Allâh and His Messenger's laws, or believing that it is permissible to rule by other than what Allâh has revealed. Allâh Almighty says:

﴿أَلَمْ تَرَ إِلَى الَّذِينَ يَزْعُمُونَ أَنَّهُمْ ءَامَنُوا بِمَا أُنزِلَ إِلَيْكَ وَمَا أُنزِلَ مِن قَبْلِكَ يُرِيدُونَ أَن يَتَحَاكَمُوا إِلَى الطَّاغُوتِ وَقَدْ أُمِرُوا أَن يَكْفُرُوا بِهِ وَيُرِيدُ الشَّيْطَانُ أَن يُضِلَّهُمْ ضَلَالًا بَعِيدًا ٦٠﴾

Have you seen those (hypocrites) who claim that they believe in that which has been sent down to you, and that which was sent down before you, and they wish to go for judgement (in their disputes) to the *Taghut* (false judges, etc.) while they have been ordered to reject them. But *Shaitan* (Satan) wishes to lead them far astray.[3]

---

[1] (*Maryam* 19:65)

[2] (*Fatir* 35:25,26)

[3] (*An-Nisa'* 4:60)

And Allâh Almighty says:

$$﴿فَلَا وَرَبِّكَ لَا يُؤْمِنُونَ حَتَّىٰ يُحَكِّمُوكَ فِيمَا شَجَرَ بَيْنَهُمْ ثُمَّ لَا يَجِدُوا فِي أَنفُسِهِمْ حَرَجًا مِّمَّا قَضَيْتَ وَيُسَلِّمُوا تَسْلِيمًا ٦٥﴾$$

But no, by your Lord, they can have no faith, until they make you (O Muhammad ﷺ) judge in all disputes between them, and find in themselves no resistance against your decisions, and accept (them) with full submission.[1]

$$﴿وَمَن لَّمْ يَحْكُم بِمَا أَنزَلَ اللَّهُ فَأُولَٰئِكَ هُمُ الْكَافِرُونَ ٤٤﴾$$

And whosoever does not judge by what Allâh has revealed, such are the *Kafirun* (i.e., disbelievers — of a lesser degree as they do not act on Allâh's Laws).[2]

7) One's faith is also nullified by not deeming the polytheists and disbelievers to actually be disbelievers, or even to doubt whether they are disbelievers, because that is to have doubt in what the Messenger of Allâh ﷺ came with. Allâh Almighty says:

$$﴿وَقَالُوا إِنَّا كَفَرْنَا بِمَا أُرْسِلْتُم بِهِ وَإِنَّا لَفِي شَكٍّ مِّمَّا تَدْعُونَنَا إِلَيْهِ مُرِيبٍ﴾$$

And said: "Verily, we disbelieve in that with which you have been sent, and we are really in grave doubt as to that to which you invite us."[3]

8) Mocking or making fun of Allâh, of the Qur'an, the religion, Islamic rewards and punishments, the Messenger of Allâh ﷺ, some of the Prophets, and so on, regardless of whether one is mocking jokingly or seriously. Allâh Almighty says:

$$﴿وَلَئِن سَأَلْتَهُمْ لَيَقُولُنَّ إِنَّمَا كُنَّا نَخُوضُ وَنَلْعَبُ قُلْ أَبِاللَّهِ وَآيَاتِهِ وَرَسُولِهِ كُنتُمْ تَسْتَهْزِئُونَ ٦٥ لَا تَعْتَذِرُوا قَدْ كَفَرْتُم بَعْدَ إِيمَانِكُمْ﴾$$

If you ask them (about this), they declare: "We were only talking idly and joking." Say: "Was it at Allâh, and His *Ayat* (proofs, evidences, verses, lessons, signs, revelations, etc.) And His Messenger that you were mocking?" Make no

---

[1] (*An-Nisa'* 4:65)

[2] (*Al-Ma'idah* 5:44)

[3] (*Ibrahim* 14:9)

excuse; you have disbelieved after you had believed.[1]

9) Helping and backing the disbelievers against the Muslims; Allâh Almighty says:

﴿وَمَن يَتَوَلَّهُم مِّنكُمْ فَإِنَّهُ مِنْهُمْ إِنَّ ٱللَّهَ لَا يَهْدِى ٱلْقَوْمَ ٱلظَّٰلِمِينَ ٥١﴾

And if any among you takes them as *Awliya'*, then surely he is one of them. Verily, Allâh guides not those people who are wrongdoers.[2]

10) Believing that it is permissible for a certain person to not follow the guidance of Prophet Muhammad ﷺ; Allâh Almighty says:

﴿وَمَن يَبْتَغِ غَيْرَ ٱلْإِسْلَٰمِ دِينًا فَلَن يُقْبَلَ مِنْهُ وَهُوَ فِى ٱلْأَخِرَةِ مِنَ ٱلْخَٰسِرِينَ ٨٥﴾

And whoever seeks a religion other than Islam, it will never be accepted of him, and in the Hereafter he will be one of the losers.[3]

11) Turning away, either completely from Allâh's religion, or turning away from those actions that are necessary to the correctness of one's Islam — neither learning nor applying those actions. Allâh Almighty says:

﴿وَمَنْ أَظْلَمُ مِمَّن ذُكِّرَ بِـَٔايَٰتِ رَبِّهِۦ ثُمَّ أَعْرَضَ عَنْهَآ إِنَّا مِنَ ٱلْمُجْرِمِينَ مُنتَقِمُونَ ٢٢﴾

And who does more wrong than he who is reminded of the *Ayat* (proofs, evidences, verses, lessons, signs, revelations, etc.) of his Lord, then he turns aside there from? Verily, We shall exact retribution from the criminals.[4]

12) Hating anything that the Prophet ﷺ came with, even if one practices that which he hates. Allâh Almighty says:

﴿ذَٰلِكَ بِأَنَّهُمْ كَرِهُوا۟ مَآ أَنزَلَ ٱللَّهُ فَأَحْبَطَ أَعْمَٰلَهُمْ ٩﴾

That is because they hate that which Allâh has sent down, so He has made their deeds fruitless.[5]

13) Practicing magic or being pleased by magic. Allâh Almighty says:

---

[1] (*At-Taubah* 9:65,66)
[2] (*Al-Ma'idah* 5:51)
[3] (*Aal 'Imran* 3:75)
[4] (*As-Sajdah* 32:22)
[5] (*Muhammad* 47:9)

﴿وَمَا يُعَلِّمَانِ مِنْ أَحَدٍ حَتَّىٰ يَقُولَا إِنَّمَا نَحْنُ فِتْنَةٌ فَلَا تَكْفُرْ﴾

But neither of these two (angels) taught anyone (such things) till they had said, "We are only for trial, so disbelieve not (by learning this magic from us)."[1]

These are the most common actions or beliefs that nullify one's faith; however, there are many others, even though most of them return to rejecting the Qur'an or a part of the Qur'an, doubting in the fact that it is a miracle, debasing the Qur'an or a part of it, deeming something lawful when there is a consensus that it is unlawful — such as fornication or drinking alcohol, finding fault in the religion or cursing it, or abandoning the prayer — and we seek refuge in Allâh from misguidance. And Allâh Almighty knows best.

---

[1] (*Al-Baqarah* 2:102)

The Pillars And Branches of Faith

The Pillars Of Faith

In Arabic, the word used for pillars is *Arkan*, the singular of which is *Rukn*: the *Rukn* of something is its strong side. There are six pillars of faith:

1) Faith in Allâh
2) Faith in the Angels
3) Faith in the Book
4) Faith in the Messengers
5) Faith in the Last Day
6) Faith in the Divine Preordainment, both the good and bad of it

The proof for these six being the pillars of faith is found in the answer Allâh's Messenger ﷺ gave when Jibril, peace be upon him, asked him about faith. He ﷺ answered:

«أَنْ تُؤْمِنَ بِاللهِ وَمَلَائِكَتِهِ وَكُتُبِهِ وَرُسُلِهِ وَالْيَوم الآخِرِ وَتُؤْمِنَ بِالْقَدَرِ خَيْرِهِ وَشَرِّهِ»

To believe in Allâh, His Angels, His Books, His Messengers, the Last Day, and to believe in Divine Preordainment, the good and bad of it. (Recorded by Muslim)

The Branches Of Faith

The Arabic word for branches is *Shu'ab*, the singular of which is *Shu'bah*, which means a characteristic or a component. The branches of faith, then, are its many components; in one *Hadith*, we learn that those components are more than seventy in number.

Abu Hurairah, may Allâh be pleased with him, related that the Prophet ﷺ said:

«الإيمَانُ بِضْعٌ وَسَبْعُونَ (أَوْ بِضْعٌ وَسِتُّونَ) شُعْبَةً، فَأَفْضَلُهَا قَوْلُ لَا إِلَهَ إِلَّا اللهُ وَأَدْنَاهَا إِمَاطَةُ الأَذَى عَنِ الطَّرِيقِ»

Faith counsits of more then seventy (or more then sixty) branches, the best of which is the saying, "None has the right to be worshipped but Allâh," and the lowest of which is to remove something harmful from the road. (Recorded by Muslim)

The Messenger of Allâh ﷺ clarified that the best of these components or branches is *Tawhid*, which is obligatory upon every person, and upon which hinges the validity of other components. The lowest of them is to remove something that might harm a Muslim. Between these two branches, there are a number of other branches — such as love for the Messenger of Allâh ﷺ, loving for a brother what one loves for himself, and *Jihad*. The branches are not clearly mentioned altogether in the Sunnah; however, some scholars, such as Al-Baihaqi in *Al-Jami' Li-Shu'abil-Iman*, have tried to infer what they are and enumerate them.

Some of the many branches are like supports, without which faith disappears in a person. For example, one's faith is invalid if he disbelieves in the Last Day, for Allâh Almighty says:

﴿زَعَمَ ٱلَّذِينَ كَفَرُوٓاْ أَن لَّن يُبْعَثُوٓاْ قُلْ بَلَىٰ وَرَبِّى لَتُبْعَثُنَّ ثُمَّ لَتُنَبَّؤُنَّ بِمَا عَمِلْتُمْ وَذَٰلِكَ عَلَى ٱللَّهِ يَسِيرٌ ۝٧﴾

The disbelievers pretend that they will never be resurrected (for the Account). Say: "Yes! By my Lord, you will certainly be resurrected, then you will be informed of what you did, and that is easy for Allâh."[1]

Some of those branches are less significant than supports, and thus one's faith does not leave due to their absence; nonetheless, one's level of faith decreases and one might even be described as a doer of wicked deeds. One example of this category is for one to treat his neighbor badly. Abu Hurairah, may Allâh be pleased with him, related that the Messenger of Allâh ﷺ said:

«مَنْ كَانَ يُؤْمِنُ بِاللهِ وَالْيَوْمِ الآخِرِ فَلْيَقُلْ خَيْرًا أَوْ لِيَصْمُتْ، وَمَنْ كَانَ يُؤْمِنُ بِاللهِ وَالْيَوْمِ الآخِرِ فَلْيُكْرِمْ جَارَهُ وَمَنْ كَانَ يُؤْمِنُ بِاللهِ وَالْيَوْمِ الآخِرِ فَلْيُكْرِمْ ضَيْفَهُ»

Whosoever believes in Allâh and the Last Day, then let him speak well or otherwise remain quiet. Whosoever believes in Allâh and the Last Day, then let him honor his neighbor. And whosoever believes in Allâh and the Last Day, then let him

[1] (*At-Taghabun* 64:7)

honor his guest. (Recorded by Al-Bukhari)

A single person may have some of the components of faith while at the same time he has some of the components of *Nifaq* (hypocrisy): for the latter category, he deserves punishment, but he will not dwell in the Hellfire for eternity because of the faith he has in his heart. And Allâh Almighty knows best.

The First Pillar of *Iman*
Belief In Allâh

Having faith in Allâh means to believe with certainty and conviction that Allâh is the Lord and Sovereign of all that exists, that He is the Creator and Planner and Sustainer of the entire universe, that He alone — and without a partner — deserves to be worshipped, that all that is worshipped other than Him is worshipped in vain, that Allâh has the most exalted and perfect attributes, and that He is far above from having any fault or defect. Faith in Allâh consists of the following:

1) *Tawhid Ar-Rububiyyah*

This means to believe that Allâh Almighty is the only Creator, King, Planner, and Sustainer of all that exists. First, that He is the sole Creator of all that exists:

﴿أَلَا لَهُ ٱلْخَلْقُ وَٱلْأَمْرُ﴾

Surely, His is the Creation and Commandment.[1]

And Allâh Almighty says:

﴿هَلْ مِنْ خَلِقٍ غَيْرُ ٱللَّهِ يَرْزُقُكُم مِّنَ ٱلسَّمَاءِ وَٱلْأَرْضِ﴾

Is there any creator other than Allâh who provides for you from the sky (rain) and the earth?[2]

﴿قُلْ مَنْ بِيَدِهِ مَلَكُوتُ كُلِّ شَيْءٍ﴾

Say: "In Whose Hand is the sovereignty of everything?"[3]

---

[1] (*Al-A'raf* 7:54)

[2] (*Fatir* 35:3)

[3] (*Al-Mu'minun* 23:88)

We must also believe that it is only Allâh Who sustains everything:

﴿قُلْ مَن يَرْزُقُكُم مِّنَ ٱلسَّمَآءِ وَٱلْأَرْضِ أَمَّن يَمْلِكُ ٱلسَّمْعَ وَٱلْأَبْصَٰرَ وَمَن يُخْرِجُ ٱلْحَيَّ مِنَ ٱلْمَيِّتِ وَيُخْرِجُ ٱلْمَيِّتَ مِنَ ٱلْحَيِّ وَمَن يُدَبِّرُ ٱلْأَمْرَ فَسَيَقُولُونَ ٱللَّهُ فَقُلْ أَفَلَا تَتَّقُونَ ﴾ (٣١)

Say: "Who provides for you from the sky and the earth? Or who owns hearing and sight? And who brings out the living from the dead and brings out the dead from the living? And who disposes the affairs?" They will say: "Allâh." Say: "Will you not then be afraid of Allâh's punishment?"[1]

The polytheists to whom Muhammad ﷺ was sent as a Messenger did not oppose this category; rather, they accepted it, for Allâh Almighty says:

﴿وَلَئِن سَأَلْتَهُم مَّنْ خَلَقَ ٱلسَّمَٰوَٰتِ وَٱلْأَرْضَ لَيَقُولُنَّ خَلَقَهُنَّ ٱلْعَزِيزُ ٱلْعَلِيمُ ﴾ (٩)

And indeed if you ask them, "Who has created the heavens and the earth?" They will surely say: "The All-Mighty, the All-Knower created them."[2]

From previous nations, the only one known to have rejected this category of *Tawhid* was Fir'awn, who did so because of his haughtiness; Allâh Almighty says to us, relating what he says:

﴿فَقَالَ أَنَا۠ رَبُّكُمُ ٱلْأَعْلَىٰ ﴾ (٢٤)

Saying: "I am your lord, most high."[3]

Another group, the Zoroastrians, set up partners with Allâh in this category, for they said that the universe has two creators: darkness and light; they believed that light was better than darkness.

2) *Tawhid Al-Uluhiyyah*

It is also called *Tawhid Al-'Ibadah* (worship), from the point of view of the worshipper. But to ascribe it to Allâh, this category is called *Al-Uluhiyyah* (from the word *Al-Ilah*, which means "the God"). This category requires one to dedicate his worship purely for Allâh, for

---

[1] (*Yunus* 10:31)

[2] (*Az-Zukhruf* 43:9)

[3] (*An-Nazi'at* 79:24)

Allâh alone deserves to be worshipped. All that is worshipped other than Him is falsely worshipped. Allâh Almighty says:

﴿ذَٰلِكَ بِأَنَّ ٱللَّهَ هُوَ ٱلْحَقُّ وَأَنَّ مَا يَدْعُونَ مِن دُونِهِ ٱلْبَٰطِلُ﴾

That is because Allâh, He is the Truth, and that which they invoke besides Him is *Al-Batil* (falsehood, Satan and all other false deities)[1]

And Allâh Almighty says:

﴿لَّا تَجْعَلْ مَعَ ٱللَّهِ إِلَٰهًا ءَاخَرَ فَتَقْعُدَ مَذْمُومًا مَّخْذُولًا ۝﴾

Set not up with Allâh any other *Ilah* (god), or you will sit down reproved, forsaken (in the Hell-fire).[2]

Most people disbelieve in and reject this category, and it was because of this that the Messengers were sent and the Books were revealed. Allâh Almighty says:

﴿وَمَآ أَرْسَلْنَا مِن قَبْلِكَ مِن رَّسُولٍ إِلَّا نُوحِىٓ إِلَيْهِ أَنَّهُۥ لَآ إِلَٰهَ إِلَّآ أَنَا۠ فَٱعْبُدُونِ ۝﴾

And We did not send any Messenger before you (O Muhammad ﷺ but We inspired him (saying): "*Laa Ilaha Illa Ana* [none has the right to be worshipped but I (Allâh)], so worship Me (Alone and none else)."[3]

3) *Tawhid Al-Asma' was-Sifat*

This category involves believing in Allâh and in His Attributes in the way that is taught to us in the Qur'an and the Sunnah, and in a way that is appropriate for Allâh, and that is achieved by affirming that which Allâh affirmed for Himself, or, what His Messenger ﷺ affirmed, and by negating what Allâh Almighty negated from Himself, or, what His Messenger ﷺ negated from Him — without distorting such attributes or negating them, and without saying "how" they are nor believing that they are similar to the attributes of the creatures. Allâh Almighty says:

﴿لَيْسَ كَمِثْلِهِۦ شَىْءٌ ۖ وَهُوَ ٱلسَّمِيعُ ٱلْبَصِيرُ ۝﴾

---

[1] (*Luqman* 31:30)
[2] (*Al-Isra'* 17:22)
[3] (*Al-Anbiya'* 21:25)

There is nothing like unto Him, and He is the All-Hearer, the All-Seer.[1]

There are many groups and sects that have gone astray regarding this category.

A topic that can be attached to faith in Allâh is faith in the unseen. We must first discuss its meaning and then its influence on the beliefs of the Muslim.

The Meaning Of Faith In The Unseen

Al-Ghaib, or the unseen, refers to anything that is hidden from the senses, whether it is known or unknown. Belief in the unseen — i.e., in that which cannot be perceived by the senses — is not gained by genius of the mind; rather, it becomes known through what the Prophets inform us. Belief in the unseen is one of the qualities of the believer, for Allâh Almighty says:

$$﴿الٓمٓ ۝ ذَٰلِكَ ٱلۡكِتَٰبُ لَا رَيۡبَ ۛ فِيهِ ۛ هُدٗى لِّلۡمُتَّقِينَ ۝ ٱلَّذِينَ يُؤۡمِنُونَ بِٱلۡغَيۡبِ وَيُقِيمُونَ ٱلصَّلَوٰةَ وَمِمَّا رَزَقۡنَٰهُمۡ يُنفِقُونَ ۝﴾$$

Alif-Lam-Mim. This is the Book (the Qur'an), whereof there is no doubt, a guidance to those who are pious. Who believe in the Ghaib and perform As-Salat, and spend out of what we have provided for them.[2]

Regarding their belief in the *Ghaib*, or the unseen, there are two views:

1) They believe in that which is hidden from the senses, and this specifically refers to those hidden matters that Allâh and His Messenger ﷺ have informed us about.

2) They believe in Allâh now that they do not see Him just as they would were they able to see Him, as opposed to the hypocrites. There is no contradiction between the two meanings, for they must both be present in the believer.

---

[1] (*Ash-Shura* 42:11)

[2] (*Al-Baqarah* 2:1-3)

The Influence of Faith In The Unseen On The Muslim's Beliefs

The belief one has in the unseen greatly influences and affects his behavior and his way of life, for it is a great incentive for doing good deeds and it inhibits one from doing evil deeds. Some of the effects of a belief in the unseen are given here:

1) Sincerity in action: If you believe in Allâh, His reward, and His punishment, you will follow His orders and stay away from His prohibitions, hoping for His reward, while fearing His punishment in the Hereafter, and not hoping for reward and thankfulness in this world from people. Allâh Almighty says regarding those who give food to others in spite of their love for it:

$$ ﴿وَيُطْعِمُونَ ٱلطَّعَامَ عَلَىٰ حُبِّهِۦ مِسْكِينًا وَيَتِيمًا وَأَسِيرًا ۝ إِنَّمَا نُطْعِمُكُمْ لِوَجْهِ ٱللَّهِ لَا نُرِيدُ مِنكُمْ جَزَآءً وَلَا شُكُورًا ۝﴾ $$

And they give food, inspite of their love for it (or for the love of Him), to *Miskin* (poor), the orphan, and the captive, (Saying): "We feed you seeking Allâh's Face only. We wish for no reward, nor thanks from you."[1]

2) Strength upon the truth: The believer knows that though he has no strength or help from people when he is obeying Allâh, calling others to the truth, and warning others against falsehood, yet he is strong because of Allâh. This world and its suffering become insignificant to him in contrast to the next life, the Hereafter. In this verse, Allâh informs us of what Ibrahim, peace be upon him, said to his people:

$$ ﴿وَتَٱللَّهِ لَأَكِيدَنَّ أَصْنَٰمَكُم بَعْدَ أَن تُوَلُّوا۟ مُدْبِرِينَ ۝ فَجَعَلَهُمْ جُذَٰذًا إِلَّا كَبِيرًا لَّهُمْ لَعَلَّهُمْ إِلَيْهِ يَرْجِعُونَ ۝﴾ $$

"And by Allâh, I shall plot a plan (to destroy) your idols after you have gone away and turned your backs." So he broke them to pieces, (all) except the biggest of them, that they might turn to it.[2]

---

[1] (*Al-Insan* 76:8,9)

[2] (*Al-Anbiya'* 21:57,58)

3) A sense of indignation for worldly appearances: This is a result of filling one's heart with faith, with belief that this world and its pleasures will vanish, that the Hereafter is the everlasting life, that happiness is not in one's mind alone, and that the eternal should be chosen over the transient. Allâh Almighty says:

﴿وَمَا هَٰذِهِ ٱلْحَيَوٰةُ ٱلدُّنْيَآ إِلَّا لَهْوٌ وَلَعِبٌ وَإِنَّ ٱلدَّارَ ٱلْأَخِرَةَ لَهِىَ ٱلْحَيَوَانُ لَوْ كَانُوا۟ يَعْلَمُونَ ٦٤﴾

And this life of the world is only an amusement and a play! Verily, the home of the Hereafter, that is the life indeed (i.e., the eternal life that will never end), if they but knew.[1]

Allâh informs us about the wife of Fir'awn. She was not content with the pleasures of life that she had, and she asked to be saved from Fir'awn and his behavior, hoping for the Hereafter because of the light of faith in Allâh Almighty and the Hereafter that was in her heart:

﴿وَضَرَبَ ٱللَّهُ مَثَلًا لِّلَّذِينَ ءَامَنُوا۟ ٱمْرَأَتَ فِرْعَوْنَ إِذْ قَالَتْ رَبِّ ٱبْنِ لِى عِندَكَ بَيْتًا فِى ٱلْجَنَّةِ وَنَجِّنِى مِن فِرْعَوْنَ وَعَمَلِهِۦ وَنَجِّنِى مِنَ ٱلْقَوْمِ ٱلظَّٰلِمِينَ ١١﴾

And Allâh has set forth an example for those who believe, the wife of Fir'awn, when she said: "My Lord! Build for me a home with You in Paradise, and save me from Fir'awn and his work, and save me from the people who are wrongdoers."[2]

4) Rancor and malice disappear: When people strive to fulfill their desires and lust, using unlawful means, rancor and malice will spread. But when one believes in the unseen — in Allâh's Promise of reward and warning of punishment — one begins to hold himself accountable for all of his deeds, hoping for reward, and fearing punishment. When one truly believes that he will get his reward from Allâh, he will work hard in doing good deeds, hoping for an everlasting reward. By following this path, people will instil love among themselves as individuals and societies; Allâh Almighty says:

---

[1] (*Al-'Ankabut* 29:64)
[2] (*At-Tahrim* 66:11)

﴿وَٱلَّذِينَ تَبَوَّءُو ٱلدَّارَ وَٱلْإِيمَٰنَ مِن قَبْلِهِمْ يُحِبُّونَ مَنْ هَاجَرَ إِلَيْهِمْ وَلَا يَجِدُونَ فِى صُدُورِهِمْ حَاجَةً مِّمَّا أُوتُوا وَيُؤْثِرُونَ عَلَىٰ أَنفُسِهِمْ وَلَوْ كَانَ بِهِمْ خَصَاصَةٌ وَمَن يُوقَ شُحَّ نَفْسِهِ فَأُولَٰئِكَ هُمُ ٱلْمُفْلِحُونَ ۝ وَٱلَّذِينَ جَاءُو مِنْ بَعْدِهِمْ يَقُولُونَ رَبَّنَا ٱغْفِرْ لَنَا وَلِإِخْوَٰنِنَا ٱلَّذِينَ سَبَقُونَا بِٱلْإِيمَٰنِ وَلَا تَجْعَلْ فِى قُلُوبِنَا غِلًّا لِّلَّذِينَ ءَامَنُوا رَبَّنَا إِنَّكَ رَءُوفٌ رَّحِيمٌ ۝﴾

And those who, before them, had homes (in Al-Madinah) and had adopted the faith, love those who emigrate to them, and have no jealousy in their breasts for that which they have been given (from the booty of Banu An-Nadhir), and give them (emigrants) preference over themselves, even though they were in need of that. And whosoever is saved from his own covetousness, such are they who will be the successful. And those who came after them say: "Our Lord! Forgive us and our brethren who have preceded us in faith, and put not in our hearts any hatred against those who have believed. Our Lord! You are indeed full of kindness, Most Merciful."[1]

These are some of the effects of having faith in the unseen, effects that will not be lacking in someone unless his faith is defective. And if these effects do not become prevalent in a given society, its members will become like animals, eating both the living and the dead, with the strong oppressing the weak. When that happens on a mass scale, evil, fear and corruption will reign — and we seek protection in Allâh Almighty from those evil results.

The Second Pillar Of *Iman*

Belief In The Angels

The Definition of Angels

The linguistic meaning: The Arabic word for angels is *Mala'ikah*, and the singular is *Malak*. They say that it is derived from the word *Ulukah*, which means the message. It is also said to have been derived from *Laaka*, meaning sent. There are other opinions as well regarding its root meaning.

[1] (*Al-Hashr* 59:9,10)

Its definition as an Islamic term: A creation from the realm of the unseen; angels are created from light and they worship Allâh.

The angels have no share in the qualities of *Rububiyyah* and *Uluhiyyah* that we discussed in the previous section. Allâh granted them the level of total submission to His Commands as well as the strength to carry out those commands. Allâh Almighty says:

﴿وَلَهُۥ مَن فِى ٱلسَّمَٰوَٰتِ وَٱلْأَرْضِ وَمَنْ عِندَهُۥ لَا يَسْتَكْبِرُونَ عَنْ عِبَادَتِهِۦ وَلَا يَسْتَحْسِرُونَ ۝ يُسَبِّحُونَ ٱلَّيْلَ وَٱلنَّهَارَ لَا يَفْتُرُونَ ۝﴾

To Him belongs whosoever is in the heavens and on the earth. And those who are near Him (i.e., the angels) are not too proud to worship Him, nor are they weary (of His worship). They (i.e., the angels) glorify His praises night and day, (and) they never slacken (to do so). [1]

﴿بَلْ عِبَادٌ مُّكْرَمُونَ ۝ لَا يَسْبِقُونَهُۥ بِٱلْقَوْلِ وَهُم بِأَمْرِهِۦ يَعْمَلُونَ ۝﴾

They, are but honored slaves. They speak not until He has spoken, and they act on His Command.[2]

The Belief Of The Arab Polytheists Regarding The Angels Before The Advent Of Islam

The people of ignorance — in the period before Islam — claimed that the angels were the daughters of Allâh — far above Allâh is from what they say. Allâh Almighty refuted them, clarifying that they have no knowledge thereof:

﴿أَمْ خَلَقْنَا ٱلْمَلَٰٓئِكَةَ إِنَٰثًا وَهُمْ شَٰهِدُونَ ۝ أَلَآ إِنَّهُم مِّنْ إِفْكِهِمْ لَيَقُولُونَ ۝ وَلَدَ ٱللَّهُ وَإِنَّهُمْ لَكَٰذِبُونَ ۝﴾

Or did We create the angels females while they were witnesses? Verily, it is of their falsehood that they (Quraish pagans) say: "Allâh has begotten (offspring or children, i.e., angels are the daughters of Allâh)?" And, verily, they are liars![3]

---

[1] (*Al-Anbiya'* 21:19,20)

[2] (*Al-Anbiya'* 21:26,27)

[3] (*As-Saffat* 37:150-152)

Belief In The Angels

Belief in the angels is the second pillar of faith, and what this pillar means is for us to believe with certainty that Allâh has angels that exist: they are created from light, and they do not disobey Allâh in what He orders them, while they perform that which they are commanded.

Proofs Indicating That It Is Obligatory To have Belief In Them

1) Allâh Almighty says:

﴿ءَامَنَ ٱلرَّسُولُ بِمَآ أُنزِلَ إِلَيْهِ مِن رَّبِّهِۦ وَٱلْمُؤْمِنُونَ ۚ كُلٌّ ءَامَنَ بِٱللَّهِ وَمَلَٰٓئِكَتِهِۦ وَكُتُبِهِۦ وَرُسُلِهِۦ﴾

The Messenger believes in what has been sent down to him from his Lord, and (so do) the believers. Each one believes in Allâh, His Angels, His Books, and His Messengers.[1]

2) Allâh Almighty says:

﴿لَّيْسَ ٱلْبِرَّ أَن تُوَلُّوا۟ وُجُوهَكُمْ قِبَلَ ٱلْمَشْرِقِ وَٱلْمَغْرِبِ وَلَٰكِنَّ ٱلْبِرَّ مَنْ ءَامَنَ بِٱللَّهِ وَٱلْيَوْمِ ٱلْءَاخِرِ وَٱلْمَلَٰٓئِكَةِ وَٱلْكِتَٰبِ وَٱلنَّبِيِّـۧنَ﴾

It is not *Al-Birr* (piety, righteousness, and each and every act of obedience to Allâh, etc.) that you turn your faces towards east and (or) west (in prayers); but *Al-Birr* is (the quality of) the one who believes in Allâh, the Last Day, the Angels, the Book, the Prophets...[2]

Allâh Almighty says:

﴿وَمَن يَكْفُرْ بِٱللَّهِ وَمَلَٰٓئِكَتِهِۦ وَكُتُبِهِۦ وَرُسُلِهِۦ وَٱلْيَوْمِ ٱلْءَاخِرِ فَقَدْ ضَلَّ ضَلَٰلًۢا بَعِيدًا﴾

And whosoever disbelieves in Allâh, His Angels, His Books, His Messengers, and the Last Day, then indeed he has strayed far away.[3]

3) When Jibril asked the Prophet ﷺ about *Iman*, he ﷺ said:

«أَنْ تُؤْمِنَ بِاللهِ وَمَلَائِكَتِهِ وَكُتُبِهِ وَرُسُلِهِ، وَالْيَوْمِ الآخِرِ، وَتُؤْمِنَ بِالْقَدَرِ

---

[1] (*Al-Baqarah* 2:205)

[2] (*Al-Baqarah* 2:177)

[3] (*An-Nisa'* 4:136)

خَيْرِهِ وَشَرِّهِ»

To believe in Allâh, in His Angels, in His Books, in His Messengers, in the Last Day, and to believe in Divine Preordainment, both the good of it and the bad of it.

So belief in the angels is part of what was included as *Iman* in this *Hadith*. Because their existence is supported by irrefutable proof, to reject their existence is disbelief, a ruling that is established by the consensus of the Muslims: disbelief in them is disbelief in the clear verses of the Qur'an and sayings of the Messenger of Allâh ﷺ.

Belief In The Angels Comprises Of The Following

1) We must believe that they exist.

2) We must believe in those angels that we know the names of (through revelation), such as Jibril. Those that we do not know, we believe in their existence in general.

3) We must believe in their qualities which we learn of through revelation, such as the description of Jibril: The Prophet ﷺ informed us that he saw him in the image that he was created — he had six hundred wings that blocked the horizon. Angels may also take the shape of man, such as happened with Jibril in the *Hadith* wherein he asks about *Iman* and Islam.

4) We must believe in those of their actions that we learn through revelation: they glorify Allâh and worship Him day and night. It is in their nature to obey Allâh, and they do not have the ability to disobey Him:

﴿لَّا يَعْصُونَ ٱللَّهَ مَآ أَمَرَهُمْ وَيَفْعَلُونَ مَا يُؤْمَرُونَ ٦﴾

Who disobey not, (from executing) the Commands they receive from Allâh, but do that which they are com-manded.[1]

For them, avoiding sins and performing acts of obedience is natural: they expend no effort in this regard because they have no desires or lust.

Some angels may have certain tasks specific to them, such as Jibril, who is the one entrusted with Allâh's revelation; Allâh

---

[1] (*At-Tahrim* 66:6)

sends him to the Prophets and Messengers. Allâh Almighty says:

﴿ نَزَلَ بِهِ ٱلرُّوحُ ٱلۡأَمِينُ ۝ عَلَىٰ قَلۡبِكَ لِتَكُونَ مِنَ ٱلۡمُنذِرِينَ ۝ ﴾

Which the trustworthy *Ruh* [Jibril (Gabriel)] has brought down; upon your heart that so you may be of the warners...[1]

Mika'il is the angel who is entrusted with the rain and vegetation. Abu Hurairah, may Allâh be pleasd with him, related this *Hadith* from the Prophet ﷺ:

«بَيْنَا رَجُلٌ بِفَلَاةٍ مِنَ الأَرْضِ فَسَمِعَ صَوْتًا فِي سَحَابَةٍ: اسْقِ حَدِيقَةَ فُلَانٍ، فَتَنَحَّىٰ ذَلِكَ السَّحَابُ فَأَفْرَغَ مَاءَهُ فِي حَرَّةٍ فَإِذَا شَرْجَةٌ مِنْ تِلْكَ الشِّرَاجِ قَدِ اسْتَوْعَبَتْ ذَلِكَ الْمَاءَ كُلَّهُ فَتَتَبَّعَ الْمَاءَ، فَإِذَا رَجُلٌ قَائِمٌ فِي حَدِيقَتِهِ يُحَوِّلُ الْمَاءَ بِمِسْحَاتِهِ. فَقَالَ لَهُ: يَا عَبْدَالله! مَااسْمُكَ؟ قَالَ: فُلَانٌ. لِلْاسْمِ الَّذِي سَمِعَ فِي السَّحَابَةِ. فَقَالَ لَهُ: يَا عَبْدَالله! لِمَ تَسْأَلُنِي عَنِ اسْمِي؟ فَقَالَ: إِنِّي سَمِعْتُ صَوْتًا فِي السَّحَابِ الَّذِي هَذَا مَاؤُهُ يَقُولُ: اسْقِ حَدِيقَةَ فُلَانٍ. لِاسْمِكَ، فَمَا تَصْنَعُ فِيهَا؟ قَالَ: أَمَّا إِذْ قُلْتَ هَذَا، فَإِنِّي أَنْظُرُ إِلَى مَا يَخْرُجُ مِنْهَا فَأَتَصَدَّقُ بِثُلْثِهِ، وَآكُلُ أَنَا وَعِيَالِي ثُلُثاً، وَأَرُدُّ فِيهَا ثُلْثَهُ»

As a man was standing in a vast open space of land, he heard a voice in the clouds saying, "Supply water to the garden of so-and-so." So, the cloud left its place and emptied its water into an area; a waterway absorbed all of the water that fell from the sky. The man followed the water, until he reached a man who was standing in his garden, diverting the water with his shovel. The man said, "O servant of Allâh! What is your name." He gave him his name. The man in the garden asked, "O servant of Allâh! Why do you ask me my name?" He said, "I indeed heard a voice in the same clouds from which this water came, saying, 'Supply water to the garden of so-and-so', and the name I heard was yours. Then what will you do with it?" He said, "Because of what you said, I will wait and see what comes out of the earth: I will give one-third of it in charity, I will eat one-

[1] (*Ash-Shu'ara* 26:193,194)

third of it along with my family, and I will return one-third..."
(Recorded by Muslim)

This *Hadith* is referring to the angels who divert the rains according to Allâh's Will.

There is an angel who is entrusted with the Trumpet, his name is Israfil, peace be upon him. He will blow into it twice by Allâh's Command: the first time he blows it, people will become terrified and swoon away, and the second blowing is for the resurrection. Allâh Almighty says:

$$﴿وَنُفِخَ فِى ٱلصُّورِ فَصَعِقَ مَن فِى ٱلسَّمَٰوَٰتِ وَمَن فِى ٱلْأَرْضِ إِلَّا مَن شَآءَ ٱللَّهُ ثُمَّ نُفِخَ فِيهِ أُخْرَىٰ فَإِذَا هُمْ قِيَامٌ يَنظُرُونَ ٦٨﴾$$

And the Trumpet will be blown, and all who are in the heavens and all who are on the earth will swoon away, except him whom Allâh wills. Then it will blown a second time and behold, they will be standing, looking on (waiting).[1]

Another angel we know of is the one entrusted with the task of taking souls, the Angel of Death, and we also know that he has helpers. Allâh Almighty says:

$$﴿قُلْ يَتَوَفَّىٰكُم مَّلَكُ ٱلْمَوْتِ ٱلَّذِى وُكِّلَ بِكُمْ ثُمَّ إِلَىٰ رَبِّكُمْ تُرْجَعُونَ ١١﴾$$

Say: "The angel of death, who is set over you, will take your souls, then you shall be brought to your Lord."[2]

Some angels are the keepers of Paradise, for Allâh Almighty says:

$$﴿وَسِيقَ ٱلَّذِينَ ٱتَّقَوْا۟ رَبَّهُمْ إِلَى ٱلْجَنَّةِ زُمَرًا حَتَّىٰ إِذَا جَآءُوهَا وَفُتِحَتْ أَبْوَٰبُهَا وَقَالَ لَهُمْ خَزَنَتُهَا سَلَٰمٌ عَلَيْكُمْ طِبْتُمْ فَٱدْخُلُوهَا خَٰلِدِينَ ٧٣﴾$$

And those who kept their duty to their Lord will be led to Paradise in groups, till, when they reach it, and its gates will be opened (before their arrival for their reception) and its keepers will say: "*Salamun 'Alaikum* (peace be upon you)! You have done well, so enter here to abide therein."[3]

---

[1] (*Az-Zumar* 39:68)
[2] (*As-Sajdah* 32:11)
[3] (*Az-Zumar* 39:73)

There are other angels who are the keepers of the Hellfire — the *Zabaniyyah* — and they are nineteen in number. At their forefront is Malik ﷺ. Allâh Almighty says:

$$﴿وَمَآ أَدْرَىٰكَ مَا سَقَرُ ۝ لَا تُبْقِي وَلَا تَذَرُ ۝ لَوَّاحَةٌ لِّلْبَشَرِ ۝ عَلَيْهَا تِسْعَةَ عَشَرَ ۝ وَمَا جَعَلْنَآ أَصْحَٰبَ ٱلنَّارِ إِلَّا مَلَٰٓئِكَةً﴾$$

And what will make you know exactly what Hellfire is? It spares not (any sinner), nor does it leave (anything unburnt)! Burning and blackening the skins! Over it are nineteen (angels as guardians and keepers of Hell). And We have set none but angels as guardians of the Fire.[1]

And Allâh Almighty says:

$$﴿وَنَادَوْا۟ يَٰمَٰلِكُ لِيَقْضِ عَلَيْنَا رَبُّكَ قَالَ إِنَّكُم مَّٰكِثُونَ ۝﴾$$

And they will cry: "O Malik (Keeper of Hell)! Let your Lord make an end of us." He will say: "Verily you shall abide forever."[2]

Then there are the angels that protect man in all situations, and they are called *Al-Mu'aqqibat*. Allâh Almighty says:

$$﴿لَهُۥ مُعَقِّبَٰتٌ مِّنۢ بَيْنِ يَدَيْهِ وَمِنْ خَلْفِهِۦ يَحْفَظُونَهُۥ مِنْ أَمْرِ ٱللَّهِ﴾$$

For each (person), there are angels in succession, before and behind him. They guard him by the Command of Allâh.[3]

$$﴿وَهُوَ ٱلْقَاهِرُ فَوْقَ عِبَادِهِۦ وَيُرْسِلُ عَلَيْكُمْ حَفَظَةً﴾$$

He is the Irresistible, Supreme over His slaves, and He sends guardians (angels guarding and writing all of one's good and bad deeds) over you.[4]

There are some angels who are entrusted with the fetus in the womb; when the fetus has spent four months in the womb, Allâh sends an angel and orders the angel to write his provision, his life-span, his deeds, and whether he will be miserable or happy. All of

---

[1] (*Al-Muddaththir* 74:27-31)

[2] (*Az-Zukhruf* 43:77)

[3] (*Ar-Ra'd* 13:11)

[4] (*Al-An'am* 6:61)

this is established in a *Hadith* related by Muslim and narrated by Ibn Mas'ud, may Allâh be pleased with him.

There are also angels that are responsible for questioning the dead person when he is put in his grave; they ask him about his Lord, his religion, and his Prophet — this too is established in the Sunnah.

Their Relation To Man

Allâh Almighty has entrusted the angels with tasks related to different kinds of creation — from among them is man. In fact, the angels have a very strong attachment with man from the very early stages of his development — from the time he is merely semen. Ibn Al-Qayyim mentions the close relationship between angels and man in *Ighathatul-Lahfan*:

"Indeed they are entrusted in shaping man and in moving him along from one stage to the next. They are entrusted to protect the fetus in the three levels of darkness. They are even responsible for writing man's provision, deeds, life-span, and whether he will be miserable or happy. Indeed angels stick close to man in all situations, listing his sayings and deeds. They are responsible for protecting man while he is alive and for taking away his soul when he dies, and then for presenting that soul before its Creator and Maker. In the grave and in the Hereafter, they are responsible for executing his punishments and rewards, and they are responsible for the instruments used to give both punishment and reward.

The angels have a special relationship with the believer, for by the Will of Allâh, they support him, and during battle, they defend him. They are his helpers in this world and in the Hereafter, and they are the ones who not only supplicate for him, but also call him to good and forbid him from evil. They are his helpers, supporters, protectors, teachers, advisors; and they are the ones who supplicate for him, ask Allâh Almighty to forgive him, and pray for him as long as he is obeying his Lord; they also continue to pray for him as long as he is teaching good to others. While he is asleep, when he is dead, and when he is resurrected — on these occasions, they give him glad tidings of Allâh's generosity and rewards. They advise him to seek little from this world and much from the Hereafter. They remind him when he forgets; invigorate him when he becomes lazy. They make him firm when he is afraid, and they strive for his welfare, in both this life and the Hereafter.

On the other hand, they do not love the disbelievers, the oppressors, and the wrongdoers; rather, they show enmity toward them, waging war against them, making their hearts shake. The angels send punishment upon them by Allâh's Will and they curse them. They are Allâh's Messengers among the creation and they are the ambassadors between Allâh and His worshippers. They execute His Commands all over the world and they raise matters up to Him."

The proofs in the Qur'an and Sunnah regarding the above require much space to enumerate; they are well-known, however, and some of them we have already mentioned.

The Fruits Of Believing In The Angels

Belief in the angels reaps many fruits; among them are the following:

1) One appreciates the greatness, strength, and power of Allâh, for greatness in the creation results from the greatness of the Creator.

2) One must be thankful to Allâh for the care He shows to the children of Adam, whereby some angels are entrusted to protect man, to write his deeds, and to do other tasks that are related to the welfare of man.

3) One must love the angels because of their prodigious worship of Allâh Almighty.

The Third Pillar Of *Iman*

Belief In The Revealed Books

In Arabic, the word for the books is *Kutub*, the plural of *Kitab*, meaning that which is written. Here books refers to those Books that Allâh Almighty revealed to His Messengers, as a mercy and guidance to all human beings, so that through the Books, they could achieve happiness in this life and in the Hereafter.

Belief in Allâh's Books is one of the pillars of *Iman*. This means that we must believe with certainty that Allâh has certain Books that He revealed to His Messengers, so that they would reach His worshippers with the clear truth. Those Books consist of Allâh's

Speech: He really spoke them — as He willed and in a way that He willed.

Proofs Indicating That Belief In The Books Is Obligatory

1) Allâh Almighty says:

﴿قُولُوٓاْ ءَامَنَّا بِٱللَّهِ وَمَآ أُنزِلَ إِلَيۡنَا وَمَآ أُنزِلَ إِلَىٰٓ إِبۡرَٰهِـۧمَ وَإِسۡمَٰعِيلَ وَإِسۡحَٰقَ وَيَعۡقُوبَ وَٱلۡأَسۡبَاطِ وَمَآ أُوتِيَ مُوسَىٰ وَعِيسَىٰ وَمَآ أُوتِيَ ٱلنَّبِيُّونَ مِن رَّبِّهِمۡ لَا نُفَرِّقُ بَيۡنَ أَحَدٍ مِّنۡهُمۡ وَنَحۡنُ لَهُۥ مُسۡلِمُونَ ١٣٦﴾

Say, "We believe in Allâh and that which has been sent down to us and that which has been sent down to Ibrahim, Isma'il, Ishaq, Ya'qub, and to *Al-Asbat* [the twelve sons of Ya'qub], and that which has been given to Musa and 'Iesa, and that which has been given to the Prophets from their Lord. We make no distinction between any of them, and to Him we have submitted (in Islam)."[1]

Indeed Allâh has ordered the believers to believe in Him and in what He has sent down to them through Prophet Muhammad ﷺ — the Noble Qur'an. He also ordered them to believe in what was revealed to the Prophets from their Lord, without differentiating between any one of them. They were required to do that, showing their submission to Allâh and their faith in what He Almighty informed them.

2) Allâh Almighty says:

﴿ءَامَنَ ٱلرَّسُولُ بِمَآ أُنزِلَ إِلَيۡهِ مِن رَّبِّهِۦ وَٱلۡمُؤۡمِنُونَ كُلٌّ ءَامَنَ بِٱللَّهِ وَمَلَٰٓئِكَتِهِۦ وَكُتُبِهِۦ وَرُسُلِهِۦ لَا نُفَرِّقُ بَيۡنَ أَحَدٍ مِّن رُّسُلِهِۦ وَقَالُواْ سَمِعۡنَا وَأَطَعۡنَا غُفۡرَانَكَ رَبَّنَا وَإِلَيۡكَ ٱلۡمَصِيرُ ٢٨٥﴾

The Messenger believes in what has been sent down to him from his Lord, and (so do) the believers. Each one believes in Allâh, His Angels, His Books, and His Messengers. They say, "We make no distinction between one and another of His Messengers" — and they say, "We hear, and we obey. (We seek) Your forgiveness, our Lord, and to You is the return (of

---

[1] (*Al-Baqarah* 2:136)

all)."[1]

This verse describes the faith of the Prophet ﷺ and of the believers; it clarifies the faith they have been ordered to have — faith in Allâh, in His Angels, in His Books, in His Messengers — without differentiation between them. Therefore disbelief in some of them is tantamount to disbelief in all of them.

3) Allâh Almighty says:

﴿يَٰٓأَيُّهَا ٱلَّذِينَ ءَامَنُوٓاْ ءَامِنُواْ بِٱللَّهِ وَرَسُولِهِۦ وَٱلْكِتَٰبِ ٱلَّذِى نَزَّلَ عَلَىٰ رَسُولِهِۦ وَٱلْكِتَٰبِ ٱلَّذِىٓ أَنزَلَ مِن قَبْلُ وَمَن يَكْفُرْ بِٱللَّهِ وَمَلَٰٓئِكَتِهِۦ وَكُتُبِهِۦ وَرُسُلِهِۦ وَٱلْيَوْمِ ٱلْءَاخِرِ فَقَدْ ضَلَّ ضَلَٰلَۢا بَعِيدًا ﴾ ﴿١٣٦﴾

O you who believe! Believe in Allâh, and His Messenger, and the Book (the Qur'an) which He has sent down to His Messenger, and the Scripture which He sent down to those before (him), and whosoever disbelieves in Allâh, His Angels, His Books, His Messengers, and the Last Day, then indeed he has strayed far away.[2]

In this verse, Allâh Almighty orders us to believe in Allâh, in His Messenger, in the Book revealed to the Messenger — the Qur'an, and in the Books revealed before the Qur'an. An important point to understand here is that Allâh joined disbelief in the Angels, Books, Messengers, and the Last Day with disbelief in Him.

4) When Jibril asked the Prophet ﷺ about faith, he ﷺ said:

«أَنْ تُؤْمِنَ بِالله وَمَلَائِكَتِهِ وَكُتُبِهِ وَرُسُلِهِ وَالْيَوْمِ الآخِرِ وَتُؤْمِنَ بِالْقَدَرِ خَيْرِهِ وَشَرِّهِ»

To believe in Allâh, His Angels, His Books, His Messengers, the Last Day, and to believe in Divine Preordainment — both the good and bad of it.

In this *Hadith*, the Prophet ﷺ informed us that belief in the Books is one of the pillars of faith.

---

[1] (*Al-Baqarah* 2:285)
[2] (*An-Nisa'* 4:136)

What Belief In The Books Includes

Belief in the Books includes four matters:

1) Belief that they were indeed sent down or revealed from Allâh.

2) Belief specifically in those Books that Allâh taught us the names of, such as the Qur'an. Allâh Almighty says:

﴿وَنَزَّلْنَا عَلَيْكَ ٱلْكِتَٰبَ تِبْيَٰنًا لِّكُلِّ شَىْءٍ وَهُدًى وَرَحْمَةً وَبُشْرَىٰ لِلْمُسْلِمِينَ﴾

And We have sent down to you the Book (the Qur'an) as an exposition of everything, a guidance, a mercy, and glad tidings for those who have submitted themselves (as Muslims).[1]

The Tawrah that Allâh revealed to Musa, peace be upon him:

﴿إِنَّآ أَنزَلْنَا ٱلتَّوْرَىٰةَ فِيهَا هُدًى وَنُورٌ﴾

Verily, We did send down the Tawrah [to Musa], therein was guidance and light.[2]

The Injil that Allâh revealed to 'Iesa, peace be upon him:

﴿وَقَفَّيْنَا عَلَىٰٓ ءَاثَٰرِهِم بِعِيسَى ٱبْنِ مَرْيَمَ مُصَدِّقًا لِّمَا بَيْنَ يَدَيْهِ مِنَ ٱلتَّوْرَىٰةِ وَءَاتَيْنَٰهُ ٱلْإِنجِيلَ فِيهِ هُدًى وَنُورٌ﴾

And in their footsteps, We sent 'Iesa, son of Maryam, confirming the Tawrah that had come before him, and We gave him the Injil, in which was guidance and light.[3]

The Zabur that Allâh gave to Dawud, peace be upon him:

﴿وَءَاتَيْنَا دَاوُۥدَ زَبُورًا ۝١٦٣﴾

And to Dawud We gave the Zabur.[4]

And the Scriptures of Ibrahim and Musa, peace be upon them:

﴿إِنَّ هَٰذَا لَفِى ٱلصُّحُفِ ٱلْأُولَىٰ ۝١٨ صُحُفِ إِبْرَٰهِيمَ وَمُوسَىٰ ۝١٩﴾

Verily! This is in the former Scriptures, the Scriptures of

---

[1] (*An-Nahl* 16:89)

[2] (*Al-Ma'idah* 5:44)

[3] (*Al-Ma'idah* 5:46)

[4] (*An-Nisa'* 4:163)

Ibrahim and Musa.[1]

3) We must apply the rulings and laws of the Qur'an; but moreover, we must be pleased with those rulings, submitting to them, regardless of whether we understand the wisdom for any given ruling or not. We must also know that all of the previous Books have been abrogated by the Noble Qur'an, for Allâh Almighty says:

﴿وَأَنزَلْنَآ إِلَيْكَ ٱلْكِتَـٰبَ بِٱلْحَقِّ مُصَدِّقًا لِّمَا بَيْنَ يَدَيْهِ مِنَ ٱلْكِتَـٰبِ وَمُهَيْمِنًا عَلَيْهِ﴾

And We have sent down to you the Book (this Qur'an) in truth, confirming the Scripture that came before it and *Muhayminan* over it (the earlier Scriptures).[2]

Muhayminan over the old Scriptures means judging over them. Therefore it is not permissible to apply any of the laws from the previous Books unless the Qur'an confirms that law. Whenever there is a matter about which we are not sure, we must not turn to those Books, but to the Qur'an, for Allâh Almighty says:

﴿فَإِن تَنَـٰزَعْتُمْ فِى شَىْءٍ فَرُدُّوهُ إِلَى ٱللَّهِ وَٱلرَّسُولِ﴾

(And) if you differ in anything among yourselves, refer it to Allâh and His Messenger.[3]

The Prophet ﷺ said:

«وَالَّذِي نَفْسُ مُحَمَّدٍ بِيَدِهِ لَا يَسْمَعُ بِي أَحَدٌ مِنْ هَذِهِ الأُمَّةِ يَهُودِيٌّ وَلَا نَصْرَانِيٌّ ثُمَّ يَمُوتُ وَلَمْ يُؤْمِنْ بِالَّذِي أُرْسِلْتُ بِهِ إِلَّا كَانَ مِنْ أَصْحَابِ النَّارِ»

By the One Who has my soul in His Hand, no one hears about me from this nation, from the Jews, or from the Christians, and then dies without believing in what I have been sent with, except that he is from the dwellers of the Fire. (Recorded by Muslim)

This *Hadith* states in the clearest of terms that the religion the Prophet ﷺ came with abrogates all that came before it, which is why

---

[1] (*Al-A'la* 87:18,19)

[2] (*Al-Ma'idah* 5:48)

[3] (*An-Nisa'* 4:59)

it includes all that mankind needs in this world until the Day of Judgement. If people follow what the Prophet ﷺ came with, they will achieve happiness in the Hereafter. And Allâh Almighty guaranteed the preservation of the Qur'an, so that it remains as a proof over mankind. Allâh Almighty says:

﴿إِنَّ ٱلَّذِينَ كَفَرُواْ بِٱلذِّكْرِ لَمَّا جَآءَهُمْ وَإِنَّهُ لَكِتَٰبٌ عَزِيزٌ ٤١ لَّا يَأْتِيهِ ٱلْبَٰطِلُ مِنۢ بَيْنِ يَدَيْهِ وَلَا مِنْ خَلْفِهِۦ تَنزِيلٌ مِّنْ حَكِيمٍ حَمِيدٍ ٤٢﴾

Verily, those who disbelieved in the Reminder (i.e., the Qur'an) when it came to them (shall receive the punishment). And verily, it is an honorable respected Book. Falsehood cannot come to it from before it or behind it (it is) sent down by the All-Wise, Worthy of all praise.[1]

The Noble Qur'an

The Meaning Of Qur'an

In the Arabic language, *Al-Qur'an* is taken from the infinitive *Qira'ah*, which means reading. From it comes the verb *Qara'a*, as in *Qara'tul-Kitab*: I read the book. Allâh uses the word Qur'an with the meaning of 'to read' in this verse:

﴿إِنَّ عَلَيْنَا جَمْعَهُ وَقُرْءَانَهُ ١٧﴾

It is for Us to collect it and to give you (O Muhammad ﷺ) the ability to recite it.[2]

Then the word Qur'an was given a new meaning — as a name for the Book that was revealed to Prophet Muhammad ﷺ. It is called the Qur'an because it embraces the fruits of all previous Books revealed by Allâh. Allâh Almighty says:

﴿وَنَزَّلْنَا عَلَيْكَ ٱلْكِتَٰبَ تِبْيَٰنًا لِّكُلِّ شَىْءٍ وَهُدًى وَرَحْمَةً وَبُشْرَىٰ لِلْمُسْلِمِينَ﴾

And We have sent down to you the Book (the Qur'an) as an exposition of everything, a guidance, a mercy, and glad tidings for those who have submitted themselves (as Muslims).[3]

---

[1] (*Fussilat* 41:41,42)

[2] (*Al-Qiyamah* 75:17)

[3] (*An-Nahl* 16:89)

The Meaning Of Qur'an As An Islamic Term

It is Allâh's Speech, it is the miracle that was sent down to His Messenger, Muhammad ﷺ as revelation, and its recitation is a form of worship.

The Qur'an is preserved in the hearts of men, it is recited on their tongues, and it is written in *Mushafs* (books), it is heard by the ears of men, and it has been transmitted to us by so many trustworthy sources that there is no doubt as to its authenticity.

The Qur'an Is Allâh's Speech

In its wording and meaning, the Qur'an is Allâh's Speech, and it is not created. Jibril, peace be upon him, heard it and conveyed it to Muhammad ﷺ, who in turn conveyed it to his Companions, may Allâh be pleased with them. It is the same Qur'an that we recite with our tongues, write in *Mushafs*, memorize in our breasts, and listen to with our ears. Allâh Almighty says:

﴿وَإِنْ أَحَدٌ مِّنَ ٱلْمُشْرِكِينَ ٱسْتَجَارَكَ فَأَجِرْهُ حَتَّىٰ يَسْمَعَ كَلَٰمَ ٱللَّهِ﴾

And if anyone of the polytheists seeks your protection then grant him protection, so that he may hear the Word of Allâh.[1]

It is recorded by Al-Bukhari and Muslim that 'Abdullah bin 'Umar ﷺ narrated that the Prophet ﷺ forbade Muslims from travelling with the Qur'an to the land of the enemy. And the Prophet ﷺ said,

«زَيِّنُوا الْقُرْآنَ بِأَصْوَاتِكُمْ»

Adorn the Qur'an with your voices. (An authentic *Hadith* recorded by Imam Ahmad.)

Belief in all that we have stated about the Qur'an is obligatory. It is also obligatory to believe that the Qur'an is the final Book revealed from Allâh: it came to confirm and support those truths that Allâh revealed in previous Books; but it was also revealed to clarify how man distorted those previous books. Therefore the Qur'an gives us an all-embracing *Shari'ah* — set of laws to live by — one that is suitable for all times and places, one that abrogates all previous laws. These beliefs are compulsory upon all those who have received the

---

[1] (*At-Tawbah* 9:6)

message until the time of the Hour. Since the time the Qur'an was revealed, Allâh Almighty informed us, that He accepts no religion other than Islam.

The Fourth Pillar of *Iman*

Belief In The Messengers

To believe in the Messengers means to believe with certainty that Allâh sent a Messenger to each nation, calling them to worship Allâh alone, without associating partners with Him, and calling them to disbelieve in all that is worshipped other than Him. We must also believe that every one of the Messengers is truthful, guided, righteous, and obedient to Allâh and that they conveyed all that Allâh sent them with: they neither hid any part of the message nor did they change any part of it. Allâh Almighty says:

﴿فَهَلْ عَلَى ٱلرُّسُلِ إِلَّا ٱلْبَلَٰغُ ٱلْمُبِينُ ۝ وَلَقَدْ بَعَثْنَا فِى كُلِّ أُمَّةٍ رَّسُولًا أَنِ ٱعْبُدُواْ ٱللَّهَ وَٱجْتَنِبُواْ ٱلطَّٰغُوتَ فَمِنْهُم مَّنْ هَدَى ٱللَّهُ وَمِنْهُم مَّنْ حَقَّتْ عَلَيْهِ ٱلضَّلَٰلَةُ فَسِيرُواْ فِى ٱلْأَرْضِ فَٱنظُرُواْ كَيْفَ كَانَ عَٰقِبَةُ ٱلْمُكَذِّبِينَ ۝﴾

Are the Messengers charged with anything but to clearly convey the Message? And verily, We have sent among every *Ummah* (community, nation) a Messenger (proclaiming): "Worship Allâh, and avoid the *Taghut* (all false deities)." Then of them were some whom Allâh guided and of them were some upon whom the straying was justified. So, travel through the land and see what was the end of those who denied (the truth).[1]

Some of the Messengers were better than others:

﴿تِلْكَ ٱلرُّسُلُ فَضَّلْنَا بَعْضَهُمْ عَلَىٰ بَعْضٍ مِّنْهُم مَّن كَلَّمَ ٱللَّهُ وَرَفَعَ بَعْضَهُمْ دَرَجَٰتٍ وَءَاتَيْنَا عِيسَى ٱبْنَ مَرْيَمَ ٱلْبَيِّنَٰتِ وَأَيَّدْنَٰهُ بِرُوحِ ٱلْقُدُسِ﴾

Those Messengers! We preferred some of them to others; to some of them Allâh spoke (directly); others He raised to degrees (of honor); and to 'Iesa, the son of Maryam, We gave clear proofs and evidences, and supported him with *Ruhul-*

---

[1] (*An-Nahl* 16:35,36)

Qudus [Jibril].[1]

The best of the Messengers are five known as *Ulul-'Azm*, or the Messengers of firm will: Nuh, Ibrahim, Musa, 'Iesa, and Muhammad, may the peace and blessings of Allâh be upon them all, and the best of these five is Muhammad ﷺ.

To have belief in all of the Messengers is obligatory; whoever disbelieves in one from them, then he has not only disbelieved in them all, but he has also disbelieved in the One Who sent them — Allâh. Allâh Almighty says:

$$﴿ إِنَّ ٱلَّذِينَ يَكْفُرُونَ بِٱللَّهِ وَرُسُلِهِۦ وَيُرِيدُونَ أَن يُفَرِّقُوا۟ بَيْنَ ٱللَّهِ وَرُسُلِهِۦ وَيَقُولُونَ نُؤْمِنُ بِبَعْضٍ وَنَكْفُرُ بِبَعْضٍ وَيُرِيدُونَ أَن يَتَّخِذُوا۟ بَيْنَ ذَٰلِكَ سَبِيلًا ۝ أُو۟لَٰٓئِكَ هُمُ ٱلْكَٰفِرُونَ حَقًّا ۚ وَأَعْتَدْنَا لِلْكَٰفِرِينَ عَذَابًا مُّهِينًا ۝ وَٱلَّذِينَ ءَامَنُوا۟ بِٱللَّهِ وَرُسُلِهِۦ وَلَمْ يُفَرِّقُوا۟ بَيْنَ أَحَدٍ مِّنْهُمْ أُو۟لَٰٓئِكَ سَوْفَ يُؤْتِيهِمْ أُجُورَهُمْ ۚ وَكَانَ ٱللَّهُ غَفُورًا رَّحِيمًا ۝ ﴾$$

Verily, those who disbelieve in Allâh and His Messengers and wish to make distinction between Allâh and His Messengers saying, "We believe in some but reject others," and wish to adopt a way in between. They are in truth disbelievers. And We have prepared for the disbelievers a humiliating torment. And those who believe in Allâh and His Messengers and make no distinction between any of them (Messengers), We shall give them their rewards, and Allâh is Ever Oft Forgiving, Most Merciful. [2]

We must believe in the Messengers in general, meaning that we believe in those that we know of and those that we don't know of. So, we must specifically believe in those Messengers that Allâh named, and we must believe that Allâh sent Messengers other than the ones He named to us:

$$﴿ وَلَقَدْ أَرْسَلْنَا رُسُلًا مِّن قَبْلِكَ مِنْهُم مَّن قَصَصْنَا عَلَيْكَ وَمِنْهُم مَّن لَّمْ نَقْصُصْ عَلَيْكَ ﴾$$

---

[1] (*Al-Baqarah* 2:253)
[2] (*An-Nisa'* 4:150-152)

And, indeed We have sent Messengers before you; of some of them We have related to you their story and of some We have not related to you their story.[1]

It is not a part of faith to raise them above the status that Allâh gave to them, for they are human beings and His creatures. They are distinct in that Allâh chose them and prepared them to carry His Message. Their nature is that of man; they have no share in the qualities specific to godhood, so they don't know the information of the unseen, except for those matters that Allâh has informed them about. Allâh ordered Muhammad ﷺ to convey to his nation:

﴿قُلْ إِنَّمَا أَنَا۟ بَشَرٌ مِّثْلُكُمْ يُوحَىٰ إِلَىَّ﴾

Say: "I am only a human being like you. It is inspired in me that your *Ilah* (God) is One *Ilah*."[2]

﴿قُل لَّا أَقُولُ لَكُمْ عِندِى خَزَآئِنُ ٱللَّهِ وَلَا أَعْلَمُ ٱلْغَيْبَ وَلَا أَقُولُ لَكُمْ إِنِّى مَلَكٌ إِنْ أَتَّبِعُ إِلَّا مَا يُوحَىٰ إِلَىَّ﴾

Say: "I don't tell you that with me are the treasures of Allâh, nor (that) I know the unseen; nor do I tell you that I am an angel. I but follow what is revealed to me by inspiration."[3]

The Definition Of *Nabi* (Prophet) and *Rasul* (Messenger)

Nabi in the Arabic language: It is taken from the word *Naba'a*, which means news or information. A Prophet is called a *Nabi* because he informs us about Allâh Almighty — i.e., he conveys to us His Orders and revelation. A Prophet is perhaps also called *Nabi* because Allâh informed him.

Rasul in the Arabic language: *Rasul* is taken from *Irsal*, which means direction. Therefore the Messengers are thus named because they are directed from Allâh. Allâh Almighty says:

﴿ثُمَّ أَرْسَلْنَا رُسُلَنَا تَتْرَا﴾

Then We sent Our Messengers in succession,[4]

---

[1] (*Ghafir* 40:78)

[2] (*Fussilat* 41:6)

[3] (*Al-An'am* 6:50)

[4] (*Al-Mu'minun* 23:44)

The Difference Between A *Nabi* (Prophet) And A *Rasul* (Messenger)

A *Rasul* is a man who is inspired with a new *Shari'ah* or set of laws, and he is sent to a transgressing people, conveying to them Allâh's Message — for example, the Messengers of firm will (*Ulul-'Azm*).

A *Nabi* is a man who is inspired with a message, but the message is to follow the *Shari'ah* of those who preceded him; he is sent to apply a previously sent *Shari'ah* (set of laws) — for example, the Prophets from the Children of Israel that came after Musa, peace be upon him. Allâh Almighty says:

﴿إِنَّآ أَنزَلْنَا ٱلتَّوْرَىٰةَ فِيهَا هُدًى وَنُورٌ يَحْكُمُ بِهَا ٱلنَّبِيُّونَ ٱلَّذِينَ أَسْلَمُوا۟﴾

Verily, We did send down the Tawrah, therein was guidance and light, by which the Prophets, who submitted themselves to Allâh's Will.[1]

Prophethood Is A Blessing Granted By Allâh

Prophethood is a blessing that Allâh bestows according to His choice:

﴿ٱللَّهُ يَصْطَفِى مِنَ ٱلْمَلَـٰٓئِكَةِ رُسُلًا وَمِنَ ٱلنَّاسِ﴾

Allâh chooses Messengers from angels and from men.[2]

Therefore Prophethood is not a goal that is achieved through man's striving or working; rather, it is a high and special rank for which Allâh chooses — purely by His grace — whomsoever He pleases from His creation. He prepares them to carry the message, He protects them from the effects of the devils, and He protects them from *Shirk*, as a favor and mercy from Him, not from the efforts they expended. It is a blessing and favor from Allâh; He says:

﴿أُو۟لَـٰٓئِكَ ٱلَّذِينَ أَنْعَمَ ٱللَّهُ عَلَيْهِم مِّنَ ٱلنَّبِيِّـۧنَ مِن ذُرِّيَّةِ ءَادَمَ وَمِمَّنْ حَمَلْنَا مَعَ نُوحٍ وَمِن ذُرِّيَّةِ إِبْرَٰهِيمَ وَإِسْرَٰٓءِيلَ وَمِمَّنْ هَدَيْنَا وَٱجْتَبَيْنَآ﴾

Those were they to whom Allâh bestowed His grace from among the Prophets, of the offspring of Adam, and of those

---

[1] (*Al-Ma'idah* 5:44)
[2] (*Al-Hajj* 22:75)

whom We carried (in the ship) with Nuh, and of the offspring of Ibrahim and Israel and from among those whom We guided and chose.[1]

Allâh said to Musa:

$$﴿إِنِّي اصْطَفَيْتُكَ عَلَى النَّاسِ بِرِسَالَاتِي وَبِكَلَامِي﴾$$

I have chosen you above men by My Messages, and by My speaking (to you).[2]

And Allâh said, relating the words of Ya'qub to his son Yusuf, peace be upon them:

$$﴿وَكَذَلِكَ يَجْتَبِيكَ رَبُّكَ﴾$$

Thus will your Lord choose you.[3]

All of the above verses clearly indicate that Prophethood is not achieved by greatness or by actions; rather, it is a blessing and mercy from Allâh. He chooses men for that ranking by His Knowledge and Wisdom; it is a ranking that is not achieved by those who wish for it or work for it.

A Description Of The Messengers And Their Miracles

1. A Description Of The Messengers

The Messengers are good examples in their characteristics and manners; a discussion about their qualities is a long one indeed, but here we will suffice by mentioning the following qualities:

1) Truthfulness: Allâh informed us that His Messengers are truthful:

$$﴿هَذَا مَا وَعَدَ الرَّحْمَنُ وَصَدَقَ الْمُرْسَلُونَ ٥٢﴾$$

This is what the Most Beneficent had promised, and the Messengers spoke truth![4]

Without a doubt, truthfulness is the core and heart of the message and calling, and with it matters are set straight and deeds reap their fruits. Lying is a defect that the best of creation — the Messengers —

---

[1] (*Maryam* 19:58)

[2] (*Al-A'raf* 7:144)

[3] (*Yusuf* 12:6)

[4] (*Ya Sin* 36:52)

are far above.

2) Patience: Calling people to the obedience of Allâh and warning them not to go against His Commands is indeed a difficult and rough path to follow, and not everyone can handle it. However, Allâh's Messengers, peace be upon them, are the best of creation. They were faced with all kinds of hardship and harm, yet their firm will was not affected, and they continued to call people to the way of Allâh. Allâh informed us about some of His Prophets and the harm that was inflicted on them because of the message they brought. Allâh informed us about the patience and forbearance they exhibited in order to raise Allâh's Word above all else. Allâh ordered the Prophet ﷺ to take example after the Messengers of firm will, when He Almighty said:

$$﴿فَٱصْبِرْ كَمَا صَبَرَ أُوْلُوا ٱلْعَزْمِ مِنَ ٱلرُّسُلِ وَلَا تَسْتَعْجِل لَّهُمْ كَأَنَّهُمْ يَوْمَ يَرَوْنَ مَا يُوعَدُونَ لَمْ يَلْبَثُوٓا إِلَّا سَاعَةً مِّن نَّهَارٍ بَلَٰغٌ فَهَلْ يُهْلَكُ إِلَّا ٱلْقَوْمُ ٱلْفَٰسِقُونَ ٣٥﴾$$

Therefore be patient as did the Messengers of firm will and be in no haste about them (disbelievers). On the Day when they will see that (torment) with which they are promised (i.e. threatened, it will be) as if they had not stayed more than an hour in a single day. (O mankind! This Qur'an is sufficient as) a clear Message (or proclamation to save yourself from destruction). But shall any be destroyed except the people who are rebellious.[1]

2. The Miracles of the Messengers ﷺ

What is meant by those miracles: The miracles of the Prophets and Messengers are those things that go against the nature or habitual pattern of occurrences; Allâh makes those miracles occur at the hand of His Prophets and Messengers, and man is unable and incapable of repeating that occurrence or causing something similar to occur. Such miracles occurred at the hands of Allâh's Prophets and Messengers so that the proof upon man becomes final; the proof of those miracles is so binding that man must surrender and believe in what the Messengers came with, regardless of whether the people asked a given Messenger to bring them a miracle or no. Those

---

[1] (*Al-Ahqaf* 46:35)

miracles are called *Ayat* in the Qur'an.

Belief In Muhammad ﷺ As A Prophet And Messenger

Belief in Muhammad ﷺ consists of the following:

1) We must believe that he was sent to all of mankind, for Allâh Almighty says:

﴿يَٰٓأَيُّهَا ٱلنَّاسُ إِنِّى رَسُولُ ٱللَّهِ إِلَيْكُمْ جَمِيعًا﴾

Say: "O mankind! Verily, I am sent to you all as the Messenger of Allâh"[1]

And the Prophet ﷺ said:

«وَكَانَ النَّبِيُّ يُبْعَثُ إِلَى قَوْمِهِ خَاصَّةً وَبُعِثْتُ إِلَى كُلِّ أَحْمَرَ وَأَسْوَدَ»

A Prophet would be sent specifically to his people, yet I was sent to every red and black (i.e., to all of mankind). (Recorded by Muslim)

Allâh has made the religion complete for us, He has completed His favors upon us, and He is pleased with Islam as a religion for us, the religion that was revealed to Muhammad ﷺ, who is a mercy for all of mankind and the seal of Prophets and Messengers. He ﷺ is the Messenger of Allâh not only to man but to jinns as well — a giver of glad tidings, a warner, and a caller to Allâh, by His Will, and a torch illuminating the way.

Whoever from mankind doesn't accept his message deserves a punishment from Allâh — just like his brother disbelievers, for Allâh Almighty says:

﴿ٱلْيَوْمَ أَكْمَلْتُ لَكُمْ دِينَكُمْ وَأَتْمَمْتُ عَلَيْكُمْ نِعْمَتِى وَرَضِيتُ لَكُمُ ٱلْإِسْلَٰمَ دِينًا﴾

This day, I have perfected your religion for you, completed My favor upon you, and have chosen for you Islam as your religion.[2]

﴿وَمَن يَبْتَغِ غَيْرَ ٱلْإِسْلَٰمِ دِينًا فَلَن يُقْبَلَ مِنْهُ﴾

And whoever seeks a religion other than Islam, it will never

---

[1] (*Al-A'raf* 7:158)
[2] (*Al-Ma'idah* 5:3)

be accepted of him.[1]

2) We must believe that he ﷺ is the final Prophet and Messenger, for Allâh Almighty says:

﴿مَّا كَانَ مُحَمَّدٌ أَبَآ أَحَدٍ مِّن رِّجَالِكُمْ وَلَٰكِن رَّسُولَ ٱللَّهِ وَخَاتَمَ ٱلنَّبِيِّـۧنَ وَكَانَ ٱللَّهُ بِكُلِّ شَىْءٍ عَلِيمًا ۝﴾

Muhammad is not the father of any man among you, but he is the Messenger of Allâh and the last (end) of the Prophets. And Allâh is Ever All-Aware of everything.[2]

The Fifth Pillar Of *Iman*

Belief In The Last Day

Belief in the Last Day is the fifth pillar of *Iman*, and what it means is that we must believe with certainty in all that Allâh informed us in His Book, and, all that the Messenger of Allâh ﷺ informed us about regarding what happens after death. This includes the following — the trial of the grave, the punishment and reward in the grave, resurrection, the gathering of mankind for accountability, the judgement, the Scale of deeds, the *Hawdh* (special basin granted to the Prophet ﷺ in the Hereafter, from which the believers will drink), the path, intercession, Paradise, Hell, and all that Allâh prepared in these two abodes for their dwellers.

Proofs Indicating That It Is Compulsory To Believe In The Last Day

1) Allâh Almighty says:

﴿إِنَّ ٱلَّذِينَ ءَامَنُوا۟ وَٱلَّذِينَ هَادُوا۟ وَٱلنَّصَٰرَىٰ وَٱلصَّٰبِـِٔينَ مَنْ ءَامَنَ بِٱللَّهِ وَٱلْيَوْمِ ٱلْأَخِرِ وَعَمِلَ صَٰلِحًا فَلَهُمْ أَجْرُهُمْ عِندَ رَبِّهِمْ وَلَا خَوْفٌ عَلَيْهِمْ وَلَا هُمْ يَحْزَنُونَ ۝﴾

Verily! Those who believe and those who are Jews and Christians, and Sabians — whoever believes in Allâh and the Last Day and does righteous good deeds — shall have their reward with their Lord, on them shall be no fear, nor shall they grieve.[3]

---

[1] (*Aal 'Imran* 3:85)

[2] (*Al-Ahzab* 33:40)

[3] (*Al-Baqarah* 2:62)

2) Allâh Almighty says:

﴿لَّيْسَ ٱلْبِرَّ أَن تُوَلُّوا وُجُوهَكُمْ قِبَلَ ٱلْمَشْرِقِ وَٱلْمَغْرِبِ وَلَٰكِنَّ ٱلْبِرَّ مَنْ ءَامَنَ بِٱللَّهِ وَٱلْيَوْمِ ٱلْءَاخِرِ وَٱلْمَلَٰٓئِكَةِ وَٱلْكِتَٰبِ وَٱلنَّبِيِّۦنَ وَءَاتَى ٱلْمَالَ عَلَىٰ حُبِّهِۦ ذَوِى ٱلْقُرْبَىٰ وَٱلْيَتَٰمَىٰ وَٱلْمَسَٰكِينَ وَٱبْنَ ٱلسَّبِيلِ وَٱلسَّآئِلِينَ وَفِى ٱلرِّقَابِ وَأَقَامَ ٱلصَّلَوٰةَ وَءَاتَى ٱلزَّكَوٰةَ وَٱلْمُوفُونَ بِعَهْدِهِمْ إِذَا عَٰهَدُوا وَٱلصَّٰبِرِينَ فِى ٱلْبَأْسَآءِ وَٱلضَّرَّآءِ وَحِينَ ٱلْبَأْسِ أُوْلَٰٓئِكَ ٱلَّذِينَ صَدَقُوا وَأُوْلَٰٓئِكَ هُمُ ٱلْمُتَّقُونَ ١٧٧﴾

It is not *Al-Birr* (piety, righteousness) that you turn your faces towards east and (or) west (in prayers); but *Al-Birr* is (the quality of) the one who believes in Allâh, the Last Day, the Angels, the Book, the Prophets and gives his wealth, in spite of love for it, to the kinsfolk, to the orphans, and to *Al-Masakin* (the poor), and to the wayfarer, and to those who ask, and to set slaves free, performs *As-Salat*, and gives the *Zakat*, and who fulfill their covenant when they make it, and who are *As-Sabirin* (the patient ones, etc.) in extreme poverty and ailment (disease) and at the time of fighting (during the battles). Such are the people of the truth and they are the pious.[1]

3) Allâh Almighty says regarding the Resurrection:

﴿ثُمَّ إِنَّكُمْ يَوْمَ ٱلْقِيَٰمَةِ تُبْعَثُونَ ١٦﴾

Then (again), surely, you will be resurrected on the Day of Resurrection.[2]

4) When Jibril, peace be upon him, asked the Prophet ﷺ about *Iman*, he ﷺ said:

«أَنْ تُؤْمِنَ بِاللهِ وَمَلَائِكَتِهِ وَكُتُبِهِ وَرُسُلِهِ وَالْيَوْمِ الآخِرِ وَتُؤْمِنَ بِالْقَدَرِ خَيْرِهِ وَشَرِّهِ»

To believe in Allâh, His Angels, His Books, His Messengers, the Last Day, and to believe in Divine Preordainment, both the good and bad of it. (Recorded by Muslim)

---

[1] (*Al-Baqarah* 2:177)
[2] (*Al-Mu'minun* 23:16)

The Punishment Of The Grave, And Its Pleasures

There are so many *Ahadith* related from the Prophet ﷺ regarding the questions of the two angels, the punishment of the grave, and its pleasures that these are positively established realities. Therefore believing in them is obligatory. One is punished in the grave if he deserves punishment, and one is given bliss if that is what he deserves. Whichever the case, one will be recompensed in the grave, regardless of whether he is buried or not, or whether he is eaten up in his grave, or whether he is cremated, or whether he drowned and is at the bottom of the sea, and so on. The proofs that establish recompense in the grave are many — from them are the following:

1) Allâh Almighty says:

$$﴿يُثَبِّتُ ٱللَّهُ ٱلَّذِينَ ءَامَنُوا۟ بِٱلْقَوْلِ ٱلثَّابِتِ فِى ٱلْحَيَوٰةِ ٱلدُّنْيَا وَفِى ٱلْأَخِرَةِ$$

$$وَيُضِلُّ ٱللَّهُ ٱلظَّٰلِمِينَ وَيَفْعَلُ ٱللَّهُ مَا يَشَآءُ ٢٧﴾$$

Allâh will keep firm those who believe, with the word that stands firm in this world (i.e., they will keep on worshipping Allâh Alone and none else), and in the Hereafter. And Allâh will cause to go astray those who are wrongdoers, and Allâh does what He wills.[1]

"With the word that stands firm...and in the Hereafter": This is a proof that we will be asked in the graves (and those among us who believe and whom Allâh favors will be blessed with "the word that stands firm").

2) Allâh Almighty says:

$$﴿ٱلنَّارُ يُعْرَضُونَ عَلَيْهَا غُدُوًّا وَعَشِيًّا وَيَوْمَ تَقُومُ ٱلسَّاعَةُ أَدْخِلُوٓا۟ ءَالَ فِرْعَوْنَ أَشَدَّ$$

$$ٱلْعَذَابِ ٤٦﴾$$

The Fire; they are exposed to it, morning and afternoon, and on the Day when the Hour will be established (it will be said to the angels): "Cause Fir'awn's people to enter the severest torment!"[2]

This verse proves that some people are punished in their graves.

---

[1] (*Ibrahim* 14:27)

[2] (*Ghafir* 40:46)

3) Al-Bukhari recorded that Ibn 'Abbas, may Allâh be pleased with them, said:

"The Prophet ﷺ passed by two graves and said:

«إِنَّهُمَا لَيُعَذَّبَانِ وَمَا يُعَذَّبَانِ فِي كَبِيرٍ»

Indeed they are being punished, and they are not being punished for something that is great.

Then he said:

«بَلَى، أَمَّا أَحَدُهُمَا فَكَانَ يَسْعَى بِالنَّمِيمَةِ، وَأَمَّا الآخَرُ فَكَانَ لَا يَسْتَتِرُ مِنْ بَوْلِهِ»

Indeed (for something that is great). As for one of them, he would spread tales in order to sow dissension among people; and as for the other, he would not properly protect himself from his urine.

The Prophet ﷺ then took a fresh stick, broke it in two, and drove each of the sticks on the grave, after which he ﷺ said:

«لَعَلَّهُ يُخَفَّفُ عَنْهُمَا مَالَمْ يَيْبَسَا»

Perhaps their punishment will be lightened as long as they (the two sticks) do not get dry.

The Hour And Its Signs

Allâh Almighty says:

﴿وَعِندَهُۥ مَفَاتِحُ ٱلْغَيْبِ لَا يَعْلَمُهَآ إِلَّا هُوَ﴾

And with Him are the keys of the *Ghaib* (all that is hidden), none knows them but He.[1]

The knowledge of when the Hour will arrive is that part of the unseen that only Allâh knows about:

﴿إِنَّ ٱللَّهَ عِندَهُۥ عِلْمُ ٱلسَّاعَةِ﴾

Verily, Allâh! With Him (Alone) is the knowledge of the Hour.[2]

---

[1] (*Al-An'am* 6:59)
[2] (*Luqman* 31:34)

There are many verses of the Qur'an, and sayings of the Prophet ﷺ, that prove the coming of the Hour; among them are the following:

1) Allâh Almighty says:

﴿ إِنَّ ٱلسَّاعَةَ لَآتِيَةٌ لَّا رَيْبَ فِيهَا وَلَٰكِنَّ أَكْثَرَ ٱلنَّاسِ لَا يُؤْمِنُونَ ٥٩ ﴾

Verily, the Hour (Day of Judgement) is surely coming, therein is no doubt, yet most men believe not.[1]

2) The Prophet ﷺ said:

«بُعِثْتُ أَنَا وَالسَّاعَةَ كَهَاتَيْنِ وَيَقْرُنُ أَصْبُعَيْهِ السَّبَّابَةَ وَالْوُسْطَى»

The time in which I have been sent and the Hour are like these two. He ﷺ then joined his index finger with his middle one.

The Resurrection

The Resurrection means bringing life to the dead at the second blowing of the Trumpet, a time when people will stand — barefooted, naked, and uncircumcised. Allâh Almighty says:

﴿ كَمَا بَدَأْنَآ أَوَّلَ خَلْقٍ نُّعِيدُهُ وَعْدًا عَلَيْنَآ إِنَّا كُنَّا فَٰعِلِينَ ١٠٤ ﴾

As We began the first creation, We shall repeat it, (it is) a promise binding upon Us. Truly, We shall do it.[2]

The Qur'an, the Sunnah, and the consensus of the Muslims establish the truth of the Resurrection. In the Qur'an, Allâh Almighty says:

﴿ ثُمَّ إِنَّكُم بَعْدَ ذَٰلِكَ لَمَيِّتُونَ ١٥ ثُمَّ إِنَّكُمْ يَوْمَ ٱلْقِيَٰمَةِ تُبْعَثُونَ ١٦ ﴾

After that, surely you will die. Then (again), surely you will be resurrected on the Day of Resurrection.[3]

As for the Sunnah, the Prophet ﷺ said:

«ثُمَّ يُنْزِلُ الله مِنَ السَّمَاءِ مَاءً فَيَنْبُتُونَ كَمَا يَنْبُتُ الْبَقْلُ»

Then Allâh will send water from the sky, and you will grow just like vegetables grow.

And the Muslims unanimously agree that it is the truth.

---

[1] (*Ghafir* 40:59)

[2] (*Al-Anbiya'* 21:104)

[3] (*Al-Mu'minun* 23:15,16)

The Gathering

After people will rise from their graves, they will be steered to the land of the Gathering. Allâh Almighty says:

﴿يَوْمَ تَشَقَّقُ ٱلْأَرْضُ عَنْهُمْ سِرَاعًا ذَٰلِكَ حَشْرٌ عَلَيْنَا يَسِيرٌ ٤٤﴾

On the Day when the earth shall be cleft, from off them, (they will come out) hastening forth. That will be a gathering, quite easy for Us. [1]

﴿وَتَرَى ٱلْأَرْضَ بَارِزَةً وَحَشَرْنَٰهُمْ فَلَمْ نُغَادِرْ مِنْهُمْ أَحَدًا ٤٧﴾

And you will see the earth as a levelled plain, and we shall gather them all together so as to leave not one of them behind.[2]

And the Prophet ﷺ said:

«يُحْشَرُ النَّاسُ يَوْمَ الْقِيَامَةِ حُفَاةً عُرَاةً غُرْلًا»

The people will be gathered on the Day of Judgement, and they will be barefooted, naked, and uncircumcised.

The Reckoning

This means that Allâh will show man the deeds he performed in this world, and he will admit what he did; at that time, people will take the rights that are due to them from others, and all of that is most easy for Allâh. That the accountability and judgement will take place is proven by many verses from the Qur'an, as well as *Ahadith* of the Prophet ﷺ, such as these two verses:

﴿فَلَنَسْئَلَنَّ ٱلَّذِينَ أُرْسِلَ إِلَيْهِمْ وَلَنَسْئَلَنَّ ٱلْمُرْسَلِينَ ٦﴾

Then surely, We shall question those (people) to whom it (the Book) was sent and verily, We shall question the Messengers.[3]

﴿وَعُرِضُوا۟ عَلَىٰ رَبِّكَ صَفًّا لَّقَدْ جِئْتُمُونَا كَمَا خَلَقْنَٰكُمْ أَوَّلَ مَرَّةٍ﴾

And they will be set before your Lord in (lines as) rows, (and

---

[1] (*Qaf* 50:44)

[2] (*Al-Kahf* 18:47)

[3] (*Al-A'raf* 7:6)

Allâh will say): "Now indeed, you have come to Us as We created you the first time."[1]

Allâh will Himself take account of man's deeds, for 'Adi bin Hatim, may Allâh be pleased with him, related that the Prophet ﷺ said:

«مَا مِنْكُمْ مِنْ أَحَدٍ إِلَّا سَيُكَلِّمُهُ اللهُ لَيْسَ بَيْنَهُ وَبَيْنَهُ تَرْجُمَانٌ فَيَنْظُرُ أَيْمَنَ مِنْهُ فَلَا يَرَى إِلَّا مَا قَدَّمَ مِنْ عَمَلِهِ وَيَنْظُرُ أَشْأَمَ مِنْهُ فَلَا يَرَى إِلَّا مَا قَدَّمَ وَيَنْظُرُ بَيْنَ يَدَيْهِ فَلَا يَرَى إِلَّا النَّارَ تِلْقَاءَ وَجْهِهِ فَاتَّقُوا النَّارَ وَلَوْ بِشِقِّ تَمْرَةٍ»

There is not one from you except that Allâh will speak to him; there will not be between Him (Allâh) and him any interpreter. He (man) will look to his right and see only that which he put forth; he will look to his left and see only that which he put forth. And he will look before him and will see only the Hellfire, which will reach his face. So, protect yourselves from the Fire, even if you do so with part of a date (by giving it in charity). (Recorded by Al-Bukhari)

The *Hawdh*

The *Hawdh* is a huge basin from which the nation of Muhammad ﷺ will drink, except for those who went against his guidance and who changed his religion after him. As the Prophet ﷺ was among his Companions, he said:

«إِنِّي عَلَى الْحَوْضِ أَنْتَظِرُ مَنْ يَرِدُ عَلَيَّ مِنْكُمْ، فَوَاللهِ لَيُقْطَعَنَّ دُونِي رِجَالٌ، فَلَأَقُولَنَّ: أَيْ رَبِّ، مِنِّي وَمِنْ أُمَّتِي، فَيَقُولُ: إِنَّكَ لَا تَدْرِي مَا عَمِلُوا بَعْدَكَ، مَازَالُوا يَرْجِعُونَ عَلَى أَعْقَابِهِمْ»

I am at the *Hawdh* waiting for whoever from you comes to me (to drink); by Allâh, some men will be blocked from coming to me, and I will say, "My Lord, they are from me and from my nation." It will be said, "Indeed, you do not know what they did after you; they continued to go back on their heels." (Recorded by Al-Bukhari)

This *Hadith* establishes the reality of the *Hawdh* and that people who innovate in religion or people who go against the guidance of

---

[1] (*Al-Kahf* 18:48)

the Prophet ﷺ will be prevented from drinking from it. The *Hadiths* regarding the *Hawdh* are so many that its existence is positively established. 'Abdul-Malik bin 'Umair said, "I heard Jundub, may Allâh be pleased with him, saying, 'I heard the Prophet ﷺ say:

$$«أَنَا فَرَطُكُمْ عَلَى الْحَوْضِ»$$

I am your predecessor at the *Hawdh*.'" (Recorded by Al-Bukhari)

The Scale (or The Balance)

A scale is an apparatus for weighing things. The Scale of the Hereafter is real: it has two real pans upon which the deeds of Allâh's worshippers will be placed. The Scale exhibits Allâh's justice, for He doesn't wrong any soul. So Allâh will bring forth the deeds of men, including deeds that in weight are equal to a grain or a mustard seed. Those deeds will be weighed: one will be rewarded according to the results of the weighing. The Scale of deeds may be one or many, and Allâh is capable over all things. Here are two of the proofs that establish the reality of the Scale:

1) Allâh Almighty says:

$$﴿وَنَضَعُ ٱلْمَوَٰزِينَ ٱلْقِسْطَ لِيَوْمِ ٱلْقِيَٰمَةِ فَلَا تُظْلَمُ نَفْسٌ شَيْئًا وَإِن كَانَ مِثْقَالَ حَبَّةٍ مِّنْ خَرْدَلٍ أَتَيْنَا بِهَا وَكَفَىٰ بِنَا حَٰسِبِينَ ۝﴾$$

And We shall set up Balances of justice on the Day of Resurrection, then none will be dealt with unjustly in anything. And if there be the weight of a mustard seed, We will bring it. And Sufficient are We as Reckoners.[1]

3) The Prophet ﷺ said:

$$«كَلِمَتَانِ حَبِيبَتَانِ إِلَى الرَّحْمَنِ خَفِيفَتَانِ عَلَى اللِّسَانِ، ثَقِيلَتَانِ فِي الْمِيزَانِ سُبْحَانَ اللهِ وَبِحَمْدِهِ سُبْحَانَ اللهِ الْعَظِيمِ»$$

Two words, beloved to the Most Merciful, light on the tongue, and heavy on the Scale: *Subhaanallahi wa Bihamdihee* (How perfect Allâh is and with His praise) and *Subhaanallahil-'Azeem* (How perfect Allâh, the Magnificent).

---

[1] (*Al-Anbiya'* 21:47)

(Recorded by Al-Bukhari)

The previous proofs establish the weighing of deeds on the Scale, the success that results from good deeds being heavy, and the loss that results from the good deeds being light.

As-Sirat

As-Sirat means the path, and here it refers to the bridge that is erected over the Hellfire and that leads to Paradise. All must pass over this bridge, and only by passing across it does one enter Paradise. The existence of the bridge is established in both the Qur'an and the Sunnah. Allâh Almighty says:

﴿وَإِن مِّنكُمْ إِلَّا وَارِدُهَا ۚ كَانَ عَلَىٰ رَبِّكَ حَتْمًا مَّقْضِيًّا ۝ ثُمَّ نُنَجِّى الَّذِينَ اتَّقَوا وَّنَذَرُ الظَّالِمِينَ فِيهَا جِثِيًّا ۝﴾

There is not one of you but will pass over it (Hell); this is with your Lord, a Decree which must be accomplished. Then We shall save those who use to fear Allâh and were dutiful to Him. And We shall leave the wrongdoers therein (humbled) to their knees (in Hell).[1]

Abu Hurairah, may Allâh be pleased with him, related in a long *Hadith* that the Prophet ﷺ said:

«وَيُضْرَبُ الصِّرَاطُ بَيْنَ ظَهْرَيْ جَهَنَّمَ فَأَكُونُ أَنَا وَأُمَّتِي أَوَّلَ مَنْ يُجِيزُهَا»

And the *Sirat* is placed over the Hellfire. I and my nation will be the first to cross it. (Recorded by Muslim)

Ash-Shafa'ah (Intercession)

Ash-Shaf' means to attach something to what is similar to it. And *Shafa'ah* signifies means or a request. Here it means to intercede for others to bring benefit or drive harm away.

In most cases, it is used to mean that someone who is higher in ranking or status intercedes for someone who is lower in ranking. And two conditions must be fulfilled for intercession to occur on the Day of Judgement with Allâh:

1) That Allâh gives permission to the intercessor to intercede. Allâh

---

[1] (*Maryam* 19:71,72)

Almighty says:

$$﴿مَن ذَا ٱلَّذِى يَشْفَعُ عِندَهُۥٓ إِلَّا بِإِذْنِهِۦۚ﴾$$

Who is he that can intercede with Him except with His Permission?[1]

2) That Allâh is pleased with the one who is being interceded for. Allâh Almighty says:

$$﴿وَلَا يَشْفَعُونَ إِلَّا لِمَنِ ٱرْتَضَىٰ﴾$$

And they cannot intercede except for him with whom He is pleased.[2]

Categories Of Intercession

There are Two Categories of Intercession:

— The first is specific to the Prophet ﷺ.

— The second is general - for him ﷺ and for others.

The First Category Includes The Following

1) The greater intercession; it is specific to the Prophet ﷺ and it is the highest position of praise and glory that Allâh promised him:

$$﴿عَسَىٰٓ أَن يَبْعَثَكَ رَبُّكَ مَقَامًا مَّحْمُودًا ۝﴾$$

It may be that your Lord will raise you to *Maqam Mahmud* (the highest position of praise and glory).[3]

This refers to when the standing becomes difficult for the people on the Day or Judgement, and they will be searching for intercession. They will go in succession to Adam, Ibrahim, Musa, and then to 'Iesa — all of these Prophets will say, "Myself, myself." Then finally, they will reach our Prophet Muhammad ﷺ, who will say:

$$«أَنَا لَهَا»$$

I am to do this. (Recorded by Al-Bukhari)

2) Intercession for entering Paradise: Anas bin Malik, may Allâh be

---

[1] (*Al-Baqarah* 2:255)

[2] (*Al-Anbiya'* 21:28)

[3] (*Al-Isra'* 17:79)

pleased with him, related that the Prophet ﷺ said:

«أَنَا أَوَّلُ النَّاسِ يُشْفَعُ فِي الْجَنَّةِ وَأَنَا أَكْثَرُ الأَنْبِيَاءِ تَبَعاً»

I am the first of people to intercede regarding Paradise and among the Prophets I have the most followers. (Recorded by Muslim)

3) The Prophet ﷺ will intercede to have punishment lightened for his uncle, Abu Talib. Abu Sa'id Al-Khudri, may Allâh be pleased with him, related that the Prophet ﷺ mentioned his uncle Abu Talib to him, and then he ﷺ said:

«لَعَلَّهُ تَنْفَعُهُ شَفَاعَتِي يَوْمَ الْقِيَامَةِ فَيَجْعَلَ فِي ضَحْضَاحٍ مِنْ نَارٍ يَغْلِي مِنْهُ دِمَاغُهُ»

Perhaps my intercession will benefit him on the Day of Judgement, so that he is placed in a shallow part of the Fire, and from it his brain will boil.

However, as one who died not upon *Tawhid*, he will not benefit from intercession to the extent of being taken out of the Hellfire. And Allâh knows best.

The Second Category Consists Of The Following

1) Intercession for those people of *Tawhid* who perpetrated great sins, people who were placed in the Hellfire but are then taken out of it. This kind of intercession has been related by a great many sources in *Ahadith*, so many so that its occurrence is positively established. The Prophet ﷺ will intercede many times for the people of this category; other intercessors in this case are the angels, the Prophets, and the believers.

The *Mu'tazilah* and the *Khawarij*, two deviant sects, reject this category of intercession. They reject it based on their false belief that one who perpetrates great sins is in the Hellfire for eternity, thus making intercession useless in his case.

2) Intercession will occur for the people of Paradise, that they may be raised to a position higher than the one that their situation calls for.

3) Some people will be interceded for, so that they can enter Paradise without being reckoned. When 'Ukashah bin Mihsan

asked the Prophet ﷺ to supplicate for him to make him from the seventy thousand who will enter Paradise without reckoning, the Prophet ﷺ said:

«اللَّهُمَّ اجْعَلْهُ مِنْهُمْ»

O Allâh, make him from them.

Paradise And Hell

Paradise is the abode that Allâh prepared for the righteous ones to inhabit in the Hereafter.

Hell is the abode that Allâh prepared for the disbelievers to inhabit in the Hereafter.

Both of them are created and exist now, for Allâh Almighty says about Paradise:

﴿أُعِدَّتْ لِلْمُتَّقِينَ ۝﴾

Prepared for the pious[1]

And about Hell:

﴿لِلْكَافِرِينَ﴾

For the disbelievers.[2]

When the Prophet ﷺ prayed the Eclipse Prayer, he ﷺ said:

«إِنِّي رَأَيْتُ الْجَنَّةَ فَتَنَاوَلْتُ مِنْهَا عُنْقُودًا وَلَوْ أَخَذْتُهُ لَأَكَلْتُمْ مِنْهُ مَا بَقِيَتِ الدُّنْيَا، وَرَأَيْتُ النَّارَ فَلَمْ أَرَ كَالْيَوْمِ مَنْظَرًا قَطُّ أَفْظَعَ»

Indeed I have seen Paradise and I reached for a cluster from it. Were I to have taken it, you would have eaten from it as long as the world would remain. I also saw the Hellfire, and I have never seen anything more horrible than it. (Agreed upon)

Paradise and Hellfire will never cease to exist, for Allâh Almighty says:

﴿جَزَآؤُهُمْ عِندَ رَبِّهِمْ جَنَّٰتُ عَدْنٍ تَجْرِى مِن تَحْتِهَا ٱلْأَنْهَٰرُ خَٰلِدِينَ فِيهَآ أَبَدًا﴾

Their reward with their Lord is *'Adn* (Eden) Paradise (Gardens

---

[1] (*Aal 'Imran* 3:133)

[2] (*Aal 'Imran* 3:131)

of Eternity), underneath which rivers flow, they will abide therein forever.[1]

The Sixth Pillar Of *Iman*

Belief In *Al-Qadar* (Divine Preordainment)

The Definition Of *Al-Qadar*: What Allâh decrees for all in existence, based on what has preceded in terms of His Knowledge and in accordance with His Wisdom.

Belief in *Al-Qadar* is the sixth pillar of faith: when Jibril, peace be upon him, asked the Prophet ﷺ about *Iman*, he ﷺ answered:

«أَنْ تُؤْمِنَ بِاللهِ وَمَلَائِكَتِهِ وَكُتُبِهِ وَرُسُلِهِ وَالْيَوْمِ الآخِرِ وَتُؤْمِنَ بِالْقَدَرِ خَيْرِهِ وَشَرِّهِ»

To believe in Allâh, His Angels, His Books, His Messengers, the Last Day, and to believe in divine Preordainment, both the good and bad of it.

Belief in *Al-Qadar* means believing with certainty that all that happens — good and bad — occurs according to Allâh's divine Preordainment and Decree. Allâh Almighty says:

﴿مَا أَصَابَ مِن مُّصِيبَةٍ فِى ٱلْأَرْضِ وَلَا فِى أَنفُسِكُمْ إِلَّا فِى كِتَٰبٍ مِّن قَبْلِ أَن نَّبْرَأَهَآ إِنَّ ذَٰلِكَ عَلَى ٱللَّهِ يَسِيرٌ ۝ لِّكَيْلَا تَأْسَوْا۟ عَلَىٰ مَا فَاتَكُمْ وَلَا تَفْرَحُوا۟ بِمَآ ءَاتَىٰكُمْ ۗ وَٱللَّهُ لَا يُحِبُّ كُلَّ مُخْتَالٍ فَخُورٍ ۝﴾

No calamity befalls on the earth or in yourselves but is inscribed in the Book of Decrees (*Al-Lawh Al-Mahfuz*), before We bring it into existence. Verily, that is easy for Allâh. In order that you may not be sad over matters that you fail to get, nor rejoice because of that which has been given to you. And Allâh likes not prideful boasters.[2]

This verse indicates that all events in existence, and in the souls of men — both the good and bad of it — are divinely preordained by Allâh and were written before the creation was created. Therefore one should not grieve for not having something he loves, nor should

---

[1] (*Al-Bayyinah* 98:8)

[2] (*Al-Hadid* 57:22,23)

he rejoice over getting that which he wants.

Zaid bin Thabit, may Allâh be pleased with him, narrated that he heard the Messenger of Allâh ﷺ say:

«لَوْ أَنَّ اللهَ عَذَّبَ أَهْلَ سَمَاوَاتِهِ وَأَهْلَ أَرْضِهِ لَعَذَّبَهُمْ غَيْرَ ظَالِمٍ لَهُمْ وَلَوْ رَحِمَهُمْ كَانَتْ رَحْمَتُهُ لَهُمْ خَيْرًا مِنْ أَعْمَالِهِمْ، وَلَوْ كَانَ لَكَ جَبَلُ أُحُدٍ - أَوْ مِثْلُ جَبَلِ أُحُدٍ - ذَهَبًا أَنْفَقْتَهُ فِي سَبِيلِ اللهِ مَا قَبِلَهُ مِنْكَ حَتَّى تُؤْمِنَ بِالْقَدَرِ، وَتَعْلَمَ أَنَّ مَا أَصَابَكَ لَمْ يَكُنْ لِيُخْطِئَكَ وَأَنَّ مَا أَخْطَأَكَ لَمْ يَكُنْ لِيُصِيبَكَ، وَأَنَّكَ إِنْ مِتَّ عَلَى غَيْرِ هَذَا دَخَلْتَ النَّارَ»

If Allâh were to punish the inhabitants of the heavens and the inhabitants of earth, He would not be doing them wrong by punishing them. And were He to have mercy on them, His mercy would be better than their deeds. And were you to have gold equal to Mount Uhud, or almost equal to Mount Uhud, and then you spent it in the way of Allâh, He would not accept it from you until you believed in divine Preordainment — until you know that what befalls you wasn't meant to miss you, and that what misses you wasn't meant to strike you. If you die upon other than this (belief), you will enter the Hellfire. (Recorded by Imam Ahmad)

Everything that Allâh decrees is by His Wisdom and Knowledge. He doesn't create pure evil in the sense that no good or benefit will result from that evil; therefore evil is not ascribed to Him in the sense that it is evil; rather, it comes under the general reality that Allâh created all things. Justice, Wisdom, and Mercy — these are some of Allâh's Qualities that we infer from His divine Decree. Allâh is categorically perfect and complete, for He says:

﴿مَّآ أَصَابَكَ مِنْ حَسَنَةٍ فَمِنَ ٱللَّهِ وَمَآ أَصَابَكَ مِن سَيِّئَةٍ فَمِن نَّفْسِكَ﴾

Whatever of good reaches you, is from Allâh, but whatever of evil befalls you, is from yourself.[1]

The meaning of this verse is that whatever blessings and good things happen to man, then it is from Allâh; and whatever evil befalls him, then it is because of his own evil deeds and sins. No one can flee

---

[1] (*An-Nisa'* 4:79)

from the divine Decree or from that which is decreed. Allâh created His creatures; nothing occurs in His dominion except what He wishes, and He is not pleased with disbelief for His creatures. But Allâh granted them the ability to choose: man's actions occur by his ability and will, yet Allâh guides whomsoever He wishes by His Mercy, and He misguides whomsoever He wills by His Wisdom. And He is not asked about what He does, but they (mankind) will be asked.

The Levels Of Belief In *Al-Qadar*

There are four levels of belief in *Al-Qadar*:

1) Knowledge

Which means that we believe in Allâh's Knowledge: that He knows all things and that His Knowledge encompasses all things. Even something as small as an ant — whether it is in the heavens or in the earth — is not hidden from His Knowledge. He indeed knew the entire creation before He even created them; He knew every situation they were in, regardless of whether it is something open or hidden. There are many proofs to support this — these are a few:

a) Allâh Almighty says:

$$﴿وَأَنَّ ٱللَّهَ قَدْ أَحَاطَ بِكُلِّ شَىْءٍ عِلْمًا ۝﴾$$

And that Allâh surrounds (comprehends) all things in (His) Knowledge.[1]

b) Allâh Almighty says:

$$﴿وَعِندَهُۥ مَفَاتِحُ ٱلْغَيْبِ لَا يَعْلَمُهَآ إِلَّا هُوَ وَيَعْلَمُ مَا فِى ٱلْبَرِّ وَٱلْبَحْرِ وَمَا تَسْقُطُ مِن وَرَقَةٍ إِلَّا يَعْلَمُهَا وَلَا حَبَّةٍ فِى ظُلُمَٰتِ ٱلْأَرْضِ وَلَا رَطْبٍ وَلَا يَابِسٍ إِلَّا فِى كِتَٰبٍ مُّبِينٍ ۝﴾$$

And with Him are the keys of the *Ghaib* (all that is hidden), none knows them but He. And He knows whatever there is in (or on) the earth and in the sea; not a leaf falls, but he knows it. There is not a grain in the darkness of the earth nor anything fresh or dry, but is written in a Clear Record.[2]

[1] (*At-Talaq* 65:12)
[2] (*Al-An'am* 6:59)

c) Ibn 'Abbas, may Allâh be pleased with them, said that the Prophet ﷺ was asked regarding those children (who die before they become adults) whose parents are disbelievers, and the Prophet ﷺ answered:

«اللهُ أَعْلَمُ بِمَا كَانُوا عَامِلِينَ إِذْ خَلَقَهُمْ»

Allâh knows best what their deeds would be when He created them. (Recorded by Muslim)

Allâh has knowledge of all things that are present and hidden, those have taken place and those that have not taken place; He even knows those things that haven't taken place, and how they would be were they to take place. There are many proofs that clearly indicate His All-Embracing Knowledge.

2) The Writing

We believe that Allâh wrote the decrees regarding His creation in *Al-Lawh Al-Mahfuz* (The Preserved Tablet); nothing is left out of that record. The proofs for this level are many indeed, and here are some of them:

a) Allâh Almighty says:

﴿أَلَمْ تَعْلَمْ أَنَّ ٱللَّهَ يَعْلَمُ مَا فِى ٱلسَّمَآءِ وَٱلْأَرْضِ إِنَّ ذَٰلِكَ فِى كِتَٰبٍ إِنَّ ذَٰلِكَ عَلَى ٱللَّهِ يَسِيرٌ ۝﴾

Know you not that Allâh knows all that is in heaven and on earth? Verily, it is (all) in the Book (*Al-Lawh Al-Mahfuz*). Verily! That is easy for Allâh.[1]

b) In a *Hadith* related by 'Ubadah bin Samit, may Allâh be pleased with him, the Prophet ﷺ said:

«أَوَّلُ مَا خَلَقَ الله – تَبَارَكَ وَتَعَالَى – الْقَلَمُ، ثُمَّ قَالَ لَهُ اكْتُبْ قَالَ: وَمَا أَكْتُبُ؟ قَالَ: الْقَدَرَ فَكَتَبَ مَايَكُونُ وَ مَا هُوَ كَائِنٌ إِلَى أَنْ تَقُومَ السَّاعَةُ»

The first thing that Allâh created was the Pen. Then He said to it, "Write." The Pen said, "What shall I write?" He said, "Write what will be and what will take place until the Hour arrives." (Recorded by Imam Ahmad)

---

[1] (*Al-Hajj* 22:70)

The previous proofs clearly show that Allâh wrote all things before creating the creation; He left nothing out of the Book — and that is easy for the One from Whom nothing is hidden.

3) His Will

We believe that Allâh's Will is executed and that His Ability is All-Embracing; whatever Allâh wills to happen, necessarily occurs; whatever He doesn't will, does not occur. The proofs that establish this level of belief are many, from them are the following:

a) Allâh Almighty says:

$$﴿وَمَا تَشَآءُونَ إِلَّآ أَن يَشَآءَ ٱللَّهُ رَبُّ ٱلْعَٰلَمِينَ ٢٩﴾$$

And you will not (will), unless (it be) that Allâh wills, the Lord of all that exists.[1]

b) Allâh Almighty says:

$$﴿إِنَّمَآ أَمْرُهُۥٓ إِذَآ أَرَادَ شَيْـًٔا أَن يَقُولَ لَهُۥ كُن فَيَكُونُ ٨٢﴾$$

Verily, His Command, when He intends a thing, is only that He says to it, "Be!" — and it is![2]

c) Al-Bukhari and Muslim recorded that Mu'awiyah bin Abi Sufyan, may Allâh be pleased with him, related that the Prophet ﷺ said:

«مَنْ يُرِدِ اللهُ بِهِ خَيْرًا يُفَقِّهْهُ فِي الدِّينِ»

Whoever Allâh wants good for, He makes him knowledgeable in the religion.

These evidences prove that Allâh's Will is manifest over all things, everything that happens in the universe happens by Allâh's Will, for He is the sole Creator, King, Planner, and Sustainer of the universe. Nothing occurs in His dominion that He doesn't wish: His Decree cannot be prevented and there is none to counter His Ruling. Whatever Allâh doesn't will, then it doesn't happen, because He doesn't will for it to happen, not because of a lack of ability. There is nothing that escapes Allâh:

$$﴿وَمَا كَانَ ٱللَّهُ لِيُعْجِزَهُۥ مِن شَيْءٍ فِي ٱلسَّمَٰوَٰتِ وَلَا فِي ٱلْأَرْضِ إِنَّهُۥ كَانَ عَلِيمًا﴾$$

---

[1] (*At-Takwir* 81:29)

[2] (*Ya Sin* 36:82)

$$﴿ \textcircled{٤٤} \ قَدِيرًا ﴾$$

Allâh is not such that anything in the heavens or in the earth escapes Him. Verily, He is All-Knowing, All-Capable.[1]

4) The Creation

We must believe that Allâh created everything, there is no creator or Lord other than Him. The following two proofs support this belief:

a) Allâh Almighty says:

$$﴿ اللَّهُ خَالِقُ كُلِّ شَيْءٍ وَهُوَ عَلَى كُلِّ شَيْءٍ وَكِيلٌ \textcircled{٦٢} ﴾$$

Allâh is the Creator of all things, and He is the *Wakil* (Trustee, Disposer of affairs, Guardian, etc.) over all things.[2]

b) The Prophet ﷺ said:

«إِنَّ اللَّهَ خَالِقُ كُلِّ صَانِعٍ وَصَنْعَتِهِ»

Indeed, Allâh is the Creator of all makers and that which they make.

These two proofs plainly show that Allâh decreed and created all things and that He encompasses all things with His care and protection. He created all things without having a previous example to base their creation upon. He granted some of His creation both ability and action; He is the Creator of the doer and his action; He is the All-Knowing and the Creator of all things.

The Effects Of *Iman* On The Individual And On Society

Iman or faith, with all of its pillars makes up one complete unit, meaning that each component is related to the other, and no single component is sufficient in itself, it needs all of the other components as well. Believing in all of the pillars of *Iman* results in having *Iman* in each of the individual pillars, so in reality, they cannot be separated from one another. The same can be said for its effects on the individual and on society, for the individual is the first brick from which society is comprised. The Messages were addressed to individuals because if they are upright, the society becomes upright. Here are some of the effects of *Iman*:

---

[1] (*Fatir* 35:44)

[2] (*Az-Zumar* 39:62)

1) Belief in Allâh Almighty is life for the hearts; it strengthens hearts as they climb to levels of completeness. *Iman* encourages man to take on good and noble characteristics, to stay away from evil and base characteristics, for Allâh Almighty says:

﴿أَوَ مَن كَانَ مَيْتًا فَأَحْيَيْنَٰهُ وَجَعَلْنَا لَهُۥ نُورًا يَمْشِى بِهِۦ فِى ٱلنَّاسِ كَمَن مَّثَلُهُۥ فِى ٱلظُّلُمَٰتِ لَيْسَ بِخَارِجٍ مِّنْهَا ۚ كَذَٰلِكَ زُيِّنَ لِلْكَٰفِرِينَ مَا كَانُوا۟ يَعْمَلُونَ ۝١٢٢﴾

Is he who was dead (without faith by ignorance and disbelief) and We gave him life (by knowledge and faith) and set for him a light (of faith) whereby he can walk amongst men, like him who is in the darkness (of disbelief, polytheism and hypocrisy) from which he can never come out? Thus it is made fair-seeming to the disbelievers that which they used to do.[1]

2) Because *Iman* conforms to the inborn nature of man, it is the source of comfort and peace for individuals; meanwhile, it is also the source of bliss and happiness for society: it strengthens the ties of one member of society to another. With faith in one's heart, one is satisfied and contented in all situations — when he is rich or poor, when he is in comfort or difficulty, when he is happy or sad, but only because he believes in Allâh's divine Preordainment and Wisdom, for Allâh Almighty says:

﴿وَعَسَىٰٓ أَن تَكْرَهُوا۟ شَيْئًا وَهُوَ خَيْرٌ لَّكُمْ ۖ وَعَسَىٰٓ أَن تُحِبُّوا۟ شَيْئًا وَهُوَ شَرٌّ لَّكُمْ ۗ وَٱللَّهُ يَعْلَمُ وَأَنتُمْ لَا تَعْلَمُونَ ۝٢١٦﴾

And it may be that you dislike a thing which is good for you and that you like a thing which is bad for you. Allâh knows but you do not know.[2]

Imam Muslim recorded that Suhaib, may Allâh be pleased with him, narrated that the Prophet ﷺ said:

«عَجَبًا لِأَمْرِ الْمُؤْمِنِ إِنَّ أَمْرَهُ كُلَّهُ خَيْرٌ، وَلَيْسَ ذَاكَ لِأَحَدٍ إِلَّا لِلْمُؤْمِنِ، إِنْ أَصَابَتْهُ سَرَّاءُ شَكَرَ، فَكَانَ خَيْرًا لَهُ، وَإِنْ أَصَابَتْهُ ضَرَّاءُ صَبَرَ فَكَانَ خَيْرًا لَهُ»

---

[1] (*Al-An'am* 6:122)

[2] (*Al-Baqarah* 2:216)

Wonderful is the affair of the believer, for his affair in its entirety is good, and that is for no one except the believer. If a good thing befalls him, he is thankful, and that is good for him; if a harmful thing befalls him, he is patient, and that is good for him.

The believer who has these qualities feels tranquility in his heart and calmness in his limbs and soul; those qualities fill his life with happiness and peace, and thus he becomes serene with Allâh's mercy and justice, serene because Allâh is his sanctuary that he seeks refuge in.

3) With *Iman*, souls are purified and cleansed; this means that faith purifies souls from false beliefs and delusions, thus making the soul pure by what it believes in. When souls truly believe and feel that Allâh created them and that He guarantees their provision, the chains are broken that make one fear and hope from creation, regardless of whether it is a real man that one fears or an illusion in the mind. Therefore one ceases to believe that planets, stars, trees, rocks, graves, or the dead can cause harm or bring benefit. One then clings to the truth, leaving all else. When many people have such faith, they will become united in their goal and objective, and they will no longer have motives to compete or fight with other members of that group.

4) Strength and honor abound when people believe that this world is a planting-ground for the Hereafter, as Allâh Almighty says:

$$﴿وَأَقِيمُوا۟ ٱلصَّلَوٰةَ وَءَاتُوا۟ ٱلزَّكَوٰةَ ۚ وَمَا تُقَدِّمُوا۟ لِأَنفُسِكُم مِّنْ خَيْرٍ تَجِدُوهُ عِندَ ٱللَّهِ ۗ إِنَّ ٱللَّهَ بِمَا تَعْمَلُونَ بَصِيرٌ ۝﴾$$

And perform *As-Salat* and give *Zakat*, and whatever of good you send forth for yourselves before you, you shall find it with Allâh. Certainly, Allâh is All-Seer of what you do.[1]

And Allâh Almighty says:

$$﴿فَمَن يَعْمَلْ مِثْقَالَ ذَرَّةٍ خَيْرًا يَرَهُ ۝ وَمَن يَعْمَلْ مِثْقَالَ ذَرَّةٍ شَرًّا يَرَهُ ۝﴾$$

---

[1] (*Al-Baqarah* 2:110)

So whosoever does good equal to the weight of an atom (or a small ant), shall see it. And whosoever does evil equal to the weight of an atom (or a small ant) shall see it.[1]

One who has true *Iman* believes that whatever he missed out on in life was not meant for him and that whatever he did achieve was meant for him all along. With such a belief, one has no reason to fear, and so one stays away from humiliating or debasing himself. When we understand the points just mentioned, we should plainly see how the Muslim nation advanced as prodigiously as it did at the hands of the Messenger of Allâh ﷺ and his Companions, may Allâh be pleased with them. The strength and power of all of the earth cannot stand before those whose hearts are filled with faith, those who are righteous because they know that Allâh is aware of all of their deeds, those whose goal is the Hereafter; just as we should appreciate how individual Prophets stood, challenging their people, without worrying about their great numbers and power. Two wonderful examples of the great power of faith are Ibrahim and Hud, may peace and blessings be upon them.

5) When one believes in a life after this life, and when one believes that he will be rewarded for his deeds, he will feel that his life has a noble purpose, a feeling that will urge him on in performing good deeds, in having good manners, and in staying away from sins. His goal is to develop himself into a noble individual, his community into a prosperous society, and his people into a productive nation.

6) When one has a correct belief in Allâh's divine Preordainment, a belief that includes knowledge in causes and their effects, one will strive and work hard in his life; moreover, one will realize the many virtues of good works. One will also appreciate that when Allâh grants guidance and success to one of His worshippers, that worshipper will take all the appropriate steps to reach his goal, without allowing hopelessness to find a way into his heart when he misses out on something, and without allowing pride or haughtiness to find a way into his heart if he achieves something in this world. For Allâh Almighty says:

---

[1] (*Az-Zalzalah* 99:7,8)

﴿مَآ أَصَابَ مِن مُّصِيبَةٍ فِي ٱلْأَرْضِ وَلَا فِيٓ أَنفُسِكُمْ إِلَّا فِي كِتَٰبٍ مِّن قَبْلِ أَن نَّبْرَأَهَآ إِنَّ ذَٰلِكَ عَلَى ٱللَّهِ يَسِيرٌ ۝ لِّكَيْلَا تَأْسَوْا۟ عَلَىٰ مَا فَاتَكُمْ وَلَا تَفْرَحُوا۟ بِمَآ ءَاتَىٰكُمْ وَٱللَّهُ لَا يُحِبُّ كُلَّ مُخْتَالٍ فَخُورٍ ۝﴾

No calamity befalls on the earth or in yourselves but it is inscribed in the Book of Decrees (*Al-Lawh Al-Mahfuz*), before We bring it into existence. Verily, that is easy for Allâh. In order that you may not be sad over matters that you fail to get, nor rejoice because of that which has been given to you. And Allâh likes not prideful boasters.[1]

---

[1] (*Al-Hadid* 57:22,23)

Lesson Four

The Categories Of *Tawhid* And *Shirk*

There are three categories of *Tawhid*:

1) *Tawhid Ar-Rububiyyah* (Lordship)
2) *Tawhid Al-Uluhiyyah* (Godhood)
3) *Tawhid Al-Asma' was-Sifat* (Names and Attributes)

Tawhid Ar-Rububiyyah: The belief that Allâh is the Creator, Ruler, and Sustainer of all things, and that He has no partners in those matters.

Tawhid Al-Uluhiyyah: The belief that Allâh is the only One Who truly deserves to be worshipped and that He has no partner in that regard. And that is the meaning of *Laa Ilaha Illallâh*, or "None has the right to be worshipped but Allâh." All acts of worship — such as prayer and fasting — must be performed sincerely for Allâh alone; it is not permissible to direct even a portion of that worship to other than Him.

Tawhid Al-Asma' was-Sifat: The belief that all that has been related in the Noble Qur'an or in the authentic Sunnah regarding Allâh's Names and Attributes must be established and affirmed for Allâh alone, in a manner that is suitable to Him — how perfect He is — without changing their meaning or ignoring them completely or twisting the meanings or giving resemblance to any of the created things. Allâh Almighty says:

﴿قُلْ هُوَ ٱللَّهُ أَحَدٌ ۝ ٱللَّهُ ٱلصَّمَدُ ۝ لَمْ يَلِدْ وَلَمْ يُولَدْ ۝ وَلَمْ يَكُن لَّهُ كُفُوًا أَحَدٌ ۝﴾

Say: "He is Allâh, (the) One, *Allâhus-Samad* (Allâh — the Self-Sufficient Master, Whom all creatures need, He neither eats nor drinks). He begets not, nor was He begotten. And there is none coequal or comparable unto Him.[1]

And He Almighty says:

$$﴿لَيْسَ كَمِثْلِهِۦ شَىْءٌۖ وَهُوَ ٱلسَّمِيعُ ٱلْبَصِيرُ ۝﴾$$

There is nothing like unto Him, and He is the All-Hearer, the All-Seer.[2]

Some of the people of knowledge hold that there are two categories of *Tawhid*, simply because they have included the third category (Names and Attributes) under the first one (*Rububiyyah*). There is no real difference in the two ways of classifying, because the goal of explaining *Tawhid* is achieved either way.

The Classification of *Tawhid*

Tawhid is a crucial topic because it is the foundation of our religion and the basis for which all of the Messengers, peace be upon them, were sent, from the first of them to the last. This topic is also so important because people who go astray or are destroyed only suffer those consequences because they turn away from this foundation, because they are ignorant of it, because they act contrary to its implications.

The polytheists of old were ignorant regarding the aspect of *Tawhid* which required them to worship Allâh alone, without associating partners with Him — and it was because of that aspect that the Messengers were sent, the Books were revealed, and jinns and humans were created.

They thought that their religion of *Shirk* was correct, and that through it, they were getting closer to Allâh Almighty. In reality, however, they were perpetrating the greatest crime and sin. But because of their ignorance, their turning away, and their blind following of their fathers and ancestors, they thought their religion

---

[1] (*Al-Ikhlas* 112:1-4)

[2] (*Ash-Shura* 42:11)

was true, they rejected the Prophets, and they fought them. Allâh Almighty says:

﴿ إِنَّهُمُ ٱتَّخَذُواْ ٱلشَّيَـٰطِينَ أَوْلِيَآءَ مِن دُونِ ٱللَّهِ وَيَحْسَبُونَ أَنَّهُم مُّهْتَدُونَ ۝ ﴾

Surely they took the *Shayatin* (devils) as *Awliya'* (protectors and helpers) instead of Allâh, and consider that they are guided.[1]

The first people who went astray and believed in *Shirk* were the people of Nuh, peace be upon him; they were the first nation to believe in *Shirk*, while those after them followed them. What led them to *Shirk* was exaggeration in venerating righteous people: Wad, Suwa', Yaghuth, Ya'uq, and Nasr. These were all righteous men who died and whose people were very sad to have lost them. The *Shaitan* embellished the idea of exaggerating in veneration for those righteous men. This lead them to make images and erect statues of them at their gathering places. They reasoned that people would look at the statues of the righteous men and follow in their way; however, rather than following in their way, they were ruined, and so were those who came after them. As time passed, people forgot the initial reason why the statues were made, and they began to worship them. Some of our pious predecessors said, "When these people (who built the statues) were destroyed, those came after them who worshipped the statues, and so Allâh revealed this verse regarding them:

﴿ وَقَالُواْ لَا تَذَرُنَّ ءَالِهَتَكُمْ وَلَا تَذَرُنَّ وَدًّا وَلَا سُوَاعًا وَلَا يَغُوثَ وَيَعُوقَ وَنَسْرًا ۝ وَقَدْ أَضَلُّواْ كَثِيرًا وَلَا تَزِدِ ٱلظَّـٰلِمِينَ إِلَّا ضَلَـٰلًا ۝ مِّمَّا خَطِيَـٰٔتِهِمْ أُغْرِقُواْ فَأُدْخِلُواْ نَارًا فَلَمْ يَجِدُواْ لَهُم مِّن دُونِ ٱللَّهِ أَنصَارًا ۝ ﴾

And they have said: "You shall not leave your gods, nor shall you leave Wadd, nor Suwa', nor Yaghuth, nor Ya'uq, nor Nasr." And indeed they have led many astray. And (O Allâh): "Grant no increase to the wrongdoers except in error." Because of their sins they were drowned, then they were made to enter the Fire, and they found none to help them instead of Allâh.[2]

[1] (*Al-A'raf* 7:30)
[2] (*Nuh* 71:23-25)

Exaggeration regarding the status of angels, Prophets, righteous men, jinns, or statues is the basis of the evil of *Shirk*. At the hands of the Messengers, peace be upon them, Allâh clarified to mankind that it is obligatory to worship Him alone, that He is the true God, and that it is forbidden to take intermediaries between Him and His creatures; rather, we must worship Him directly without any intermediary. This is the message the Messengers were sent to deliver, and for which the Books were revealed, and for which creation was created. Allâh Almighty says:

﴿وَمَا خَلَقْتُ ٱلْجِنَّ وَٱلْإِنسَ إِلَّا لِيَعْبُدُونِ ۝﴾

And I created not the jinns and humans except they should worship Me (Alone).[1]

﴿يَـٰٓأَيُّهَا ٱلنَّاسُ ٱعْبُدُواْ رَبَّكُمُ ٱلَّذِى خَلَقَكُمْ وَٱلَّذِينَ مِن قَبْلِكُمْ﴾

O mankind! Worship your Lord, Who created you and those who were before you.[2]

Tawhid is an issue that at all times and on all occasions requires much attention, especially when we are calling others to the religion of Allâh and to worship Him alone, and especially considering that *Shirk* is the greatest sin, a sin that most people of the past and present are guilty of. Therefore, Muslims must strive to call others to the way of *Tawhid* and warn them about *Shirk* and its different categories, so that people may be wary of it. The last Prophet, Muhammad ﷺ, delivered that message completely, both in Makkah and in Al-Madinah.

When calling others to Islam, the people of knowledge must give *Tawhid* priority over all else because it is the foundation: if it is spoiled in any way by *Shirk*, all other deeds are nullified.

﴿وَلَوْ أَشْرَكُواْ لَحَبِطَ عَنْهُم مَّا كَانُواْ يَعْمَلُونَ ۝﴾

But if they had joined in worship others with Allâh, all that they used to do would have been of no benefit to them.[3]

---

[1] (*Ath-Thariyat* 51:56)

[2] (*Al-Baqarah* 2:21)

[3] (*Al-An'am* 6:88)

The Definition Of *Tawhid*

It is to single out Allâh with *Ar-Rububiyyah* (Lordship), *Al-Uluhiyyah* (Godhood), and *Al-Asma' was-Sifat* (Names and Attributes). To believe that He is One in His Self and in His Attributes, that He is One in His Sovereignty and in His actions. Indeed, He is One in His Self, in His Names, and in His Attributes; there is none that is coequal, comparable, or similar to Him.

﴿لَيْسَ كَمِثْلِهِ شَيْءٌ وَهُوَ ٱلسَّمِيعُ ٱلْبَصِيرُ ۝﴾

There is nothing like Him, and He is the All-Hearer, the All-Seer.[1]

He is One in His kingdom and actions; as Creator, Planner, and Sustainer of all that exists, He has no partner:

﴿قُلِ ٱللَّهُمَّ مَٰلِكَ ٱلْمُلْكِ تُؤْتِى ٱلْمُلْكَ مَن تَشَآءُ وَتَنزِعُ ٱلْمُلْكَ مِمَّن تَشَآءُ﴾

Say: "O Allâh! Possessor of the kingdom, You give the kingdom to whom You will, and You take the kingdom from whom You will."[2]

As the One Who deserves worship alone, He is One, for there is none that deserves worship but Him. Allâh Almighty says:

﴿قُلْ إِنِّىٓ أُمِرْتُ أَنْ أَعْبُدَ ٱللَّهَ مُخْلِصًا لَّهُ ٱلدِّينَ ۝﴾

Say: "Verily, I am commanded to worship Allâh, making all religion purely for Him."[3]

The Virtue Of *Tawhid*

It is a great virtue to have belief in *Tawhid*; indeed, Allâh made that belief to be a saving ship for His worshippers in this life and in the Hereafter.

As for this life — when one is from the people of *Tawhid*, living his life according to its implications, and not associating any partners with Allâh whatsoever, Allâh will shower him with safety, peace, guidance, and a good life, for He says:

---

[1] (*Ash-Shura* 42:11)

[2] (*Aal 'Imran* 3:26)

[3] (*Az-Zumar* 39:11)

﴿ٱلَّذِينَ ءَامَنُواْ وَلَمْ يَلْبِسُوٓاْ إِيمَٰنَهُم بِظُلْمٍ أُوْلَٰٓئِكَ لَهُمُ ٱلْأَمْنُ وَهُم مُّهْتَدُونَ ٨٢﴾

It is those who believe and confuse not their belief with wrong, for them (only) there is security and they are the guided.[1]

"Wrong" here means to mix one's faith with *Shirk*. When one avoids that wrong, one will have achieved security and guidance. Allâh Almighty says:

﴿مَنْ عَمِلَ صَٰلِحًا مِّن ذَكَرٍ أَوْ أُنثَىٰ وَهُوَ مُؤْمِنٌ فَلَنُحْيِيَنَّهُ حَيَوٰةً طَيِّبَةً﴾

Whoever works righteousness, whether male or female, while he (or she) is a true believer verily, to him We will give a good life.[2]

As for the Hereafter — when one dies upon *Tawhid* and meets his Lord, not associating any partners with Him, He enters Paradise and Allâh Almighty saves him from the Hellfire. In an authentic *Hadith*, in the Two *Sahihs* it is recorded that the Prophet ﷺ said:

«إِنَّ اللهَ حَرَّمَ عَلَى النَّارِ مَنْ قَالَ لَا إِلَهَ إِلَّا اللهُ يَبْتَغِي بِذَلِكَ وَجْهَ اللهِ»

Indeed, Allâh has forbidden upon the Fire he who says, 'None has the right to be worshipped but Allâh,' seeking from that Allâh's Face.

The Shaikh mentioned that "there are three categories of *Tawhid*," a fact that the scholars derived through studying and contemplating verses of the Qur'an, the sayings of the Prophet ﷺ, and the situation of the polytheists.

Of the three categories, the polytheists acknowledged two and rejected one, the one around which they disputed with the Messengers, fought with them, and showed enmity and hatred toward them, a fact that one appreciates when he reflects on the Qur'an, the life of the Prophet ﷺ, and the history of all Messengers, peace be upon them.

Some have added a fourth category, called *Tawhid Al-Mutaba'ah* (Following) meaning that it is obligatory to follow the Messenger of Allâh ﷺ and adhere to the *Shari'ah*. None is followed other than the

---

[1] (*Al-An'am* 6:82)

[2] (*An-Nahl* 16:97)

Prophet ﷺ, for he is the greater Imam that is always followed. It is not permissible, therefore, to go outside of the boundaries of his *Shari'ah*, for the *Shari'ah* is one and its Imam is one. Every jinn and man must follow and submit to his *Shari'ah* and they must follow his way in *Tawhid*. Though this fourth category is understood, it really falls under the category called *Tawhid Al-Uluhiyyah*, for the Lord ordered His worshippers to follow the Book and the Sunnah, and following the Sunnnah is *Tawhid Al-Mutaba'ah* Muslim scholars agree that it is obligatory to follow the way of the Messenger of Allâh ﷺ and that no one is excused from following that way.

Then the Shaikh mentioned the three categories:

1) *Tawhid Ar-Rububiyyah*

2) *Tawhid Al-Uluhiyyah*

3) *Tawhid Al-Asma' was-Sifat*

1. *Tawhid Ar-Rububiyyah*

What this means to single out regarding His actions. For example, creating, providing, giving life, causing death, sending down rain, causing crops to grow. The monotheistic Muslim believes that Allâh is the Creator, the Provider, the One Who brings benefit, and the Only One Who can harm, the One Who brings to life, the One Who causes death, the King of the entire dominion — in His Hands are the reins of the heavens and the earth.

The polytheists believed in this category of *Tawhid*, for Allâh Almighty says about them:

$$﴿قُلْ مَن يَرْزُقُكُم مِّنَ ٱلسَّمَآءِ وَٱلْأَرْضِ أَمَّن يَمْلِكُ ٱلسَّمْعَ وَٱلْأَبْصَٰرَ وَمَن يُخْرِجُ ٱلْحَىَّ مِنَ ٱلْمَيِّتِ وَيُخْرِجُ ٱلْمَيِّتَ مِنَ ٱلْحَىِّ وَمَن يُدَبِّرُ ٱلْأَمْرَ فَسَيَقُولُونَ ٱللَّهُ فَقُلْ أَفَلَا تَتَّقُونَ ﴾ (٣١)$$

Say: "Who provides for you from the sky and the earth? Or who owns hearing and sight? And who brings out the living from the dead and brings out the dead from the living? And who disposes the affairs?" They will say: "Allâh." Say: "Will you not then be afraid of Allâh's punishment?"[1]

---

[1] (*Yunus* 10:31)

2. *Tawhid Al-Uluhiyyah*

This means to single out Allâh with those actions that His worshippers perform as a form of worship — in ways that Allâh and His Messenger ﷺ have legislated. It means to believe that Allâh alone is the One Who deserves to be worshipped and obeyed, and that there is none that deserves to be worshipped other than Him. Therefore, all acts of worship must be performed purely for Him. So when one prays, he must pray only to Allâh; when one supplicates, he must supplicate only to Him. When one slaughters an animal, it must be done by Allâh's Name only. When one makes a vow, one must do it only for Allâh. When one seeks help, one must seek it from Allâh in those matters that only Allâh is capable of. When one calls out for help, one must call out for help from Allâh — in those matters that only Allâh is capable of.

To believe and apply *Tawhid* in this sense requires one to:
- Worship none except Allâh
- Fear none except Allâh
- Submit to none except Allâh
- Seek refuge in none except Allâh
- Seek help from none except Allâh
- Rely upon none except in Allâh
- Seek judgement from none except Allâh's *Shari'ah*
- To not make lawful except that which Allâh has allowed
- To not make forbidden except that which Allâh has prohibited

It is confirmed that 'Adi bin Hatim — who was a Christian in the Days of Ignorance — heard the Prophet ﷺ recite this verse:

﴿ٱتَّخَذُوٓاْ أَحْبَارَهُمْ وَرُهْبَـٰنَهُمْ أَرْبَابًا مِّن دُونِ ٱللَّهِ وَٱلْمَسِيحَ ٱبْنَ مَرْيَمَ﴾

They (Jews and Christians) took their rabbis and their monks to be their lords besides Allâh, and the Messiah, son of Maryam.[1]

'Adi said, "O Messenger of Allâh, they did not worship them." The Messenger of Allâh ﷺ said:

---
[1] (*At-Tawbah* 9:31)

«بَلَى إِنَّهُمْ حَرَّمُوا عَلَيْهِمُ الْحَلَالَ، وَأَحَلُّوا لَهُمُ الْحَرَامَ، فَاتَّبَعُوهُمْ. فَذَلِكَ عِبَادَتُهُمْ إِيَّاهُمْ»

"Indeed, they (the rabbis and monks) would forbid them from that which was lawful, and they would permit them to do that which was forbidden. They followed them: that was their worship of them."

The *Tawhid* With Which The Messengers Were Sent

Tawhid Al-Uluhiyyah is the *Tawhid* that the Messengers invited people to accept, and it is that category of *Tawhid* that people rejected, from the time of Nuh, peace be upon him, until that of Muhammad ﷺ. Allâh Almighty says:

﴿وَمَا أَرْسَلْنَا مِن قَبْلِكَ مِن رَّسُولٍ إِلَّا نُوحِي إِلَيْهِ أَنَّهُ لَا إِلَهَ إِلَّا أَنَا فَاعْبُدُونِ﴾

And We did not send any Messenger before you but We inspired him (saying): "*Laa Ilaha Illa Ana* [none has the right to be worshipped but I], so worship Me."[1]

And Allâh Almighty says:

﴿وَلَقَدْ بَعَثْنَا فِي كُلِّ أُمَّةٍ رَّسُولًا أَنِ اعْبُدُوا اللَّهَ وَاجْتَنِبُوا الطَّاغُوتَ﴾

And verily, We have sent among every *Ummah* (community, nation) a Messenger (proclaiming): "Worship Allâh, and avoid the *Taghut* (all false deities)..."[2]

Whosoever worships Allâh alone, leaving the worship of all else, has indeed followed the straight path, and has grasped the most trustworthy handhold:

﴿فَمَن يَكْفُرْ بِالطَّاغُوتِ وَيُؤْمِنۢ بِاللَّهِ فَقَدِ اسْتَمْسَكَ بِالْعُرْوَةِ الْوُثْقَىٰ لَا انفِصَامَ لَهَا﴾

Whoever disbelieves in *Taghut* and believes in Allâh, then he has grasped the most trustworthy handhold that will never break. [3]

﴿لَا تَتَّخِذُوٓا إِلَٰهَيْنِ اثْنَيْنِ إِنَّمَا هُوَ إِلَٰهٌ وَٰحِدٌ فَإِيَّٰىَ فَارْهَبُونِ ۝٥١﴾

---

[1] (*Al-Anbiya'* 21:25)

[2] (*An-Nahl* 16:36)

[3] (*Al-Baqarah* 2:256)

And Allâh said: "Take not *ilahain* (two gods in worship, etc.). Verily, He is only One *Ilah* (God). Then, fear Me much."[1]

The polytheists among the Arabs acknowledged that Allâh created all things, while their gods neither created, nor provided, nor brought things to life, nor caused death; Allâh Almighty says:

$$ ﴿وَلَئِن سَأَلْتَهُم مَّنْ خَلَقَ ٱلسَّمَوَٰتِ وَٱلْأَرْضَ لَيَقُولُنَّ خَلَقَهُنَّ ٱلْعَزِيزُ ٱلْعَلِيمُ ۝﴾ $$

And indeed if you ask them, "Who has created the heavens and the earth?" They will surely say: "The All-Mighty, the All-Knower created them."[2]

Nevertheless, they were polytheists because they worshipped other gods along with Allâh, gods that in their estimation were intermediaries between them and Allâh. So, because they rejected *Tawhid Al-Uluhiyyah*, their belief in *Tawhid Ar-Rububiyyah* didn't benefit them at all:

$$ ﴿وَمَا يُؤْمِنُ أَكْثَرُهُم بِٱللَّهِ إِلَّا وَهُم مُّشْرِكُونَ ۝﴾ $$

And most of them believe not in Allâh except that they attribute partners unto Him.[3]

They didn't single Allâh out for worship, supplication and seeking help; rather, they associated partners with Him in their worship:

$$ ﴿مَا نَعْبُدُهُمْ إِلَّا لِيُقَرِّبُونَا إِلَى ٱللَّهِ زُلْفَىٰٓ﴾ $$

"We worship them only that they may bring us near to Allâh."[4]

$$ ﴿هَٰٓؤُلَآءِ شُفَعَٰٓؤُنَا عِندَ ٱللَّهِ﴾ $$

"These are our intercessors with Allâh."[5]

So again, it becomes clear that although one may believe in *Tawhid Ar-Rububiyyah*, one is a polytheist, not a Muslim, as long as one doesn't believe in *Tawhid Al-Uluhiyyah*.

---

[1] (*An-Nahl* 16:51)

[2] (*Az-Zukhruf* 43:9)

[3] (*Yusuf* 12:106)

[4] (*Az-Zumar* 39:3)

[5] (*Yunus* 10:18)

Who Is Allâh?

Indeed Allâh is the One True God: He has no partner and there is no one who is equal or similar to Him, not similar to His Self, to His Attributes, or to His actions. With this belief, we are different from those who ascribe a wife or a child to Allâh:

﴿قُلْ هُوَ ٱللَّهُ أَحَدٌ ۝ ٱللَّهُ ٱلصَّمَدُ ۝ لَمْ يَلِدْ وَلَمْ يُولَدْ ۝ وَلَمْ يَكُن لَّهُۥ كُفُوًا أَحَدٌ ۝﴾

Say: "He is Allâh, (the) One, *Allâhus-Samad* (Allah — the Self-Sufficient Master, Whom all creatures need, He neither eats nor drinks). He begets not, nor was He begotten, And there is none coequal or comparable unto Him.[1]

With our belief that is explained above, we are different from those who claim that Allâh is the third of three — far, far is Allâh above the evil they ascribe to Him:

﴿لَّقَدْ كَفَرَ ٱلَّذِينَ قَالُوٓاْ إِنَّ ٱللَّهَ ثَالِثُ ثَلَٰثَةٍ وَمَا مِنْ إِلَٰهٍ إِلَّآ إِلَٰهٌ وَٰحِدٌ﴾

Surely, disbelievers are those who said: "Allâh is the third of the three." But there is no *ilah* (god) (none who has the right to be worshipped) but One *Ilah* (God — Allâh)[2]

﴿وَإِلَٰهُكُمْ إِلَٰهٌ وَٰحِدٌ لَّآ إِلَٰهَ إِلَّا هُوَ ٱلرَّحْمَٰنُ ٱلرَّحِيمُ ۝﴾

And your *Ilah* (God) is One *Ilah* (God — Allâh), *La Ilaha Illa Huwa* (there is none who has the right to be worshipped but He), the Most Beneficent, the Most Merciful.[3]

And with that same belief, we are opposite of those who believe that a god other than Allâh has any power in the universe:

﴿لَوْ كَانَ فِيهِمَآ ءَالِهَةٌ إِلَّا ٱللَّهُ لَفَسَدَتَا فَسُبْحَٰنَ ٱللَّهِ رَبِّ ٱلْعَرْشِ عَمَّا يَصِفُونَ ۝﴾

Had there been therein (in the heavens and the earth) gods besides Allâh, then verily both would have been ruined. Glorified be Allâh, the Lord of the Throne, (High is He) above what they attribute to Him![4]

---

[1] (*Al-Ikhlas* 112:1-4)

[2] (*Al-Ma'idah* 5:73)

[3] (*Al-Baqarah* 2:163)

[4] (*Al-Anbiya'* 21:22)

3. *Tawhid Al-Asma' was-Sifat* (Names and Attributes)

Under this category, we affirm for Allâh all that He affirmed about Himself and all that His Messenger Muhammad ﷺ affirmed about Him — all of His Beautiful Names, and all of the Attributes that those Names indicate, without resembling them to the attributes of creatures, without comparisons, without distortions and without denying those attributes. Allâh Almighty has Names and Attributes that indicate His Perfection and Greatness, and no one is similar to Him in those Names and Attributes.

Allâh's Names and Attributes are mentioned in the Qur'an and in the authentic Sunnah of the Prophet ﷺ, and we must believe that they are real, for Allâh said:

$$﴿لَيْسَ كَمِثْلِهِ شَيْءٌ وَهُوَ السَّمِيعُ الْبَصِيرُ ١١﴾$$

There is nothing like Him, and He is the All-Hearer, the All-Seer.[1]

Examples Of Allâh's Names And Attributes

1) Some Of His Names: Ar-Rahman, Ar-Rahim, Al-Qahir, Al-Qadir, As-Sami', Al-Basir, Al-Quddus.

2) Some Of His Attributes: Highness, Hearing, Seeing, Ability, that He has a Face and Hand, and that He descends (during the last-third of every night).

After explaining the different categories of *Tawhid*, we can now explain the objective of sending the Messengers and the wisdom of their Messages.

The Messengers

Allâh sent the Messengers to the people to call them to His religion, to worship Him alone — without associating partners with Him, and to avoid the worship of others. The first Messenger was Nuh and the last one was Muhammad ﷺ.

The Wisdom Behind Sending The Messengers

Allâh sent them as a proof upon mankind, to convey the message of the religion to the people, to give glad tidings of Paradise and of a

---

[1] (*Ash-Shura* 42:11)

great reward to the obedient one, and to warn the disobedient one of a severe punishment and the Hellfire. Allâh Almighty says:

﴿رُّسُلًا مُّبَشِّرِينَ وَمُنذِرِينَ لِئَلَّا يَكُونَ لِلنَّاسِ عَلَى ٱللَّهِ حُجَّةٌۢ بَعْدَ ٱلرُّسُلِ﴾

Messengers as bearers of good news as well as of warning in order that mankind should have no plea against Allâh after the Messengers.[1]

There are three different kinds of *Shirk*:

1) The Greater *Shirk*
2) The Lesser *Shirk*
3) The Hidden *Shirk*

The Greater *Shirk*:

For the one who dies upon it, the Greater *Shirk* results in the nullification of deeds and eternity in the Hellfire. Allâh Almighty says:

﴿وَلَوْ أَشْرَكُوا۟ لَحَبِطَ عَنْهُم مَّا كَانُوا۟ يَعْمَلُونَ ٨٨﴾

But if they had joined in worship others with Allâh, all that they used to do would have been of no benefit to them.[2]

And Allâh Almighty says:

﴿مَا كَانَ لِلْمُشْرِكِينَ أَن يَعْمُرُوا۟ مَسَٰجِدَ ٱللَّهِ شَٰهِدِينَ عَلَىٰٓ أَنفُسِهِم بِٱلْكُفْرِ أُو۟لَٰٓئِكَ حَبِطَتْ أَعْمَٰلُهُمْ وَفِى ٱلنَّارِ هُمْ خَٰلِدُونَ ١٧﴾

It is not for the polytheists to maintain the *Masjids* of Allâh while they witness against their own selves of disbelief. The works of such are in vain and in Fire shall they abide.[3]

Whoever dies upon the Greater *Shirk* will not be forgiven, and Paradise will be forbidden for him, as Allâh Almighty

[1] (*An-Nisa'* 4:165)

[2] (*Al-An'am* 6:88)

[3] (*At-Tawbah* 9:17)

says:

﴿إِنَّ اللَّهَ لَا يَغْفِرُ أَن يُشْرَكَ بِهِ وَيَغْفِرُ مَا دُونَ ذَٰلِكَ لِمَن يَشَآءُ﴾

Verily, Allâh forgives not that partners should be set up with him in worship, but He forgives except that (anything else) to whom He pleases.[1]

And Allâh Almighty says:

﴿إِنَّهُ مَن يُشْرِكْ بِاللَّهِ فَقَدْ حَرَّمَ اللَّهُ عَلَيْهِ ٱلْجَنَّةَ وَمَأْوَىٰهُ ٱلنَّارُ وَمَا لِلظَّٰلِمِينَ مِنْ أَنصَارٍ ٧٢﴾

Verily, whosoever sets up partners in worship with Allâh, then Allâh has forbidden Paradise for him, and the Fire will be his abode. And for the wrongdoers there are no helpers.[2]

Here are some of the forms of the Greater *Shirk*:

i)   Supplicating to the dead
ii) Praying or supplicating to idols
iii) Seeking help from idols or the dead
iv) Making an oath by an idol or a dead person
v)   Slaughtering an animal for an idol or a dead person

The Lesser *Shirk*:

It is that which is called *Shirk* in either the Qur'an or the Sunnah, but which is not from the category of the Greater *Shirk*. For example doing certain deeds for show-off, swearing by other than Allâh, saying, 'Whatever Allâh wills and whatever so-and-so wills,' and so on. The Prophet ﷺ said:

«أَخْوَفُ مَا أَخَافُ عَلَيْكُمُ الشِّرْكُ الأَصْغَرُ»

What I fear most for you is the Lesser *Shirk*.

When asked what it was, he ﷺ said:

«الرِّيَاءُ»

---

[1] (*An-Nisa'* 4:48)
[2] (*Al-Ma'idah* 5:72)

Riya' (showing off).

It was recorded by Imam Ahmad, At-Tabarani, and Al-Bayhaqi from Mahmud bin Lubayd Al-Ansari, may Allâh be pleased with him, with a good chain of narration. It was also recorded by At-Tabarani with a good chain, from Mahmud bin Lubayd from Rafi' bin Khadij from the Prophet ﷺ.

The Prophet ﷺ said:

«مَنْ حَلَفَ بِشَيْءٍ دُونَ اللهِ فَقَدْ أَشْرَكَ»

Whoever swears by anything other than Allâh has committed *Shirk*.

It was recorded by Imam Ahmad with an authentic chain, from 'Umar bin Al-Khattab, may Allâh be pleased with him.

Abu Dawud and At-Tirmithi recorded an authentic chain from a narration of Ibn 'Umar, may Allâh be pleased with them, from the Prophet ﷺ that he said:

«مَنْ حَلَفَ بِغَيْرِ اللهِ فَقَدْ كَفَرَ أَوْ أَشْرَكَ»

Whoever swears by other than Allâh has indeed disbelieved or committed *Shirk*.

And the Prophet ﷺ said:

«لَا تَقُولُوا: مَاشَاءَ اللهُ وَشَاءَ فُلَانٌ، وَلَكِنْ قُولُوا: مَاشَاءَ اللهُ ثُمَّ شَاءَ فُلَانٌ»

Do not say, "What Allâh wills and what so and so wills." Rather, say, "What Allâh wills, and then what so and so wills."

It was recorded by Abu Dawud with an authentic chain of narration from Huthaifah bin Al-Yaman, may Allâh be pleased with him.

Though this category does not mean that one has left the religion, or that one will spend eternity in the Hellfire, it does mean that one is lacking in the obligatory complete level of *Tawhid*.

The Hidden *Shirk*:

This third category is indicated by the following saying of the Prophet ﷺ:

«أَلَا أُخْبِرُكُمْ بِمَا هُوَ أَخْوَفُ عَلَيْكُمْ عِنْدِي مِنَ الْمَسِيحِ الدَّجَّالِ؟»

"Shall I not inform you of what I fear more for you than the Masih Ad-Dajjal?"

His Companions said, "Yes, O Messenger of Allâh." He ﷺ said:

«الشِّرْكُ الْخَفِيُّ، يَقُومُ الرَّجُلُ فَيُصَلِّي فَيُزَيِّنُ صَلَاتَهُ لِمَا يَرَى مِنْ نَظَرِ الرَّجُلِ إِلَيْهِ»

"Hidden *Shirk*: a man stands to pray and adorns his prayer because he sees another man watching him."

It was recorded by Imam Ahmad in his *Musnad* from Abu Sa'id Al-Khudri, may Allâh be pleased with him.

It is also possible to divide *Shirk* into two categories only, the Greater, and the Lesser.

As for Hidden *Shirk*, it is general in both, because it sometimes occurs in the Greater *Shirk*, such as the *Shirk* of the hypocrites — they hide their false beliefs, showing belief in Islam. This is because they want to show off to others and they are afraid for themselves.

Hidden *Shirk* also occurs in the Lesser *Shirk*, for instance in *Riya'* (doing deeds for show-off). Examples of when this happens can be found in the two above-mentioned *Ahadith*, one related by Muhammad bin Lubayd Al-Ansari, may Allâh be pleased with him, and the other by Abu Sa'id, may Allâh be pleased with him. And success is from Allâh.

Shirk And Its Kinds

1. The first kind of *Shirk* the Shaikh mentioned is the Greater *Shirk*, which means either to worship other than Allâh, or to make partners with Allâh in something that is specifically His. For example, to take someone as His partner in worship, obedience, love, fear, supplication, and seeking help.

When one associates partners with Allâh — regardless of who that partner is, such as a man, animal, plant, or inanimate object — one has perpetrated the Greater *Shirk*, examples of which are as follows:

- To supplicate to that partner as one supplicates to Allâh.

- To love that partner as one loves Allâh.

- To hope from that partner as one hopes from Allâh.

- To submit oneself in obedience to that partner as one submits in obedience to Allâh.

- To fear that partner as one fears Allâh.

- To seek someone's judgement instead of the judgement of Allâh's *Shari'ah*.

Allâh Almighty says:

$$﴿وَٱعْبُدُوا۟ ٱللَّهَ وَلَا تُشْرِكُوا۟ بِهِۦ شَيْـًٔا﴾$$

Worship Allâh and join none with Him in worship.[1]

Of course, the Greater *Shirk* is the worst and most severe kind of *Shirk*; indeed, it is the greatest sin with Allâh, for Allâh does not accept any deed from its perpetrator, regardless of how pious he may be otherwise. If one dies, associating partners with Allâh, Allâh will not forgive him, for He says:

$$﴿إِنَّ ٱللَّهَ لَا يَغْفِرُ أَن يُشْرَكَ بِهِۦ وَيَغْفِرُ مَا دُونَ ذَٰلِكَ لِمَن يَشَآءُ وَمَن يُشْرِكْ بِٱللَّهِ فَقَدِ ٱفْتَرَىٰ إِثْمًا عَظِيمًا ٤٨﴾$$

Verily, Allâh forgives not that partners should be set up with Him in worship, but He forgives except that (anything else) to whom He pleases, and whoever sets up partners with Allâh in worship, he has indeed invented a tremendous sin.[2]

---

[1] (*An-Nisa'* 4:36)

[2] (*An-Nisa'* 4:48)

Whoever dies upon this form of *Shirk* is from the dwellers of the Hellfire, for the Prophet ﷺ said:

«مَنْ مَاتَ وَهُوَ يَدْعُو مِنْ دُونِ اللهِ نِدًّا دَخَلَ النَّارَ»

Whoever dies and he is calling upon other than Allâh as a rival then he enters the Hellfire. (Recorded by Al-Bukhari and Muslim from Ibn Mas'ud)

In another *Hadith*, the Prophet ﷺ said,

«مَنْ لَقِيَ اللهَ لَا يُشْرِكُ بِهِ شَيْئاً دَخَلَ الْجَنَّةَ . وَ مَنْ لَقِيَهُ يُشْرِكُ بِهِ شَيْئاً دَخَلَ النَّارَ»

Whoever meets Allâh without associating any partner with Him enters Paradise. Whoever meets Him, associating any partner with Him enters the Hellfire. (Recorded by Muslim, from Jabir.)

The Muslim, therefore, worships and invokes only Allâh, and submits only to Him, for Allâh Almighty says:

﴿قُلْ إِنَّ صَلَاتِي وَنُسُكِي وَمَحْيَايَ وَمَمَاتِي لِلَّهِ رَبِّ ٱلْعَٰلَمِينَ ۝ لَا شَرِيكَ لَهُۥ وَبِذَٰلِكَ أُمِرْتُ وَأَنَا۠ أَوَّلُ ٱلْمُسْلِمِينَ ۝﴾

Say: "Verily, my *Salat* (prayer), my sacrifice, my living, and my dying are for Allâh, the Lord of all that exists. He has no partner. And of this I have been commanded, and I am the first of the Muslims."[1]

2. The second kind is the Lesser *Shirk*. It consists of various categories:

1) A little *Riya'* (doing good deeds for show-off); for example, when one prays, fasts, or gives charity, he is seeking other than Allâh's Face; hence, he is mixing good deeds with bad ones. The Prophet ﷺ said:

«أَخْوَفُ مَا أَخَافُ عَلَيْكُمُ الشِّرْكُ الأَصْغَرُ»

What I fear most for you is the lesser *Shirk*.

When asked about it, he ﷺ said,

---

[1] (*Al-An'am* 6:162,163)

«الرِّيَاءُ»

Riya'. (Recorded by Ahmad from Shaddad bin Aws.)

When one performs any good deed or act of worship to impress or please people, then he has committed *Riya'*, which is forbidden. In another *Hadith* related by Shaddad bin Aws, the Prophet ﷺ said:

«مَنْ صَلَّى يُرَائِي فَقَدْ أَشْرَكَ، وَمَنْ صَامَ يُرَائِي فَقَدْ أَشْرَكَ، وَمَنْ تَصَدَّقَ يُرَائِي فَقَدْ أَشْرَكَ»

Whoever prays, showing off to others, he has indeed committed *Shirk*. Whoever fasts, showing off to others, he has indeed committed *Shirk*. Whoever gives charity, showing off to others, he has indeed committed *Shirk*.

2) Another form of the Lesser *Shirk* is to swear by anyone other than Allâh, for instance, to swear by the Prophet ﷺ, by the Ka'bah, or by one's parents. In the Two *Sahihs* it is recorded that Ibn 'Umar narrated from the Prophet ﷺ:

«إِنَّ الله يَنْهَاكُمْ أَنْ تَحْلِفُوا بِآبَائِكُمْ. مَنْ كَانَ حَالِفاً فَلْيَحْلِفْ بِالله أَوْ لِيَصْمُتْ»

Indeed, Allâh has forbidden you from swearing by your fathers; whoever makes an oath, let him swear by Allâh or remain silent.

3) Another form of the Lesser *Shirk* is for one to say the following expressions:

- "What Allâh wills and what you will."
- "This is from Allâh and from you."
- "I am what I am because of Allâh and because of you."
- "I have no one except Allâh and you."
- "I place my trust upon Allâh and upon you."
- "Were it not for Allâh and you, such and such would (or wouldn't) have happened."

Based on one's intention when saying these phrases, such statements may even become a form of the Greater *Shirk*.

Protecting The Belief In *Tawhid*

The Prophet ﷺ strove hard to keep the belief in *Tawhid* clean and pure in the hearts of Muslims, making every effort to allow no doubt or *Shirk* to enter those hearts. He ﷺ taught his Companions to turn with their hearts to Allâh only, to seek help in Him alone, and to put their trust in Him alone. As soon as the Prophet ﷺ saw anything that might weaken the relationship between the Muslims and their Lord, that might damage the belief of *Tawhid* in their hearts, he ﷺ raced to warn the Muslims of the effect of that matter on their faith. Some examples of such matters are as follows:

1) Magic

Incantations, spells, or charms that are used to have an effect on hearts and bodies, intended to make them sick, to make people kill one another, to divide between a man and his wife, and so on. Magic is a matter that depends on secrecy and concealment. Magicians use the above-mentioned techniques to inflict harm on people, and in the plainest of terms, Islam forbade magic when the Prophet ﷺ said:

«اجْتَنِبُوا السَّبْعَ الْمُوبِقَاتِ»

"Stay away from the seven grave (and deadly) sins."

The Companions asked, "And what are they, O Messenger of Allâh?" He ﷺ said:

«الشِّرْكُ بِاللهِ وَالسِّحْرُ وَقَتْلُ النَّفْسِ الَّتِي حَرَّمَ اللهُ إِلَّا بِالْحَقِّ. وَأَكْلُ الرِّبَا. وَأَكْلُ مَالِ الْيَتِيمِ. وَالتَّوَلِّي يَوْمَ الزَّحْفِ. وَقَذْفُ الْمُحْصَنَاتِ الْغَافِلَاتِ»

"Associating partners with Allâh, magic, killing a soul that Allâh has forbidden unless it is by a right, consuming usury, consuming the wealth of an orphan, fleeing on the day of battle, and accusing chaste, innocent women."

Recorded by Al-Bukhari and Muslim from Abu Hurairah, may Allâh be pleased with him.

In Islam, the magician's punishment is execution — by being struck on his neck with a sword. The Messenger of Allâh ﷺ said:

«حَدُّ السَّاحِرِ ضَرْبُهُ بِالسَّيْفِ»

The punishment of the magician is striking him with the sword.

The one who is deceived by magicians, believing in them, going to them, and seeking a cure from an ailment or help in any matter that involves the unseen, has indeed disbelieved in what was revealed to Muhammad ﷺ.

The proof for that: The Prophet ﷺ said:

«لَيْسَ مِنَّا مَنْ تَطَيَّرَ أَوْ تُطُيِّرَ لَهُ أَوْ تَكَهَّنَ أَوْ تُكُهِّنَ لَهُ، أَوْ سَحَرَ أَو سُحِرَ لَهُ»

These are not from us: one who interprets an omen or has one interpreted for him, one who predicts the future or has someone predict it for him, and one who performs magic or it has been performed for him.

It was mentioned by Shaikh Muhammad bin 'Abdul-Wahhab in *Kitab At-Tawhid* and he attributed it to Al-Bazzar with a good chain.

And Abu Hurairah, may Allâh be pleased with him, related that the Prophet ﷺ said:

«مَنْ أَتَى كَاهِنًا فَصَدَّقَهُ بِمَا يَقُولُ فَقَدْ كَفَرَ بِمَا أُنْزِلَ عَلَى مُحَمَّدٍ»

Whoever goes to a soothsayer and believes in what he says, has indeed disbelieved in what has been revealed to Muhammad.

It was recorded by Abu Dawud, and the remainder of the four *Sunan* compilers.

2) *Ruqya* (Incantations)

These are known as incantations and spells that one recites. From this category, Islam forbade that which involves *Shirk*, such as invoking anyone other than Allâh, seeking help from anyone other than Allâh, or seeking protection from anyone other than Allâh. Examples of such spells are those that use the names of angels, of devils, of jinns, and so on.

However, if, for the same purpose, one recites verses of the Qur'an, says Allâh's Names or Attributes, or supplicates to Allâh alone, then that is permissible because it doesn't involve *Shirk*.

'Awf bin Malik said that they used to recite incantations during the days of ignorance and so he asked, "O Messenger of Allâh, how do you view that?'' The Prophet ﷺ answered:

«اعْرِضُوا عَلَيَّ رُقَاكُمْ لَا بَأْسَ بِالرُّقَى مَا لَمْ يَكُنْ فِيهِ شِرْكٌ»

"Present your *Ruqya* to me; there is no harm in using *Ruqya* as long as there is no *Shirk* involved.'' (Muslim and Abu Dawud)

The *Ruqya* Of The Prophet ﷺ:

The Messenger of Allâh ﷺ would use *Ruqya*; one form that is related to us from him is the following:

«اللَّهُمَّ رَبَّ النَّاسِ أَذْهِبِ الْبَأْسَ، وَاشْفِ أَنْتَ الشَّافِي لَا شِفَاءَ إِلَّا شِفَاؤُكَ. شِفَاءً لَا يُغَادِرُ سَقَماً»

O Allâh, Lord of mankind, take away the severe sickness and cure. You are the Curer; there is no cure except Your cure, a cure that leaves behind no sickness. (Recorded by Muslim)

3) *At-Tama'im*

The plural of *Tamimah* (a talisman). This is something that one hangs on the neck of children; it consists of beads or other materials. They claimed that it would protect them from evil and jealousy.

The Prophet ﷺ forbade the use of such things, because no one drives away evil and envy except Allâh. The Messenger of Allâh ﷺ said:

«مَنْ تَعَلَّقَ تَمِيمَةً فَلَا أَتَمَّ اللهُ لَهُ، وَمَنْ عَلَّقَ وَدَعَةً فَلَا أَوْدَعَ اللهُ لَهُ»

Whoever wears a *Tamimah*, then may Allâh not complete for him his affair, and whoever wears a shell (a good-luck charm) may Allâh not protect him.

According to the correct view, it is not only forbidden to hang a *Tamimah* around one's neck, but it is also forbidden to hang a small copy of the Qur'an around one's neck. First because of the general prohibition, and second because we must block the door to further evils. This opinion is held by Ibn Mas'ud, Ibn 'Abbas, some of the *Tabi'in*, and the noble Shaikh, 'Abdul-'Aziz bin Baz.

To hang other things around one's neck, seeking some sort of benefit is an act of *Shirk*. It has been reported that the Prophet ﷺ said:

«مَنْ عَلَّقَ تَمِيمَةً فَقَدْ أَشْرَكَ»

Whoever wears a *Tamimah* has indeed committed *Shirk*.

4) At-Tiwalah:

It is an item that a woman makes, thinking that it has power to make her more beloved to her husband. The Prophet ﷺ forbade this practice because it is one in which one seeks benefit or seeks to ward off harm from other than Allâh. This is why it has been related in a *Hadith*:

«إِنَّ الرُّقَى وَالتَّمَائِمَ وَالتِّوَلَةَ شِرْكٌ»

Indeed, *Ar-Ruqya'*, *At-Tama'im*, and *At-Tiwalah* are *Shirk*.
(Recorded by Abu Dawud and Ibn Majah from Ibn 'Abbas)

Whoever Depends On Something, Then He is Entrusted to It

Whoever believes that some of the forbidden matters mentioned above have a special effect on things, such as the ability to cure the sick, to fulfill needs, to ward off evil, to bring back the lost, or so on, then Allâh forsakes that person, leaving him to what he believes. The Messenger of Allâh ﷺ said:

«مَنْ تَعَلَّقَ شَيْئًا وُكِلَ إِلَيْهِ»

Whoever hangs something (a charm), he is entrusted to it.

This means whoever turns to other than Allâh and attaches his heart to that thing, forsaking His Lord, then Allâh entrusts him to it.

But whoever relies upon Allâh from his heart, entrusts his affairs with Him, and relies upon Him, then Allâh suffices him, protecting him from all evil, granting him ease in every difficult matter, and saving him from every trial. Allâh Almighty says:

﴿وَمَن يَتَوَكَّلْ عَلَى ٱللَّهِ فَهُوَ حَسْبُهُ﴾

And whosoever puts his trust in Allâh, then He will suffice him.[1]

---

[1] (*At-Talaq* 65:3)

Exaggerating In Honoring People

Islam forbids us from exceeding the proper bounds when it comes to praising people or glorifying them. Muslims know that no matter how high the level of a person is, he is still a slave of Allâh. Allâh Almighty says:

﴿إِن كُلُّ مَن فِى ٱلسَّمَـٰوَٰتِ وَٱلۡأَرۡضِ إِلَّآ ءَاتِى ٱلرَّحۡمَـٰنِ عَبۡدًا ۝﴾

There is none in the heavens and the earth but comes to the Most Beneficent as a slave.[1]

Islam forbade us from exceeding the proper bounds in this matter so that *Tawhid* may remain pure and clean, and so that deeds may be performed purely for Allâh. Exaggerating the good qualities of people most definitely leads to associating partners with Allâh.

In this regard, we have the example of the Christians, who continued to exaggerate the qualities of 'Iesa, peace be upon him, until they made him a god on one occasion, and the son of a god on another, and a part of a god on yet another occasion — all of which is disbelief itself. Allâh Almighty says:

﴿لَّقَدۡ كَفَرَ ٱلَّذِينَ قَالُوٓاۡ إِنَّ ٱللَّهَ هُوَ ٱلۡمَسِيحُ ٱبۡنُ مَرۡيَمَ﴾

Surely, they have disbelieved who say: "Allâh is the Messiah, son of Maryam."[2]

﴿لَّقَدۡ كَفَرَ ٱلَّذِينَ قَالُوٓاۡ إِنَّ ٱللَّهَ ثَالِثُ ثَلَـٰثَةٍ﴾

Surely, disbelievers are those who said: "Allâh is the third of the three."[3]

They only deviated so far away from the correct path because they exceeded the proper bounds regarding 'Iesa, peace be upon him. Allâh clarified that fact and explained the way of the truth to them, saying:

﴿يَـٰٓأَهۡلَ ٱلۡكِتَـٰبِ لَا تَغۡلُواۡ فِى دِينِكُمۡ وَلَا تَقُولُواۡ عَلَى ٱللَّهِ إِلَّا ٱلۡحَقَّ﴾

O People of the Scripture (Jews and Christians)! Do not

---

[1] (*Maryam* 19:93)

[2] (*Al-Ma'idah* 5:72)

[3] (*Al-Ma'idah* 5:73)

exceed the limits in your religion, nor say about Allâh but the truth.[1]

So the Muslims would be saved from what other nations have fallen into; the Prophet ﷺ said:

«لَا تُطْرُونِي كَمَا أَطْرَتِ النَّصَارَى ابْنَ مَرْيَمَ. إِنَّمَا أَنَا عَبْدٌ. فَقُولُوا: عَبْدُاللهِ وَرَسُولُهُ»

Do not praise me as the Christians praised the son of Maryam; indeed, I am only a slave, so say, "the slave of Allâh and His Messenger." (Recorded by Al-Bukhari in the Book of the Prophets)

Exaggerating Over the Righteous People Is The Basis of Idol Worship

It has been related that the names of the idols that were worshipped are the names of righteous people; they had followers who would glorify them, and when they died, those followers said, "Let us erect statues where they used to gather so that we may continue to remember them." When that generation died and when much time passed, future generations came, not knowing the purpose of the statues; the *Shaitan* seduced them into believing that their fathers and grandfathers used to worship the statues, and so they began to do the same.

---

[1] (*An-Nisa'* 4:171)

Lesson Five

Ihsan

The pillar of *Ihsan* is to worship Allâh as if you see Him, although you don't see Him, He certainly sees you.

Know — may Allâh have mercy on you — that Allâh knows everything about every creature; He knows their circumstances and their deeds; He misses nothing, and nothing is hidden from Him, not even the smallest ant — nothing smaller than that nor greater. Allâh Almighty says:

$$﴿وَمَا تَكُونُ فِي شَأْنٍ وَمَا تَتْلُواْ مِنْهُ مِن قُرْءَانٍ وَلَا تَعْمَلُونَ مِنْ عَمَلٍ إِلَّا كُنَّا عَلَيْكُمْ شُهُودًا إِذْ تُفِيضُونَ فِيهِ وَمَا يَعْزُبُ عَن رَّبِّكَ مِن مِّثْقَالِ ذَرَّةٍ فِي ٱلْأَرْضِ وَلَا فِي ٱلسَّمَآءِ وَلَا أَصْغَرَ مِن ذَٰلِكَ وَلَا أَكْبَرَ إِلَّا فِي كِتَٰبٍ مُّبِينٍ ﴾ ٦١$$

Whatever you may be doing, and whatever portion you may be reciting from the Qur'an, — and whatever deed you (mankind) may be doing (good or evil), We are Witness thereof, when you are doing it. And nothing is hidden from your Lord (so much as) the weight of an atom (or small ant) on the earth or in the heaven. Not what is less than that or what is greater than that but is (written) in a Clear Record.[1]

Other than affirming Allâh's complete Knowledge, Ability, and Care regarding His creatures, this verse teaches Allâh's worshippers to always feel that He is aware of their actions or lack of action, their sayings and deeds, and all that circulates in their hearts.

$$﴿وَأَسِرُّواْ قَوْلَكُمْ أَوِ ٱجْهَرُواْ بِهِۦٓ إِنَّهُۥ عَلِيمٌۢ بِذَاتِ ٱلصُّدُورِ ﴾ ١٣$$

And whether you keep your talk secret or disclose it, verily, He is the All-Knower of what is in the breasts (of men).[2]

The feeling that Allâh knows all, should become more acute when a

---

[1] (*Yunus* 10:61)
[2] (*Al-Mulk* 67:13)

Muslim performs an act of worship, a time when he is standing before his Lord, when he grasps that Allâh sees him and when it is as if he sees Allâh: this is the highest level of religion, which the Messenger ﷺ clarified when he explained Islam, *Iman*, and *Ihsan*. He ﷺ said:

«الإِحْسَانُ أَنْ تَعْبُدَ اللهَ كَأَنَّكَ تَرَاهُ فَإِنْ لَمْ تَكُنْ تَرَاهُ فَإِنَّهُ يَرَاكَ»

Ihsan is to worship Allâh as if you see Him, and though you do not see Him, He indeed sees you.

The Definition Of *Ihsan*

In the Arabic language, *Ihsan* is the opposite of a wrong or an offence. A person who does good deeds is called a *Muhsin* or, according to the famous grammarian Sibawayh, *Mihsan*. Deeds that are good are called *Mahasin*, just as deeds that are bad are called *Masawa'*. When you say that one has *Hassana* something, you mean that he has adorned it. *Ihsan* means proficiency in action, and sincerity, and truthfulness.

As used in the *Shari'ah*, *Ihsan* changes in meaning according to the context it is used in. When mentioned along with Islam and *Iman*, it means good obedience and watching what one does. Al-Manawi said, "*Ihsan* is outward Islam, which is held up by inward *Iman*, which is perfected by the observing *Ihsan*."

Ihsan means to perform deeds, knowing that Allâh is aware of one's deeds, and it also means to be obedient to Him. When one performs deeds, knowing that Allâh is watching him, one will perform good deeds in a better way. In *Ihsan*, then, is the essence and spirit of *Iman*.

The Reality Of *Ihsan*

When Jibril, peace be upon him, asked the Prophet ﷺ about *Ihsan*, he explained:

«هُوَ أَنْ تَعْبُدَ اللهَ كَأَنَّكَ تَرَاهُ، فَإِنْ لَمْ تَكُنْ تَرَاهُ فَإِنَّهُ يَرَاكَ»

It is to worship Allâh as if you see Him, and though you do not see Him, He indeed sees you.

This means that a person will perform deeds in a good way when he is cognizant of the fact that Allâh sees him, and that is the interpretation of this verse:

$$﴿إِنَّ ٱللَّهَ يَأْمُرُ بِٱلْعَدْلِ وَٱلْإِحْسَانِ﴾$$

Verily, Allâh enjoins *Al-Adl* (justice) and *Al-Ihsan*.[1]

That is why Allâh magnified the rewards of the people of *Ihsan*, for He said:

$$﴿إِنَّ ٱللَّهَ يُحِبُّ ٱلْمُحْسِنِينَ (١٩٥)﴾$$

Truly, Allâh loves *Al-Muhsinun* (the good-doers).[2]

And He Almighty says:

$$﴿هَلْ جَزَآءُ ٱلْإِحْسَانِ إِلَّا ٱلْإِحْسَانُ (٦٠)﴾$$

Is there any reward for good other than good?[3]

Meaning, what reward is there in the Hereafter for those who do good in this world other than good being done to them.

Ihsan is one of the best levels of worship, because it is not only the essence and spirit of faith, but it is also its completion; all other levels of *Iman* are included in it. *Ihsan* in this sense, then, signifies a complete level of attentiveness before Allâh, making one fear Allâh and perform deeds sincerely and purely for Him alone.

The Levels Of *Ihsan*

Ihsan comes at many different levels, the highest of which is one feeling that he is in the presence of Allâh Almighty as the Prophet ﷺ explained in the *Hadith*. The level beneath that is seeking closeness to Allâh by performing voluntary deeds; then other acts of *Ihsan* follow after that, regardless of whether those are represented by intention, objective, or action.

$$«. . . أَنْ تَعْبُدَ اللهَ كَأَنَّكَ تَرَاهُ»$$

To worship Allâh as if you see Him

The Prophet's explanation here indicates that the worshipper should worship Allâh in this manner — feeling His closeness, that He is before Him, and feeling as if he sees Him. What follows

---

[1] (*An-Nahl* 16:90)

[2] (*Al-Baqarah* 2:195)

[3] (*Ar-Rahman* 55:60)

necessarily are reverence, fear, awe, and glorification. The wording in the narration of Abu Hurairah, may Allâh be pleased with him, is,

$$«أَنْ تَخْشَى اللهَ كَأَنَّكَ تَرَاهُ»$$

To fear Allâh as if You see Him.

What also necessarily follows is sincerity in worship, which makes one strive to improve his worship of Allâh, making it more complete. Ibn 'Umar, may Allâh be pleased with them, said, "When we would make *Tawaf*, we would imagine that Allâh was before our eyes." (Recorded by Abu Nu'aym in *Hilyatul-Awliya'* 1:309)

$$«فَإِنْ لَمْ تَكُنْ تَرَاهُ فَإِنَّهُ يَرَاكَ»$$

And though you do not see Him, He indeed sees you.

This encourages the worshipper to feel Allâh's closeness to him when he is worshipping Him — so that he reaches such a level that it is as if he sees Him. If that is difficult, the worshipper seeks help through his faith that Allâh is watching him and is aware of not only his outer deeds, but also of his innermost secrets. The worshipper knows that none of his deeds are hidden from Allâh. When this level is achieved, it is easy for one to move on to the next level, and that is to always act as if he sees Allâh and according to the knowledge that Allâh is near and close to him. Know that *Ihsan* is made up of two ranks:

1) The rank of sincerity, and that is for one to worship Allâh, cognizant of the fact that Allâh sees him and is near to him. When one applies this, he becomes sincere to Allâh. Remembering that Allâh is near him and knows his deeds when he is actually performing an act of worship prevents one from doing that act for anyone other than Allâh.

2) The rank of the *Mushahid* (observer), and that means for the worshipper to act in conformity to the feeling in his heart that Allâh sees him. This is for the heart to be illuminated with *Iman* and for one to penetrate the depths of knowledge, until the unseen to him becomes like the seen. And this is the reality of the *Ihsan* explained in the *Hadith* of Jibril, peace be upon him.[1]

---

[1] This was taken from *Jami' Al-'Ulum wal-Hikam* [by Ibn Rajab] 1:75-76, with some editing.

Lesson Six

The Conditions For Prayer

There are nine conditions or requisites for prayer: Islam, sanity, (the age of) discernment, the removal of *Hadath*, removal of any impurity, the covering of one's *'Awrah* (any area of that body the must be covered), the entrance of its time, facing the *Qiblah*, and intention.

❖ ❖ ❖

In Arabic, the conditions are called *Shurut*, the plural of *Shart*, which linguistically means a sign. However, in the *Shari'ah*, it has another meaning: When it is nonexistent it necessitates nonexistence, but when it is existent, it does not necessitate existence. Put more simply, if there is no purity, then there is no prayer, but if one is pure, it is not necessarily the case that he has to pray (at that specific moment). And by the conditions of prayer, we are referring to those conditions upon which the correctness of one's prayer depends.

The Nine Conditions For Prayer:

1) Islam, the opposite of which is disbelief (*Kufr*). The disbeliever's actions are rejected, no matter what deed it is he performs, for Allâh Almighty says:

It is not for the polytheists to maintain the *Masjids* of Allâh, while they witness against their own selves of disbelief. The works of such are in vain and in Fire shall they abide.[1]

And in another verse, Allâh Almighty says:

﴿وَقَدِمْنَآ إِلَىٰ مَا عَمِلُوا۟ مِنْ عَمَلٍ فَجَعَلْنَٰهُ هَبَآءً مَّنثُورًا ٢٣﴾

And We shall turn to whatever deeds they (disbelievers) did, and We shall make such deeds as scattered floating particles

---

[1] (*At-Tawbah* 9:17)

of dust.[1]

The only prayer that is accepted is the Muslim's prayer, a reality that is proven by this verse:

﴿وَمَن يَبْتَغِ غَيْرَ ٱلْإِسْلَٰمِ دِينًا فَلَن يُقْبَلَ مِنْهُ وَهُوَ فِي ٱلْآخِرَةِ مِنَ ٱلْخَٰسِرِينَ ٨٥﴾

And whoever seeks a religion other than Islam, it will never be accepted of him, and in the Hereafter he will be one of the losers.[2]

2) Sanity, the opposite of which is obviously insanity or madness. The Pen is raised for the insane person, which means that he is not held accountable for his deeds until he returns to his senses. The Messenger of Allâh ﷺ said:

«رُفِعَ الْقَلَمُ عَنْ ثَلَاثَةٍ: النَّائِمِ حَتَّى يَسْتَيْقِظَ، وَالْمَجْنُونِ حَتَّى يُفِيقَ، وَالصَّغِيرِ حَتَّى يَبْلُغَ»

The Pen has been raised from three: the one who is sleeping, until he awakens; the insane person, until he returns to his senses; and the child, until he reaches puberty.

Recorded by Ahmad in his *Musnad*, and Abu Dawud, An-Nasa'i and Ibn Majah.

3) The age of discernment, the opposite of which is early childhood years. The age of discernment is realized at the age of seven, the time when a child must be ordered to pray, for the Messenger of Allâh ﷺ said:

«مُرُوا أَبْنَاءَكُمْ بِالصَّلَاةِ لِسَبْعٍ، وَاضْرِبُوهُمْ عَلَيْهَا لِعَشْرٍ، وَفَرِّقُوا بَيْنَهُمْ فِي الْمَضَاجِعِ»

Order your sons to pray when they turn seven, and hit them (if they refuse) when they turn ten, and at that time, make them sleep in separate beds.

Recorded by Al-Hakim, Imam Ahmad, and Abu Dawud, and in one version it is:

[1] (*Al-Furqan* 25:23)
[2] (*Aal 'Imran* 3:85)

«مُرُوا أَوْلَادَكُمْ»

Order your children....

4) The removal of *Hadath*, and there are two kinds of *Hadath*: (i) the greater one, (ii) the lesser one. The former includes menstruation and sexual intercourse; one purifies himself from these forms of *Hadath* by performing *Ghusl*. An example of the latter is the passing of wind, and this form of *Hadath* is removed by ablution; the Messenger of Allâh ﷺ said:

«لَا يَقْبَلُ اللهُ صَلَاةً بِغَيْرِ طُهُورٍ»

Allâh does not accept prayer without purification. (Recorded by Muslim and others)

He ﷺ also said:

«لَا يَقْبَلُ اللهَ صَلَاةَ مَنْ أَحْدَثَ حَتَّى يَتَوَضَّأَ»

Allâh does not accept the prayer of one in a state of *Hadath* until he performs ablution. (Agreed upon)

5) The removal of impurities from three: from one's body, from one's clothing, and from the place one prays in.

﴿ وَثِيَابَكَ فَطَهِّرْ ٤ ﴾

And your garments purify![1]

The Messenger of Allâh ﷺ said:

«تَنَزَّهُوا مِنَ الْبَوْلِ فَإِنَّ عَامَّةَ عَذَابِ الْقَبْرِ مِنْهُ»

Purify yourselves from urine because verily, it is the most common reason for punishment in the grave.

6) The covering of one's *'Awrah* (any area of the body that must be covered) with clothing that doesn't reveal one's shape, skin, or complexion. The Messenger of Allâh ﷺ said:

«لَا يَقْبَلُ اللهُ صَلَاةَ حَائِضٍ إِلَّا بِخِمَارٍ»

Allâh does not accept the prayer of a woman who has reached the age of menstruation unless she wears a veil. (Recorded by Abu Dawud)

---

[1] (*Al-Muddaththir* 74:4)

The people of knowledge concur that if one is able to wear clothes, but prays naked instead, then his prayer is invalid. The *'Awrah* for man, or the area of his body that must be covered, is the area between his belly button and his knees, and the same goes for the female slave. The *'Awrah* of the free woman is her entire body except for her face, and even that must be covered when she is in the presence of strange men.[1] In a *Hadith* related by Salamah bin Al-Akwa', the Messenger of Allâh ﷺ ordered him to cover himself, even if he had only one garment to accomplish that. And Allâh Almighty says:

﴿يَٰبَنِىٓ ءَادَمَ خُذُواْ زِينَتَكُمۡ عِندَ كُلِّ مَسۡجِدٍ﴾

O children of Adam! Take your adornment to every *Masjid*.[2]

That means, for the prayer.

7) The entrance of the prayer's time. The proof for this condition is taken from the *Hadith* of Jibril, peace be upon him, wherein he led the Prophet ﷺ in each prayer, once at the beginning of the time for each prayer, and then at the end of its time. He said, "O Muhammad, the prayer is between these two times." Allâh Almighty says:

﴿إِنَّ ٱلصَّلَوٰةَ كَانَتۡ عَلَى ٱلۡمُؤۡمِنِينَ كِتَٰبٗا مَّوۡقُوتٗا ۝﴾

Verily, the prayer is enjoined on the believers at fixed hours.[3]

﴿أَقِمِ ٱلصَّلَوٰةَ لِدُلُوكِ ٱلشَّمۡسِ إِلَىٰ غَسَقِ ٱلَّيۡلِ وَقُرۡءَانَ ٱلۡفَجۡرِۖ إِنَّ قُرۡءَانَ ٱلۡفَجۡرِ كَانَ مَشۡهُودٗا ۝﴾

Perform *As-Salat* from midday till the darkness of the night, and recite the Qur'an in the early dawn. Verily, the recitation of the Qur'an in the early dawn is ever witnessed (attended by the angels in charge of mankind of the day and the

---

[1] A strange man is any man that is not her *Mahram*; a *Mahram* to her is a man whom she may never marry and who is allowed to be in seclusion with her.

[2] *(Al-A'raf* 7:31)

[3] *(An-Nisa'* 4:103)

night).[1]

8) Facing the *Qiblah*:

﴿قَدْ نَرَىٰ تَقَلُّبَ وَجْهِكَ فِى ٱلسَّمَآءِ فَلَنُوَلِّيَنَّكَ قِبْلَةً تَرْضَىٰهَا فَوَلِّ وَجْهَكَ شَطْرَ ٱلْمَسْجِدِ ٱلْحَرَامِ وَحَيْثُ مَا كُنتُمْ فَوَلُّواْ وُجُوهَكُمْ شَطْرَهُ﴾

Verily! We have seen the turning of your face towards the heaven. Surely, We shall turn you to a *Qiblah* (prayer direction) that shall please you, so turn your face in the direction of Al-Masjid Al-Haram (in Makkah). And wherever you people are, turn your faces (in prayer) in that direction.[2]

9) Intention: it resides in the heart and its utterance is an innovation. The Prophet ﷺ said:

«إِنَّمَا الأَعْمَالُ بِالنِّيَّاتِ، وَإِنَّمَا لِكُلِّ امْرِىءٍ مَا نَوَىٰ»

Indeed, deeds are by intentions, and for every person is what he intended.

---

[1] (*Al-Isra'* 17:78)
[2] (*Al-Baqarah* 2:144)

Lesson Seven

The Pillars (*Arkan*) of Prayer

There are fourteen pillars of prayer: standing, if able; the opening *Takbir*; recitation of *Al-Fatihah*; bowing; standing up straight after bowing; prostrating, with seven specific body parts touching the ground; rising from the prostration; sitting between the two prostrations; tranquility in all of the prayer's actions; performing these pillars in order; the final *Tashahhud*; sitting down for it; sending *Salat* upon the Prophet ﷺ; and the two *Taslims*.

❖ ❖ ❖

1) Standing, if able: this is a pillar in the obligatory prayers. That this is a pillar of prayer is taken from this verse:

﴿حَٰفِظُوا۟ عَلَى ٱلصَّلَوَٰتِ وَٱلصَّلَوٰةِ ٱلْوُسْطَىٰ وَقُومُوا۟ لِلَّهِ قَٰنِتِينَ ﴾ (٢٣٨)

Guard strictly As-Salawat (the prayers) especially the middle Salat (i.e., the best prayer 'Asr). And stand before Allâh with obedience.[1]

«صَلِّ قَائِمًا»

Pray in a standing position.

2) The opening *Takbir*, i.e., to begin the prayer by saying, "*Allâhu Akbar*," and no other phrase can act as a substitute for this one. The Prophet ﷺ said:

«تَحْرِيمُهَا التَّكْبِيرُ وَتَحْلِيلُهَا التَّسْلِيمُ»

Its sacred state is entered with its *Takbir* and it is ended with its *Taslim*.

In the famous, long *Hadith* regarding the one who didn't pray correctly, the Prophet ﷺ said:

«إِذَا قُمْتَ إِلَى الصَّلَاةِ فَكَبِّرْ»

---

[1] (*Al-Baqarah* 2:238)

When you stand for prayer, then say, "*Allâhu Akbar*."

3) Reciting *Al-Fatihah*. It must be recited in every unit of prayer. The Prophet ﷺ said:

«لَا صَلَاةَ لِمَنْ لَمْ يَقْرَأْ بِفَاتِحَةِ الْكِتَابِ»

There is no prayer for one who does not recite *Al-Fatihah* of the Book.

4) Bowing.

5) Standing up straight after bowing.

6) Prostrating, with seven specific body parts touching the ground.

7) Rising from the prostration.

8) Sitting between the two prostrations. The proof for these pillars can be found in this verse:

﴿يَـٰٓأَيُّهَا ٱلَّذِينَ ءَامَنُواْ ٱرْكَعُواْ وَٱسْجُدُواْ﴾

O you who believe! Bow down, and prostrate yourselves.[1]

Another proof is the saying of the Prophet ﷺ:

«أُمِرْتُ أَنْ أَسْجُدَ عَلَى سَبْعَةِ أَعْظُمٍ»

I have been ordered to prostrate on seven bones. (Recorded by Al-Bukhari and Muslim)

9) Tranquility in all of the prayer's actions.

10) Performing all of these pillars in order. The *Hadith* about the one who prayed incorrectly can be considered a comprehensive proof for this and for all preceding pillars. Abu Hurairah, may Allâh be pleased with him, said, "As we were sitting with the Prophet ﷺ, a man entered and prayed. He then stood and gave greetings of peace to the Prophet ﷺ, who replied:

«ارْجِعْ فَصَلِّ فَإِنَّكَ لَمْ تُصَلِّ»

Go back and pray, for indeed you have not prayed.

The man went back, but the same occurred three times, after which the man said, 'By He Who has sent you as a Prophet with the truth, I can do no better than this, so teach me.' The Prophet

---

[1] (*Al-Hajj* 22:77)

ﷺ said:

«إِذَا قُمْتَ إِلَى الصَّلَاةِ فَكَبِّرْ، ثُمَّ اقْرَأْ مَا تَيَسَّرَ مَعَكَ مِنَ الْقُرْآنِ، ثُمَّ ارْكَعْ حَتَّى تَطْمَئِنَّ رَاكِعًا، ثُمَّ ارْفَعْ حَتَّى تَعْتَدِلَ قَائِمًا، ثُمَّ اسْجُدْ حَتَّى تَطْمَئِنَّ سَاجِدًا، ثُمَّ ارْفَعْ حَتَّى تَطْمَئِنَّ جَالِسًا، ثُمَّ افْعَلْ ذَلِكَ فِي صَلَاتِكَ كُلِّهَا»

When you stand for prayer, say: "*Allâhu Akbar*," then recite what is easy for you from the Qur'an. Then bow down until you become tranquil in your bowing. Then rise until you are standing upright. Next, prostrate until you become tranquil in your prostration. Then rise and sit until you become tranquil in the seated position. And then continue to do that for the rest of your prayer."

11) The final *Tashahhud*; This pillar is taken from the *Hadith* of Ibn Mas'ud, may Allâh be pleased with him, who said, "Before the *Tashahhud* became obligatory upon us, we used to say: 'Peace upon Allâh from His worshippers, and peace upon Jibril and Mika'il.' But then the Prophet ﷺ said:

«لَا تَقُولُوا: السَّلَامُ عَلَى اللهِ مِنْ عِبَادِهِ، فَإِنَّ اللهَ هُوَ السَّلَامُ، وَلَكِنْ قُولُوا: التَّحِيَّاتُ لِلهِ وَالصَّلَوَاتُ وَالطَّيِّبَاتُ»

Do not say: 'Peace upon Allâh from His worshippers,' for indeed Allâh is As-Salam; rather, you should say: '*At-Tahiyyat* is for Allâh. All acts of worship and good deeds are for Him.' "

We will give the exact wording of the *Tashahhud* mentioned in this *Hadith*, along with its meaning in the next lesson — if Allâh wills.

12) Sitting down for it, i.e., sitting down for the *Tashahhud*. The Prophet ﷺ said:

«إِذَا قَعَدَ أَحَدُكُمْ فِي الصَّلَاةِ فَلْيَقُلِ التَّحِيَّاتُ»

When one of you sits for the prayer, then let him say *At-Tahiyyat*. (Agreed upon)

13) Sending *Salat* (blessings) upon the Prophet ﷺ. In one narration the Prophet ﷺ said:

«إِذَا صَلَّى أَحَدُكُمْ - وَفِيهِ - ثُمَّ يُصَلِّي عَلَى النَّبِيِّ»

When one of you prays, then in it let him send blessing upon the Prophet.

In another narration:

«لِيُصَلِّ عَلَى النَّبِيِّ ثُمَّ يَدْعُو»

Then let him send blessings upon the Prophet then supplicate... (Recorded by Ahmad and Abu Dawud)

14) The two *Taslims* (i.e. to say *As-Salamu 'Alaikum wa Rahmatullah*, turning one's head to the right, and then saying the same, turning to the left), for the Prophet ﷺ said:

«وَتَحْلِيلُهَا التَّسْلِيمُ»

...it is ended with its *Taslim*.

Lesson Eight

The Obligatory Elements Of Prayer

There are eight obligatory elements in the prayer: All of the *Takbirs*, except for the opening *Takbir* (because it is one of the pillars of prayer); to say: *Sami'-Allâhu Liman Hamidah* (Allâh listens to those who praise Him), both for the *Imam* and for the one who prays alone; to say: *Rabbana wa Lakal-Hamd* (Our Lord, and for You is all praise), for everyone. During the bowing position, to say: *Subhana Rabbiyal-'Azeem* (How perfect my Lord is, the Supreme); during prostration, to say: *Subhana Rabbiyal-'Ala* (How perfect my Lord is, the Most High). Between the two prostrations, to say: *Rabbigh-fir Lee* (My Lord, forgive me); the first *Tashahhud*; and sitting down for it.

❖ ❖ ❖

1) All of the *Takbirs*, except for the opening *Takbir* — Ibn Mas'ud said, "I saw that the Prophet ﷺ would say *Allâhu Akbar* whenever he would rise or descend, and whenever he would stand or sit." (Recorded by Ahmad, An-Nasa'i, and At-Tirmithi who said it was *Sahih*.) And the Prophet ﷺ used the imperative when he said:

«إِذَا كَبَّرَ الْإِمَامُ فَكَبِّرُوا»

When the *Imam* says, "*Allâhu Akbar*," say (all of you), "*Allâhu Akbar*."

When the imperative is used, it indicates an obligatory.

2) During the bowing position, to say: *Subhana Rabbiyal-'Azeem* (How perfect my Lord is, the Supreme). In a *Hadith* related by Huthaifah, in which the Prophet's prayer is described, the Prophet ﷺ would say while bowing:

«سُبْحَانَ رَبِّيَ الْعَظِيم»

Subhana Rabbiyal-'Azeem.

and while he was prostrating:

«سُبْحَانَ رَبِّيَ الْأَعْلَى»

Subhana Rabbiyal-'Ala.

3) To say: *Sami'-Allâhu Liman Hamidah* (Allâh listens to those who praise Him), both for the *Imam* and for the one who prays alone. As he was describing the Prophet's prayer, Abu Hurairah said that when the Prophet ﷺ would raise his backbone from the bowing position, he would say:

«سَمِعَ الله لِمَنْ حَمِدَهُ»

Sami'- Allâhu Liman Hamidah. (Agreed upon)

4) To say: *Rabbana wa Lakal-Hamd* (Our Lord, and for You is all praise), for everyone: for the *Imam*, for the one following the *Imam*, and for the one who is praying individually. In the previous *Hadith* related by Abu Hurairah, we learn exactly what the Prophet ﷺ would say as he was rising, which indicates that he would say:

«رَبَّنَا وَلَكَ الْحَمْدُ»

Rabbana wa Lakal-Hamd

when he reached the standing position.

5) During prostration, to say: *Subhana Rabbiyal-'Ala* (How perfect my Lord is, the Most High). That this is an obligatory element of prayer is also indicated by the previous *Hadith*.

6) Between the two prostrations, to say: *Rabbigh-fir Lee* (My Lord, forgive me). That the Prophet ﷺ would say this phrase between the two prostrations is related in a *Hadith* narrated by Huthaifah. Recorded by An-Nasa'i and Ibn Majah.[1]

7) The first *Tashahhud*.

8) And sitting down for it, i.e., for the first *Tashahhud*. These last two are based on a *Hadith*, wherein the Prophet ﷺ is described as follows: He used to read the *Tahiyyat* (i.e., the *Tashahhud*) after every two units. And the Prophet ﷺ said.

«إِذَا قَعَدْتُمْ فِي كُلِّ رَكْعَتَيْنِ فَقُولُوا التَّحِيَّاتُ»

When you sit after each two units, say *At-Tahiyyat.* (Ahmad

---

[1] See *Shurutus-Salat wa Arkanuha* by Shaikh Al-Islam Muhammad bin 'Abdul Wahhab, and *Al-'Uddah Sharhul-'Umdah*, 13-71, and *Manarus-Sabil* 70:87.

and An-Nisa'i)

The difference between the pillars of prayer (*Arkan*) and the obligatory elements (*Wajibat*) of prayer, is that when one leaves out any pillar of prayer, regardless of whether he leaves it out on purpose or because he forgets, his prayer is nullified. But only when one purposefully leaves out one of the obligatory elements of prayer is his prayer void. If one forgets to perform one of the obligatory elements of prayer, one may make it up by performing the prostration that is legislated for forgetfulness.[1]

---

[1] *Shurutus-Salat* by Imam Muhammad bin 'Abdul Wahhab.

Lesson Nine

An Explanation Of The *Tashahhud*

The *Tashahhud* is to say, "Greetings to Allâh, and blessings and goodness. Peace be upon you, O Prophet, and the mercy of Allâh and His blessings. Peace be upon us and all of Allâh's righteous servants. I bear witness that none has the right to be worshipped except Allâh and I bear witness that Muhammad is His servant and Messenger."

Then the worshipper sends peace and blessings upon the Prophet ﷺ, saying, "O Allâh, bestow Your favor on Muhammad and on the family of Muhammad as You have bestowed Your favor on Ibrahim and on the family of Ibrahim, You are full of praise, Most Glorious. O Allâh, bless Muhammad and the family of Muhammad as You have blessed Ibrahim and the family of Ibrahim, You are full of praise, Most Glorious."

Then in the final *Tashahhud*, which is in the last unit of prayer, the worshipper seeks refuge in Allâh from four: from the punishment of the Fire, from the punishment of the grave, from the trials of life and death, and from the evil trial of Al-Masih Ad-Dajjal. And then finally, one may supplicate as he wishes, but especially using those invocations that have been related from the Prophet ﷺ, such as the following: "O Allâh, help me to remember You, to give You thanks, and to be Your good servant. O Allâh, I have greatly wronged myself and no one forgives sins but You. So grant me forgiveness and have mercy on me. Surely, You are Most Forgiving, Most Merciful."

As for the first *Tashahhud* (which is in the second unit of prayer), after having said, "I bear witness that none has the right to be worshipped except Allâh and I bear witness that Muhammad is His servant and Messenger," one rises to the third unit — in the *Zuhr*, *'Asr*, *Maghrib*, and *'Isha'* prayers. But because there are *Ahadith*, which in general, indicate that one should send peace and blessings upon the Prophet ﷺ, it is better for one to send peace and blessings upon him and then to rise to the third unit of prayer.

The *Tashahhud*: The Shaikh chose the *Tashahhud* that was related by Ibn Mas'ud, may Allâh be pleased with him, who said, "When the Messenger of Allâh ﷺ taught me the *Tashahhud*, my hands were clenched in his, in the same way that he would teach me a *Surah* of the Qur'an." (Recorded by Ahmad (1:114) Al-Bukhari (4:175) Muslim (2:14) and others.) Yet there are other wordings to the *Tashahhud*: whichever one the worshipper chooses, his prayer is correct. If he varies, using this one sometimes and that one others, then this is good. And Allâh Almighty knows best. Nonetheless, among the different narrations regarding the *Tashahhud*, Ibn Mas'ud's narration is most authentic.

Abu Mas'ud Al-Badri, may Allâh be pleased with him, related that Bashir bin Sa'd asked, "O Messenger of Allâh, Allâh ordered us to send blessings upon you, so how should we send blessings upon you?" At first, the Prophet ﷺ remained silent, and then he said:

«اللَّهُمَّ صَلِّ عَلَى مُحَمَّدٍ وَعَلَى آلِ مُحَمَّدٍ كَمَا صَلَّيْتَ عَلَى آلِ إِبْرَاهِيمَ، وَبَارِكْ عَلَى مُحَمَّدٍ وَعَلَى آلِ مُحَمَّدٍ كَمَا بَارَكْتَ عَلَى آلِ إِبْرَاهِيمَ فِي الْعَالَمِينَ إِنَّكَ حَمِيدٌ مَجِيدٌ. وَالسَّلَامُ كَمَا عَلِمْتُمْ»

Say: "O Allâh, bestow Your favor on Muhammad and on the family of Muhammad as You have bestowed Your favor on the family of Ibrahim, and bless Muhammad and the family of Muhammad as You have blessed the family of Ibrahim from all that exists, You are full of praise, Most Glorious... And *Taslim* is as you know." (Recorded by Muslim)

Both Al-Bukhari and Muslim related another narration, which is narrated by Ka'b bin 'Ujirah. In it, the Prophet ﷺ said:

«اللَّهُمَّ صَلِّ عَلَى مُحَمَّدٍ وَعَلَى آلِ مُحَمَّدٍ كَمَا صَلَّيْتَ عَلَى آلِ إِبْرَاهِيمَ إِنَّكَ حَمِيدٌ مَجِيدٌ»

Say: "O Allâh, bestow Your favor on Muhammad and the family of Muhammad, as You have bestowed Your favor on Ibrahim and the family of Ibrahim. Verily, You are full of praise, Most Glorious... And he mentioned the rest of the *Hadith*. Recorded by Al-Bukhari (3:15) and Muslim (2:16)

Abu Hurairah, may Allâh be pleased with him, narrated that the Messenger of Allâh ﷺ said:

«إِذَا تَشَهَّدَ أَحَدُكُمْ فَلْيَسْتَعِذْ مِنْ أَرْبَعٍ يَقُولُ: اللَّهُمَّ إِنِّي أَعُوذُ بِكَ مِنْ عَذَابِ جَهَنَّمَ، وَمِنْ عَذَابِ الْقَبْرِ، وَمِنْ فِتْنَةِ الْمَحْيَا وَالْمَمَاتِ، وَمِنْ فِتْنَةِ الْمَسِيحِ الدَّجَّالِ»

When one of you says the *Tashabhud*, seek he should seek refuge in Allâh from four, saying, "O Allâh, I seek refuge in You from the punishment of the grave, from the torment of the Fire, from the trials and tribulations of life and death, and from the evil trial of Al-Masih Ad-Dajjal."

This *Hadith* indicates that after one sends peace and blessings upon the Prophet ﷺ, one should seek refuge in Allâh Almighty from the four mentioned above.

In another narration, Abu Bakr, may Allâh be pleased with him, related that he said to the Messenger of Allâh ﷺ, "Teach me a supplication that I can use in my prayer." He said:

«قُلْ: اللَّهُمَّ إِنِّي ظَلَمْتُ نَفْسِي ظُلْمًا كَثِيرًا وَلَا يَغْفِرُ الذُّنُوبَ إِلَّا أَنْتَ فَاغْفِرْ لِي مَغْفِرَةً مِنْ عِنْدِكَ وَارْحَمْنِي إِنَّكَ أَنْتَ الْغَفُورُ الرَّحِيمُ»

Say: "O Allâh, I have greatly wronged myself and no one forgives sins but You. So grant me forgiveness and have mercy on me. Surely, You are Most Forgiving, Most Merciful." (Agreed upon)

This *Hadith* clearly proves the categorical permissibility of supplication during prayer: one of the times to supplicate during prayer is at the end of the *Tashahhud* — after one has already made the *Tashahhud*, has sent peace and blessings on the Prophet ﷺ, and has sought refuge in Allâh from the four above-mentioned afflictions. And it is okay to choose another supplication that has been related from the Prophet ﷺ, for he said in Ibn Mas'ud's narration:

«ثُمَّ لِيَتَخَيَّرْ مِنَ الدُّعَاءِ أَعْجَبَهُ إِلَيْهِ فَيَدْعُو»

Then he may supplicate with that invocation that is most beloved to him.

And this *Hadith* indicates even more: that not only is it permissible to supplicate with an invocation that has been related from the Prophet ﷺ, but it is also permissible to supplicate with any other invocation, as long as the invocation does not consist of that which is prohibited. In yet another narration, the Prophet ﷺ said:

«ثُمَّ لِيَتَخَيَّرْ مِنَ الْمَسْأَلَةِ مَا شَاءَ»

Then let him choose to ask whatever he wishes.

One of the supplications that can be said after the *Tashahhud* is the following recorded by Muslim and Abu 'Awanah:

«اللَّهُمَّ اغْفِرْ لِي مَا قَدَّمْتُ وَمَا أَخَّرْتُ وَمَا أَسْرَرْتُ، وَمَا أَعْلَنْتُ وَمَا أَسْرَفْتُ، وَمَا أَنْتَ أَعْلَمُ بِهِ مِنِّي، أَنْتَ الْمُقَدِّمُ وَأَنْتَ الْمُؤَخِّرُ لَا إِلَهَ إِلَّا أَنْتَ»

O Allâh, forgive me for those sins which have come to pass as well as those which shall come to pass, and those I have committed in secret as well as those I have made public, and where I have exceeded all bounds as well as those things about which You are more knowledgeable. You are *Al-Muqaddim* (the First) and *Al-Mu'akhkhir* (the Last). None has the right to be worshipped except You.

The *Imam* may make these supplications as long as it does not become burdensome on those that are following him in prayer.

You may pray for a specific person, just as the Prophet ﷺ supplicated for the weak from Makkah.

(الـتَّـحِـيَّـاتُ) *At-Tahiyyat* means everything that indicates the glorification of Allâh, such as bowing and prostrating. And everything by which Allâh is glorified belongs to Him alone; if one performs anything that is solely for Allâh's glorification to anyone else, then he is a polytheist, a disbeliever.

(الصلوات) *As-Salawaat* means all supplications, though it has been said to mean the five prayers.

(الطيبات لله) *At-Tayyibatu Lillah* means all good deeds.

Allâh is glorified, but peace is not sent upon Him, because by seeking to send peace upon someone, one is making supplication. Allâh is pure and good and He doesn't accept sayings or deeds unless they are good and pure.

(السلام عليك أيها النبي ورحمة الله وبركاته) *As-Salamu 'Alaika Ayyuhannabiyyu wa Rahmatullahi wa Barakaatuhu* means that one is supplicating for peace, mercy, and blessings to be sent on the Prophet ﷺ. From this, we take a lesson: since we can pray for the Prophet ﷺ, we cannot pray to him.

(السلام علينا وعلى عباد الله الصالحين) *As-Salamu 'Alaina wa 'Ala 'Ibaadillahis-Saliheen*: Here, you are sending peace upon yourself and upon every righteous servant of Allâh, whether that servant be on earth or in the heavens. And again, the fact that we are supplicating for the righteous clearly indicates that we cannot supplicate to them.

(أشهد أن لا إله إلا الله وحده لا شريك له) *Ashhaadu Al-Laa Ilaha Illallâhu Wahdahu Laa Shareeka Lahu wa Ashhadu Anna Muhammadan 'Abduhu wa Rasooluhu*: Here, you bear witness with certainty that no one in the heavens or the earth deserves to be worshipped except Allâh Almighty, and that Muhammad ﷺ is Allâh's Messenger and worshipper — a worshipper is not worshipped, and a Messenger should not be disbelieved in; rather, he should be obeyed and followed. Allâh honored the Prophet ﷺ by calling him His servant:

﴿تَبَارَكَ ٱلَّذِي نَزَّلَ ٱلْفُرْقَانَ عَلَىٰ عَبْدِهِۦ لِيَكُونَ لِلْعَالَمِينَ نَذِيرًا ۝﴾

Blessed is He Who sent down the Criterion (of right and wrong, i.e., this Qur'an) to His servant (Muhammad ﷺ that he may be a warner to the *'Alamin* (mankind and jinns).[1]

(اللهم صل على محمد وعلى آل محمد كما صليت على إبراهيم إنك حميد مجيد) *Allâhumma Salli 'Ala Muhammadin wa 'Ala Aali Muhammadin Kama Sallaita 'Ala Ibrahima Innaka Hameedum Majeed*: *Salat* from Allâh means for Him to praise his servant in the highest gathering, as Al-Bukhari mentioned in his *Sahih*, from Abu Al-'Aliyah, who said "Allâh's *Salat* is His praising His servant in the highest of gatherings." And they say that it means mercy. But the first view is correct. *Salat* from the angels means for them to ask Allâh to forgive His servant. And *Salat* from human beings means supplication for them.

(آل محمد) *Aali Muhammad* means the family of the Prophet ﷺ from the children of Hashim, the children of Al-Muttalib, and his wives. It is forbidden for any of them to accept *Zakat*. And the family of Ibrahim means those believers that are from his progeny.

Just as one can send *Salat* upon the Prophet ﷺ from what has been related, one may also send *Salat* upon others as well, but as long as one doesn't do so often. It is permissible to send *Salat* upon other people because the Prophet ﷺ did so when he said,

«اللَّهُمَّ صَلِّ عَلَى آلِ أَبِي أَوْفَى»

O Allâh, send *Salat* on the family of Abi Awfa.

But one must not make someone recognized as a person upon whom *Salat* are sent: that is something specific to the Prophet ﷺ; nor should one choose a specific Companion or a set of Companions, by sending *Salat* only on him or on them, leaving out the rest.

---

[1] (*Al-Furqan* 25:1)

Lesson Ten

The *Sunan* Elements Of Prayer

The following are the *Sunan* elements of prayer:

1) The opening supplication.

2) While standing, placing one's right hand on one's left, over the chest; before bowing and after rising from that position.

3) With joined and outstretched fingers, raising one's hands, so that they are parallel to his shoulders or to his ears, in the following situations: the opening *Takbir*, when going down to bow, when rising from the bowing position, and when rising from the first *Tashahhud*, i.e., standing for the third unit of prayer.

4) Saying the statements of glorification more than once while bowing and prostrating.

5) What may be added to *Rabbana wa Lakal-Hamd* after standing from the bowing position, and supplicating for forgiveness more than once between the two prostrations.

6) To place the head at the same angle and level of one's back during the bowing position.

7) While prostrating, one should distance his upper arms from his sides, his stomach from his thighs, and his thighs from his calves.

8) Keeping the forearms away from the ground while prostrating.

9) During the first *Tashahhud* and between the two prostrations, one should place his buttocks on his left calf and foot, while his right foot should be erected, with his toes on the ground holding the foot up, and with the bottom of his foot facing the opposite direction of the *Qiblah*.

10) Specifically in the last *Tashahhud* of the three-unit and four-unit prayer, one should let his buttocks rest on the ground, while his left calf is resting under his right leg, once again

resting the weight of the right foot on its toes, with the bottom of the foot facing away from the *Qiblah*.

11) Pointing one's right index finger during both the first and last *Tashahhud*, from the time one sits until the time he finishes the *Tashahhud*; and in the same position, he should move that finger when he is supplicating.

12) During the first *Tashahhud*, sending blessings on the Prophet ﷺ, his family, on Ibrahim and on his family.

13) To supplicate during the final *Tashahhud*.

14) Audible recitation during the *Fajr* prayer, the *Jumu'ah* prayer, the two *'Eid* prayers, the prayer for rain, and in the first two units of the *Maghrib* and *'Isha'* prayers.

15) Quiet recitation during the *Zuhr* prayer, the *'Asr* prayer, the third unit of the *Maghrib* prayer, and the last two units of the *'Isha'* prayer.

16) Reciting more than *Al-Fatihah* during prayer. Just as one should follow those *Sunan* mentioned above, one should also follow those not mentioned among them: saying more than *Rabbana wa Lakal-Hamd*, for the *Imam*, his follower, and the one who is reading alone, for that is a Sunnah. Another example is to place one's hands on one's knees during the bowing position, with his fingers spread out.

The *Sunan* Elements of Prayer:

The *Sunan* elements of prayer are divided into two categories: 1) sayings, 2) actions. It is not binding upon the worshipper to perform the Sunnah sayings or actions of prayer: if the worshipper performs them, he is rewarded; if he doesn't, then just as in all other deeds that are Sunnah, there is no sin upon him. Nonetheless, the Muslim should perform them, following the Prophet's command:

«عَلَيْكُمْ بِسُنَّتِي وَسُنَّةِ الْخُلَفَاءِ الرَّاشِدِينَ الْمَهْدِيِّينَ عَضُّوا عَلَيْهَا بِالنَّوَاجِذِ»

Follow my Sunnah (way) and the Sunnah of the rightly —
guided caliphs — cling to that way by biting on it with your
molars.

The Opening Supplication:

It is so called because with it, one begins the prayer. This is one of
the opening supplications that has been related from the Prophet ﷺ:

«سُبْحَانَكَ اللَّهُمَّ وَبِحَمْدِكَ، وَتَبَارَكَ اسْمُكَ وَتَعَالَى جَدُّكَ وَلَا إِلَهَ غَيْرُكَ»

Subhaanaka Allâhumma wa Bihamdika wa Tabaarakasmu-
ka wa Ta'aala Jadduka wa Laa Ilaaha Ghairuka.

meaning: "Glory is to You, O Allâh, and praise, Blesssed is Your
Name and Exalted is Your Majesty, and none has the right to be
worshipped except You."

Phrase by Phrase Translation:

(سبحانك اللهم) *Subhaanaka Allâhumma*: With your Sublimity, I
consider You far too exalted to have any faults, O Allâh.

(وبحمدك) *Wa Bihamdika*: It has been said to mean that I join
between two: I consider you free from having any faults and I
praise You.

(وتبارك اسمك) *Wa Tabaarakasmuka*: Blessings are achieved by Your
remembrance.

(و تعالى جدك) *Wa Ta'aala Jadduka*: Your Exaltedness is Sublime.

(ولا إله غيرك) *Wa Laa Ilaaha Ghairuka*: There is no one on the earth
or in the sky that is rightfully worshipped except You.

Because there are different opening supplications that have been
related from the Prophet ﷺ, it is recommended for a Muslim to
sometimes supplicate with one version and sometimes with another,
so that his adherence to the Sunnah is more complete.

Another opening supplication that has been authentically related
from the Prophet ﷺ:

«اللَّهُمَّ بَاعِدْ بَيْنِي وَبَيْنَ خَطَايَايَ كَمَا بَاعَدْتَ بَيْنَ الْمَشْرِقِ وَالْمَغْرِبِ،
اللَّهُمَّ نَقِّنِي مِنْ خَطَايَايَ كَمَا يُنَقَّى الثَّوْبُ الأَبْيَضُ مِنَ الدَّنَسِ، اللَّهُمَّ
اغْسِلْنِي مِنْ خَطَايَايَ بِالْمَاءِ وَالثَّلْجِ وَالْبَرَدِ»

O Allâh, distance me from my sins just as you have distanced the East from the West; O Allâh, purify me of my sins as a white robe is purified of filth; O Allâh, cleanse me of my sins with water, snow and ice pellets. (Recorded by Al-Bukhari and Muslim)

"Placing one's right hand on one's left": In a *Hadith* related by Wa'il bin Hujr, the Prophet ﷺ is described as having placed his right hand on his left hand. It was recorded by Ahmad and Muslim. And the Messenger of Allâh ﷺ said:

«إِنَّا مَعْشَرَ الأَنْبِيَاءِ أُمِرْنَا بِتَعْجِيلِ فِطْرِنَا وَتَأْخِيرِ سَحُورِنَا وَأَنْ نَضَعَ أَيْمَانَنَا عَلَى شَمَائِلِنَا فِي الصَّلَاةِ»

We, the Prophets, have been ordered to hasten to break our fast, and to delay our *Suhur*; and to place our right (hands) on our left (hands) in prayer.

Recorded by Abu Dawud with a *Hasan Mursal* chain of narration from Tawus. It was also narrated from 'Ali with a chain of narration that contains some unreliable narrators. In it he said, "Indeed from the Sunnah in prayer is to place the hand over the hand under the navel..." It was recorded by Ahmad and it mentions matters other than that, and the first narration is the more preferred. Allâh knows best.

"With joined and ourtstretched fingers, raising one's hands": The Prophet ﷺ used to raise his hands with his fingers stretched. (Recorded by Abu Dawud). In a *Hadith* related by Abu Humaid, he says that the Prophet ﷺ used to raise his hands until they were parallel with his shoulders. (Agreed upon). Similar was recorded by Abu Dawud from Malik bin Al-Huwairith, who said that the Prophet ﷺ would raise his hands until they were parallel to his earlobes. And by raising his hands, the Prophet ﷺ indicated raising the veil between him and his Lord, just as the index finger is used in the seated position to signify the Oneness of Allâh.

In the *Hadith* reported by 'Ali, may Allâh be pleased with him, he said that when the Messenger of Allâh ﷺ would stand up for an obligatory prayer, he would say, *Allâhu Akbar* and raise his hands to the level of his shoulders; he would do the same when he finished his recitation, and he wanted to bow, and he would do that when he raised his head from bowing. He would not raise his hands in any portion of the prayer while he was sitting. And when he stood from the two prostrations, he would raise his hands with that *Takbir*. It was recorded by Ahmad, Abu Dawud, and At-Tirmithi who said it is *Sahib*. The meaning of "the two prostrations" is the two units of prayer.

"more than once": In the *Hadith* of Huthaifah, he reported that when the Messenger of Allâh ﷺ bowed, he would say:

«سُبْحَانَ رَبِّيَ الْعَظِيم»

Subhana Rabbiyal-'Azeem.

And when he would prostrate, he would say:

«سُبْحَانَ رَبِّيَ الْأَعْلَى»

Subhana Rabbiyal-'Ala. (Recorded by Abu Dawud)

It is compulsory, then, to say them once; the least level of completeness is to say them three times; and the highest level of completeness is to say them ten times.

"and supplicating for forgiveness more than once": This is because it is compulsory to ask Allâh for forgiveness once between the two prostrations: Huthaifah, may Allâh be pleased with him, related that between the two prostrations, the Prophet ﷺ would say:

«رَبِّ اغْفِرْ لِي»

O my Lord, forgive me. (Recorded by An-Nasa'i and Ibn Majah).

"To place the head at the same angle and level of one's back during the bowing position": 'Aishah, may Allâh be pleased with her, said that when he ﷺ would bow, he would neither point his head (down) nor hang it back, but would remain between the two. (This was recorded by Muslim)

"While prostrating, one should distance his upper arms from his sides...and one should keep his forearms away from the ground": It has been related that, during prostration, the Prophet ﷺ would not let his arms lie down. (This was recorded by Al-Bukhari and Abu Dawud.) Rather, he would raise them above the ground and he would distance them from his two sides until the whiteness of his armpits could be seen from behind him. (Recorded by Al-Bukhari and Muslim)

"...one should place his buttocks on his left calf and foot...": When the Prophet ﷺ taught the person who prayed incorrectly, he said:

«فَإِذَا جَلَسْتَ فِي وَسَطِ الصَّلَاةِ فَاطْمَئِنْ وَافْتَرِشْ فَخِذَكَ الْيُسْرَى ثُمَّ تَشَهَّدْ»

And when you sit down in the middle of the prayer, be serene, lay down your left thigh, and make the *Tashahhud*. [Recorded by Abu Dawud and Al-Baihaqi with a good (*Jayyid*) chain of narration.]

And 'Aishah, may Allâh be pleased with her, said that the Prophet ﷺ would lay down his left leg, and erect his right (foot). (Recorded by Muslim)

"One should let his buttocks rest on the ground...": As he was describing the prayer of the Prophet ﷺ, Abu Humaid As-Sa'idi, may Allâh be pleased with him, said:

«وَإِذَا جَلَسَ فِي الرَّكْعَةِ الْأَخِيرَةِ قَدَّمَ رِجْلَهُ الْيُسْرَى وَنَصَبَ الْأُخْرَىٰ وَقَعَدَ عَلَى مَقْعَدَتِهِ»

"When he would sit for the last unit of prayer, he would put forward his left leg, erecting the other, and he would then rest his weight on his buttocks." (It was recorded by Al-Bukhari 2:828)

And in the *Hadith* of Rifa'ah bin Rafi', recorded by Abu Dawud (no. 860) the Prophet ﷺ said:

«فَإِذَا جَلَسْتَ فِي وَسَطِ الصَّلَاةَ فَاطْمَئِنْ وَافْتَرِشْ فَخِذَكَ الْيُسْرَى ثُمَّ تَشَهَّد»

And when you sit in the middle of the prayer, be serene, let your left thigh rest, and then make *Tashahhud*.

"sending blessings on the Prophet ﷺ": It is Sunnah for the one praying to send blessings upon the Prophet ﷺ just as he does in the last *Tashahhud*, for the Prophet ﷺ would send blessings on himself not only in the last *Tashahud*, but in the first *Tashahhud* as well (and on other occasions as well). (This was recorded by Abu 'Awanah in his *Sahib* and An-Nasa'i)

"To supplicate during the final *Tashahhud*": As has been related in the *Hadith*:

«ثُمَّ لِيَتَخَيَّرْ مِنَ الدُّعَاءِ مَا شَاءَ»

Then he may choose whatever supplication he wishes. (Recorded by Al-Bukhari)

Earlier some supplications were mentioned for this position. See lesson number nine.

"Audible recitation...": Imam Ibn Qudamah said, "There is a consensus among the Muslims that it is recommended to read out loud and to read quietly, each in their respective places. The basis for this is the practice of the Prophet ﷺ, the knowledge of which has been transmitted from earlier to later generations."

"Reciting more than *Al-Fatihah*": Imam Ibn Qudamah said, "That it is Sunnah to recite a *Surah* after *Al-Fatihah* in the first two units of every prayer, and it is a practice about which we know no dissension."

Another Sunnah is the *Imam* to say, "*Allâhu Akbar*" out loud, for the Prophet ﷺ said:

«إِذَا كَبَّرَ الإِمَامُ فَكَبِّرُوا»

When the *Imam* says, "*Allâhu Akbar*," then all of you should say "*Allâhu Akbar*."

He ﷺ also said:

«وَإِذَا قَالَ سَمِعَ اللهُ لِمَنْ حَمِدَهْ فَقُولُوا: رَبَّنَا وَلَكَ الْحَمْدُ»

And when he says, "*Sami'-Allâhu Liman Hamidah*" then all of you should say, "*Rabbana wa Lakal-Hamd*."

However, the follower of the *Imam* and the one who is praying alone should say both of these phrases quietly.

It is also Sunnah to quietly seek refuge in Allâh from the accursed *Shaitan*: "*A'uthu Billahi Minash-Shaitaanir-Rajeem* (I take refuge in Allâh from the accursed *Shaitan*)." You may take refuge in Allâh from the *Shaitan* using this invocation, or using any other that has been related from the Prophet ﷺ.

After seeking refuge from the *Shaitan*, you should quietly read *Bismillah* (i.e., *Bismillahir-Rahmaanir-Raheem*), even though *Bismillah* is neither from *Surat Al-Fatihah* nor from any other *Surah*; rather, it is a verse from the Qur'an that comes before and between *Surahs* of the Qur'an, except for *Surahs Bara'ah* and *Al-Anfal*.

It is Sunnah to write *Bismillah* at the beginning of books and letters, just as Sulaiman, peace be upon him, did, and just as the Prophet ﷺ used to do. It repels the *Shaitan*, you should also read it before performing all actions.

As you are reciting *Surat Al-Fatihah* it is recommended that you stop at the end of each verse (as opposed to reading the chapter through, without pausing, and without stopping to take a breath after the end of the verses). After reading the last verse, and then after pausing slightly, you should say, "*Aameen*," which means, "O Allâh, answer." By pausing, you allow it to be known that the "*Aameen*" is not a part of the Qur'an. Both the *Imam* and his follower may say it after the audible prayers, and in the same prayers, based on Samurah's *Hadith*, it is recommended for the *Imam* to remain quiet after that. It is then recommended for the *Imam* to recite an entire chapter, and though reading one verse only is sufficient, *Imam* Ahmad preferred it to be long. And outside of the prayer, you may recite the *Bismillah* either out loud or quietly.

The recitation in the *Fajr* prayer should be from the longer *Mufassal* section of the Qur'an, or the beginning of *Surah Qaf* since Aws asked the Companions of Muhammad ﷺ about how the Qur'an was divided and they said, "A third, a fifth, a seventh, a ninth, an eleventh, a thirteenth — and the *Mufassal* section as one."

The recitation in the *Maghrib* prayer should be from the shorter *Surahs* and in the remainder of the prayers from those of moderate length as long as there is no reason to prevent that. Otherwise, recitation should be from the shorter *Surahs*.

For the loud prayers, a woman may recite out loud as long as no strange man can hear her. When you pray voluntary prayers late at night, you must consider the general good: if someone is nearby who will be disturbed by your recitation, then you should recite quietly; if the one who is nearby would like to listen, then you may recite out loud. If, by mistake, you recite out loud when you should have recited quietly or, recited quietly when you should have recited out loud, then you can correct yourself by simply changing the volume of your voice to what is appropriate, continuing in your recitation, without beginning all over. And finally, because the verses of the Qur'an are in a particular order, you must recite them in order.

"Saying the statements of glorification more than once...": The scholars say that, in terms of the *Imam*, he may reach the lowest level of completeness by reading those phrases three times and the highest level of completeness by reading them ten times. Also, you should know that the Prophet ﷺ forbade us from reciting the Qur'an during both the bowing and the prostrating positions.

"What may be added to *Rabbana-walakal-Hamd*": For example, saying:

«مِلْءَ السَّمَاوَاتِ وَالْأَرْضِ وَمِلْءَ مَا شِئْتَ مِنْ شَيْءٍ بَعْدُ»

The heavens and the earth and all between them abound with Your praises, and all that You will abound with Your praises.

If one likes, one may add:

«أَهْلَ الثَّنَاءِ وَالْمَجْدِ أَحَقُّ مَا قَالَ الْعَبْدُ وَكُلُّنَا لَكَ عَبْدٌ لَا مَانِعَ لِمَا أَعْطَيْتَ وَلَا مُعْطِيَ لِمَا مَنَعْتَ وَلَا يَنْفَعُ ذَا الْجَدِّ مِنْكَ الْجَدُّ»

O Posessor of praise and majesty, the truest thing a servant has said (of You) and we are all Your servants. O Allâh, none can prevent what You have willed to bestow and none can bestow what You have willed to prevent, and no wealth or majesty can benefit anyone, as from You is all wealth and majesty.

You may say any other phrase that has been related from the Prophet ﷺ, such as the one in Abu Sa'id's *Hadith*:

«اللَّهُمَّ رَبَّنَا لَكَ الْحَمْدُ»

Allâhumma Rabbana Lakal-Hamd.

A slight variation, which means, "O Allâh, Our Lord, for You is all praise."

It is also recommended, when you go down for prostration, that your hands touch the ground directly, with your fingers joined together, pointed in the direction of the *Qiblah*. In that position, your fists should not be clenched, nor should your elbows be resting on the ground; rather, they should be raised.

"and supplicating for forgiveness more than once...": Not only may you ask for forgiveness more than once, you may also read an additional supplication: Ibn 'Abbas, may Allâh be pleased with them, said that the Prophet ﷺ would say the following between the two prostrations:

«رَبِّ اغْفِرْ لِي وَارْحَمْنِي وَاهْدِنِي وَارْزُقْنِي وَعَافِنِي»

My Lord forgive me, have mercy upon me, guide me, give me sustenance, and give me health. (Recorded by Abu Dawud)

You may make the same supplication when you are prostrating, for the Prophet ﷺ said:

«وَأَمَّا السُّجُودُ فَأَكْثِرُوا فِيهِ مِنَ الدُّعَاءِ فَقَمِنٌ أَنْ يُسْتَجَابَ لَكُمْ»

As for the prostration, when you are in that position, supplicate much — and it will be worthy for you to be answered. (Recorded by Muslim)

Abu Hurairah related that the Messenger of Allâh ﷺ would say when he was prostrating:

«اللَّهُمَّ اغْفِرْ لِي ذَنْبِي كُلَّهُ دِقَّهُ وَجُلَّهُ وَأَوَّلَهُ وَآخِرَهُ وَعَلَانِيَتَهُ وَسِرَّهُ»

O Allâh, forgive me all of my sins, the small and great of them, the first and last of them, and the seen and hidden of them.

Shaikh Muhammad bin 'Abdul-Wahhab said, "Then he should sit for the *Tashahhud*, with his hands on his legs, stretching and joining the fingers of his left hand, so that they are facing the *Qiblah*. As for his right hand, his pinky finger (little finger) and the one next to it should be clenched, while thumb and middle finger should touch, making the shape of a ring. Then he should make *Tashahhud*, pointing with his index finger, signifying *Tawhid*. He may point with that finger when supplicating either during prayer or outside of prayer, for Ibn Zubair said, 'The Prophet ﷺ would point with his finger when he supplicated, and he wouldn't move it.'" (It was recorded by Abu Dawud)

It is also Sunnah to turn towards your right and left when making *Taslim* (i.e., saying *As-Salamu 'Alaikum wa Rahmatullah*). The *Imam* says the *Taslim* out loud, and his followers should say it quietly. While he shouldn't prolong his voice when he says the *Taslim*, he should make intention first to exit the prayer and second to send peace on the protecting angels and on those who are present.

After making *Taslim*, the *Imam* should not prolong facing the *Qiblah*; rather, it is Sunnah for him to turn toward those who followed him in prayer, either turning to his right or to his left. And no follower should leave the place of prayer before him, for the Prophet ﷺ said:

«إِنِّي إِمَامُكُمْ فَلَا تَسْبِقُونِي بِالرُّكُوعِ وَلَا بِالسُّجُودِ وَلَا بِالانْصِرَافِ»

I am your *Imam*, so do not precede me — neither in the bowing position, nor in the prostrating position, nor in leaving.

If women are praying with men, the women should leave first, while the men wait for a short while, so that they don't accost the women or get in their way.

After the prayer is finished, it is Sunnah for you to remember Allâh, to invoke Him, and to ask His forgiveness, saying,

(استغفر الله) *Astaghfirullah* (I ask Allâh for forgiveness) three times. Then you should say:

«اللَّهُمَّ أَنْتَ السَّلَامُ وَمِنْكَ السَّلَامُ تَبَارَكْتَ يَا ذَا الْجَلَالِ وَالإِكْرَامِ لَا إِلَهَ إِلَّا اللهُ وَحْدَهُ لَا شَرِيكَ لَهُ لَهُ الْمُلْكُ وَلَهُ الْحَمْدُ وَهُوَ عَلَى كُلِّ شَيْءٍ قَدِيرٌ، وَلَا حَوْلَ وَلَا قُوَّةَ إِلَّا بِاللهِ لَا إِلَهَ إِلَّا اللهُ وَلَا نَعْبُدُ إِلَّا إِيَّاهُ لَهُ النِّعْمَةُ وَلَهُ الْفَضْلُ وَلَهُ الثَّنَاءُ الْحَسَنُ لَا إِلَهَ إِلَّا اللهُ مُخْلِصِينَ لَهُ الدِّينَ وَلَوْ كَرِهَ الْكَافِرُونَ، اللَّهُمَّ لَا مَانِعَ لِمَا أَعْطَيْتَ وَلَا مُعْطِيَ لِمَا مَنَعْتَ وَلَا يَنْفَعُ ذَا الْجَدِّ مِنْكَ الْجَدُّ»

"*Allâhumma Antas-Salaamu wa Minkas-Salaamu, Tabaarakta Yaa
Thal-Jalaali wal-Ikraam. Laa Ilaha Illallâhu Wahdahu Laa Share-
eka Lahu. Lahul-Mulku wa Lahul-Hamdu wa Huwa 'Ala Kulli
Shay'in Qadeer. Wa Laa Hawla wa Laa Quwwata Illa Billah. Laa
Ilaha Illallahu wa Laa Na'budu Illa Iyyaahu. Lahun-Ni'matu wa
Lahul-Fadhlu wa Lahuth-Thana'ul-Hasan. Laa Ilaha Illallâhu
Mukhliseena Lahud-Deena wa Law Karihal-Kaafiroon. Allâhumma
La Maani'a Limaa A'taita, wa Laa Mu'tiya Limaa Mana'ta, wa Laa
Yanfa'u Thal-Jaddi Minkal-Jadd.*"

(O Allâh, You are As-Salaam (The One Who is free from all defects)
and from You is all peace, Blessed are You, O Possessor of majesty
and honor. None has the right to be worshipped except Allâh, alone,
without partner, to Him belongs all sovereignty and praise, and He is
capable over all things. And there is no power nor ability except by
Allâh. None has the right to be worshipped except Allâh, and we do
not worship any other besides Him. His is grace, and His is bounty
and to Him belongs the most excellent praise. None has the right to
be worshipped but Allâh. (We are) sincere in making our religious
devotion to Him, even though the desbelievers may dislike it. O
Allâh, none can prevent what You have willed to bestow and none
can bestow what You have willed to prevent, and no wealth or
majesty can benefit anyone, as from You is all wealth and majesty:

Then you should say,

(سبحان الله) "*Subhaanallah* (How perfect Allâh is!)" thirty-three
times.

(الحمد لله) "*Al-Hamdulillah* (All praise is for Allâh)" thirty-three
times, and:

(الله اكبر) "*Allâhu Akbar* (Allâh is the Most Great)" thirty-three times.
To complete the hundred, say:

(لا إله إلا الله وحده لا شريك له له الملك وله الحمد وهو على كل شيء قدير) "*Laa Ilaha
Illallâh wahdahu la shareeka lahu. Lahul-Mulku, wa Lahul-
Hamdu, wa Huwa 'Ala Kulli Shay'in Qadeer.* (None has the right
to be worshipped except Allâh, alone, without partner, to Him
belongs all sovereignty and praise and He is Capable over all
things).''

After having finished the *Fajr* and *Maghrib* prayers, and before speaking to any person, say:

(اللهم أجرني من النار) *Allâhummajurnee Minan-Naar* (O Allâh, protect me from the fire), seven times.

Know that to supplicate quietly is better than to supplicate out loud, and moreover, you should supplicate with what is narrated from the Prophet ﷺ, and with a present heart, both hoping and fearing, for the Prophet ﷺ said:

«لَا يُسْتَجَابُ الدُّعَاءُ مِنْ قَلْبِ غَافِلٍ»

The supplication of a heedless heart is not answered.

Ask Allâh Almighty by His Beautiful Names and Attributes, and ask Him, mentioning your belief in *Tawhid*.

When you supplicate, try supplicating during those times when you are more likely to be answered: the last third of the night, between the *Athan* (call to prayer) and the *Iqamah*, after the obligatory prayers, the last hour of (daylight on) Friday and between the *Athan* and *Iqamah* during the Friday prayer.

You should patiently wait for your supplication to be answered, not rushing, and not saying, "I supplicated and I supplicated but I was not answered." And it is okay to specify yourself when you supplicate, but it is disliked to do so when others are saying *Aameen* after you. And it is also disliked to supplicate out loud.

You should know that the Shaikh mentioned only some of the Sunnah elements of prayer, whereas there are more, and as I mentioned earlier, the people of knowledge classify those elements into sayings and deeds. There are seventeen sayings in prayer that are Sunnah:

1) The Opening Supplication.

2) Seeking refuge in Allâh from the *Shaitan*.

3) The *Basmalah*.

4) Saying "*Aameen*" after the Opening Chapter.

5-9) Reciting a *Surah* of the Qur'an in the first two units, and in the *Fajr, Jumu'ah*, voluntary, and two 'Eid prayers.

10-11) Reciting out loud when required; reciting quietly when required.

12) After standing from bowing, reading, *"Mil'as-Samawaati wal-Ardh..."* to the end of that supplication

13-14) Saying the statements of glorification more than once when bowing and when prostrating.

15) Between the two prostrations, asking Allâh for forgiveness more than once.

16) In the last *Tashahhud*, seeking refuge in Allâh from four trials.

17) In the first *Tashahhud*, sending prayers and blessings on Muhammad ﷺ and his family.

All other Sunnah elements of the prayer are actions, such as the following:

- (Raising the hands with) the fingers being stretched and joined and (palms) facing the *Qiblah* when beginning the prayer, when going down to the bowing position, and when rising from that position. Also, lowering the hands after raising them.

- Placing the right hand on the left wrist, and putting them under the navel.[1]

- Looking at the place of prostration.

- Separating one's feet at a comfortable distance during the standing position.

- Reciting in a metered pace (*Tarteel*).

- That the *Imam's* recitation in the first unit is longer than in the second, and the length of his recitation should correspond to the condition of his followers.

- Holding one's knees during the bowing position, with the fingers stretched open.

- During the bowing position, making one's back straight; also, in the same position, one's head should be parallel to one's back.

- When going down for prostration, one's knees should touch the ground before one's hands.

---

[1] Publisher's Note: The *Hadith* from which this act is mentioned is weak. Please check the book *Nailul-Awtaar*, Volume 2, pages 207-211.

- When rising from the prostrating position, one's hands should precede one's knees in being lifted.

- While prostrating, placing one's forehead and nose firmly on the ground, while one's arms are spread away from one's sides; one's stomach should be away from one's thighs and one's thighs should be away from one's calves.

- During prostration, one's feet should be erected, with the tips of the toes separated and touching the ground.

- During prostration, one's hands should be parallel to one's shoulders; also, one's fingers should be stretched, joined, and facing the *Qiblah*.

- One's hands should directly touch the place of prostration.

- Standing to the next unit of prayer on the soles of the feet putting the hands on the thighs for support.

- Sitting on the left foot with the right foot erect between the two prostrations and in *Tashahhud*.

- Sitting on the buttocks (as described earlier) in the last *Tashahhud*.

- Turning to one's right and left when making *Taslim*.

- Putting his hands on his thighs with the fingers extended and together and the index finger pointing toward the *Qiblah* between the two prostrations and in *Tashahhud*.

- During the *Tashahhud*, to clench one's pinky finger and the one next to it from one's right hand, to make the shape of a ring with the thumb and middle finger, and to point with the index finger.

- Giving preference to turning away from the *Qiblah* from the left rather than the right.

Sajdah As-Sahw: The Prostration For Forgetfulness

Imam Ahmad said that, from the narrations we have, the Prophet ﷺ made this special prostration five times:

1) When he ended the prayer after two units.
2) When he ended the prayer after three units.
3) When he did an extra action during prayer.
4) When he missed one of the actions of prayer.
5) When he stood after two units without making prostration.

Al-Khattabi said, "What is trusted among the scholars are these five *Ahadith*," referring to two related by Ibn Mas'ud, one related by Abu Sa'id, one by Abu Hurairah, and one by Ibn Buhainah.

One makes this prostration when one performs extra units or too few units, when one is doubtful during a compulsory prayer or a voluntary prayer, except if these things happen often: when they do, they are most probably whispers from the devil, and they should be disregarded, a ruling that applies to ablution, taking a shower, and removing impurities.

When one performs the actions of prayer more times than is prescribed on purpose, such as standing, bowing, or sitting, then that prayer is void; but if one does it by mistake, then he may perform the prostration for forgetfulness. The Prophet ﷺ said:

«إِذَا زَادَ الرَّجُلُ أَوْ نَقَصَ فِي صَلَاتِهِ فَلْيَسْجُدْ سَجْدَتَيْنِ»

If a man increases or decreases from his prayer, let him make two prostrations. (Recorded by Muslim)

If one forgets, but then remembers, he should return to the proper order of prayer without saying "*Allahu Akbar*." If one prays an additional unit, one should stop as soon as one remembers and base his prayer on those actions he performed before doing what was additional.

Whether one is an *Imam* or someone who is praying alone, one must return to a previous position when two trustworthy people prompt him to do so; if only one person prompts him to return, he does not have to do so unless he is sure that that person is right. The Prophet ﷺ did not return when Thul-Yadain told him to do so.

Small or few physical actions do not render one's prayer void, for the

Prophet ﷺ opened a door for 'Aishah while he was praying; on another occasion, he carried Umamah while he was praying. If one says one of the phrases of prayer, not in its place, but during another part of prayer, one's prayer is not rendered void.

When one forgets during prayer, one must prostrate twice, for the Prophet ﷺ said:

«إِذَا نَسِيَ أَحَدُكُمْ فَلْيَسْجُدْ سَجْدَتَيْنِ»

If one of you forgets, let him make two prostrations.

If one says the *Taslim* on purpose before the prayer actually ends, it becomes void; but if he said the *Taslim* by mistake, and then during a short period of time, he remembered, he can simply complete his prayer, even if he exited from the *Masjid* or spoke briefly for some benefit. If one speaks by mistake, sleeps, or if he speaks a word that slips out (i.e., a word that is not from the Qur'an) accidentally during recitation, his prayer is not rendered void. But if one laughs, then his prayer is nullified, a ruling that has *Ijma'* (consensus) behind it; but one's prayer is not nullified by merely smiling.

If one forgets one of the pillars of prayer (other than the opening *Takbir*) while he is reciting for the next unit, then the unit in which he forgot the pillar becomes nullified and the new unit replaces it. In such a situation, the opening supplication is not repeated, an opinion that is held by Ahmad. If one remembers that he missed a pillar before reciting, then he should return and repeat it and what comes after it.

When one forgets the first *Tashahhud* by standing after the prostrations of the second unit, he must return to the *Tashahhud* unless he has reached the standing position and stands erect. This was recorded by Abu Dawud. The follower must follow the *Imam*; he does not have to do the *Tashahhud* but he does have to make prostration.

When one is not sure how many units he prayed, he should base the number on what he is sure of, and when the follower doubts, he should just continue to follow the *Imam*.

If a follower joins the prayer when the *Imam* is bowing, and he is not sure whether he reached the prayer on time, he should disregard that unit and repeat it. The follower does not have to prostrate for forgetfulness unless his *Imam* has to do so, and he does it with him.

Actions That Are Disliked During The Prayer:

- To turn one's head slightly or to raise it to the sky is disliked.
- To pray toward a picture, fire, or lamp.
- Resting one's elbows on the ground during prostration.
- To pray when one has to relieve himself.
- To pray when food one desires is served; in this situation, one should delay the prayer even if one misses the congregation.
- To play with pebbles or to intertwine the fingers of his two hands.
- To rest on one's hand during the seated position.
- To touch one's beard.
- If one has to yawn, one should hold it back as much as possible; if he cannot control himself, he should simply put his hand on his mouth.
- To level the dirt on the ground without an excuse.
- When one passes in front of you while you are praying, don't let him pass; hold him back, and if need be, push him back, whether the one trying to pass is a human or an animal, whether the prayer is compulsory or voluntary. If the one trying to pass by refuses to desist, you may even fight him. It is forbidden to walk between one who is praying and his *Sutrah* (an object he places before him, so that people may walk by him after that object, and not before it). It is also forbidden to walk right in front of him even if he doesn't have a *Sutrah*.
- During prayer, one may kill a snake, scorpion, or louse. One may even straighten out his garment or turban.
- It is not disliked to give greetings of peace to one who is praying, but he may return your greeting by gesture.
- When the *Imam* makes an error, you may correct him; men should say '*Subhaanallah*' to point out his mistake and women should clap.
- While in the *Masjid*, if one has to spit, one should do so in his

garment; outside of the *Masjid*, he should do so on his left; it is hated to spit to one's right or straight ahead.

- It is disliked for one who is praying individually not to have a *Sutrah*, even if one does not fear a passerby. One may use a wall, a stick, or something else that is readily available. One should pray close to one's *Sutrah*, for the Prophet ﷺ said:

«إِذَا صَلَّى أَحَدُكُمْ فَلْيُصَلِّ إِلَى سُتْرَةٍ وَلْيَدْنُ مِنْهَا»

When one of you prays, he should pray toward a *Sutrah* and he should get close to it.

He should turn slightly so as not to face it directly, since the Prophet ﷺ did that, and if there is a need he may just make a line and if anything passes beyond it then it is not disliked.

Lesson Eleven

Actions That Nullify One's Prayer

There are eight actions that nullify one's prayer:

1) Speaking, but only when: (1) one is conscious that he is in prayer, (2) one has knowledge of what he is doing, and (3) one does it on purpose. But when one speaks forgetfully or from ignorance, then his prayer is not nullified.
2) Laughing.
3) Eating.
4) Drinking.
5) Part of one's *'Awrah* being exposed.
6) A significant turning from the direction of the *Qiblah*.
7) Much and continuous frivolous movement or fiddling around.
8) Exiting from the state of purity.

❖ ❖ ❖

"*Speaking... one does it on purpose*": Zaid bin Arqam said, "We used to talk during prayer; one of us would speak to the man praying beside him, until this verse was revealed:

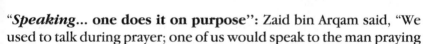

And stand before Allâh with obedience [and do not speak to others during the *Salat* (prayers)].[1]

We were ordered to remain quiet and we were forbidden from talking."

"**But when one speaks forgetfully or from ignorance, then his prayer is not nullified**": When Mu'awiyyah bin Al-Hakam As-Sulami spoke during prayer, not knowing the ruling thereof, the Prophet ﷺ said to him:

---
[1] (*Al-Baqarah* 2:238)

«إِنَّ هَذِهِ الصَّلَاةَ لَا يَصْلُحُ فِيهَا شَيْءٌ مِنْ كَلَامِ النَّاسِ إِنَّمَا هِيَ التَّسْبِيحُ
وَالتَّكْبِيرُ وَقِرَاءَةُ الْقُرْآنِ»

Indeed man's talk is not appropriate to this prayer; verily, it
(i.e., the prayer) is only glorification, exaltation (of Allâh), and
the recitation of Qur'an. (Recorded by Muslim)

Even though the Prophet ﷺ ordered him not to talk during prayer,
he didn't order him to repeat the prayer.

"Laughing": Ibn Al-Munthir stated that there is *Ijma'* (consensus) in
this issue: laughing renders one's prayer void.

"Eating and Drinking": Ibn Al-Munthir said, "Everyone that we
know of agrees that whoever eats or drinks on purpose during a
compulsory prayer has to repeat that prayer."

"Part of one's *'Awrah'* being exposed": As I already mentioned in
lesson six, to cover one's *'Awrah'* is one of the conditions of prayer.
So if one exposes his *'Awrah'* on purpose, his prayer is nullified.

"A significant turning from the direction of the *Qiblah*": Facing
the *Qiblah* is also one of the conditions of prayer (refer to lesson
six), so if one turns significantly away from that direction on
purpose, his prayer is nullified.

"Much and continuous frivolous movement or fiddling around":
If one makes many extraneous movements continuously, movements
that are not connected to the prayer, then by consensus of the
scholars, his prayer is void. After mentioning this ruling, the author of
Al-Kafi says, "If the movements are few, then the prayer is not
nullified...because the Prophet ﷺ carried Umamah during prayer -
when he would stand, he would carry her, and when he would go
down for prostration, he would place her on the ground...and in the
Eclipse prayer, he moved forward and backward."

"Exiting from the state of purity": Purity is one of the conditions of
prayer: if it is nullified, so too is the prayer. And the Prophet ﷺ said:

«لَا يَقْبَلُ اللهُ صَلَاةَ أَحَدِكُمْ إِذَا أَحْدَثَ حَتَّى يَتَوَضَّأَ»

Allâh does not accept the prayer of one of you when he
commits *Hadath* until he then performs ablution.

Lesson Twelve

The Conditions Of *Wudhu'* (Islamic Ablution)

The Conditions Of *Wudhu'* are ten:

1) Islam.
2) Sanity.
3) Age of discernment,
4) Intention.
5) That the one performing it intends to fulfill it, not having the intention (to wash) for some other reason, until he has complete the processes of purification.
6) That what caused one to have to make *Wudhu'* has stopped
7) Before making *Wudhu'*, the performance of *Istinja'* or *Istijmar*.
8) Purity of water being used, and its being lawful.
9) Removing anything (a stain, for example) that prevents the water from reaching one's skin.
10) That when one makes ablution, the time of prayer has arrived: This condition is particular to one who is afflicted with a sickness whereby he loses control of his bladder — for instance, causing him to urinate frequently.

Al-Wadhu' refers to the water that is used for ablution; *Al-Wudhu'* refers to actions involved in performing ablution. The definition of *Al-Wudhu'* in the *Shari'ah* is as follows: using pure water on those body parts that Allâh has clarified and legislated.

"Islam, Sanity, Age of Discernment, and Intention": The first three have been clarified in lesson six — the Conditions of Prayer.

Intention is special because it is a condition for all deeds, and by intention, I am referring to the resolve in one's heart to perform

Wudhu', the resolve to apply Allâh's Commands and His Messenger's commands. It is not, however, legislated to utter one's intention, for doing so is an innovation. Shaikh Al-Islam Ibn Taymiyyah said, "Intention resides in the heart, and not on the tongue, a principle that the Muslim Imams (i.e., scholars) not only agree upon, but agree upon for all acts of worship." Even were one to wash all of the required body parts for the *Wudhu'*, it would not be correct unless he actually intended to make the *Wudhu'*. So, if one were to wash those body parts, say, only to remove impurities, then his *Wudhu'* would not be correct. Furthermore, the intention has to continue all the way through, until he finishes purifying himself; if, in the middle of making *Wudhu'*, he changes his intention from the *Wudhu'* to something else, his *Wudhu'* is cancelled.

"That what caused one to have to make *Wudhu'* has stopped": This means that if one has to perform *Wudhu'* because he defecated, for example, then his stool should completely stop flowing before he makes *Wudhu'*. The same can be said for vomiting: he should completely finish vomiting before starting to make *Wudhu'*.

"Before making *Wudhu'*, the performance of *Istinja'* or *Istijmar*": *Istinja'* means to purify oneself from urine or stool, using water, and in some contexts, it could mean *Istijmar* as well. *Istijmar* means to purify oneself from the same impurities using stones or what carries the same ruling as stones (such as toilet paper in the present day). Whoever, then, has relieved himself, must perform *Istinja'* or *Istijmar* before making *Wudhu'*. But contrary to what some people think, if one wishes to make *Wudhu'*, it is not necessary to perform *Istinja'* or *Istijmar* when one hasn't actually relieved oneself.

"Purity of water being used, and its being lawful": It is not permissible to use impure water, water that has been wrongfully usurped, or water that has been stolen. The Prophet ﷺ said:

«مَنْ أَحْدَثَ فِي أَمْرِنَا هَذَا مَا لَيْسَ مِنْهُ فَهُوَ رَدٌّ»

Whosoever introduces into this matter of ours that which does not belong to it, then it is rejected.

"Removing anything (a stain, for example) that prevents the water from reaching one's skin": So that one's ablution is performed properly, as the Prophet ﷺ advised his nation to perform it, one should remove any stain or particles, that prevent the water from directly reaching one's skin.

"That when one makes ablution, the time of prayer has arrived...": This is particularly for those who continually release impurities from their bodies, such as one who is afflicted with enuresis, a condition wherein one urinates uncontrollably. When a woman was afflicted not with her monthly bleeding, but with another kind of bleeding that was a result of sickness, the Prophet ﷺ ordered her to make ablution for every prayer. (Recorded by Abu Dawud and At-Tirmithi).

Lesson Thirteen

Elements That Are Obligatory (*Fardh*) In The *Wudhu'*

There are six elements that are obligatory in *Wudhu'*:

1) Washing one's face, including *Al-Madhmadhah* and *Al-Istinshaq* (These terms will be clarified in the explanation, if Allâh wills)
2) Washing one's hands, elbows, and whatever is in between.
3) Wiping one's entire head, including one's ears.
4) Washing one's feet, including one's ankles.
5) Performing these elements in order.
6) Performing them at one time, without too long of a pause between one body part and another.

It is recommended to repeat the washing of one's face, hands, and feet three times; the same goes for the *Madhmadhah* and the *Al-Istinshaq*. However, it is obligatory to perform each of those elements only once. And based on the meanings of authentic *Ahadith*, one should wipe his head once only.

❖ ❖ ❖

"Washing one's face, including *Al-Madhmadhah* and *Al-Istinshaq*": The limits of one's face: from where the hair begins to grow on one's head to below one's cheekbones on each side of the face, until they meet at the chin, and until the base of one's ears. Allâh Almighty says:

﴿إِذَا قُمْتُمْ إِلَى ٱلصَّلَوٰةِ فَٱغْسِلُوا۟ وُجُوهَكُمْ وَأَيْدِيَكُمْ إِلَى ٱلْمَرَافِقِ وَٱمْسَحُوا۟ بِرُءُوسِكُمْ وَأَرْجُلَكُمْ إِلَى ٱلْكَعْبَيْنِ﴾

When you intend to offer *As-Salat* (the prayer), wash your faces and your hands (forearms) up to the elbows, rub (by passing wet hands over) your heads, and (wash) your feet up to the ankles.[1]

In a *Hadith*, Humran describes the *Wudhu'* of 'Uthman, may Allâh be pleased with him, who is describing the *Wudhu'* of the Prophet ﷺ. 'Uthman said, "Then he washed his face three times."

We must perform *Madhmadhah* (washing out the mouth) and *Istinshaq* (snuffing water into the nose and blowing it out) based on two proofs: 1) everyone who described the Prophet's *Wudhu'* mentioned them, and 2) the nose and the mouth are parts of the face.

'Aishah, may Allâh be pleased with her, related that the Prophet ﷺ said:

«إِذَا تَوَضَّأْتَ فَمَضْمِضْ»

When you make *Wudhu'*, perform the *Madhmadhah*.

Abu Hurairah, may Allâh be pleased him, related that the Prophet ﷺ said:

«إِذَا تَوَضَّأَ أَحَدُكُمْ فَلْيَجْعَلْ فِي أَنْفِهِ مَاءً ثُمَّ لِيَسْتَنْثِرْ»

When one of you makes *Wudhu'*, he should put water into his nose and then blow it out. (Agreed upon).

Based on what has been related from the Sunnah, the water is taken into the nose with the right hand, and blown out with the assistance of the left.

To follow the Sunnah, one should perform *Al-Madhmadhah* and *Al-Istinshaq* with one handful of water; when one of the Prophet's Companions described his *Wudhu'*, he said, "He then made *Madhmadhah* and *Istinshaq*." As long as one is not fasting, one should exaggerate in both, working the water inside one's mouth and inhaling water through one's nose to a high level. The Prophet ﷺ said:

«وَبَالِغْ فِي الْمَضْمَضَةِ وَالِاسْتِنْشَاقِ إِلَّا أَنْ تَكُونَ صَائِمًا»

And exaggerate when performing the *Madhmadhah* and

---

[1] (*Al-Ma'idah* 5:6)

Istinshaq unless you are fasting. (Recorded by Abu Dawud and At-Tirmithi via a narration from Luqit bin Saburah).

"Washing one's hands, elbows, and whatever is in between": One should wash his hands until (and including) his elbows. Allâh Almighty says:

$$﴿ وَأَيْدِيَكُمْ إِلَى ٱلْمَرَافِقِ ﴾$$

And your hands (forearms) up to the elbows [1]

In Humran's narration: "He then washed his right hand up to the elbow three times, and then the left in the same way." The elbow must be washed along with the hand, first because the Prophet ﷺ used to wash his elbow as well, and second because the scholars say that "up to" here means "with."

"Wiping one's entire head, including one's ears":

Allâh Almighty says:

$$﴿ وَٱمْسَحُوا۟ بِرُءُوسِكُمْ ﴾$$

Rub (by passing wet hands over) your heads.[2]

'Abdullah bin Zaid said when he described the *Wudhu'* of the Prophet ﷺ, "Indeed, the Prophet ﷺ wiped his head with his hands, bringing them toward the front and taking them toward the back. He began with the front of his head, working his hands up until he reached the back of his head, and then he brought them back to their starting place." (Recorded by Al-Bukhari and Muslim.) It is enough to wipe one's head once.

The ears take the same ruling for the Prophet ﷺ said:

«الأُذُنَانِ مِنَ الرَّأْسِ»

The ears are part of the head.

Recorded by At-Tirmithi and Abu Dawud with a *Sahih* chain of narration.

The Prophet ﷺ would wipe both his head and ears when making *Wudhu'*.

---

[1] (*Al-Ma'idah* 5:6)

[2] (*Al-Ma'idah* 5:6)

It is not legislated, however, to use new water for one's ears; rather, one should use what remains after one wipes his head. The way to wipe one's ears is described in Ibn 'Umar's *Hadith*, wherein he said, "Then he wiped his head, inserting his two index fingers into his ears, wiping with his thumbs the exterior of his ears." (Recorded by Abu Dawud and An-Nasa'i).

"Washing one's feet, including one's ankles": Allâh Almighty says:

$$ ﴿وَأَرْجُلَكُمْ إِلَى ٱلْكَعْبَيْنِ﴾ $$

And (wash) your feet up to the ankles.[1]

In Humran's *Hadith*: "Then he washed his right foot until the ankles three times, and then he did the same with his left." (Agreed upon).

One's ankles, the two bones that are protruding just above one's feet, must be washed as well.

"Performing these elements in order": This is because Allâh Almighty mentioned the *Wudhu'* in order, and the Prophet ﷺ would perform *Wudhu'* in that same order. When I say "in order," I mean that one must perform *Wudhu'* the way Allâh Almighty and His Messenger ﷺ ordered us to perform it, without advancing certain body parts before their time, which, if done, nullifies the *Wudhu'*.

By washing one's elbows before his face, one invalidates his *Wudhu'*; similarly, by washing one's feet before wiping one's head, one invalidates his *Wudhu'*, and so on. The verse clearly indicates the order of *Wudhu'*, and the Prophet ﷺ said:

$$ «تَوَضَّأْ كَمَا أَمَرَكَ اللهُ» $$

Perform *Wudhu'* in the way Allâh ordered you (to perform it).

"Performing them at one time, without too long of a pause": This is the sixth obligatory element of *Wudhu'*, and what it means is this: while making *Wudhu'*, one should not delay one body part so long that the previous body part has become dry. The body parts of *Wudhu'* must not only be performed in sequence, but also without too long of a pause between one part and the next.

---

[1] (*Al-Ma'idah* 5:6)

Khalid bin Ma'dan related that when the Prophet ﷺ saw a man praying, he noticed that an area about the size of a coin on the back of his foot was unwashed. The Prophet ﷺ ordered him to repeat his *Wudhu'*. (Recorded by Ahmad and Abu Dawud with a *Sahih* chain of narration.)

This *Hadith* clearly indicates that it is necessary to wash one part after another, without pausing too long; had it not been necessary, the Prophet ﷺ would have ordered him to wash only that spot. Moreover, everyone who described the Prophet's *Wudhu'* mentioned that he would perform it continuously, without taking breaks in between body parts, and the Prophet ﷺ is the one who delivers that legislation to his nation.

Finally, it is obligatory to wash all of the body parts for ablution once; twice is better; and three times is best. Ibn Majah recorded that on one occasion, the Prophet ﷺ made ablution, washing each body part once, and he then said:

«هَذَا وُضُوءٌ، مَنْ لَمْ يَتَوَضَّأْهُ لَمْ يَقْبَلِ اللهُ لَهُ صَلَاةً»

This is the ablution, that were one not to perform it, Allâh would not accept his prayer from him.

He then made ablution, washing each body part twice, and he then said:

«هَذَا وُضُوئِي وَوُضُوءُ الْمُرْسَلِينَ قَبْلِي»

This is my *Wudhu'* and the *Wudhu'* of the Messengers before me.

The proof for washing each body part three times is found in the *Hadith* related by 'Uthman which preceded as well as others.

Lesson Fourteen
Actions That Nullify One's Ablution

There are six ways in which one's ablution becomes nullified:

1) Anything that comes out of the two passages.
2) Any impurity that comes out of one's body excessively.
3) When one loses consciousness, during sleep or otherwise.
4) When one touches his private parts directly with his hand, without a barrier separating the two, be it the private part in the front or the one in the back.
5) Eating the meat of a camel.
6) Apostasy, we seek refuge in Allâh from that.

Important note: It is true that when you wash the body of a dead person, your *Wudhu'* is not nullified, because there is no proof to the contrary, this is the view of most scholars, but if your hand touches his private part without a barrier between the two (such as a cloth), you must perform *Wudhu'* again. Notwithstanding the previous ruling, you must not touch the private parts of a dead person unless it is behind a barrier.

Similarly, touching a woman does not nullify *Wudhu'*, regardless of whether it was accompanied by desire or not, according to the more correct view of the scholars, as long as nothing is emitted. From the two scholarly opinions in this issue, this one is correct. The Prophet ﷺ kissed some of his wives and then he would go for prayer without making ablution. The scholars who are of the other opinion refer to this verse:

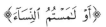

﴿أَوْ لَمَسْتُمُ ٱلنِّسَاءَ﴾

Or if you have been in contact with women.[1]

However, the correct opinion is that this verse is alluding to

---
[1] (*Al-Ma'idah* 5:6)

sexual intercourse, an interpretation that is upheld by Ibn 'Abbas, may Allâh be pleased with them, and a group of scholars from both early and later generations. And guidance lies with Allâh.

In the last lesson, the Shaikh spoke about *Wudhu'*; here, he mentions ways in which one's *Wudhu'* becomes nullified. The first way in which one loses his *Wudhu'* is when anything comes out of the two passages, regardless of whether what comes out is a little or a lot. There are two categories of material that come out of the two passages:

1) What is regular, such as urine and feces. The scholars agree that these discharges nullify one's *Wudhu'*. Ibn 'Abdul-Barr mentioned this consensus in relation to this verse:

﴿أَوْ جَاءَ أَحَدٌ مِّنكُم مِّنَ ٱلْغَآئِطِ﴾

Or any of you comes from answering the call of nature.[1]

In a *Hadith*, the Prophet ﷺ mentioned:

«وَلَكِنْ مِنْ غَائِطٍ وَبَوْلٍ»

But from feces and urine.

And in regards to the passing of wind, he ﷺ said:

«فَلَا يَنْصَرِفْ حَتَّى يَسْمَعَ صَوْتًا أَوْ يَجِدَ رِيحاً»

He should not leave (the prayer) until he hears a noise or detects a smell. (Agreed upon).

2) Things that rarely come out of the two passages, such as hair, stones, or worms. Here again one's *Wudhu'* becomes nullified. When a woman was bleeding from her private parts because of sickness and not because of her monthly period, the Prophet ﷺ said:

«تَوَضَّئِي لِكُلِّ صَلَاةٍ»

Make *Wudhu'* for each prayer.

Because the discharge of that blood was abnormal or rare, the same ruling applies to all abnormal matters that come out of the two

[1] (*Al-Ma'idah* 5:6)

passages. Furthermore, there is another analogy that we can make. The first category of material, i.e., what is normal, requires one to make ablution, and so the same can be said of the second category, i.e., what is rare or abnormal, because both share one common factor: both involve material coming out of the two passages.

"Any impurity that comes out of one's body excessively": If an impurity comes out not from the two passages, but from some other area of the body, one's *Wudhu'* becomes nullified when the matter that comes out is excessive. If the discharge is small, then one remains in a state of purity, for Ibn 'Abbas said regarding blood, "If it is excessive, then he must make *Wudhu'* again." When Ibn 'Umar squeezed a blister causing blood to come out, he prayed without making ablution. In regards to this issue, there is no one known to have differed with the two of them. Therefore, Ibn Qudamah, in *Al-Mughni*, as well as others, mentioned that there is a consensus for that.

"When one loses consciousness, during sleep or otherwise": Other examples are insanity, when one becomes unconscious due to a blow, or when one is drunk. The Prophet ﷺ said:

«الْعَيْنُ وِكَاءُ السَّهِ فَمَنْ نَامَ فَلْيَتَوَضَّأْ»

The eye is the drawstring of the anus. So, whoever sleeps should then perform *Wudhu'*:

The control one loses is not only limited to sleep, for unconsciousness, insanity, and drunkenness are more extreme ways of losing consciousness, so they too (in a way more deserving than sleep) nullify one's *Wudhu'*. The Prophet ﷺ said:

«وَلَكِنْ مِنْ غَائِطٍ وَبَوْلٍ وَنَوْمٍ»

But from feces and urine and sleep.

Here, the meaning of sleep is deep sleep, whereby the one who is sleeping is no longer aware of those who are around him.

"When one touches his private part directly with his hand...": The Prophet ﷺ said:

«مَنْ مَسَّ فَرْجَهُ فَلْيَتَوَضَّأْ»

Whoever touches his private part, then let him perform *Wudhu'*.

Recorded by An-Nasa'i, Ibn Majah, Al-Hakim, Ad-Daraqutni, and

Imam Ahmad, from a narration of Busrah bint Safwan. It was graded *Sahih* by Al-Albani in *Al-Irwa'*.

"**Eating the meat of a camel**": Jabir bin Samurah related that a man asked the Prophet ﷺ, "Should I make *Wudhu'* after eating the meat of a camel?" He said:

«نَعَمْ تَوَضَّأْ مِنْ لُحُومِ الإِبِلِ»

Yes, make *Wudhu'* after eating the meat of a camel. (Recorded by Muslim)

But one does not have to make *Wudhu'* after drinking the milk of a camel or after eating gravy, the source of which is a camel.

"**Apostasy, we seek refuge in Allâh from that**": Allâh Almighty said:

﴿لَئِنْ أَشْرَكْتَ لَيَحْبَطَنَّ عَمَلُكَ﴾

If you join others in worship with Allâh, (then) surely (all) your deeds will be in vain.[1]

﴿وَمَن يَكْفُرْ بِالإِيمَانِ فَقَدْ حَبِطَ عَمَلُهُ﴾

And whosoever rejects faith, then fruitless is his work.[2]

"**Important note: It is true that when you wash the body of a dead person, your *Wudhu'* is not nullified...**": Ibn Qudamah said, "This is the opinion of the majority of jurists, and - if Allâh wills - it is correct, because only from the revealed texts of the *Shari'ah* can we say that something is compulsory, and in regards to this issue, there is no revealed text.

"**An interpretation that is upheld by Ibn 'Abbas and a group of scholars from both early and late generations**": From them, are the following: 'Aishah, and 'Ali, may Allâh be pleased with them, 'Ata, Al-Hasan, Tawus, Ash-Sha'bi, 'Ikrimah, and Sa'id bin Jubair, may Allâh have mercy on them all.

The Shaikh mentioned two issues at the end of this section about which there is disagreement: 1) washing a dead person, and 2) touching a woman. In both issues, he deemed that the stronger opinion is that the *Wudhu'* is not nullified. And Allâh knows best.

---

[1] (*Az-Zumar* 39:65)
[2] (*Al-Ma'idah* 5:5)

Lesson Fifteen

Every Muslim Must Adorn Himself With Manners That Are Legislated By Islam

From those manners are the following:

1) Truthfulness
2) Trustworthiness
3) Chastity.
4) Modesty or shyness.
5) Bravery.
6) Generosity.
7) Fulfilling one's word.
8) Staying away from all that Allâh has forbidden.
9) Being good to one's neighbor.
10) Helping those in need, as much as one is able.

And all other manners that the Qur'an and Sunnah legislate.

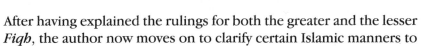

After having explained the rulings for both the greater and the lesser *Fiqh*, the author now moves on to clarify certain Islamic manners to the general population of Muslims.

My brother Muslim — may Allâh Almighty grant us success in all that is good — you must apply those manners and become an excellent example for the people, an example of Islam's high morals and manners.

From the very beginning, Islam spread throughout the populated lands of the earth by way of Muslim merchants and other traveling Muslims — people who were truthful and who fulfilled their trust. My hope is with Allâh Almighty, and then with you, my brother Muslim, in that you should be from those who are adorned with the greatest of manners — Islamic manners.

You must adorn yourself with every manner that Allâh or His Messenger ﷺ ordered you to apply or encouraged you to apply, for the Messenger of Allâh ﷺ said:

«إِنَّمَا بُعِثْتُ لأُتَمِّمَ مَكَارِمَ الأَخْلَاقِ»

Indeed, I have only been sent to complete the noblest of manners.

Recorded by Al-Bukhari in *Al-Adab Al-Mufrad* as well as Ahmad and Al-Hakim with a *Sahih* chain.

In another *Hadith*, the Prophet ﷺ said:

«إِنَّ اللهَ كَرِيمٌ يُحِبُّ الْكَرَمَ وَيُحِبُّ مَعَالِي الأَخْلَاقِ وَيَكْرَهُ سَفَاسِفَهَا»

Indeed, Allâh is Generous: He loves generosity, He loves the highest of manners, while He hates the base ones.

Recorded by Al-Hakim and Abu Nu'aym with a *Sahih* chain.

Allâh Almighty described the Prophet ﷺ, saying:

﴿وَإِنَّكَ لَعَلَى خُلُقٍ عَظِيمٍ ٤﴾

And verily, you (O Muhammad ﷺ) are on exalted standard of character.[1]

When 'Aishah, may Allâh be pleased with her, was asked about the Prophet's manners, she said, "His manners were the Qur'an." (Recorded by Muslim).

The Messenger of Allâh ﷺ would ask his Lord to guide him to righteous manners, to keep him far away from bad ones. In a *Hadith*, he ﷺ said:

«اللَّهُمَّ اغْفِرْ لِي ذُنُوبِي وَخَطَايَايَ كُلَّهَا، اللَّهُمَّ انْعَشْنِي وَاجْبُرْنِي، اللَّهُمَّ اهْدِنِي لِصَالِحِ الأَعْمَالِ وَالأَخْلَاقِ فَإِنَّهُ لَا يَهْدِي لِصَالِحِهَا إِلَّا أَنْتَ وَلَا يَصْرِفُ سَيِّئَهَا إِلَّا أَنْتَ»

O Allâh, forgive me all of my sins and errors; O Allâh, rejuvenate me and protect me from poverty; O Allâh, guide me to good deeds and manners, for no one can guide to the good

---

[1] (*Al-Qalam* 68:4)

ones except You, and no one can ward off the bad ones except You.

Recorded by Al-Hakim and there is a witnessing narration for it according to Ibn As-Sunni, so it is a *Hasan Hadith* due to its many routes of transmission.

The following *Hadith* clearly shows the superiority of good manners:

«أَكْمَلُ الْمُؤْمِنِينَ إِيمَاناً أَحْسَنُهُمْ خُلُقاً»

The most complete of believers in terms of faith is the best of them in manners.

Recorded by At-Tirmithi and Abu Dawud with a *Hasan* chain.

And in another narration:

«خِيَارُكُمْ أَحَاسِنُكُمْ أَخْلَاقاً»

The best of you is the best from you in manners.

Recorded by Al-Bukhari and Muslim.

The Prophet ﷺ also said:

«أَفْضَلُ الْمُؤْمِنِينَ أَحْسَنُهُمْ خُلُقاً»

The most virtuous of the believers are the best of them in manners. (Recorded by Al-Hakim with a *Hasan* chain).

Good manners can help you get into Paradise, for the Prophet ﷺ said:

«أَنَا زَعِيمٌ بِبَيْتٍ فِي أَعْلَى الْجَنَّةِ لِمَنْ حَسَّنَ خُلُقَهُ»

I am the guarantor of a house in the highest part of Paradise for the one who has good manners. (Recorded by Abu Dawud with a *Hasan* chain).

Good manners can also bring about Allâh's love for His worshipper, for the Prophet ﷺ said:

«أَحَبُّ عِبَادِ اللهِ إِلَى اللهِ أَحْسَنُهُمْ خُلُقاً»

The most beloved of Allâh's worshippers to Him are the ones with the best manners. (Recorded by At-Tabarani with a *Sahih* chain).

Good manners can also help you gain the Prophet's love and his closeness on the Day of Judgement; the Prophet ﷺ said:

«إِنَّ مِنْ أَحَبِّكُمْ إِلَيَّ وَأَقْرَبِكُمْ مِنِّي مَجْلِساً يَوْمَ الْقِيَامَةِ أَحَاسِنُكُمْ أَخْلَاقاً»

Indeed, the most beloved of you to me and the ones seated closest to me from you on the Day of Judgement are those from you who have the best manners. (Recorded by At-Tirmithi with a *Hasan* chain)

Good manners are very heavy on your Scale of deeds; indeed, the Prophet ﷺ said:

«مَا مِنْ شَيْءٍ فِي الْمِيزَانِ أَثْقَلُ مِنْ حُسْنِ الْخُلُقِ»

There is nothing heavier on the Scale than good manners. (Recorded by Abu Dawud with a *Sahih* chain)

By having good manners, you can reach the level of the one who fasts and the one who stands late in the night to pray. The Prophet ﷺ said:

«إِنَّ الرَّجُلَ لَيُدْرِكُ بِحُسْنِ خُلُقِهِ دَرَجَاتِ قَائِمِ اللَّيْلِ صَائِمِ النَّهَارِ»

Indeed, through his good manners, a man reaches the levels of the one who stands at night (to pray) and the one who fasts during the day. (Recorded by Abu Dawud and Al-Hakim with a *Sahih* chain)

And finally, good manners can help increase you in your age and can help bring life into your home. The Prophet ﷺ said:

«حُسْنُ الْخُلُقِ وَحُسْنُ الْجِوَارِ يُعَمِّرَانِ الدِّيَارَ وَيَزِيدَانِ فِي الأَعْمَارِ»

Good manners and being good to neighbors — both of these bring life to homes and cause one's life span to be prolonged. (Recorded by Ahmad with a *Sahih* chain).

"**Truthfulness**": The Shaikh began a list of good manners with truthfulness, a characteristic that Allâh ordered us apply:

﴿يَٰٓأَيُّهَا ٱلَّذِينَ ءَامَنُوا۟ ٱتَّقُوا۟ ٱللَّهَ وَكُونُوا۟ مَعَ ٱلصَّٰدِقِينَ ۝﴾

O you who believe! Be afraid of Allâh, and be with those who are true (in the words and deeds).[1]

---

[1] (*At-Tawbah* 9:119)

The Messenger of Allâh ﷺ said:

«إِنَّ الصِّدْقَ يَهْدِي إِلَى الْبِرِّ وَإِنَّ الْبِرَّ يَهْدِي إِلَى الْجَنَّةِ، وَإِنَّ الرَّجُلَ لَيَصْدُقُ حَتَّى يُكْتَبَ عِنْدَ اللهِ صِدِّيقاً»

Indeed, truthfulness guides to righteousness; indeed, righteousness guides to Paradise. And a man continues to tell the truth until He is written with Allâh as a truthful one. (Recorded by Al-Bukhari and Muslim).

The Prophet ﷺ said:

«الصِّدْقُ طُمَأْنِينَةٌ وَالْكَذِبُ رِيبَةٌ»

Truth is serenity while lying is uncertainty. (Recorded by At-Tirmithi).

Truthfulness involves many traits — truthfulness in speech, in promises, in appointments, in buying, and in selling. Let your slogan, my brother, be truthfulness, and in all situations, train yourself to be truthful, for it will serve as a protection.

"Trustworthiness": In many ways man is entrusted with duties, and Allâh Almighty has ordered man to fulfill the most primary of duties — all religious obligations and commandments — after the heavens and the earth declined to bear those duties:

﴿إِنَّا عَرَضْنَا الْأَمَانَةَ عَلَى السَّمَوَاتِ وَالْأَرْضِ وَالْجِبَالِ فَأَبَيْنَ أَن يَحْمِلْنَهَا وَأَشْفَقْنَ مِنْهَا وَحَمَلَهَا الْإِنسَانُ إِنَّهُ كَانَ ظَلُومًا جَهُولًا ۝﴾

Truly We did offer *Al-Amanah* (the trust) to the heavens and the earth, and the mountains, but they declined to bear it and were afraid of it. But man bore it. Verily, he was unjust (to himself) and ignorant (of its results).[1]

You fulfill your trust by performing deeds as Allâh Almighty ordered you to perform them. Then at another level, you have been entrusted with your wife and children; it is your responsibility to give those children a righteous upbringing. You have been entrusted with both a body and senses: therefore you must use them only in the obedience of Allâh. The Prophet ﷺ said:

---

[1] (*Fatir* 33:72)

«الْمَجَالِسُ بِالأَمَانَةِ إِلَّا ثَلَاثَةَ مَجَالِسٍ: مَجْلِسُ سَفْكِ دَمٍ حَرَامٍ، أَوْ فَرْجٍ
حَرَامٍ، أَوِ اقْتِطَاعِ مَالٍ بِغَيْرِ حَقٍّ»

Gatherings must be with trust, except for three gatherings: a gathering wherein blood is wrongfully spilled, (a gathering wherein) the unlawful occurs with the private parts, (or a gathering wherein) wealth is taken from another without a right to do so. (Recorded by Abu Dawud)

At yet another level, there is a trust between husband and wife; the Prophet ﷺ said:

«مِنْ أَعْظَمِ الْأَمَانَةِ عِنْدَ اللهِ يَوْمَ الْقِيَامَةِ الرَّجُلُ يُفْضِي إِلَى امْرَأَتِهِ وَتُفْضِي
إِلَيْهِ ثُمَّ يُنْشِرُ سِرَّهَا»

From the greatest of trusts (which are broken) with Allâh on the Day of Judgement is a man who has intimate relations with his wife and a wife who has intimate relations with her husband, and then he spreads her secrets. (Recorded by Ahmad)

Finally, one must return those things which were kept with him for safekeeping, or those things which were lent to him, returning them according to the agreement that was made, for Allâh Almighty says:

﴿إِنَّ اللَّهَ يَأْمُرُكُمْ أَن تُؤَدُّواْ الْأَمَٰنَٰتِ إِلَىٰٓ أَهْلِهَا﴾

Verily, Allâh commands that you should render back the trust to those whom they are due.[1]

The Prophet ﷺ said:

«أَدِّ الْأَمَانَةَ إِلَى مَنِ ائْتَمَنَكَ وَلَا تَخُنْ مَنْ خَانَكَ»

Return the trust to the person who entrusted you, and do not deceive the one who has deceived you. (Recorded by At-Tirmithi and Abu Dawud with a *Sahih* chain).

We should try to fulfill all trusts that are given to us because, since not doing so is an indication of hypocrisy. When the Prophet ﷺ was describing the signs of a hypocrite, he said:

---
[1] (*An-Nisa'* 4:58)

«وَإِذَا اؤْتُمِنَ خَانَ»

And if he is trusted, he deceives.

"Chastity": In one context, the Arabic word for chastity means to protect oneself from sexual wrongdoing, a characteristic that is a must for a Muslim:

﴿وَلْيَسْتَعْفِفِ ٱلَّذِينَ لَا يَجِدُونَ نِكَاحًا حَتَّىٰ يُغْنِيَهُمُ ٱللَّهُ مِن فَضْلِهِ﴾

And let those who find not the financial means for marriage keep themselves chaste, until Allâh enriches them of His bounty.[1]

A Muslim protects himself from perpetrating vile and evil deeds, hoping to receive reward from Allâh. When the Prophet ﷺ was describing the seven categories of people who will be in Allâh's Shade, one of the categories he mentioned was:

«وَرَجُلٌ دَعَتْهُ امْرَأَةٌ ذَاتُ مَنْصِبٍ وَجَمَالٍ فَقَالَ: إِنِّي أَخَافُ اللهَ»

And a man whom a woman possessing both status and beauty invites (to herself), and he says, "Indeed, I fear Allâh."

In another context, the Arabic word that generally means chastity takes on the meaning of modesty and self-respect; Allâh Almighty says:

﴿يَحْسَبُهُمُ ٱلْجَاهِلُ أَغْنِيَآءَ مِنَ ٱلتَّعَفُّفِ تَعْرِفُهُم بِسِيمَٰهُمْ لَا يَسْـَٔلُونَ ٱلنَّاسَ إِلْحَافًا﴾

The one who knows them not, thinks that they are rich because of their modesty. You may know them by their mark, they do not beg of people at all.[2]

The Prophet ﷺ said:

«الْيَدُ الْعُلْيَا خَيْرٌ مِنَ الْيَدِ السُّفْلَى وَابْدَأْ بِمَنْ تَعُولُ، وَخَيْرُ الصَّدَقَةِ مَا كَانَ عَنْ ظَهْرِ غِنًى، وَمَنْ يَسْتَعْفِفْ يُعِفَّهُ اللهُ وَمَنْ يَسْتَغْنِ يُغْنِهِ اللهُ»

The upper hand is better than the lower one, and begin with

---

[1] (*An-Nur* 24:33)

[2] (*Al-Baqarah* 2:273)

those who are under your guardianship (or care). The best charity is to give that which is left after one spends on one's needs (and on one's family's needs); whoever stays away from the unlawful and from asking people, Allâh protects him; and whoever seeks independence from people (seeking total dependence on Allâh), Allâh makes him rich. (Recorded by Al-Bukhari and Muslim)

"Modesty or shyness": Shyness helps prevent one from perpetrating evil deeds, acting as a barrier between man and sin. Furthermore, it prevents one from being negligent with Allâh's rights and the rights of His creatures. The Prophet ﷺ said:

«إِنَّ مِمَّا أَدْرَكَ النَّاسَ مِنْ كَلَامِ النُّبُوَّةِ الأُولَى إِذَا لَمْ تَسْتَحِ فَاصْنَعْ مَا شِئْتَ»

From what the people know regarding the earliest sayings of the Prophets is, 'If you have no shame, then do as you please.'' (Recorded by Al-Bukhari)

Shyness is one of the branches of faith, for the Prophet ﷺ said:

«الإِيمَانُ بِضْعٌ وَسَبْعُونَ شُعْبَةً، فَأَفْضَلُهَا قَوْلُ لَا إِلَهَ إِلَّا اللهُ وَأَدْنَاهَا إِمَاطَةُ الأَذَى عَنِ الطَّرِيقِ، وَالْحَيَاءُ شُعْبَةٌ مِنَ الإِيمَانِ»

Iman consists of more then seventy branches; the best of them is the saying, 'None has the right to be worshipped but Allâh.' The lowest one is to remove something harmful from a path, and shyness is one of the branches of faith. (Recorded by Al-Bukhari and Muslim)

To emphasize the importance of shyness, the Prophet ﷺ said:

«الْحَيَاءُ خَيْرٌ كُلُّهُ»

Shyness is everything that is good. (Recorded by Muslim)

And:

«إِنَّ اللهَ حَيِيٌّ سِتِّيرٌ يُحِبُّ الْحَيَاءَ وَالسِّتْرَ»

Indeed Allâh is modest and concealed, He loves shyness and loves to cover the faults of His creatures. (Recorded by Abu Dawud, An-Nasa'i and Ahmad)

The greatest form of shyness is to be shy from Allâh Almighty, for the Prophet ﷺ said:

«اسْتَحْيُوا مِنَ اللهِ حَقَّ الْحَيَاءِ، وَمَنِ اسْتَحْيَىٰ مِنَ اللهِ حَقَّ الْحَيَاءِ فَلْيَحْفَظِ الرَّأْسَ وَمَا وَعَىٰ وَالْبَطْنَ وَمَا حَوَى، وَلْيَذْكُرِ الْمَوْتَ وَالبِلَى، وَمَنْ أَرَادَ الآخِرَةَ تَرَكَ زِينَةَ الدُّنْيَا، فَمَنْ فَعَلَ ذَلِكَ فَقَدِ اسْتَحْيَا مِنَ اللهِ حَقَّ الْحَيَاءِ»

Be shy from Allâh with a true shyness; whoever is truly shy from Allâh, should be careful regarding his head and what it stores, and regarding his stomach and what it stores; (such a person) should remember death and passing away; whoever desires the Hereafter, leaves the beautiful things of this world. Whoever has done all of that, then he has been shy from Allâh with true shyness. (Recorded by At-Tirmithi, Ahmad, and Al-Hakim, and it is a *Hasan Hadith*).

"Bravery": Bravery is also one of the noble characteristics of the Muslim. You should know, however, that bravery lies in the heart, while strength lies in the body. The Muslim is one who says the word of truth for Allâh, without fearing the blame of anyone.

"Generosity": We have in this regard the example of the Prophet ﷺ, about whom Ibn 'Abbas, may Allâh be pleased with them, who said, "The Messenger of Allâh was the most generous of people." And Allâh gave glad tidings to those believers who are generous:

﴿ٱلَّذِينَ يُنفِقُونَ أَمْوَٰلَهُم بِٱلَّيْلِ وَٱلنَّهَارِ سِرًّا وَعَلَانِيَةً فَلَهُمْ أَجْرُهُمْ عِندَ رَبِّهِمْ وَلَا خَوْفٌ عَلَيْهِمْ وَلَا هُمْ يَحْزَنُونَ ٢٧٤﴾

Those who spend their wealth (in Allâh's cause) by night and day, in secret and in public, they shall have their reward with their Lord. On them shall be no fear, nor shall they grieve.[1]

One of the best forms of generosity is that which is shown to one's neighbors and guests, for the Prophet ﷺ said:

«مَنْ كَانَ يُؤْمِنُ بِاللهِ وَالْيَوْمِ الآخِرِ فَلْيُكْرِمْ ضَيْفَهُ»

Whoever believes in Allâh and in the Last Day, then let him honor his guest.

---

[1] (*Al-Baqarah* 2:274)

When given a choice between spending in the way of Allâh and between holding on to our wealth, we should consider this *Hadith*:

«يَا ابْنَ آدَمَ إِنَّكَ إِنْ تَبْذُلِ الْفَضْلَ خَيْرٌ لَكَ وَإِنْ تُمْسِكْهُ شَرٌّ لَكَ»

O son of Adam, if you give in charity from your excess wealth then that is good for you, and if you keep it, then that is evil for you. (Recorded by Muslim and At-Tirmithi)

Whenever one spends for a good cause, Allâh rewards him with that which is better than what he spent, for Allâh Almighty says:

﴿وَمَا تُنفِقُوا مِنْ خَيْرٍ فَلِأَنفُسِكُمْ وَمَا تُنفِقُونَ إِلَّا ابْتِغَاءَ وَجْهِ اللَّهِ وَمَا تُنفِقُوا مِنْ خَيْرٍ يُوَفَّ إِلَيْكُمْ وَأَنتُمْ لَا تُظْلَمُونَ ۝﴾

And whatever you spend in good, it is for yourselves, when you spend not except seeking Allâh's Face. And whatever you spend in good, it will be repaid to you in full, and you shall not be wronged.[1]

In a *Qudsi Hadith*, the Prophet ﷺ related that Allâh Almighty said:

«أَنْفِقْ يَا ابْنَ آدَمَ يُنْفَقْ عَلَيْكَ»

Spend, O son of Adam, and He (Allâh) will spend on you. (Recorded by Al-Bukhari and Muslim)

"Fulfilling one's word or promise": To fulfill one's word or promise is one of the greatest characteristics of a Muslim; Allâh Almighty says:

﴿يَأَيُّهَا الَّذِينَ ءَامَنُوا أَوْفُوا بِالْعُقُودِ﴾

O you who believe! Fulfill (your) obligations.[2]

And:

﴿وَأَوْفُوا بِعَهْدِ اللَّهِ إِذَا عَاهَدتُّمْ﴾

And fulfill the covenant of Allâh when you have made a covenant.[3]

---

[1] (*Al-Baqarah* 2:272)
[2] (*Al-Ma'idah* 5:1)
[3] (*An-Nahl* 16:91)

To not fulfill one's promises is from the characteristics of the hypocrite; as the Prophet ﷺ was describing the traits of the hypocrite, he said:

«وَإِذَا عَاهَدَ غَدَرَ»

If he promises, he betrays.

He ﷺ also said:

«وَإِذَا وَعَدَ أَخْلَفَ»

When he makes a promise, he breaks it.

Regardless of whether it is in buying, selling, or even in matters related to marriage, one should fulfill not only the agreement in general, but all of the conditions that were stipulated and agreed upon. The Prophet ﷺ said:

«إِنَّ أَحَقَّ الشُّرُوطِ مَا اسْتَحْلَلْتُمْ بِهِ الْفُرُوجَ»

Indeed, the most deserving of conditions are those that make another person's private parts lawful (to you).

He ﷺ also said,

«الْمُسْلِمُونَ عَلَى شُرُوطِهِمْ»

The Muslims held to the conditions (they agree upon).

So let the Muslim beware of a stern punishment awaiting those who betray their brothers and usurp their rights.

"Staying away from all that Allâh has forbidden": It is the responsibility of every Muslim to seek out lawful sustenance, while leaving anything that Allâh has declared to be unlawful. In a *Hadith* related by Abu Hurairah, may Allâh be pleased with him, the Prophet ﷺ said:

«إِنَّ اللهَ تَعَالَى طَيِّبٌ لَا يَقْبَلُ إِلَّا طَيِّباً، وَإِنَّ اللهَ تَعَالَى أَمَرَ الْمُؤْمِنِينَ بِمَا أَمَرَ بِهِ الْمُرْسَلِينَ»

Indeed Allâh is good and pure and He doesn't accept other than what is good and pure. And Allâh ordered the believers with the same command with which he ordered the Messengers.

For Allâh Almighty said:

﴿يَٰٓأَيُّهَا ٱلَّذِينَ ءَامَنُوا۟ كُلُوا۟ مِن طَيِّبَٰتِ مَا رَزَقْنَٰكُمْ وَٱشْكُرُوا۟ لِلَّهِ إِن كُنتُمْ إِيَّاهُ تَعْبُدُونَ ۝١⁷²﴾

O you who believe! Eat of the lawful things that We have provided you with, and be grateful to Allâh, if it is indeed He Whom you worship. [1]

Then the Prophet ﷺ mentioned:

«الرَّجُلُ يُطِيلُ السَّفَرَ أَشْعَثَ أَغْبَرَ يَمُدُّ يَدَيْهِ إِلَى السَّمَاءِ يَا رَبِّ يَا رَبِّ وَمَطْعَمُهُ حَرَامٌ وَمَشْرَبُهُ حَرَامٌ وَمَلْبَسُهُ حَرَامٌ وَغُذِيَ بِالْحَرَامِ فَأَنَّى يُسْتَجَابُ لِذَلِكَ»

...A man on long journey, who was disheveled and dust-covered; he would raise his hands to the sky, and say, "O my Lord, O my Lord." However, his food was unlawful, his drink was unlawful, his clothes were unlawful — he was sustained by unlawful. How is it that his prayer could be answered? (Recorded by Muslim)

The Muslim is ordered to stay far away from the unlawful, like consuming *Riba* (interest and usury):

﴿يَٰٓأَيُّهَا ٱلَّذِينَ ءَامَنُوا۟ ٱتَّقُوا۟ ٱللَّهَ وَذَرُوا۟ مَا بَقِىَ مِنَ ٱلرِّبَوٰٓا۟ إِن كُنتُم مُّؤْمِنِينَ ۝²⁷⁸﴾

O you who believe! Be afraid of Allâh and give up what remains (due to you) from *Riba* (interest and usury) (from now onward), if you are (really) believers.[2]

Another example is to wrongfully consume the wealth of an orphan; Allâh Almighty says:

﴿إِنَّ ٱلَّذِينَ يَأْكُلُونَ أَمْوَٰلَ ٱلْيَتَٰمَىٰ ظُلْمًا إِنَّمَا يَأْكُلُونَ فِى بُطُونِهِمْ نَارًا وَسَيَصْلَوْنَ سَعِيرًا ۝١⁰﴾

Verily, those who unjustly consume the property of orphans, they eat up only fire into their bellies, and they will be burnt in

---

[1] (*Al-Baqarah* 2:172)

[2] (*Al-Baqarah* 2:278)

the blazing Fire.[1]

And yet another example is eating from money taken through bribery:

﴿وَلَا تَأْكُلُوٓاْ أَمْوَٰلَكُم بَيْنَكُم بِٱلْبَٰطِلِ وَتُدْلُواْ بِهَآ إِلَى ٱلْحُكَّامِ لِتَأْكُلُواْ فَرِيقًا مِّنْ أَمْوَٰلِ ٱلنَّاسِ بِٱلْإِثْمِ وَأَنتُمْ تَعْلَمُونَ ١٨٨﴾

And consume not one another's property unjustly, nor give bribery to the rulers that you may knowingly consume a part of the property of others sinfully.[2]

The Muslim leaves not only what is forbidden, but also what is doubtful. The Prophet ﷺ said:

«دَعْ مَا يَرِيبُكَ إِلَى مَا لَا يَرِيبُكَ»

Leave that which you doubt thereof, for which you have no doubt. (Recorded by An-Nasa'i and At-Tirmithi with a *Sahih* chain).

By perpetrating that which is doubtful, one is led to perpetrating that which is unlawful. The Prophet ﷺ said:

«إِنَّ الْحَلَالَ بَيِّنٌ وَالْحَرَامَ بَيِّنٌ وَبَيْنَهُمَا أُمُورٌ مَشْتَبِهَاتٌ لَا يَعْلَمُهُنَّ كَثِيرٌ مِنَ النَّاسِ فَمَنِ اتَّقَى الشُّبُهَاتِ فَقَدِ اسْتَبْرَأَ لِدِينِهِ وَعِرْضِهِ وَمَنْ وَقَعَ فِي الشُّبُهَاتِ وَقَعَ فِي الْحَرَامِ كَالرَّاعِي يَرْعَىٰ حَوْلَ الْحِمَى يُوشِكُ أَنْ يَرْتَعَ فِيهِ أَلَا وَإِنَّ لِكُلِّ مَلِكٍ حِمًى أَلَا إِنَّ حِمَى اللهِ مَحَارِمُهُ . . . الحديث»

Indeed, the lawful is clear and the unlawful is clear; however, between them are matters that are not clear, not many people know about those matters. Whoever avoids the unclear matters, he has protected both his religion and his honor. Whoever deals with the unclear matters, he deals with the unlawful. Like a shepherd, grazing around the limits of a sanctuary, coming close to entering it. Indeed every king has such a sanctuary; indeed the unlawful are the sanctuary of Allâh. (Recorded by Al-Bukhari and Muslim).

---

[1] (*An-Nisa'* 4:10)

[2] (*Al-Baqarah* 2:188)

"Being good to one's neighbor": Allâh Almighty says:

﴿وَٱعْبُدُوا۟ ٱللَّهَ وَلَا تُشْرِكُوا۟ بِهِۦ شَيْـًٔا ۖ وَبِٱلْوَٰلِدَيْنِ إِحْسَٰنًا وَبِذِى ٱلْقُرْبَىٰ وَٱلْيَتَٰمَىٰ وَٱلْمَسَٰكِينِ وَٱلْجَارِ ذِى ٱلْقُرْبَىٰ وَٱلْجَارِ ٱلْجُنُبِ وَٱلصَّاحِبِ بِٱلْجَنۢبِ وَٱبْنِ ٱلسَّبِيلِ﴾

Worship Allâh and join none with Him in worship, and do good to parents, kinsfolk, orphans, *Al-Masakin* (the poor), the neighbor who is near of kin, the neighbor who is a stranger, the companion by your side, the wayfarer (you meet).[1]

Al-Qurtubi (*Al-Jami' Al-Ahkam Al-Qur'an Al-Karim* 5:183) said, "It is correct that the order to be good to the neighbor means that it is recommended to be good to him whether he is a Muslim or a disbeliever. To do good to one's neighbor may mean to console him, and it may mean to deal well with him, by not harming him, and by defending him."

Allâh's Messenger ﷺ ordered being good to the neighbor, saying:

«كُنْ وَرِعاً تَكُنْ أَعْبَدَ النَّاسِ، وَكُنْ قَنِعاً تَكُنْ أَشْكَرَ النَّاسِ، وَأَحِبَّ لِلنَّاسِ مَا تُحِبُّ لِنَفْسِكَ تَكُنْ مُؤْمِناً، وَأَحْسِنْ جِوَارَ مَنْ جَاوَرَكَ تَكُنْ مُسْلِمًا»

Be one who avoids certain things that are lawful for fear that they will lead to that which is forbidden, and you will be from those who are best in worship; be content, and you will be the most thankful of people. Love for others what you love for yourself, and you will be a believer. Be good to your neighbors, and you will be a Muslim. (Recorded by Ibn Majah, Abu Ya'la, and Abu Nu'aym in *Al-Hilyah* and it is *Hasan*.)

'Aishah, may Allâh be pleased with her, related that the Prophet ﷺ said:

«مَازَالَ جِبْرِيلُ يُوصِينِي بِالْجَارِ حَتَّى ظَنَنْتُ أَنَّهُ سَيُوَرِّثُهُ»

Jibril continued to advise me to be good to my neighbor, so much so, that I thought he would make him one of my heirs. (Agreed upon)

One way to do good to one's neighbor is to give him a gift. On one occasion, the Prophet ﷺ said to Abu Tharr, may Allâh be pleased

---

[1] (*An-Nisa'* 4:36)

with him:

«إِذَا طَبَخْتَ مَرَقاً فَأَكْثِرْ مَاءَهُ ثُمَّ انْظُرْ أَهْلَ بَيْتٍ مِنْ جِيرَانِكَ فَأَصِبْهُمْ مِنْهَا بِمَعْرُوفٍ»

When you cook broth, add more water to it, then go to your neighbor's household, and give them a good portion thereof. (Recorded by Muslim)

Do not limit yourself in this regard, giving a gift only to the poor; rather, give gifts to your rich neighbors as well; the Prophet ﷺ said,

«خَيْرُ الْجِيرَانِ عِنْدَ اللهِ خَيْرُهُمْ لِجَارِهِ»

The best neighbor with Allâh is the one from them who deals most honorably with his neighbor. (Recorded by At-Tirmithi, Ahmad, Ad-Darimi, and Al-Hakim with a *Sahih* chain).

Having a good neighbor can even help one achieve happiness, for the Messenger of Allâh ﷺ said:

«أَرْبَعٌ مِنَ السَّعَادَةِ: الْمَرْأَةُ الصَّالِحَةُ، وَالْمَسْكَنُ الْوَاسِعُ، وَالْجَارُ الصَّالِحُ، وَالْمَرْكَبُ الْهَنِيءُ»

Four are from happiness: a righteous wife, a spacious home, a righteous neighbor, and a comfortable mount. (Recorded by Ibn Hibban with a *Sahih* chain)

It is not only in giving things that one shows kindness to his neighbor, but it is also in ordering him to do good, forbidding him from evil, and advising him in general.

"Helping those in need, as much as one is able": This is from the noblest of deeds, for the Prophet ﷺ said,

«وَاللهُ فِي عَوْنِ الْعَبْدِ مَا كَانَ الْعَبْدُ فِي عَوْنِ أَخِيهِ»

Allâh continues to help the worshipper as long as the worshipper is helping his brother. (Recorded by Muslim)

He ﷺ also said,

«مَنْ كَانَ فِي حَاجَةِ أَخِيهِ كَانَ اللهُ فِي حَاجَتِهِ»

Whoever is there for his brother's need, Allâh is there for his need. (Recorded by Al-Bukhari and Muslim)

The poor, the widows, the orphans, and those, who though not poor, in some areas are in need: all of these categories of people need help. The Prophet ﷺ said:

«السَّاعِي عَلَى الْأَرْمَلَةِ وَالْمِسْكِينِ كَالْمُجَاهِدِ فِي سَبِيلِ اللهِ»

The one who seeks to help the widows and the poor is like the one who is fighting in the way of Allâh.

The narrator of the *Hadith* said, "and I think he said:

«وَكَالْقَائِمِ لَا يَفْتُرُ وَكَالصَّائِمِ لَا يُفْطِرُ»

and like the one who stands for prayer without tiring and the one who fasts without breaking his fast." (Recorded by Al-Bukhari and Muslim)

Some people do not need material help in as much as they need someone to intercede for them; the Prophet ﷺ said:

«اشْفَعُوا تُؤْجَرُوا»

Intercede (for others when the cause is good and lawful) and you will be rewarded. (Recorded by Al-Bukhari and Muslim)

Anytime a brother needs help from you, whether it be in a great matter or a small one, you should help him, for the Prophet ﷺ said:

«وَ تُعِينُ الرَّجُلَ فِي دَابَّتِهِ فَتَحْمِلُهُ عَلَيْهَا أَوْ تَرْفَعُ لَهُ عَلَيْهَا مَتَاعَهُ صَدَقَةٌ»

To help your brother onto his mount or to raise to him his belongings is charity. (Recorded by Al-Bukhari and Muslim)

Lesson Sixteen
Taking On Islamic Manners

Here are only some of the many Islamic manners:

1) Greeting (*As-Salam*)
2) A smiling, cheerful face
3) Eating with your right hand, and drinking with the same
4) Before eating or drinking, one should say, "*Bismillah* (In the Name of Allâh)."
5) After eating or drinking, say, "*Al-Hamdulillah* (All praise is for Allâh)"
6) After sneezing, say, "*Al-Hamdulillah*."
7) If another person sneezes and says "*Al-Hamdulillah*," say, "*Yarhamukallâh* (May Allâh have mercy on you)."
8) Visiting the sick
9) Following a funeral — by praying the funeral prayer and attending the burial.
10) Following Islamic manners when you enter the *Masjid* or your home, and when you leave them.
11) Following Islamic manners when you travel, when you deal with your parents, your relatives, your neighbors, your elders, and those younger than you.
12) Congratulating parents upon the birth of a child.
13) Saying an invocation of blessings when there is a marriage.
14) Consoling the afflicted.
15) And all other Islamic manners, including the way we wear or remove our dress and shoes.

❖ ❖ ❖

Other than the characteristics mentioned by the Shaikh, there are many other good qualities that are mentioned in the Qur'an and the Sunnah, such as gentleness, forgiveness, honor, mercy, a heart free from rancor, patience, good speech, and humility. Shaikh 'Abdul-'Aziz bin Baz, may Allâh have mercy on him, wrote a valuable dissertation entitled, "The Manners of Believing Men and Believing Women." It should be read, for it is full of great benefit.

"Greeting (As-Salam)": To create a sense of love and unity between Muslims, it is legislated in Islam that we give greetings of peace to one another:

﴿وَإِذَا حُيِّيتُم بِتَحِيَّةٍ فَحَيُّواْ بِأَحْسَنَ مِنْهَآ أَوْ رُدُّوهَآ﴾

When you are greeted with a greeting, greet in return with what is better than it, or (at least) return it equally.[1]

When asked which Islam is best, the Prophet ﷺ said:

«تُطْعِمُ الطَّعَامَ وَتَقْرَأُ السَّلَامَ عَلَى مَنْ عَرَفْتَ وَمَنْ لَمْ تَعْرِفْ»

To feed others and to give greetings of peace to both he whom you know and he whom you know not. (Recorded by Al-Bukhari and Muslim)

Al-Bara' said, "The Prophet ﷺ ordered us with seven matters; one of the matters he mentioned was

«وَإِفْشَاءُ السَّلَام»

to spread greetings of peace." (Al-Bukhari)

And the Prophet ﷺ said:

«إِنَّ مِنْ حَقِّ الْمُسْلِمِ عَلَى الْمُسْلِمِ: إِذَا لَقِيتَهُ فَسَلِّمْ عَلَيْهِ»

Indeed, from the rights of a Muslim over another Muslim is that when one meets the other, he should give him greetings of peace. (Agreed upon)

Spreading greetings of peace causes Muslim brothers to love one another, which is what we need to enter Paradise, for the Prophet ﷺ said:

«لَا تَدْخُلُوا الْجَنَّةَ حَتَّى تُؤْمِنُوا وَلَا تُؤْمِنُوا حَتَّى تَحَابُّوا أَوَ لَا أَدُلُّكُمْ عَلَى

---
[1] (*An-Nisa'* 4:86)

شَيْءٍ إِذَا فَعَلْتُمُوهُ تَحَابَبْتُمْ، أَفْشُوا السَّلَامَ بَيْنَكُمْ»

You will not enter Paradise until you believe, and you will not believe until you love one another. Shall I not guide you to something, that were you to do it, you would love one another: Spread greetings of peace among yourselves. (Recorded by Muslim)

The method of greeting your brother is to say, "*As-Salaamu 'Alaikum wa Rahmatullahi wa Barakatuhu* (Peace be upon you, and Allâh's mercy and blessings [also be upon you])."

'Imran bin Husain, may Allâh be pleased with him, said that on one occasion, while the Prophet ﷺ was seated, a man came to him and said, "*As-Salaamu 'Alaikum* (Peace be upon you)." After the Prophet ﷺ returned the greeting and after the man sat down, the Prophet ﷺ said, "Ten." Then another man came and said, "*As-Salaamu 'Alaikum wa Rahmatullah.*" After the Prophet ﷺ returned his greeting and after the man sat down, the Prophet ﷺ said, "Twenty." Finally, another man came and said the full greeting: "*As-Salaamu 'Alaikum wa Rahmatullahi wa Barakaatuhu* (Peace be upon you, and Allâh's mercy and blessings [also be upon you])." He answered him, the man sat down, and then the Prophet ﷺ said "Thirty," each time referring to the number of rewards achieved by the one who greeted him. It was recorded by Abu Dawud, and At-Tirmithi with a *Sahih* chain.

There are a number of manners we should keep in mind regarding the Islamic greeting:

1) We should not gesture when we greet one another, unless the gesture is accompanied by the verbal saying.

2) When you enter a room where some people are awake and others are sleeping, give greeting of peace, but in a low voice. The Prophet ﷺ would give greetings in such a way as to not wake up one who was sleeping, yet allowing the one who was awake to hear. (Recorded by Muslim).

3) The Prophet ﷺ said:

«يُسَلِّمُ الرَّاكِبُ عَلَى الْمَاشِي وَالْمَاشِي عَلَى الْقَاعِدِ وَالْقَلِيلُ عَلَى الْكَثِيرِ»

The rider should greet the one walking, the one who is

walking should greet the one who is sitting, and those that are few in number should greet those who are greater in number. (Recorded by Al-Bukhari and Muslim).

In the narration of Al-Bukhari, the Prophet ﷺ also said:

«وَالصَّغِيرُ عَلَى الْكَبِيرِ»

And the young one should greet his elder.

4) When you enter your home, it is recommended for you to give greetings of peace, for Allâh says:

﴿فَإِذَا دَخَلْتُم بُيُوتًا فَسَلِّمُوا عَلَى أَنفُسِكُمْ تَحِيَّةً مِّنْ عِندِ اللَّهِ مُبَارَكَةً طَيِّبَةً﴾

But when you enter the houses, greet one another with a greeting from Allâh, blessed and good.[1]

5) You are not permitted to initiate greetings of peace when you meet a disbeliever, for the Prophet ﷺ said:

«لَا تَبْدَؤُوا الْيَهُودَ وَلَا النَّصَارَىٰ بِالسَّلَام»

Do not initiate greetings of peace when you meet the Jews or the Christians.

However, if they extend to you greetings of peace, you may answer them with, *"Wa 'Alaikum* (and upon you)." In a *Hadith* related by Anas, the Prophet ﷺ said:

«إِذَا سَلَّمَ عَلَيْكُمْ أَهْلُ الْكِتَابِ فَقُولُوا وَعَلَيْكُمْ»

If someone from the People of the Book gives you a greeting of peace, then say, *"Wa 'Alaikum."* (Recorded by Al-Bukhari and Muslim)

6) Not only should you greet people when you enter a gathering, you should also greet them when you leave that gathering. The Prophet ﷺ said:

«إِذَا انْتَهَى أَحَدُكُمْ إِلَى الْمَجْلِسِ فَلْيُسَلِّمْ فَإِذَا أَرَادَ أَنْ يَقُومَ فَلْيُسَلِّمْ فَلَيْسَتِ الأُولَى بِأَحَقَّ مِنَ الآخِرَةِ»

If one of you stops at a gathering, let him give greetings of peace; and if he wishes to leave, let him give greetings of

---

[1] (*An-Nur* 24:61)

peace: the first greeting is not more worthy than the second (i.e., it is important to give both). (Recorded by Abu Dawud and At-Tirmithi).

"A smiling, cheerful face": In a *Hadith* related by Abu Tharr, may Allâh be pleased with him, the Prophet ﷺ said:

«لَا تَحْقِرَنَّ مِنَ الْمَعْرُوفِ شَيْئاً وَلَوْ أَنْ تَلْقَى أَخَاكَ بِوَجْهٍ طَلِقٍ»

Do not look down upon any good deed, not even to meet your brother with a cheerful face. (Recorded by Muslim)

In another *Hadith*, he ﷺ said:

«تَبَسُّمُكَ فِي وَجْهِ أَخِيكَ لَكَ صَدَقَةٌ»

To smile in the face of your brother is charity given on your behalf. (Recorded by Al-Bukhari in *Al-Adab Al-Mufrad* and At-Tirmithi with a *Sahih* chain).

So cheerful was the countenance of the Prophet ﷺ that one of his Companions, Jarir bin 'Abdullah, said, "Since the day I accepted Islam, the Messenger of Allâh ﷺ would never meet me without smiling in my face." (Recorded by Al-Bukhari in *Al-Adab Al-Mufrad* with a *Sahih* chain).

A smiling face indicates a good quality and causes blessed results — it indicates that one's heart is free of rancor and it causes affection to grow between Muslims.

"Eating with your right hand, and drinking with the same": The Prophet ﷺ said:

«إِذَا أَكَلَ أَحَدُكُمْ فَلْيَأْكُلْ بِيَمِينِهِ وَإِذَا شَرِبَ فَلْيَشْرَبْ بِيَمِينِهِ فَإِنَّ الشَّيْطَانَ يَأْكُلُ بِشِمَالِهِ وَيَشْرَبُ بِشِمَالِهِ»

When one of you eats, let him eat with his right hand; and when one of you drinks, let him drink using his right hand, for verily, the *Shaitan* eats with his left and drinks with his left. (Recorded by Muslim)

Here are some more manners to keep in mind when you eat:

1) To mention Allâh's Name and to eat what is closest to you, for the Prophet ﷺ said:

«يَا غُلَامُ سَمِّ اللهَ وَكُلْ بِيَمِينِكَ وَكُلْ مِمَّا يَلِيكَ»

O young boy, mention Allâh's Name, eat with your right
(hand), and eat that which is closest to you. Recorded by Al-
Bukhari and Muslim

2) While you are eating, do not lean on something to relax. The
Prophet ﷺ said,

«إِنِّي لَا آكُلُ مُتَّكِئاً»

Indeed, I do not eat, reclining (on something). (Recorded by
Al-Bukhari)

3) If a morsel of food falls to the ground, eat it nonetheless. Jabir,
may Allâh be pleased with him, related that the Prophet ﷺ said:

«إِذَا وَقَعَتْ لُقْمَةُ أَحَدِكُمْ فَلْيَأْخُذْهَا فَلْيُمِطْ مَا كَانَ بِهَا مِنْ أَذًى وَلْيَأْكُلْهَا
وَلَا يَدَعْهَا لِلشَّيْطَانِ»

If a morsel of food belonging to one of you should fall down,
pick it up, clean off any filth that may have attached itself, and
then eat it, but don't leave it for the *Shaitan*. (Recorded by
Muslim)

4) Do not find fault with the food you eat. Abu Hurairah, may Allâh
be pleased with him, said, "The Messenger of Allâh ﷺ never
found fault with food: if he desired something, he would eat it; if
he disliked something, he would (simply) leave it." (Recorded by
Al-Bukhari and Muslim).

5) It is recommended to lick clean both the plate one eats from and
his fingers. In a *Hadith* related by Muslim, the Prophet ﷺ
ordered us to do so and then said:

«إِنَّكُمْ لَا تَدْرُونَ فِي أَيِّهِ الْبَرَكَةُ»

Indeed, you do not know where the blessing is.

In the narration of At-Tirmithi, it is:

«إِنَّكُمْ لَا تَدْرُونَ فِي أَيِّ طَعَامِكُمُ الْبَرَكَةُ»

Indeed you do not know in which portion of your food is the
blessing.

6) When you finish your meal, you should do as the Prophet ﷺ did: he would supplicate, saying:

«الْحَمْدُ للهِ الَّذِي كَفَانَا وَأَرْوَانَا غَيْرَ مَكْفِيٍّ وَلَا مَكْفُورٍ»

All the praisec and thanks are to Allâh Who has satisfied our needs and quenched our thirst. Your favor cannot be compensated or denied. (Recorded by Al-Bukhari).

"Following Islamic manners when you enter the *Masjid* or your home and when you leave them": As the Muslim is entering the *Masjid*, it is recommended for him to enter with his right foot first, and then for him to say:

«بِسْمِ اللهِ وَالصَّلَاةُ وَالسَّلَامُ عَلَى رَسُولِ اللهِ اللَّهُمَّ افْتَحْ لِي أَبْوَابَ رَحْمَتِكَ»

In the Name of Allâh, and prayers and peace be upon the Messenger of Allâh. O Allâh, open the gates of Your mercy for me. (Recorded by Muslim and Abu Dawud).

When a Muslim enters his home, he should mention Allâh's Name, for the Prophet ﷺ said:

«إِذَا دَخَلَ الرَّجُلُ بَيْتَهُ فَذَكَرَ اسْمَ اللهِ تَعَالَى حِينَ يَدْخُلُ وَحِينَ يَطْعَمُ قَالَ الشَّيْطَانُ: لَا مَبِيتَ لَكُمْ وَلَا عَشَاءَ هَاهُنَا، وَإِنْ دَخَلَ فَلَمْ يَذْكُرِ اسْمَ اللهِ عِنْدَ دُخُولِهِ قَالَ الشَّيْطَانُ: أَدْرَكْتُمُ الْمَبِيتَ، وَإِنْ لَمْ يَذْكُرِ اسْمَ اللهِ عِنْدَ مَطْعَمِهِ قَالَ: أَدْرَكْتُمُ الْمَبِيتَ وَالْعَشَاءَ»

When a man enters his home and mentions Allâh's Name upon entering and upon eating a meal, the *Shaitan* says (to his fellow devils), "There is no place for you to sleep here and there is no dinner for you over here." If he doesn't mention Allâh's Name upon entering, the *Shaitan* says (to his fellow devils), "You have found your place of rest for the night." And if he doesn't mention Allâh's Name upon eating, the *Shaitan* says, "You have reached your place of rest for the night and your dinner." (Recorded by Muslim, Abu Dawud, and Ibn Majalı).

It is also recommended to say the supplication mentioned in the following *Hadith*:

«إِذَا وَلَجَ الرَّجُلُ بَيْتَهُ فَلْيَقُلْ: اللَّهُمَّ إِنِّي أَسْأَلُكَ خَيْرَ الْمَوْلَجِ وَخَيْرَ الْمَخْرَجِ بِسْمِ اللهِ وَلَجْنَا وَبِسْمِ اللهِ خَرَجْنَا وَعَلَى رَبِّنَا تَوَكَّلْنَا ثُمَّ يُسَلِّمُ عَلَى أَهْلِهِ»

When one of you enters his home, he should say, "O Allâh, I ask of you the best of entrances and the best of exits. In the Name of Allâh we enter and in the Name of Allâh we leave, and upon our Lord we place our trust." Thereafter he should give greetings of peace to his family. (Recorded by Abu Dawud with a *Sahih* chain).

When a Muslim leaves the *Masjid*, he should begin with his left foot, saying:

«بِسْمِ اللهِ وَالصَّلَاةُ وَالسَّلَامُ عَلَى رَسُولِ اللهِ اللَّهُمَّ إِنِّي أَسْأَلُكَ مِنْ فَضْلِكَ»

In the Name of Allâh, and blessings and peace be upon the Messenger of Allâh. O Allâh, I ask You from Your favor. (Recorded by Muslim and Abu Dawud)

In the following *Hadith*, the Prophet ﷺ also told us what to say when we leave our home:

«إِذَا خَرَجَ الرَّجُلُ مِنْ بَيْتِهِ فَقَالَ: بِسْمِ اللهِ تَوَكَّلْتُ عَلَى اللهِ لَاحَوْلَ وَلَا قُوَّةَ إِلَّا بِاللهِ، فَيُقَالُ: حَسْبُكَ قَدْ هُدِيتَ وَكُفِيتَ وَوُقِيتَ، فَيَتَنَحَّىٰ لَهُ الشَّيْطَانُ فَيَقُولُ لَهُ شَيْطَانٌ آخَرُ: كَيْفَ لَكَ بِرَجُلٍ قَدْ هُدِيَ وَكُفِيَ وَوُقِيَ؟»

When a man leaves his home, he should say, "In the Name of Allâh; I place my trust in Allâh, and there is no might nor power except with Allâh." It will be said, "That is sufficient for you: you have been guided, sufficed, and protected." The *Shaitan* (devil) will move out of his way and another devil will say to the first, "How can you get to a man who has been guided, sufficed, and protected?" (Recorded by Abu Dawud and An-Nasa'i with a *Sahih* chain)

"Following Islamic manners when you travel": There are certain manners that you must adhere to when you travel:

1) In an Islamic way, you should bid farewell to those you leave behind. The Prophet ﷺ said:

«مَنْ أَرَادَ أَنْ يُسَافِرَ فَلْيَقُلْ لِمَنْ يُخَلِّفُ: أَسْتَوْدِعُكُمُ اللهَ الَّذِي لَا تَضِيعُ وَدَائِعُهُ»

Whoever is about to travel should say to those he leaves
behind, "I place you in the trust of Allâh, whose trust is never
misplaced." (Recorded by Abu Dawud with a *Sahib* chain)

2) As you are about to travel, say the supplication that is specific to
traveling. 'Abdullah bin 'Umar, may Allâh be pleased with them,
said:

«إِنَّ رَسُولَ الله صَلَّى اللهُ عَلَيْهِ وَسَلَّمَ كَانَ إِذَا اسْتَوَى عَلَى بَعِيرِهِ خَارِجًا إِلَى سَفَرٍ كَبَّرَ ثَلَاثًا ثُمَّ قَالَ: سُبْحَانَ الَّذِي سَخَّرَ لَنَا هَذَا وَمَا كُنَّا لَهُ مُقْرِنِينَ وَإِنَّا إِلَى رَبِّنَا لَمُنْقَلِبُونَ. اللَّهُمَّ إِنَّا نَسْأَلُكَ فِي سَفَرِنَا هَذَا الْبِرَّ وَالتَّقْوَى وَمِنَ الْعَمَلِ مَا تَرْضَى، اللَّهُمَّ هَوِّنْ عَلَيْنَا سَفَرَنَا هَذَا وَاطْوِ عَنَّا بُعْدَهُ، اللَّهُمَّ أَنْتَ الصَّاحِبُ فِي السَّفَرِ وَالْخَلِيفَةُ فِي الْأَهْلِ اللَّهُمَّ إِنِّي أَعُوذُ بِكَ مِنْ وَعْثَاءِ السَّفَرِ وَكَآبَةِ الْمَنْظَرِ وَسُوءِ الْمُنْقَلَبِ فِي الْمَالِ وَالْأَهْلِ»

Indeed, when the Messenger of Allâh ﷺ would be seated upon
his mount, about to travel, he would say "*Allâhu Akbar*" (Allâh
is the Most Great) three times, and then he would say, "How
perfect He is, the One Who has placed this (transport) at our
service, and we ourselves would not have been capable of that,
and to our Lord is our final destiny. O Allâh, we ask You for
righteousness and piety in this journey of ours, and we ask
You for deeds which please You. O Allâh, facilitate our journey
and let us cover its distance quickly. O Allâh, You are the
Companion on the journey, and the Successor over the family.
O Allâh, I take refuge with You from the difficulties of travel,
from having a change of heart and being in a bad predicament,
and I take refuge in You from an ill — fated outcome in terms
of wealth and family."

When he would start his return journey, he would say the same,
except he would add:

«آيِبُونَ تَائِبُونَ عَابِدُونَ لِرَبِّنَا حَامِدُونَ»

We return, repenting to, worshipping, and praising our Lord." (Recorded by Muslim).

4) Because it is from Allâh's favor that He has lightened certain rulings for the traveler, when you travel you should apply those lightened rulings; for instance, you should shorten your prayers; if needed, you may join them; you may continue to wipe over your socks for three days along with their nights; and you may break your fast.

"when you deal with your parents": Being good to your parents is one of the greatest forms of worship; in fact, Allâh mentioned His right along with the right of parents, and He mentioned ill-treatment of parents along with the association of partners with Him. Allâh Almighty says:

﴿وَمَن كَفَرَ فَلَا يَحْزُنكَ كُفْرُهُ إِلَيْنَا مَرْجِعُهُمْ فَنُنَبِّئُهُم بِمَا عَمِلُوٓاْ إِنَّ ٱللَّهَ عَلِيمٌۢ بِذَاتِ ٱلصُّدُورِ ٢٣﴾

And whoever disbelieved, let not his disbelief grieve you, to Us is their return, and We shall inform them what they have done. Verily, Allâh is the All-Knower of what is in the breasts (of men).[1]

And:

﴿وَوَصَّيْنَا ٱلْإِنسَٰنَ بِوَٰلِدَيْهِ حَمَلَتْهُ أُمُّهُۥ وَهْنًا عَلَىٰ وَهْنٍ وَفِصَٰلُهُۥ فِى عَامَيْنِ أَنِ ٱشْكُرْ لِى وَلِوَٰلِدَيْكَ إِلَىَّ ٱلْمَصِيرُ ١٤﴾

And We have enjoined on man (to be dutiful and good) to his parents. His mother bore him in weakness and hardship upon weakness and hardship, and his weaning is in two years, give thanks to Me and to your parents, to Me is the final destination.[2]

There are many instances in the Sunnah wherein the Prophet ﷺ highlighted the importance of being good to one's parents.

---

[1] (*Luqman* 31:23)

[2] (*Luqman* 31:14)

Ibn Mas'ud, may Allâh be pleased with him, once said, "I asked the Messenger of Allâh ﷺ, which deed is most beloved to Allâh?" He said:

«الصَّلَاةُ فِي وَقْتِهَا»

"Prayer in its time."

Ibn Mas'ud then asked, "And then which?" He said,

«بِرُّ الْوَالِدَيْنِ؟»

"Dutifulness to one's parents."

"Then which?" He said,

«الْجِهَادُ فِي سَبِيلِ اللهِ»

"Fighting in the way of Allâh." (Recorded by AL-Bukhari and Muslim)

'Abdullah bin 'Amr related that a man said, "O Messenger of Allâh, I pledge allegiance to you: to emigrate and to perform *Jihad.*" The Prophet ﷺ asked:

«هَلْ مِنْ وَالِدَيْكَ أَحَدٌ حَيٌّ؟»

"Are any of your parents alive?"

He said, "Yes, both of them." The Prophet ﷺ asked,

«فَتَبْتَغِي الأَجْرَ مِنَ اللهِ تَعَالَى»

"And you seek reward from Allâh?"

He said, "Yes." And then the Prophet ﷺ commanded:

«فَارْجِعْ إِلَى وَالِدَيْكَ وَأَحْسِنْ صُحْبَتَهُمَا»

"Then go back to your parents and be a good companion to them." (Recorded by Muslim)

Being dutiful to one's parents is one of the causes to enter Paradise. Abu Hurairah, may Allâh be pleased with him, related that he heard the Messenger of Allâh ﷺ say:

«رَغِمَ أَنْفُهُ رَغِمَ أَنْفُهُ رَغِمَ أَنْفُهُ»

"Ignominy upon him, ignominy upon him, ignominy upon him."

He was asked, "Upon whom, O Messenger of Allâh?" He ﷺ said:

«مَنْ أَدْرَكَ وَالِدَيْهِ عِنْدَ الْكِبَرِ أَحَدَهُمَا أَوْ كِلَاهُمَا ثُمَّ لَمْ يَدْخُلِ الْجَنَّةَ»

"Whoever has one or both of his parents with him when they reach old age and then does not enter Paradise." (Recorded by Muslim)

The Prophet ﷺ also said:

«الْوَالِدُ أَوْسَطُ أَبْوَابِ الْجَنَّةِ»

The father is the middle door (from among the doors) of Paradise. (Recorded by At-Tirmithi and Ibn Majah with a *Sahih* chain)

Mu'awiyyah bin Jahimah, may Allâh be pleased with them, related that his father, Jahimah, went to the Prophet ﷺ and said, "O Messenger of Allâh, I wished to fight, so I came here seeking your counsel." The Prophet ﷺ asked:

«هَلْ لَكَ مِنْ أُمٍّ»

"Do you have a mother (who is alive)?"

He said, "Yes."

«فَالْزَمْهَا فَإِنَّ الْجَنَّةَ عِنْدَ رِجْلِهَا»

"Stick close to her, for verily, Paradise is at her leg." (Recorded by An-Nasa'i and Ahmad with a *Sahih* chain.)

In another narration, the Prophet ﷺ said:

«الْزَمْهَا فَإِنَّ الْجَنَّةَ تَحْتَ أَقْدَامِهَا»

"Stick close to her, for verily, Paradise is under her feet." (Recorded by An-Nasa'i and Ahmad with a *Sahih* chain).

Being dutiful to one's parents is a cause which leads to Allâh's pleasure, for the Prophet ﷺ said:

«رِضَا الرَّبِّ فِي رِضَا الْوَالِدَيْنِ وَسُخْطُهُ فِي سُخْطِهِمَا»

The pleasure of the Lord is in the parents' pleasure; His anger is in their anger.

Moreover, being dutiful to one's parents leads to an increase in sustenance and life; the Prophet ﷺ said:

«مَنْ سَرَّهُ أَنْ يُمَدَّ لَهُ فِي عُمُرِهِ وَيُزَادُ فِي رِزْقِهِ فَلْيَبَرَّ وَالِدَيْهِ وَلْيَصِلْ رَحِمَهُ»

Whoever wishes to have his life extended and his sustenance increased, then let him be dutiful to his parents and let him nurture relations with his relatives. (Recorded by Ahmad)

In fact, being dutiful to one's parents causes all good, wards off all evil; here are a number of ways in which you can fulfill your duty to them:

1) Feed them, clothe them, serve them, and answer them when they call you.

2) Obey them, for the Prophet ﷺ said:

«. . . وَأَطِعْ وَالِدَيْكَ وَإِنْ أَمَرَاكَ أَنْ تَخْرُجَ مِنْ دُنْيَاكَ فَاخْرُجْ لَهُمَا»

Obey your parents, if they command you to leave your land then leave it for them. (Recorded by Al-Bukhari in *Al-Adab Al-Mufrad* with a *Sahih* chain)

3) Be humble with them and speak gently with them.

4) Do not call them by their names.

5) When you walk with them, walk behind them.

6) Do to them what you would like to be done to you, and hate for them what you would hate for yourself.

7) Whenever you pray to Allâh, ask Him to forgive them.

8) Honor your parents' friends.

But know that whatever you do to show your duty toward them, you can never fulfill the rights they have upon you, so great are their rights. The Prophet ﷺ said:

«لَا يُجْزِي وَلَدٌ وَالِدَهُ إِلَّا أَنْ يَجِدَهُ مَمْلُوكًا فَيَشْتَرِيَهُ فَيُعْتِقَهُ»

A son cannot pay his father back unless he finds him a slave, buys him, and then sets him free. (Recorded by Muslim)

"your relatives": Abu Ayyub, may Allâh be pleased with him, related that when a desert Arab asked the Prophet ﷺ to inform him of what would bring him closer to Paradise and farther away from the Fire, He ﷺ said:

«تَعْبُدُ اللَّهَ وَلَا تُشْرِكُ بِهِ شَيْئاً وَتُقِيمُ الصَّلَاةَ، وَتُؤْتِي الزَّكَاةَ، وَتَصِلُ الرَّحِمَ»

Worship Allâh, and do not associate any partners with Him; establish the prayer; pay the compulsory charity; and join relations with your relatives. (Recorded by Al-Bukhari and Muslim).

Abu Hurairah, may Allâh be pleased with him, reported that the Prophet ﷺ said:

«خَلَقَ اللَّهُ عَزَّ وَجَلَّ الْخَلْقَ فَلَمَّا فَرَغَ مِنْهُ قَامَتِ الرَّحِمُ فَقَالَ: مَهْ؟ قَالَتْ: هَذَا مَقَامُ الْعَائِذِ بِكَ مِنَ الْقَطِيعَةِ. قَالَ: أَلَا تَرْضَيْنَ أَنْ أَصِلَ مَنْ وَصَلَكِ وَأَقْطَعَ مَنْ قَطَعَكِ قَالَتْ: بَلَى يَارَبِّ، قَالَ: فَذَلِكِ لَكِ»

Allâh Almighty created the creation, and when He finished doing so, the womb stood. Allâh said, "What is this?" It said, "This is where refuge is sought in You from those who cut off relations." He said, "Are you not pleased that I will join those that are good to you and that I will cut off those who cut you off." It said, "Indeed, yes, O my Lord." And then He said, "Then that is for you."

After mentioning the *Hadith*, Abu Hurairah said, "And recite, if you wish:

﴿فَهَلْ عَسَيْتُمْ إِن تَوَلَّيْتُمْ أَن تُفْسِدُواْ فِي ٱلْأَرْضِ وَتُقَطِّعُوٓاْ أَرْحَامَكُمْ ٢٢﴾

Would you then, if you were given the authority, do mischief in the land, and sever your ties of kinship?[1] (Recorded by Al-Bukhari and Muslim)

Like in obedience to one's parents, joining relations with relatives by dealing honorably and kindly with them also causes one's life to be prolonged, for the Prophet ﷺ said:

«مَنْ أَحَبَّ أَنْ يُبْسَطَ لَهُ فِي رِزْقِهِ وَأَنْ يُنْسَأَ لَهُ فِي أَثَرِهِ فَلْيَصِلْ رَحِمَهُ»

Whoever would love for his sustenance to be made abundant for him and for his time (of death) to be delayed, then let him

---
[1] (*Muhammad* 47:22)

join ties with relatives. (Recorded by Al-Bukhari and Abu Dawud)

To join ties means to avoid hurting one's relatives; it means to visit them, to pray for them, to help them financially, to order them to do good, to forbid them from evil, and to advise them. Allâh Almighty said to His Prophet:

$$﴿وَأَنذِرْ عَشِيرَتَكَ ٱلْأَقْرَبِينَ ٢١٤﴾$$

And warn your tribe of near kindred[1]

"your neighbors": Refer to lesson fifteen, where this topic has been discussed.

"your elders": During a dispute, when one was required to speak before the Prophet ﷺ, the youngest one present attempted to speak; the Prophet ﷺ said:

$$«كَبِّرْ كَبِّرْ»$$

Older, older.

Admonishing the young man for having spoken before his elders had the opportunity to speak. (Recorded by Al-Bukhari and Muslim)

The Prophet ﷺ said:

$$«إِنَّ مِنْ إِجْلَالِ اللهِ تَعَالَى إِكْرَامَ ذِي الشَّيْبَةِ الْمُسْلِمِ وَحَامِلِ الْقُرْآنِ غَيْرِ الْغَالِي فِيهِ وَالْجَافِي عَنْهُ وَإِكْرَامَ ذِي السُّلْطَانِ الْمُقْسِطِ»$$

Indeed, from the ways of glorifying Allâh is to honor graying Muslim; the one who carries with him the Qur'an, who neither deals extremely with it nor turns away from it; and the just leader. (Recorded by Abu Dawud, and it is *Sahih*)

He ﷺ also said:

$$«لَيْسَ مِنَّا مَنْ لَمْ يَرْحَمْ صَغِيرَنَا وَيَعْرِفْ شَرَفَ كَبِيرِنَا»$$

He is not from us who neither shows mercy to the young from us nor knows the honor of the old from us. (Recorded by Abu Dawud and At-Tirmithi and it is *Sahih*).

---

[1] (*Ash-Shu'ara* 26:214)

To honor our elders also means to honor our scholars, because by their knowledge and virtues, they too deserve veneration.

"and those younger then you": The Prophet ﷺ said:

«لَيْسَ مِنَّا مَنْ لَمْ يَرْحَمْ صَغِيرَنَا»

He is not from us who does not show mercy to the young from us. (Recorded by Abu Dawud and At-Tirmithi)

He ﷺ used to show compassion and mercy to children, playing with them and showing kind patience in the face of their whims. For instance, he carried his granddaughter, Umamah, during prayer. He would play with Al-Hasan and Al-Husain. On one occasion he used rhythmic words to make the brother of Anas bin Malik, Abu 'Umair feel better. The latter was perhaps feeling sad after his pet bird, Nughair, died, and the Prophet ﷺ said jokingly:

«يَا أَبَا عُمَيْرٍ مَا فَعَلَ النُّغَيْرُ»

O Aba 'Umair, what has An-Nughair done.

"Congratulating someone upon the birth of a child": Because this practice brings happiness into the heart of a Muslim, one should strive to congratulate the new parents, praying for them and for their newborn. Muslim related that Al-Hasan Al-Basri taught a man how to congratulate another on the occasion of a new born: "May you be blessed in what you have been bestowed with; may you thank He that gave; may your child reach the age of reason, and may you be blessed by him being dutiful to you." In another narration Al-Hasan taught him to say, "May Allâh make him blessed for you and for the nation of Muhammad ﷺ." (Recorded by At-Tabarani with a *Hasan* chain)

After saying that it is recommended to give congratulations upon the birth of a child, Imam An-Nawawi said, "Our companions (i.e., those who are from his school of thought in jurisprudence) said, 'It is recommended to give congratulations upon the birth of a child, just as Al-Husain, may Allâh be pleased with him, taught a man to say the following: "May Allâh bless you in what you have been given; may He make you thankful to the One Who gave; may your child grow up to maturity; and may you be blessed by him being dutiful to you." If you are the father and have been congratulated, it is recommended for you to answer, "May Allâh bless you and send blessings upon you; may He reward you well; may He provide you with one similar; and may He increase your rewards." It is recommended to say this or something similar.

"Consoling the afflicted": The Messenger of Allâh ﷺ said:

«مَنْ عَزَّى أَخَاهُ الْمُؤْمِنَ فِي مُصِيبَةٍ كَسَاهُ اللهُ حُلَّةً خَضْرَاءَ وِيُخْبَرُ بِهَا يَوْمَ الْقِيَامَةِ»

Whoever consoles his brother believer in his adversity, Allâh will attire him with a green dress on the Day of Judgement, for which he will be envied.

It was recorded by Al-Khattib in *Tarikh Baghdad* and Ibn 'Asakir, and there is a supporting narration for it with Ibn Abu Shaybah. It is a *Hasan Hadith* which Al-Albani graded *Hasan* in *Al-Irwa'* no. 15.

When you console people who are afflicted, you should say those words that will bring them comfort, that will drive away their grief — words that strengthen those that are grieved, making them patient, and satisfied with Allâh's Decree. You can either use words that have been related from the Prophet ﷺ or you can say any kind words, as long as they do not contradict the *Shari'ah*. When the Prophet ﷺ was comforting his daughter for her loss, he said:

«إِنَّ لِلهِ مَا أَخَذَ وَلِلهِ مَا أَعْطَى وَكُلُّ شَيْءٍ عِنْدَهُ إِلَى أَجَلٍ مُسَمًّى فَلْتَصْبِرْ وَلْتَحْتَسِبْ»

Indeed to Allâh belongs what He takes, and to Allâh belongs what He gives; everything with him is until an appointed term, so be patient and seek your reward from Him. (Recorded by Al-Bukhari and Muslim).

An-Nawawi said, "This *Hadith* is the best form of consoling someone."

When the Prophet ﷺ met Umm Salamah after her loss, he ﷺ said:

«اللَّهُمَّ اغْفِرْ لِأَبِي سَلَمَةَ وَارْفَعْ دَرَجَتَهُ فِي الْمَهْدِيِّينَ وَاخْلُفْهُ فِي عَقِبِهِ فِي الْغَابِرِينَ وَاغْفِرْ لَنَا وَلَهُ يَا رَبَّ الْعَالَمِينَ وَافْسَحْ لَهُ فِي قَبْرِهِ وَنَوِّرْ لَهُ فِيهِ»

O Allâh, forgive Abu Salamah; raise him in ranking with those whom you have guided, and leave behind for him from his progeny from those who remain. Forgive us and him, O Lord of all that exists; make his grave spacious for him and illuminate it for him. (Recorded by Muslim).

There is no set period, beyond which one should not console someone — some people mistakenly think that the limit is three days, while others have mentioned other limits. In one narration, the Prophet ﷺ consoled the family of Ja'far after three nights.

"And all other Islamic manners...": Islam has legislated many manners for the Muslim, manners that cover every aspect of his life: manners for going to the washroom, for going to the *Masjid*, for visiting the sick, for sitting in a gathering, for seeking knowledge, for walking in the road, for visiting brothers, for talking, and so on. Though we have mentioned some Islamic manners here, we have certainly not mentioned them all; there are books that deal specifically with Islamic manners, such as *Al-Adab Ash-Shar'iyah* by Ibn Muflih, and *Al-Adab Al-Mufrad* by Al-Bukhari.

Lesson Seventeen

A Warning Against *Shirk* (Associating partners with Allâh) And Different Kinds Of Sins

One category of sins is called "The seven grave (and deadly) sins":

1) Associating partners with Allâh (*Shirk*).
2) Magic.
3) Killing a person, an act which Allâh has forbidden, unless there is an Islamic reason.
4) Consuming usury (interest).
5) Consuming the wealth of orphans.
6) Fleeing on the day of battle.
7) Accusing chaste, innocent, believing women of wrongdoing.

These are also great sins:

- Being undutiful to one's parents.
- Cutting off ties with relatives.
- Giving false testimony.
- Making false oaths.
- Hurting one's neighbor.
- Wrongfully shedding the blood of others.
- Wrongfully taking the wealth of others.
- Wrongfully attacking the honor of others.
- Drinking any form of alcohol.
- Gambling.
- Backbiting.
- Spreading false rumors.
- And all other sins that Allâh Almighty and His Messenger ﷺ have prohibited.

❖ ❖ ❖

"The seven grave and deadly sins": The Prophet ﷺ mentioned them all in one *Hadith* when he ﷺ said:

«اجْتَنِبُوا السَّبْعَ الْمُوبِقَاتِ: الشِّرْكُ بِاللهِ، وَالسِّحْرُ، وَقَتْلُ النَّفْسِ الَّتِي حَرَّمَ اللهُ إِلَّا بِالْحَقِّ، وَأَكْلُ الرِّبَا، وَأَكْلُ مَالِ الْيَتِيمِ، وَالتَّوَلِّي يَوْمَ الزَّحْفِ، وَقَذْفُ الْمُحْصَنَاتِ الْمُؤْمِنَاتِ الْغَافِلَاتِ»

Stay away from the seven grave sins: associating partners with Allâh; magic; killing a person whose life Allâh has made sacred except with a right; consuming usury; consuming the wealth of orphans; fleeing on the day of battle; slandering chaste, innocent, believing women. (Agreed upon)

"Associating partners with Allâh (*Shirk*)": *Shirk* means to dedicate any kind of worship to other than Allâh. (Refer to lesson four, where we have already discussed *Shirk* and its different categories.) Both Allâh — in His Book — and the Prophet ﷺ — in his Sunnah — have warned us against *Shirk*. Relating to us the words of Luqmân, Allâh Almighty says:

﴿يَٰبُنَىَّ لَا تُشْرِكْ بِٱللَّهِ إِنَّ ٱلشِّرْكَ لَظُلْمٌ عَظِيمٌ﴾

"O my son! Join not in worship others with Allâh. Verily! Joining others in worship with Allâh is a great wrong indeed."[1]

The Prophet ﷺ said to his Companions:

«... أَلَا أُنَبِّئُكُمْ بِأَكْبَرِ الْكَبَائِرِ»

"Should I inform you of the greatest of the great sins."

They said, "Yes, O Messenger of Allâh." He ﷺ said:

«الإِشْرَاكُ بِاللهِ»

"To associate partners with Allâh." (Agreed upon)

One form of *Shirk* is to prostrate to anyone other than Allâh; another is to supplicate to anyone other than Allâh or to ask for one's needs to be fulfilled by anyone other than Allâh; and yet another form is to sacrifice an animal, seeking closeness not to Allâh, but to another.

---

[1] (*Luqmân* 31:13)

Basically, it is *Shirk* to dedicate any form of worship to any one other than Allâh, regardless of what the object of worship is: the living, the dead, a grave, a statue, a stone, a tree, an angel, a Prophet, a pious man, an animal, or anything else. This is the only sin that Allâh does not forgive: it requires one to not only repent, but to also re-enter the fold of Islam. Allâh says:

$$﴿إِنَّ ٱللَّهَ لَا يَغْفِرُ أَن يُشْرَكَ بِهِۦ وَيَغْفِرُ مَا دُونَ ذَٰلِكَ لِمَن يَشَآءُ وَمَن يُشْرِكْ بِٱللَّهِ فَقَدِ ٱفْتَرَىٰٓ إِثْمًا عَظِيمًا ٤٨﴾$$

Verily, Allâh forgives not that partners should be set up with Him in worship, but He forgives except that (anything else) to whom He pleases, and whoever sets up partners with Allâh in worship, he has indeed invented a tremendous sin.[1]

The Muslim submits only to Allâh, prays only to Allâh, and supplicates only to Allâh:

$$﴿قُلْ إِنَّ صَلَاتِي وَنُسُكِي وَمَحْيَايَ وَمَمَاتِي لِلَّهِ رَبِّ ٱلْعَٰلَمِينَ ١٦٢ لَا شَرِيكَ لَهُۥ وَبِذَٰلِكَ أُمِرْتُ وَأَنَا۠ أَوَّلُ ٱلْمُسْلِمِينَ ١٦٣﴾$$

Say: "Verily, my *Salat* (prayer), my sacrifice, my living, and my dying are for Allâh, the Lord of the *'Alamin* (mankind, jinns and all that exists)."[2]

One also perpetrates *Shirk* when one believes that Allâh has a wife or a child, far above is Allâh from any of that. Allâh says:

$$﴿قُلْ هُوَ ٱللَّهُ أَحَدٌ ١ ٱللَّهُ ٱلصَّمَدُ ٢ لَمْ يَلِدْ وَلَمْ يُولَدْ ٣ وَلَمْ يَكُن لَّهُۥ كُفُوًا أَحَدٌ ٤﴾$$

Say: "He is Allâh, (the) One; *Allâhus-Samad* (Allâh — the Self-Sufficient Master, Whom all creatures need, He neither eats nor drinks). He begets not, nor was He begotten. And there is none coequal or comparable to Him."[3]

"Magic (soothsaying, or claiming to know the unseen): Magic involves things that occur without us knowing how — the means or

---

[1] (*An-Nisa'* 4:48)
[2] (*Al-An'am* 6:162,163)
[3] (*Al-Ikhlas* 112:1-4)

the reality is hidden. The ostensible reason for these happenings is when the magician, for instance, ties a knot, says a phrase, or writes something down, all of which he does, intending to affect the person (either his mind, heart, or body) whom he wishes to make the object of nefarious activities, all of which he performs without actually taking physical measures to harm that person.

Both magic and soothsaying are forms of *Kufr* (disbelief): the magician cannot really be a magician unless he has ties with devils, whom he worships instead of worshipping Allâh. Allâh Almighty says:

و قال : ﴿وَمَا كَفَرَ سُلَيْمَنُ وَلَكِنَّ ٱلشَّيَطِينَ كَفَرُوا يُعَلِّمُونَ ٱلنَّاسَ ٱلسِّحْرَ﴾

﴿وَمَا يُعَلِّمَانِ مِنْ أَحَدٍ حَتَّىٰ يَقُولَا إِنَّمَا نَحْنُ فِتْنَةٌ فَلَا تَكْفُرْ﴾

Sulaiman did not disbelieve, but the *Shayatin* (devils) disbelieved, teaching men magic... but neither of these two (angels) taught anyone (such things) till they had said, "We are only for trial, so disbelieve not (by learning this magic from us)."[1]

A Muslim is forbidden from going to magicians and soothsayers, from asking them, from believing what lies they speak regarding the unseen, from believing their predictions about the future, regardless of what methods they use (reading palms or crystal balls). Allâh Almighty says:

﴿قُل لَّا يَعْلَمُ مَن فِي ٱلسَّمَوَٰتِ وَٱلْأَرْضِ ٱلْغَيْبَ إِلَّا ٱللَّهُ﴾

Say: "None in the heavens and the earth knows the *Ghaib* (unseen) except Allâh"[2]

And:

﴿عَٰلِمُ ٱلْغَيْبِ فَلَا يُظْهِرُ عَلَىٰ غَيْبِهِۦ أَحَدًا ۝ إِلَّا مَنِ ٱرْتَضَىٰ مِن رَّسُولٍ فَإِنَّهُۥ يَسْلُكُ مِنۢ بَيْنِ يَدَيْهِ وَمِنْ خَلْفِهِۦ رَصَدًا ۝﴾

"(He Alone) the All-Knower of the *Ghaib* (unseen), and He reveals to none His *Ghaib* (unseen)." Except to a Messenger

---

[1] (*Al-Baqrah* 2:102)
[2] (*An-Naml* 27:65)

(from mankind) whom He has chosen (He informs him of unseen as much as He likes), and then He makes a band of watching guards (angels) to march before him and behind him.[1]

The Islamic punishment for the magician is execution by sword, a ruling that has been related from three of the Prophet's Companions.

"Killing a person, an act which Allâh has forbidden, unless there is an Islamic reason": In Islam, it is a grave deed indeed to take the life another, a sin regarding which Allâh has given a stern warning, a warning that involves a painful torment in the Hereafter and a severe punishment in this world — the murderer is executed unless the relatives or guardians of the murdered forgive him. Allâh says:

﴿مِنۡ أَجۡلِ ذَٰلِكَ كَتَبۡنَا عَلَىٰ بَنِىٓ إِسۡرَٰٓءِيلَ أَنَّهُۥ مَن قَتَلَ نَفۡسَۢا بِغَيۡرِ نَفۡسٍ أَوۡ فَسَادٍ فِى ٱلۡأَرۡضِ فَكَأَنَّمَا قَتَلَ ٱلنَّاسَ جَمِيعًا وَمَنۡ أَحۡيَاهَا فَكَأَنَّمَآ أَحۡيَا ٱلنَّاسَ جَمِيعًا وَلَقَدۡ جَآءَتۡهُمۡ رُسُلُنَا بِٱلۡبَيِّنَٰتِ ثُمَّ إِنَّ كَثِيرًا مِّنۡهُم بَعۡدَ ذَٰلِكَ فِى ٱلۡأَرۡضِ لَمُسۡرِفُونَ ٣٢﴾

Because of that We ordained for the Children of Israel that if anyone killed a person not in retaliation of murder, or (and) to spread mischief in the land — it would be as if he killed all mankind, and if anyone saved a life, it would be as if he saved the life of all mankind. And indeed, there came to them Our Messengers with clear proofs, evidences, and signs, even then after that many of them continued to exceed the limits (e.g., by doing oppression unjustly and exceeding beyond the limits set by Allâh by committing the major sins) in the land![2]

And:

﴿وَمَن يَقۡتُلۡ مُؤۡمِنًا مُّتَعَمِّدًا فَجَزَآؤُهُۥ جَهَنَّمُ خَٰلِدًا فِيهَا وَغَضِبَ ٱللَّهُ عَلَيۡهِ وَلَعَنَهُۥ وَأَعَدَّ لَهُۥ عَذَابًا عَظِيمًا ٩٣﴾

And whoever kills a believer intentionally, his recompense is

---

[1] (*Al-Jinn* 72:26,27)

[2] (*Al-Ma'idah* 5:32)

Hell to abide therein, and the wrath and the curse of Allâh are upon him, and a great punishment is prepared for him.[1]

The Prophet ﷺ said:

«إِذَا الْتَقَى الْمُسْلِمَانِ بِسَيْفَيْهِمَا فَالْقَاتِلُ وَالْمَقْتُولُ فِي النَّارِ»

"If two Muslims meet each other, each with his sword, then the murderer and the murdered are in the Fire."

Someone asked, "O Messenger of Allâh, (I understand about) the murderer, but why (is) the murdered (punished as well)?" He ﷺ said:

«إِنَّهُ كَانَ حَرِيصًا عَلَى قَتْلِ صَاحِبِهِ»

"He was indeed eager to kill his opponent." (Recorded by Al-Bukhari and Muslim)

The Prophet ﷺ also said:

«لَا يَزَالُ الْعَبْدُ فِي فُسْحَةٍ مِنْ دِينِهِ مَا لَمْ يُصِبْ دَمًا حَرَامًا»

The slave continues to liberty in his religion, as long as he does not spill unlawful blood. (Recorded by Al-Bukhari and Ahmad)

"Consuming usury (interest)": Usury is one of the greatest of sins: it destroys the economy and it takes wrongful advantage of those who are in need of money, regardless of whether it is the businessman for his business or the poor man for his basic needs.

Basically, usury occurs (at least in one of its forms) when one person lends money to another person for a set period, stipulating that when that period arrives, he pays a specific amount more than what was originally loaned. Therefore the lender and those like him take advantage of those who are in need of money, forcing them to live a life of debt. Taking advantage of businessman, and without incurring any risks in case of losses, the usurer takes a percentage over and above profits received. When the business declines and the businessman is drowned in debt, the usurer will destroy him. But had they been partners, both sharing in profit and loss, one striving with his wealth the other with his business acumen, the wheels of the economy would continue to turn, but this time, for the benefit of all. Allâh says:

---

[1] (*An-Nisa'* 4:93)

﴿يَٰٓأَيُّهَا ٱلَّذِينَ ءَامَنُوا۟ ٱتَّقُوا۟ ٱللَّهَ وَذَرُوا۟ مَا بَقِىَ مِنَ ٱلرِّبَوٰٓا۟ إِن كُنتُم مُّؤْمِنِينَ ۝ فَإِن
لَّمْ تَفْعَلُوا۟ فَأْذَنُوا۟ بِحَرْبٍ مِّنَ ٱللَّهِ وَرَسُولِهِۦ وَإِن تُبْتُمْ فَلَكُمْ رُءُوسُ أَمْوَٰلِكُمْ لَا
تَظْلِمُونَ وَلَا تُظْلَمُونَ ۝ وَإِن كَانَ ذُو عُسْرَةٍ فَنَظِرَةٌ إِلَىٰ مَيْسَرَةٍ وَأَن تَصَدَّقُوا۟
خَيْرٌ لَّكُمْ إِن كُنتُمْ تَعْلَمُونَ ۝ ﴾

O you who believe! Be afraid of Allâh and give up what remains
(due to you) from *Riba* (usury) (from now onward), if you are
(really) believers. And if you do not do it, then take a notice of
war from Allâh and His Messenger but if you repent, you shall
have your capital sums. Deal not unjustly (by asking more than
your capital sums), and you shall not be dealt with unjustly (by
receiving less than your capital sums). And if the debtor is in a
hard time (has no money), then grant him time till it is easy for
him to repay, but if you remit it by way of charity, that is better
for you if you did but know.[1]

The Prophet ﷺ said:

«لَعَنَ اللهُ آكِلَ الرِّبَا وَمُوكِلَهُ»

Allâh has cursed both the one who eats usury and the one who
gives it. (Recorded by Muslim).

At-Tirmithi recorded it with a *Sahih* chain and the addition:

«وَشَاهِدَيْهِ وَكَاتِبَهُ»

...and the witnesses and the one who records it.

Usury, in all of its forms, is forbidden, for the Prophet ﷺ said:

«الرِّبَا اثْنَانِ وَسَبْعُونَ بَابًا أَدْنَاهَا مِثْل إِتْيَانِ الرَّجُلِ أُمَّهُ»

Usury (*Riba*) is seventy-two doors, the least of which is equal
to a man committing incest with his mother. (Recorded by At-
Tabarani in *Al-Awsat* with a *Sahih* chain)

"Consuming the wealth of orphans": Allâh Almighty says:

﴿إِنَّ ٱلَّذِينَ يَأْكُلُونَ أَمْوَٰلَ ٱلْيَتَٰمَىٰ ظُلْمًا إِنَّمَا يَأْكُلُونَ فِى بُطُونِهِمْ نَارًا وَسَيَصْلَوْنَ
سَعِيرًا ۝ ﴾

---

[1] (*Al-Baqarah* 2:278-280)

Verily, those who unjustly consume the property of orphans, they eat up only fire into their bellies, and they will be burnt in the blazing Fire![1]

When one consumes the wealth of an orphan, he perpetrates one of the great sins, but only if he takes that wealth unlawfully. If the guardian of the orphan is poor, he may take according to need, and the amount he takes that corresponds to his needs is governed by custom. Allâh says:

$$﴿وَمَن كَانَ فَقِيرًا فَلْيَأْكُلْ بِالْمَعْرُوفِ﴾$$

But if he is poor, let him have for himself what is just and reasonable (according to his work).[2]

And:

$$﴿وَلَا تَقْرَبُوا مَالَ ٱلْيَتِيمِ إِلَّا بِٱلَّتِي هِيَ أَحْسَنُ﴾$$

And come not near to the orphan's property, except to improve it.[3]

The warning regarding those, "who unjustly consume the property of orphans" includes those who literally do so, and those guardians, who because of their dereliction and not because of their greed, allow the orphan's wealth to dwindle away. For instance, in clearly unsound investments; the words "consume" are used because that is what happens in most cases.

"Fleeing on the day of battle": Allâh Almighty says:

$$﴿وَمَن يُوَلِّهِمْ يَوْمَئِذٍ دُبُرَهُ إِلَّا مُتَحَرِّفًا لِّقِتَالٍ أَوْ مُتَحَيِّزًا إِلَىٰ فِئَةٍ فَقَدْ بَآءَ بِغَضَبٍ مِّنَ ٱللَّهِ وَمَأْوَىٰهُ جَهَنَّمُ وَبِئْسَ ٱلْمَصِيرُ ﴿١٦﴾﴾$$

And whoever turns his back to them on such a day — unless it be a stratagem of war, or to retreat to a troop (of his own), — he indeed has drawn upon himself wrath from Allâh. And his abode is Hell, and worst indeed is that destination![4]

If one flees when there is a battle between Muslims fighting in *Jihad*

---

[1] (*An-Nisa'* 4:10)

[2] (*An-Nisa'* 4:6)

[3] (*Al-An'am* 6:152)

[4] (*Al-Anfal* 8:16)

in the cause of Allâh against their enemies, when the two armies face one another, then one is perpetrating a grave sin, for he has forsaken the Muslims and weakened their ranks. When a battle is about to begin and the two armies are present at the place of battle, *Jihad* becomes obligatory on those who are present.

"Slandering chaste, innocent, believing women": Allâh Almighty says:

﴿إِنَّ ٱلَّذِينَ يَرْمُونَ ٱلْمُحْصَنَـٰتِ ٱلْغَـٰفِلَـٰتِ ٱلْمُؤْمِنَـٰتِ لُعِنُوا۟ فِى ٱلدُّنْيَا وَٱلْـَٔاخِرَةِ وَلَهُمْ عَذَابٌ عَظِيمٌ ﴾ (٢٣)

Verily, those who accuse chaste women, who never even think of anything touching their chastity and are good believers, are cursed in this life and in the Hereafter, and for them will be a great torment.[1]

And:

﴿وَٱلَّذِينَ يَرْمُونَ ٱلْمُحْصَنَـٰتِ ثُمَّ لَمْ يَأْتُوا۟ بِأَرْبَعَةِ شُهَدَآءَ فَٱجْلِدُوهُمْ ثَمَـٰنِينَ جَلْدَةً﴾

And those who accuse chaste women, and produce not four witnesses, flog them with eighty stripes.[2]

And:

﴿وَٱلَّذِينَ يُؤْذُونَ ٱلْمُؤْمِنِينَ وَٱلْمُؤْمِنَـٰتِ بِغَيْرِ مَا ٱكْتَسَبُوا۟ فَقَدِ ٱحْتَمَلُوا۟ بُهْتَـٰنًا وَإِثْمًا مُّبِينًا ﴾ (٥٨)

And those who annoy believing men and women undeservedly, bear on themselves the crime of slander and plain sin.[3]

The Prophet ﷺ said:

«مَنْ قَذَفَ مَمْلُوكَهُ بِالزِّنَا أُقِيمَ عَلَيْهِ الْحَدُّ يَوْمَ الْقِيَامَةِ إِلَّا أَنْ يَكُونَ كَمَا قَالَ»

Whoever accuses a slave he owns, of fornication, will be punished for that on the Day of Judgement (i.e., for accusing) unless what he says is true. (Agreed upon)

---

[1] (*An-Nur* 24:23)

[2] (*An-Nur* 24:4)

[3] (*Al-Ahzab* 33:58)

Therefore the Muslim must be careful not to harm believing men and women with his tongue, especially since the Prophet ﷺ said:

«الْمُسْلِمُ مَنْ سَلِمَ الْمُسْلِمُونَ مِنْ لِسَانِهِ وَيَدِهِ»

The Muslim is the one from whom the Muslims are safe, from his tongue and hand. (Recorded by Al-Bukhari and Muslim).

"Being undutiful to one's parents": After the Prophet ﷺ asked:

«أَلَا أُنَبِّئُكُمْ بِأَكْبَرِ الْكَبَائِرِ؟»

Shall I not inform you of the greatest of great sins...

He mentioned being undutiful to one's parents among them. (Agreed upon).

It has been related that the Prophet ﷺ said:

«لَا يَدْخُلُ الْجَنَّةَ عَاقٌّ وَلَا مَنَّانٌ وَلَا مُدْمِنُ خَمْرٍ وَلَا مُؤْمِنٌ بِسِحْرٍ»

The disobedient (to his parents) does not enter Paradise, nor does the one who reminds others of his favors (in a harmful way), the one who is addicted to alcohol, and the one who believes in magic. (Recorded by Al-Hakim and Ath-Thahabi graded its chain *Hasan* in *Al-Kaba'ir*).

In another narration, the Prophet ﷺ said:

«لَعَنَ اللهُ الْعَاقَ لِوَالِدِيهِ»

Allâh cursed the one who is undutiful to his parents. (Recorded by An-Nasa'i with a *Hasan* chain)

Being undutiful to one's parents means that one rejects the good that has been done to him and it means that one is disobedient to Allâh, so beware, brother Muslim, of this grave sin.

"Cutting off ties with relatives": Allâh Almighty says:

﴿فَهَلْ عَسَيْتُمْ إِن تَوَلَّيْتُمْ أَن تُفْسِدُوا فِي الْأَرْضِ وَتُقَطِّعُوا أَرْحَامَكُمْ ۝ أُولَٰئِكَ الَّذِينَ لَعَنَهُمُ اللَّهُ فَأَصَمَّهُمْ وَأَعْمَىٰ أَبْصَارَهُمْ ۝﴾

Would you then, if you were given the authority, do mischief in the land, and sever your ties of kinship? Such are they whom Allâh has cursed, so that He has made them deaf and blinded their sight.[1]

The Prophet ﷺ said:

«لَا يَدْخُلُ الْجَنَّةَ قَاطِعُ رَحِمٍ»

He doesn't enter Paradise who severs ties with relatives. (Recorded by Al-Bukhari and Muslim)

One can sever ties by doing something, and by neglecting to do something, by harming a relative or by not helping him when he is in need.

Az-Zain Al-'Iraqi said, "To sever ties with kinship means to do harm to them." Others have said, "To sever ties with kinship means to abstain from doing good to them." When one breaks off ties with relatives, one only harms himself, for the Prophet ﷺ said:

«إِنَّ أَعْمَالَ بَنِي آدَمَ تُعْرَضُ كُلَّ خَمِيسٍ لَيْلَةَ الْجُمُعَةِ فَلَا يُقْبَلُ عَمَلُ قَاطِعِ رَحِمٍ»

Indeed, the deeds of the children of Adam are displayed every Thursday night; no deed from the one who severs ties with relatives will be accepted from him. (Recorded by Ahmad)

"Wrongfully taking the wealth of others...": The *Shaikh* refers here to oppression, which is of many kinds: a man can wrong himself, those around him, society, even his enemies. Indeed, Allâh does not love those who oppress; in a *Qudsi Hadith*, the Prophet ﷺ related that Allâh Almighty said:

«يَا عِبَادِي إِنِّي حَرَّمْتُ الظُّلْمَ عَلَى نَفْسِي وَجَعَلْتُهُ بَيْنَكُمْ مُحَرَّماً فَلَا تَظَالَمُوا»

O my worshippers, Indeed I have forbidden Myself from oppression, and I have made it forbidden among you, so do not wrong one another. (Recorded by Muslim, with the explanation of An-Nawawi 16:133)

Wrongdoing is forbidden in all of its forms: the Prophet ﷺ said:

«الظُّلْمُ ظُلُمَاتٌ يَوْمَ الْقِيَامَةِ»

---

[1] (*Muhammad* 47:22,23)

Wrongdoing will come as darkness on the Day of Judgement. (Recorded by Al-Bukhari and Muslim)

In summary, oppression is one of the major sins.

One form of oppression is to wrongfully take other people's wealth: by stealing, usurping, deceiving, or even bribing. Allâh says:

$$﴿وَٱلسَّارِقُ وَٱلسَّارِقَةُ فَٱقْطَعُوٓاْ أَيْدِيَهُمَا جَزَآءًۢ بِمَا كَسَبَا نَكَٰلٗا مِّنَ ٱللَّهِۗ وَٱللَّهُ عَزِيزٌ حَكِيمٞ ﴿٣٨﴾﴾$$

And the male thief and the female thief, cut off their hands, as a recompense for that which they committed, a punishment by way of example from Allâh. And Allâh is All-Powerful, All-Wise.[1]

And Allâh Almighty says:

$$﴿وَلَا تَأْكُلُوٓاْ أَمْوَٰلَكُم بَيْنَكُم بِٱلْبَٰطِلِ﴾$$

And consume not one another's property unjustly.[2]

The Prophet ﷺ said:

$$«كُلُّ الْمُسْلِمِ عَلَى الْمُسْلِمِ حَرَامٌ، دَمُهُ وَمَالُهُ وَعِرْضُهُ»$$

All of the Muslim is sacred to the Muslim: his blood, his wealth, and his honor. (Recorded by At-Tirmithi who graded it as *Hasan*)

Islam has strong safeguards to prevent people from unjustly taking other peoples' wealth: the punishments are so severe in this regard, that those who desire to take away from the safety of society are forced to hesitate, and most of the time desist altogether.

Other forms of wrongdoing include cheating, deception, or betrayal, all of which are forbidden, in business deals, contracts, or in any other dealing. Allâh Almighty says:

$$﴿وَيْلٞ لِّلْمُطَفِّفِينَ ﴿١﴾ ٱلَّذِينَ إِذَا ٱكْتَالُواْ عَلَى ٱلنَّاسِ يَسْتَوْفُونَ ﴿٢﴾ وَإِذَا كَالُوهُمْ أَو وَّزَنُوهُمْ يُخْسِرُونَ ﴿٣﴾ أَلَا يَظُنُّ أُوْلَٰٓئِكَ أَنَّهُم مَّبْعُوثُونَ ﴿٤﴾ لِيَوْمٍ عَظِيمٖ ﴿٥﴾ يَوْمَ يَقُومُ ٱلنَّاسُ لِرَبِّ ٱلْعَٰلَمِينَ ﴿٦﴾﴾$$

---

[1] (*Al-Ma'idah* 5:38)

[2] (*Al-Baqarah* 2:188)

Woe to *Al-Mutaffifin* [those who give less in measure and
weight (decrease the rights of others)] Those who, when they
have to receive by measure from men, demand full measure
And when they have to give by measure or weight to men, give
less than due. Think they not that they will be resurrected (for
reckoning). On a Great Day The Day when (all) mankind will
stand before the Lord of the *'Alamin* (mankind, jinns and all
that exists)[1]

And Allâh Almighty says:

$$﴿ إِنَّ ٱللَّهَ لَا يُحِبُّ مَن كَانَ خَوَّانًا أَثِيمًا ۝ ﴾$$

Verily, Allâh does not like anyone who is a betrayer of his trust,
and indulges in crime.[2]

Another form of oppression is to attack people's honor, cursing
them, backbiting them, spreading rumors about them, mocking
them, or being jealous of them. Islam promotes the building of a
pure society, one based on love, brotherhood, and mutual
cooperation, which is why Islam is stern regarding those diseases
that lead to a decay in society — diseases that make every member
think only about his personal benefit. Allâh Almighty says:

$$﴿ يَٰٓأَيُّهَا ٱلَّذِينَ ءَامَنُوا۟ لَا يَسْخَرْ قَوْمٌ مِّن قَوْمٍ عَسَىٰٓ أَن يَكُونُوا۟ خَيْرًا مِّنْهُمْ وَلَا نِسَآءٌ مِّن نِّسَآءٍ عَسَىٰٓ أَن يَكُنَّ خَيْرًا مِّنْهُنَّ وَلَا تَلْمِزُوٓا۟ أَنفُسَكُمْ وَلَا تَنَابَزُوا۟ بِٱلْأَلْقَٰبِ بِئْسَ ٱلِٱسْمُ ٱلْفُسُوقُ بَعْدَ ٱلْإِيمَٰنِ وَمَن لَّمْ يَتُبْ فَأُو۟لَٰٓئِكَ هُمُ ٱلظَّٰلِمُونَ ۝ يَٰٓأَيُّهَا ٱلَّذِينَ ءَامَنُوا۟ ٱجْتَنِبُوا۟ كَثِيرًا مِّنَ ٱلظَّنِّ إِنَّ بَعْضَ ٱلظَّنِّ إِثْمٌ وَلَا تَجَسَّسُوا۟ وَلَا يَغْتَب بَّعْضُكُم بَعْضًا أَيُحِبُّ أَحَدُكُمْ أَن يَأْكُلَ لَحْمَ أَخِيهِ مَيْتًا فَكَرِهْتُمُوهُ وَٱتَّقُوا۟ ٱللَّهَ إِنَّ ٱللَّهَ تَوَّابٌ رَّحِيمٌ ۝ ﴾$$

O you who believe! Let not a group scoff at another group, it
may be that the latter are better than the former; nor let
(some) women scoff at other women, it may be that the latter
are better than the former, nor defame one another, nor insult
one another by nicknames. How bad is it, to insult one's
brother after having faith. And whosoever does not repent,
then such are indeed wrongdoers. O you who believe! Avoid

---

[1] (*Al-Mutaffifin* 83:1-6)

[2] (*An-Nisa'* 4:107)

much suspicion, indeed some suspicions are sins. And spy not, neither backbite one another. Would one of you like to eat the flesh of his dead brother? You would hate it (so hate backbiting). And fear Allâh. Verily, Allâh is the One Who accepts repentance, Most Merciful.[1]

Islam also fights against racism or class division in society; all are equal: the Arab has no superiority over the non-Arab, neither the white over the black. The only means by which one's value is measured is the religion and piety that is in one's heart; therefore all compete equally in performing good, righteous deeds. Allâh Almighty says:

$$﴿يَٰٓأَيُّهَا ٱلنَّاسُ إِنَّا خَلَقْنَٰكُم مِّن ذَكَرٍ وَأُنثَىٰ وَجَعَلْنَٰكُمْ شُعُوبًا وَقَبَآئِلَ لِتَعَارَفُوٓاْ إِنَّ أَكْرَمَكُمْ عِندَ ٱللَّهِ أَتْقَىٰكُمْ إِنَّ ٱللَّهَ عَلِيمٌ خَبِيرٌ ﴿١٣﴾ ﴾$$

O mankind! We have created you from a male and a female, and made you into nations and tribes, that you may know one another. Verily, the most honorable of you with Allâh is the one with the most *Taqwa*. Verily, Allâh is All-Knowing, All-Aware.[2]

One of the worst ways of attacking the honor of another is to perpetrate fornication. Fornication ruins one's character, destroys society, causes one to be ignorant of his own father's identity, wastes away families, and wreaks havoc on societal morals. The children that result from fornication feel the true bitterness of the crime when society looks down upon them. Allâh Almighty says:

$$﴿وَلَا تَقْرَبُواْ ٱلزِّنَىٰٓ إِنَّهُۥ كَانَ فَٰحِشَةً وَسَآءَ سَبِيلًا ﴿٣٢﴾ ﴾$$

And come not near to the unlawful sexual intercourse. Verily, it is a *Fahishah* [i.e., anything that transgresses its limits (a great sin)], and an evil way.[3]

As we can clearly perceive today, widespread fornication results in the spread of sexually transmitted diseases; the Prophet ﷺ said,

---

[1] (*Al-Hujurat* 49:11,12)

[2] (*Al-Hujurat* 49:13)

[3] (*Al-Isra'* 17:32)

«مَا انْتَشَرَتِ الْفَاحِشَةُ فِي قَوْمٍ قَطُّ حَتَّى يُعْلِنُوا بِهَا إِلَّا فَشَا فِيهِمُ الطَّاعُونُ
وَالأَمْرَاضُ الَّتِي لَمْ تَكُنْ فِي أَسْلَافِهِمْ»

When *Fahishah* pervades a society so much so that people begin to practice it openly, plague will spread among them and so will sicknesses, sicknesses that were nonexistent among their predecessors. (Recorded by Ibn Majah (2:1332) with a *Sahih* chain)

That is why Islam closed the door to all ways that lead to it: Muslims are commanded to lower their gazes because the forbidden look is the beginning of the path which leads to fornication. Muslim women must cover themselves, protecting themselves and society from the spread of wickedness. At the same time, Islam orders Muslims to marry early. This is in the hope that chaste and honorable families may flourish, the guardians of which provide good training to the children of today so that they may become the noble men of tomorrow.

To harm a Muslim in any way is considered to be a form of oppression. Allâh Almighty says:

﴿وَٱلَّذِينَ يُؤْذُونَ ٱلْمُؤْمِنِينَ وَٱلْمُؤْمِنَٰتِ بِغَيْرِ مَا ٱكْتَسَبُوا۟ فَقَدِ ٱحْتَمَلُوا۟ بُهْتَٰنًا وَإِثْمًا
مُّبِينًا (٥٨)﴾

And those who annoy believing men and women undeservedly, bear on themselves the crime of slander and plain sin.[1]

The Prophet ﷺ said:

«إِنَّ شَرَّ النَّاسِ مَنْزِلَةً عِنْدَ اللهِ مَنْ وَدَعَهُ النَّاسُ اتِّقَاءَ فُحْشِهِ»

The people who are in the most miserable position in terms of their ranking with Allâh are those that the people abandon, fearing their evil. (Recorded by Al-Bukhari and Muslim)

He ﷺ also said:

«إِنَّ اللهَ يُبْغِضُ الْفَاحِشَ الْبَذِيءَ»

Indeed, Allâh hates the obscene evil. (Recorded by At-Tirmidhi

---

[1] (*Al-Hazab* 33:58)

and Abu Dawud with a *Hasan* chain)

In yet another narration, he ﷺ said,

«الْمُسْلِمُ أَخُو الْمُسْلِمِ لَا يَظْلِمُهُ وَلَا يَخْذُلُهُ وَلَا يَحْقِرُهُ، بِحَسَبِ امْرِىءٍ مِنَ الشَّرِّ أَنْ يَحْقِرَ أَخَاهُ الْمُسْلِمَ»

The Muslim is the brother of the Muslim: He neither wrongs him, forsakes him, nor belittles him. Enough evil for a person is to belittle his brother Muslim. (Recorded by Muslim)

He ﷺ also said:

«سِبَابُ الْمُسْلِمِ فُسُوقٌ وَقِتَالُهُ كُفْرٌ»

To verbally abuse a Muslim is wickedness, to fight him is disbelief. (Recorded by Al-Bukhari and Muslim)

Other ways to attack someone regarding his honor is backbiting, spreading false rumors, and falsely accusing someone.

"Giving false testimony": Describing the believers, Allâh Almighty said:

﴿وَٱلَّذِينَ لَا يَشْهَدُونَ ٱلزُّورَ﴾

And those who do not bear witness to falsehood.[1]

And:

﴿فَٱجْتَنِبُوا۟ ٱلرِّجْسَ مِنَ ٱلْأَوْثَٰنِ وَٱجْتَنِبُوا۟ قَوْلَ ٱلزُّورِ ۝﴾

So shun the abomination (worshipping) of idol, and shun lying speech (false statements).[2]

In a *Hadith* related by Abu Bakrah, may Allâh be pleased with him, the Prophet ﷺ said:

«أَلَا أُنَبِّئُكُمْ بِأَكْبَرِ الْكَبَائِرِ: الإِشْرَاكُ بِاللهِ، وَعُقُوقُ الْوَالِدَيْنِ، وَقَوْلُ الزُّورِ وَشَهَادَةُ الزُّورِ»

Shall I not inform you of the greatest of great sins: to associate partners with Allâh, to be undutiful toward one's parents, to speak a lie, and to bear false testimony.

---

[1] (*Al-Furqan* 25:72)
[2] (*Al-Hajj* 22:30)

The narrator, Abu Bakrah, said, "He continued repeating this phrase until (we became so afraid of his warning that) we wished that he would stop talking." (Agreed upon).

Imam Ath-Thahabi said that the one who gives a false testimony commits a number of grave wrongs:

1) Lying and slander; Allâh says:

$$﴿إِنَّ ٱللَّهَ لَا يَهْدِى مَنْ هُوَ مُسْرِفٌ كَذَّابٌ﴾$$

Verily, Allâh guides not one who is a transgressing liar![1]

2) He has wronged the one who suffered because of his false testimony, the one who lost his wealth, his honor, or sometimes even his soul.

3) He wrongs the one who benefits by his testimony, because he helps him attain forbidden wealth.

4) He has made permissible that which Allâh has made inviolable, for the Prophet ﷺ said:

$$«كُلُّ الْمُسْلِمِ عَلَى الْمُسْلِمِ حَرَامٌ مَالُهُ وَدَمُهُ وَعِرْضُهُ»$$

All of the Muslim is sacred to the Muslim: his wealth, his blood, and his honor. (Recorded by Al-Bukhari and Muslim).

"Making false oaths": Allâh Almighty says:

$$﴿وَلَا تَتَّخِذُوٓا أَيْمَٰنَكُمْ دَخَلًا بَيْنَكُمْ فَتَزِلَّ قَدَمٌ بَعْدَ ثُبُوتِهَا وَتَذُوقُوا ٱلسُّوٓءَ بِمَا صَدَدتُّمْ عَن سَبِيلِ ٱللَّهِ وَلَكُمْ عَذَابٌ عَظِيمٌ ۝﴾$$

And make not your oaths, a means of deception among yourselves, lest a foot may slip after being firmly planted, and you may have to taste the evil of having hindered (others) from the path of Allâh, and yours will be a great torment.[2]

'Abdullah bin 'Umar, may Allâh be pleased with them, related that the Messenger of Allâh ﷺ said:

$$«الْكَبَائِرُ: الإِشْرَاكُ بِاللهِ وَعُقُوقُ الْوَالِدَيْنِ وَقَتْلُ النَّفْسِ وَالْيَمِينُ الْغَمُوسُ»$$

The great sins are associating partners with Allâh, being

---

[1] (*Ghafir* 40:28)

[2] (*An-Nahl* 16:94)

undutiful to one's parents, killing someone, and a lying oath. (Recorded by Al-Bukhari)

In Arabic, the word used to describe this oath is *Ghamus*, which comes from *Ghamasa*, which means to dip; therefore it is an oath that dips the one who made it into sin (or into the Hellfire).

In another *Hadith*, the Messenger of Allâh ﷺ said:

«ثَلَاثَةٌ لَا يُكَلِّمُهُمُ اللهُ يَوْمَ الْقِيَامَةِ وَلَا يُزَكِّيهِمْ وَلَهُمْ عَذَابٌ أَلِيمٌ: الْمُسْبِلُ إِزَارَهُ، وَالْمَنَّانُ، وَالْمُنَفِّقُ سِلْعَتَهُ بِالْحَلِفِ الْكَاذِبِ»

On the Day of Judgement, there are three people that Allâh will neither speak to nor purify, and for them is a painful punishment: the one who lets his garment hang down below his ankles, the one who does favors and then in a harmful way reminds others about those favors, and the one who pushes the sale of his goods by making false oaths. (Recorded by Muslim)

The Prophet ﷺ also said:

«مَنْ حَلَفَ عَلَى يَمِينٍ لِيَقْتَطِعَ بِهَا مَالَ امْرِىءٍ مُسْلِمٍ لَقِيَ اللهَ وَهُوَ عَلَيْهِ غَضْبَانُ، قِيلَ: وَإِنْ كَانَ شَيْئًا يَسِيرًا؟»

Whoever makes an oath, intending to (unjustly) take away the wealth of a Muslim, he will meet Allâh, Who will be angry with him.

It was asked, "What if he intends to take something small?" He answered:

«وَإِنْ كَانَ قَضِيبًا مِنْ أَرَاكٍ»

Even it were a small stick taken from the Arak tree. (Recorded by Muslim)

"Hurting one's neighbor": The Prophet ﷺ said:

«وَاللهِ لَا يُؤْمِنُ وَاللهِ لَا يُؤْمِنُ وَاللهِ لَا يُؤْمِنُ»

"By Allâh, he does not believe; by Allâh, he does not believe; by Allâh, he does not believe."

He was asked, "Who, O Messenger of Allâh." He ﷺ said,

«الَّذِي لَا يَأْمَنُ جَارُهُ بَوَائِقَهُ»

"The one whose neighbor is not safe from his trouble making." (Agreed upon).

In the narration of Muslim:

«لَا يَدْخُلُ الْجَنَّةَ مَنْ لَا يَأْمَنُ جَارُهُ بَوَائِقَهُ»

"The one whose neighbor is not safe from his trouble making will not enter Paradise."

Meaning that his neighbor is not safe from his harm.

The Prophet ﷺ would supplicate:

«اللَّهُمَّ إِنِّي أَعُوذُ بِكَ مِنْ جَارِ السَّوءِ فِي دَارِ الْمُقَامِ فَإِنَّ جَارَ الدُّنْيَا يَتَحَوَّلُ»

O Allâh! Indeed I seek refuge with You from the evil neighbor in the prestigious abode; for indeed the near neighbor is influential. (Recorded by An-Nasa'i and Al-Bukhari in *Al-Adab Al-Mufrad* with a *Sahih* chain)

On one occasion, the Prophet ﷺ was told about a woman who prayed at night, who fasted during the day, who gave charity, but despite all of that, she would inflict harm on her neighbor with her tongue. The Prophet ﷺ said:

«لَا خَيْرَ فِيهَا هِيَ مِنْ أَهْلِ النَّارِ»

There is no good in her; she is from the inhabitants of the Fire.

Then the Prophet ﷺ was told about a woman who prayed the compulsory prayers and who would give pieces of cheese for charity; she was further described as being a woman who didn't harm others. The Messenger of Allâh ﷺ said:

«هِيَ مِنْ أَهْلِ الْجَنَّةِ»

She is from the dwellers of Paradise.

Recorded by Al-Bukhari in *Al-Adab Al-Mufrad* with a *Sahih* chain.

He ﷺ said on another occasion:

«مَنْ كَانَ يُؤْمِنُ بِاللهِ وَالْيَومِ الآخِرِ فَلَا يُؤْذِ جَارَهُ»

Whoever believes in Allâh and in the Last Day, then he should not harm his neighbor. (Agreed upon).

Then the Shaikh said, "And other deeds that Allâh has forbidden": Though there are many other forbidden deeds, there is one specific that I will mention:

"Miserliness": This sin indicates the wrong kind of individualism: the extreme love of one's self. The miser hoards his wealth, refusing to give even the compulsory charity to the poor and needy, showing his disdain for society, declining to accept the principles of mutual cooperation and brotherhood, principles that both Allâh and His Messenger have ordered us to adopt. Allâh says:

$$﴿وَلَا يَحْسَبَنَّ الَّذِينَ يَبْخَلُونَ بِمَا ءَاتَىٰهُمُ اللَّهُ مِن فَضْلِهِ هُوَ خَيْرًا لَّهُم بَلْ هُوَ شَرٌّ لَّهُمْ سَيُطَوَّقُونَ مَا بَخِلُوا بِهِ يَوْمَ الْقِيَٰمَةِ وَلِلَّهِ مِيرَٰثُ السَّمَٰوَٰتِ وَالْأَرْضِ وَاللَّهُ بِمَا تَعْمَلُونَ خَبِيرٌ ﴿١٨٠﴾﴾$$

And let not those who covetously withhold of that which Allâh has bestowed on them of His bounty think that it is good for them (and so they do not pay the obligatory *Zakat*). Nay, it will be worse for them; the things which they covetously withheld shall be tied to their necks like a collar on the Day of Resurrection. And to Allâh belongs the heritage of the heavens and the earth; and Allâh is Well-Acquainted with all that you do.[1]

Other examples of forbidden actions are to eat the meat of a dead carcass, to eat blood, to eat the meat of a pig, and to slaughter animals, seeking closeness to other than Allâh. Allâh says:

$$﴿يَٰٓأَيُّهَا الَّذِينَ ءَامَنُوا كُلُوا مِن طَيِّبَٰتِ مَا رَزَقْنَٰكُمْ وَاشْكُرُوا لِلَّهِ إِن كُنتُمْ إِيَّاهُ تَعْبُدُونَ ﴿١٧٢﴾ إِنَّمَا حَرَّمَ عَلَيْكُمُ الْمَيْتَةَ وَالدَّمَ وَلَحْمَ الْخِنزِيرِ وَمَا أُهِلَّ بِهِ لِغَيْرِ اللَّهِ فَمَنِ اضْطُرَّ غَيْرَ بَاغٍ وَلَا عَادٍ فَلَا إِثْمَ عَلَيْهِ إِنَّ اللَّهَ غَفُورٌ رَّحِيمٌ ﴿١٧٣﴾﴾$$

O you who believe! Eat of the lawful things that We have provided you with, and be grateful to Allâh, if it is indeed He Whom you worship. He has forbidden you only the *Maytah* (dead animals), and blood, and the flesh of swine, and that

---

[1] (*Al 'Imran* 3:180)

which is slaughtered as a sacrifice for others than Allâh. But if one is forced by necessity without willful disobedience nor transgressing due limits, then there is no sin on him. Truly, Allâh is Oft-Forgiving, Most Merciful.[1]

Repentance From Perpetrating What Is Forbidden

Because you will be held accountable for all of your deeds on the Day of Judgement — being rewarded for good and punished for evil — you should stay away from the grave sins and from all other sins. But if you do perpetrate any sin, you should be quick to repent to Allâh, asking Him for forgiveness and protection from further perpetrating evil deeds. A true repentance requires you to do the following:

1) To desist from the sin that you are repenting from.
2) To feel remorse for having perpetrated that sin.
3) To make a firm resolve not to return to it.

And there is a fourth condition if the sin you perpetrated involves the rights of others:

4) To return that which you wrongfully took to its owner or to seek forgiveness from the one you wronged.

These are the conditions of true repentance: if they are met, Allâh will forgive you and not punish you for them. The one who repents from a sin is like he who has no sin. Thereafter, you should continue to ask Allâh for forgiveness; indeed, every Muslim should continually ask for forgiveness, for the grave sins he commits and for the small ones. Allâh says:

$$﴿فَقُلْتُ ٱسْتَغْفِرُوا۟ رَبَّكُمْ إِنَّهُۥ كَانَ غَفَّارًا ۞﴾$$

I said (to them), "Ask forgiveness from your Lord; verily, He is Oft-Forgiving."[2]

When one repents often, he shows one of the characteristics of the true believer; Allâh says:

$$﴿قُلْ يَٰعِبَادِىَ ٱلَّذِينَ أَسْرَفُوا۟ عَلَىٰٓ أَنفُسِهِمْ لَا تَقْنَطُوا۟ مِن رَّحْمَةِ ٱللَّهِ إِنَّ ٱللَّهَ يَغْفِرُ﴾$$

---

[1] (*Al-Baqarah* 2:172,173)

[2] (*Nuh* 71:10)

ٱلذُّنُوبَ جَمِيعًا إِنَّهُ هُوَ ٱلْغَفُورُ ٱلرَّحِيمُ ۝ وَأَنِيبُوٓا۟ إِلَىٰ رَبِّكُمْ وَأَسْلِمُوا۟ لَهُۥ مِن قَبْلِ
أَن يَأْتِيَكُمُ ٱلْعَذَابُ ثُمَّ لَا تُنصَرُونَ ۝ ۞

Say: "O My worshippers who have transgressed against
themselves! Despair not of the mercy of Allâh, verily Allâh
forgives all sins. Truly, He is Oft-Forgiving, Most Merciful."
And turn in repentance and in obedience with true faith to
your Lord and submit to Him (in Islam), before the torment
comes upon you, then you will not be helped.[1]

In general, the following are some of the more prevalent sins that
many people take lightly:

- To deem lawful that which Allâh has forbidden, or to deem
  forbidden that which Allâh has made permissible.

- To believe that the stars and planets have some kind of effect on
  the lives of people.

- To believe that certain things benefit, when in fact the Creator
  did not make them so.

- To believe in evil omens — because you hear or see something,
  for example, to believe that evil will befall you; that is a form of
  Shirk (associating partners with Allâh).

- For you to keep company with hypocrites or wicked people,
  seeking closeness to them or finding comfort in their company

- To not pray in a calm and peaceful fashion.

- To make a lot of frivolous, extraneous movements during prayer

- For the follower to precede the *Imam* on purpose during any
  stage of the prayer.

- To come to the *Masjid* after having eaten onion or garlic or
  anything else that has a foul odor.

- Without having just cause, for a woman to refuse her husband's
  desire to have sexual relations.

- For a woman to seek a divorce from her husband without a
  legislated reason.

- A practice known in Arabic as *Az-Zihar*, i.e., for a man to say to his

---

[1] (*Az-Zumar* 39:53,54)

wife, "You are to me like my mother," when he intends to make her forbidden for him: this practice is forbidden based on the Qur'an, the Sunnah, and consensus.

- To have intercourse with one's wife during her monthly period.
- To have anal sex.
- For you to be unjust with your wives, treating some better than others.
- To be alone with a strange woman, in other words, a woman who is not a *Mahram* (someone who you can never marry) for you. This practice has become prevalent nowadays, especially in families that keep female servants.
- For a man to shake hands with a strange woman (i.e., one who is not a *Mahram*).
- As she leaves her home, for a woman to wear perfume, knowing that she will pass by men.
- For a woman to travel without a *Mahram*.
- For a man to look at a strange woman on purpose.
- For one to feel it is okay when one of his relatives (wives or children) fornicates.
- For one to lie about who his parents really are, or for a man to refuse to acknowledge his true son.
- When one is selling a product, to hide its defects.
- For one to be bid on a product, intending to raise its price, but not intending to actually purchase it.
- After the second call to Friday prayer is made, to engage in trade.
- To give or take bribes.
- To wrongfully usurp land.
- For you to accept a gift when intercession is required of you.
- To receive full services from an employee without paying him his due.
- To give to some of one's children more than the others.
- Without actually being in need, to ask others for money.
- To seek a loan without intending to pay it back.

- To eat or drink that which is forbidden.
- To use gold and silver utensils or dishes and to eat using them.
- To give a false testimony.
- To listen to musical instruments.
- Backbiting, which is to say about your brother that which he dislikes.
- To spread false rumors between people, intending to create dissension between them.
- To look inside the homes of others without their permission.
- When three are present, for two to speak to the exclusion of the third.
- For men to wear gold, regardless of how they wear it.
- For men to let their garments fall down below the level of their ankles.
- For a woman to wear thin, short, tight, or transparent clothing.
- For a man or a woman to attach false hair to the end of their natural hair, regardless whether that false hair is human or otherwise.
- For men to imitate women or vice versa.
- To dye your hair black.
- To make pictures of that which has a spirit (man or animal); this includes on clothes, on walls, on paper, and so on.
- To lie about one's dreams.
- Sitting or walking on a grave.
- To relieve yourself in a graveyard.
- When you are relieving yourself, for you to not take cover properly, so that others cannot see you.
- To listen in on other peoples' conversations when they dislike for you to do that.
- To deal badly with your neighbor.
- To harm people on purpose in the writing of your will.
- Playing dice, a game that relies on chance.
- To curse a believer and to curse someone who doesn't deserve to

be cursed.

- To wail loudly when mourning.

- To hit someone on the face; or to stamp someone's face.

- Without a valid Islamic reason, to shun a Muslim for more than three days.

- Haughtiness, pride, vanity, or self-conceit are the qualities that are most disliked in Islam. Allâh says about people who have such qualities:

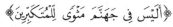

Is there not in Hell an abode for the arrogant ones?[1]

The arrogant one is hated by Allâh and by His creation.

---

[1] (*Az-Zumar* 39:60)

Lesson Eighteen

Preparing The Dead Person's Body, Praying Over Him, And Burying Him

The Details of which are as follows:

❖ ❖ ❖

The Shaikh said, "Preparing the dead person's body...":

Because of widespread ignorance regarding the Islamic rulings for funerals, the Shaikh will — in the following sections — explain those rulings for you. To introduce the topic, however, I wish to discuss the following points:

1) It is compulsory for the Muslim to be patient when he is afflicted with a trial. Therefore he should neither be angry nor show vexation. Allâh Almighty and His Messenger ﷺ often ordered us in the Qur'an and Sunnah to be patient. But even though patience is required, one may make clear to others his situation or how he feels, with statements such as the following: "I am sick," or "I am in pain" or "In every situation, all praise is for Allâh."

2) The Muslim must visit his brother Muslim when he is sick, for the Prophet ﷺ said:

«أَطْعِمُوا الْجَائِعَ وَعُودُوا الْمَرِيضَ، وَفُكُّوا الْعَانِي - الأَسِيرَ»

Feed the hungry, visit the sick, and provide means for ransoming the captive. (Recorded by Al-Bukhari)

When you visit a sick Muslim, it is recommended that you invoke Allâh Almighty to cure him and that you counsel him to be patient. Say those words that will be pleasant for him to hear; also, you should not sit with him for too long. When the Prophet ﷺ used to visit the sick, he would say:

«لَا بَأْسَ، طَهُورٌ إِنْ شَاءَ اللهُ»

It is alright; this (sickness) will purify you (from your sins) — if Allâh wills. (Recorded by Al-Bukhari)

You should say this phrase whenever you visit anyone who is sick.

3) Brother Muslim, remember your final destination. To help you do so, reflect on the following topics:

First: What Allâh's Book Says Regarding Death

In different ways, death is mentioned 164 times in the Qur'an; here are some of those verses:

﴿ كُلُّ نَفْسٍ ذَآئِقَةُ ٱلْمَوْتِ وَإِنَّمَا تُوَفَّوْنَ أُجُورَكُمْ يَوْمَ ٱلْقِيَـٰمَةِ فَمَن زُحْزِحَ عَنِ ٱلنَّارِ وَأُدْخِلَ ٱلْجَنَّةَ فَقَدْ فَازَ وَمَا ٱلْحَيَوٰةُ ٱلدُّنْيَآ إِلَّا مَتَـٰعُ ٱلْغُرُورِ ۝ ﴾

Everyone shall taste death. And only on the Day of Resurrection shall you be paid your wages in full. And whoever is removed away from the Fire and admitted to Paradise, he indeed is successful. The life of this world is only the enjoyment of deception (a deceiving thing).[1]

And:

﴿ وَجَآءَتْ سَكْرَةُ ٱلْمَوْتِ بِٱلْحَقِّ ذَٰلِكَ مَا كُنتَ مِنْهُ تَحِيدُ ۝ ﴾

And the stupor of death will come in truth: "This is what you have been avoiding!"[2]

﴿ فَلَوْلَآ إِذَا بَلَغَتِ ٱلْحُلْقُومَ ۝ وَأَنتُمْ حِينَئِذٍ تَنظُرُونَ ۝ وَنَحْنُ أَقْرَبُ إِلَيْهِ مِنكُمْ وَلَـٰكِن لَّا تُبْصِرُونَ ۝ ﴾

Then why do you not (intervene) when (the soul of a dying person) reaches the throat? And you at the moment are looking on, But We (i.e., Our angels who take the soul) are nearer to him than you, but you see not.[3]

And:

﴿ كَلَّآ إِذَا بَلَغَتِ ٱلتَّرَاقِيَ ۝ وَقِيلَ مَنْ رَاقٍ ۝ وَظَنَّ أَنَّهُ ٱلْفِرَاقُ ۝ وَٱلْتَفَّتِ ٱلسَّاقُ بِٱلسَّاقِ ۝ إِلَىٰ رَبِّكَ يَوْمَئِذٍ ٱلْمَسَاقُ ۝ ﴾

---

[1] (*Aal 'Imran* 3:185)

[2] (*Qaf* 50:19)

[3] (*Al-Waqi'ah* 56:83-85)

Nay, when (the soul) reaches to the collar bone (i.e., up to the throat in its exit), and it will be said: "Who can cure him and save him from death?" And he (the dying person) will conclude that it was (the time) of departing (death); and leg will be joined with another leg (shrouded); the drive will be, on that Day, to your Lord.[1]

Second: What the Prophet's Sunnah says about death

In a *Hadith* related by Abu Hurairah, may Allâh be pleased with him, the Prophet ﷺ said:

«أَكْثِرُوا ذِكْرَ هَاذِمِ اللَّذَّاتِ»

Remember often the destroyer of pleasures (i.e., death). (Recorded by At-Tirmithi)

Regarding this *Hadith*, the scholars have said that though its words are few, its meanings are profound and far-reaching, for when one remembers death in a true sense, the present pleasures he is experiencing are spoiled for him, and he is prevented or at least hindered from having long-term expectations about this world.

In another *Hadith*, Abu Hurairah, may Allâh be pleased with him, related that the Prophet ﷺ once visited the grave of his mother: he cried and made those around him cry as well. He ﷺ said:

«اسْتَأْذَنْتُ رَبِّي أَنْ أَسْتَغْفِرَ لَهَا فَلَمْ يَأْذَنْ لِي، وَاسْتَأْذَنْتُهُ فِي أَنْ أَزُورَ قَبْرَهَا فَأَذِنَ لِي، فَزُورُوا الْقُبُورَ فَإِنَّهَا تُذَكِّرُ الْمَوْتَ»

I sought permission from my Lord to ask forgiveness for her, and He didn't permit me, and I asked Him permission to visit her grave, and he permitted me, so visit graves, for verily, doing so reminds one of death. (Recorded by Muslim 3:65, 6:82, Abu Dawud 2:72, An-Nasa'i and Al-Baihaqi)

In a *Hadith* related by Ibn Mas'ud, may Allâh be pleased with him, the Prophet ﷺ said:

«كُنْتُ نَهَيْتُكُمْ عَنْ زِيَارَةِ الْقُبُورِ فَزُورُوهَا، فَإِنَّهَا تُزْهِدُ فِي الدُّنْيَا وَتُذَكِّرُ الآخِرَةَ»

---

[1] (*Al-Qiyamah* 75:26-30)

I used to forbid you from visiting graves, but visit them (now), for doing so makes one turn away from the world while it reminds one of the Hereafter.

Third: Death And Its Severity

1) The scholars' definition of death: a cutting off, a separation, a transformation, a change of state, and a move from one abode to another.

2) Abu Hudbah Ibrahim bin Hudbah related from Anas bin Malik that the Prophet ﷺ said:

«إِنَّ الْعَبْدَ لَيُعَالِجُ كَرْبَ الْمَوْتِ وَسَكَرَاتِ الْمَوْتِ، وَأَنَّ مَفَاصِلَهُ لَيُسَلِّمُ بَعْضُهَا عَلَى بَعْضٍ تَقُولُ عَلَيْكَ السَّلَامُ تُفَارِقُنِي وَأُفَارِقُكَ إِلَى يَوْمِ الْقِيَامَةِ»

Indeed, the worshipper experiences the agonies and pangs of death; his joints bid one another peace, saying, "And peace be upon you; you part from me and I part from you until the Day of Judgement." (It was mentioned by Ibn 'Iraq in *Tanzih Ash-Shari'ah* 2:375, and he attributed it to Ad-Dailami, from Anas.)

In *Al-Hilyah*, Al-Hafiz Abu Nu'aym recorded a narration from Makhul, who related from Wathilah bin Al-Asqa' that the Prophet ﷺ said:

«وَالَّذِي نَفْسِي بِيَدِهِ لَمُعَايَنَةُ مَلَكِ الْمَوْتِ أَشَدُّ مِنْ ضَرْبَةٍ بِالسَّيْفِ»

By the One Who has my soul in His Hand, facing the Angel of Death is more severe than the striking of a sword.

3) 'Aishah, may Allâh be pleased with her, said, "(While he was on his deathbed), the Prophet ﷺ had with him a container of water; he would put his hands into it and then wipe them on his face, saying:

«لَا إِلَهَ إِلَّا اللهُ إِنَّ لِلْمَوْتِ لَسَكَرَاتٍ»

None has the right to be worshipped but Allâh; indeed, death has its stupors.

Then he raised his hands and said:

«فِي الرَّفِيقِ الأَعْلَى»

With the exalted companions.

Until he died and his hands lowered." (Recorded by Al-Bukhari in the Book of Battles, the chapter on the Illness of the Prophet ﷺ.)

4) Some of our scholars have said (may Allâh have mercy on them), "If even the Prophets, the Messengers, and the righteous ones are thus afflicted, then with what are we so busy that we do not think about that time, and why do we delay in preparing ourselves for that situation."

﴿قُلْ هُوَ نَبَؤٌا عَظِيمٌ ۝ أَنتُمْ عَنْهُ مُعْرِضُونَ ۝﴾

Say: "That is a great news, from which you turn away."[1]

Fourth: Preparing For Death

As a Muslim, you should be prepared for death at all times: whether it is day or night, whether you are sleeping or awake. You can practically prepare for it with the following:

1) Faith in the phrase of *Tawhid* and applying it.

2) You must be steadfast in performing your five compulsory, daily prayers in congregation. Regarding the prayer, you should also pray those prayers that are highly recommended, that are voluntary in nature, that are performed in the night — and that includes both the *Witr* prayer and the *Sunnah* prayers in general.

3) You must recite the Qur'an, contemplate its meanings, and apply its commands and laws. You should recite it late at night and at the beginning and end of the day; it is also recommended for you to recite it before the compulsory prayers. Finally, you should finish reading the Qur'an in its entirety at least once or twice a month.

4) Study the Sunnah of the Prophet ﷺ: follow what he orders and abstain from what he forbids.

5) Keep company with the righteous; seek to gain benefit from them, to improve both your worldly and your religious situation. One way to do that is to study both Allâh's Book and the

---

[1] (*Sad* 38:67,68)

Prophet's Sunnah with them.

Fifth: Death And Its Signs; A Good Ending Versus An Evil One

First, it is compulsory upon one who is on his deathbed and upon everyone else to do the following:

1) To write a final testament, for the Prophet ﷺ said:

$$\text{«مَا حَقُّ امْرِىءٍ مُسْلِم يَبِيتُ لَيْلَتَيْن وَلَهُ شَيْءٌ يُرِيدُ أَنْ يُوصِيَ فِيهِ إِلَّا وَوَصِيَّتُهُ مَكْتُوبَةٌ عِنْدَ رَأْسِهِ»}$$

No Muslim should sleep two nights when he wants to write something in his final testament except that his will is written down and placed by his head. (Agreed upon)

2) To combine fear with hope: one should fear Allâh's punishment, punishment which one deserves because of his wrongdoings, while one should also hope for mercy and forgiveness. On one occasion, the Prophet ﷺ went to meet a young man who was dying and he said to him:

$$\text{«كَيْفَ تَجِدُكَ»}$$

"How do you find yourself?"

The young man said, "By Allâh: O Messenger of Allâh, I indeed hope from Allâh and indeed, I fear because of my sins." The Prophet ﷺ said:

$$\text{«لَا يَجْتَمِعَانِ فِي قَلْبِ عَبْدٍ فِي مِثْلِ هَذَا الْمَوْطِنِ إِلَّا أَعْطَاهُ الله مَا يَرْجُو، وَأَمِنَهُ مِمَّا يَخَافُ»}$$

"In this situation, when the heart of a worshipper combines those two, Allâh gives him what he hopes and keeps him safe from what he fears." (Recorded by At-Tirmithi, Ibn Majah, 'Abdullah bin Ahmad and Ibn Abi Ad-Dunya). See *Al-Wajazah* by Shaikh 'Abdur-Rahman Al-Ghaith.

3) When one is sick and is on the verge of dying, one should especially have hope in Allâh: that He will forgive him, that He will have mercy on him, for indeed, His forgiveness is vast and

His mercy embraces all things. The Prophet ﷺ said:

«لَا يَمُوتَنَّ أَحَدُكُمْ إِلَّا وَهُوَ يُحْسِنُ بِاللهِ الظَّنَّ»

Let one of you not die except with good thoughts (and hopes) about Allâh.

The Sign of a Good Ending

1) Buraidah bin Al-Husaib, may Allâh be pleased with him, related that he heard the Prophet ﷺ say:

«مَوْتُ الْمُؤْمِنِ بِعَرَقِ الْجَبِينِ»

The death of a believer is with sweat on his forehead. (Recorded by Ahmad, An-Nasa'i, At-Tirmithi, Ibn Majah, Ibn Hibban, Al-Hakim and others.)

2) In a *Hadith* related by 'Abdullah bin 'Amr, the Prophet ﷺ said:

«مَا مِنْ مُسْلِمٍ يَمُوتُ يَوْمَ الْجُمُعَةِ أَوْ لَيْلَةَ الْجُمُعَةِ إِلَّا وَقَاهُ اللهُ فِتْنَةَ الْقَبْرِ»

No Muslim dies on Friday or on Thursday night except that Allâh protects him from the trials of the grave. (Recorded by Ahmad, and Al-Fasawi and it was graded *Sahih* by Al-Albani in *Ahkamul-Jana'iz*)

3) One of the signs of a good ending is for one to die while one is performing a good deed, an act of obedience to Allâh Almighty and His Messenger ﷺ, such as to die while praying, fasting, performing *Hajj* or *Umrah*, fighting in the way of Allâh, or while calling others to the way of Allâh. If Allâh wishes good for someone, He guides him to perform good deeds when He is about to take his life.

4) Another good indication for someone who has died is for Muslims after him to praise him kindly. Anas, may Allâh be pleased with him, related that when some Muslims passed by a funeral, they praised the deceased in a good way. Upon hearing them, the Prophet ﷺ said:

«وَجَبَتْ»

"It has become binding."

Then they passed by another funeral and they described the dead person as having bad qualities. So the Prophet ﷺ said:

«وَجَبَتْ»

"It has become binding."

Then 'Umar bin Al-Khattab, may Allâh be pleased with him, asked, "What has become binding." He ﷺ answered:

«هَذَا أَثْنَيْتُمْ عَلَيْهِ خَيْرًا، فَوَجَبَتْ لَهُ الْجَنَّةُ، وَهَذَا أَثْنَيْتُمْ عَلَيْهِ شَرًّا فَوَجَبَتْ لَهُ النَّارُ، أَنْتُمْ شُهَدَاءُ الله فِي أَرْضِهِ»

"This one you praised in a good way, and so Paradise became binding for him. And this one you evaluated as being bad, and so the Fire became binding for him: You are Allâh's witnesses on His earth." (Agreed upon)

5) Other good signs you may read on the face or body of someone right after he dies:

i)   A smile on his face

ii) His index finger is pointed

iii) A shining or illuminated face, which results from hearing glad tidings from the Angel of Death

6. There are also a number of signs that indicate an evil ending; among them are the following:

i)   To die while one is associating partners with Allâh or is neglectful in one's prayers or in any other of Allâh and His Messenger's commands. Some examples of this is for one to die while one is singing, listening to music, watching lewd films, drinking alcohol, or taking drugs.

ii) After death, some bad signs can be seen on one's face or body, such as a frown, darkness, a darkness that results from having the Angel of Death giving him news of Allâh's anger. Another sign is blackness on one's face and body — and we seek protection with Allâh from all evil. (*Al-Wajazah* by Shaikh 'Abdur-Rahman Al-Ghaith 46-48.)

Supplication And Patience

The loved ones of the deceased who remain after his death must be patient, especially in the early hours after his death, and more especially when one is just given news of a loved one's death. The

Prophet ﷺ said:

«إِنَّمَا الصَّبْرُ عِنْدَ الصَّدْمَةِ الأُولَى»

Indeed patience is only during the initial shock.

Furthermore, one should supplicate for the deceased and say a well-known phrase that is given in this *Hadith*:

«مَا مِنْ عَبْدٍ تُصِيبُهُ مُصِيبَةٌ فَيَقُولُ: إِنَّا لله وَإِنَّا إِلَيْهِ رَاجِعُونَ، اللَّهُمَّ أُجْرِنِي فِي مُصِيبَتِي وَأَخْلِفْ لِي خَيْرًا مِنْهَا، إِلَّا أَجَرَهُ اللهُ تَعَالَى فِي مُصِيبَتِهِ، وَأَخْلَفَ لَهُ خَيْرًا مِنْهَا»

Whenever a worshipper is afflicted with a calamity and then says, "Indeed we belong to Allâh, and indeed, to Him we are returning; O Allâh, reward me in this calamity of mine and substitute for me that which is better (than what I have lost)," Allâh rewards him because of his calamity and substitutes for him that which is better than what he lost. (Recorded by Muslim)

The Prophet ﷺ also said:

«يَقُولُ الله تَعَالَى: مَا لِعَبْدِي الْمُؤْمِنِ عِنْدِي جَزَاءٌ إِذَا قَبَضْتُ صَفِيَّهُ مِنْ أَهْلِ الدُّنْيَا ثُمَّ احْتَسَبَهُ إِلَّا الْجَنَّةَ»

Allâh says, "When I take the prized one from this world of one of my believing worshippers, and when that believing worshipper then seeks reward from me (for that calamity), there is no other reward for him except Paradise." (Recorded by Ahmad with a *Sahih* chain)

First: As one is dying, others should prompt him to say, "None has the right to be worshipped but Allâh," for the Prophet ﷺ said:

«لَقِّنُوا مَوْتَاكُمْ: لَا إِلَهَ إِلَّا اللهُ»

Prompt those from you who are dying (those upon whom the

signs of death are visible) to say, "None has the right to be worshipped except Allâh." (Recorded by Muslim in his *Sahih*)

Second: When you are sure that someone has just died, close his eyes and tie his mouth shut, because the Sunnah indicates these two actions.

"Prompt those from you who are dying": If you are with a brother Muslim when he is about to die, you should gently instruct him to say the phrase of purity: "None has the right to be worshipped except Allâh." Remind him until he remembers and says it, and when he says it, say no more to him. But if he then speaks other words, remind him again to say the phrase of purity, in the hope that they will be his last words, so that he enters Paradise. The Prophet ﷺ said:

«لَقِّنُوا مَوْتَاكُمْ: لَا إِلَهَ إِلَّا اللهُ»

Prompt those from you who are dying to say, "*Laa Ilaha Illallâh*" (None has the right to be worshipped except Allâh). (Recorded by Muslim). In another *Hadith*, he ﷺ said:

«مَنْ كَانَ آخِرُ كَلَامِهِ لَا إِلَهَ إِلَّا اللهُ دَخَلَ الْجَنَّةَ»

Whoever's last words are "*Laa Ilaha Illallâh*" enters Paradise. (Recorded by Abu Dawud and it is *Sahih*)

"When you are sure that someone has just died": The Shaikh said that:

1) You should close his eyes. In a *Hadith* related by Umm Salamah, she said, "When the Prophet ﷺ entered upon Abu Salamah, whose eyes were still open, he ﷺ closed them and said:

«إِنَّ الرُّوحَ إِذَا قُبِضَ تَبِعَهُ الْبَصَرُ»

When the soul is taken, the sight follows it.

2) You should close his mouth, tying them shut — for example, with a piece of cloth, so that when the body is washed, water does not enter it, and so that the features of the face do not

become distorted.

3) In addition to what the Shaikh mentioned, you should somehow relax the joints of the body immediately after death, making it easier to move the body around, to wash it, and to wrap it up.

4) Some sort of weight should be placed on the stomach of the dead, preventing any waste matter from exiting when the washing is delayed.

5) The body should be covered; 'Aishah, may Allâh be pleased with her, related that when the Prophet ﷺ died, he was enshrouded. (Recorded by Al-Bukhari and Muslim)

6) The dead should be buried quickly, for the Prophet ﷺ said:

«أَسْرِعُوا بِالْجَنَازَةِ فَإِنْ تَكُ صَالِحَةً فَخَيْرٌ تُقَدِّمُونَهَا إِلَيْهِ، وَإِنْ تَكُ سِوَى ذَلِكَ فَشَرٌّ تَضَعُونَهُ عَنْ رِقَابِكُمْ»

Hasten the funeral, for if it (the soul) is righteous, then you are leading it to what is good; and if it is otherwise, then it is evil that you are ridding yourselves of. (Agreed upon)

7) Those who remain behind should be quick in paying off the debts of the deceased. Abu Hurairah related that the Prophet ﷺ said:

«نَفْسُ الْمُؤْمِنِ مُعَلَّقَةٌ بِدَيْنِهِ حَتَّى يُقْضَى عَنْهُ»

The soul of a believer is suspended by his debt, until it is paid off for him. (Recorded by At-Tirmithi. See *Al-Wajazah*, p. 46.)

❖ ❖ ❖

Third: It is compulsory to wash the body of the dead Muslim, unless he was a martyr who died on the battlefield, for he is neither washed nor prayed upon; rather, he is simply buried in the clothes he was wearing. The Prophet ﷺ neither washed the dead (Muslims) of Uhud nor did he pray over them.

Fourth: the *'Awrah* of the dead should be covered with a cloth. That cloth should be raised slightly and his stomach should be squeezed gently. Then the one who is washing the body should take a piece of cloth, wrap it around his hands, and wash the private areas of the body. Next, he should perform ablution on him — the same ablution that is made for prayer. Then he should wash his head and beard with water and *Sidr* (a special plant, whose leaves are crushed and then are used for cleaning) or something similar to it. Next, he should wash the right side of the body, following that with the left. Then he should repeat the whole process for a second and a third time — each time passing his hands on the deceased's stomach. When he passes his hands over the stomach, some waste matter may be discharged, and if that happens, he should clean it and then block the orifices with cotton or something similar. If the orifice doesn't hold together (discharges keep coming out), he may cover them with special clay or he may use any other technique or material known in modern-day medicine, such as plaster.

❖ ❖ ❖

"It is compulsory to wash...": When a Muslim dies, whether he be young or old, whether part of his body remains or the whole of it, it is compulsory to wash his corpse, the exception being the martyr of the battlefield, who died at the hands of the disbelievers while he was fighting in the way of Allâh. The Prophet ﷺ said,

«لَا تُغَسِّلُوهُمْ فَإِنْ كُلَّ جُرْحٍ، أَوْ كُلَّ دَمٍ يَفُوحُ مِسْكًا يَوْمَ الْقِيَامَةِ»

Do not wash them, for every injury and every drop of blood will exude the odor of musk on the Day of Judgement. (Recorded by Ahmad with a *Sahih* chain)

The Virtues Of Washing A Corpse

In a *Hadith* related by Abu Rafi', may Allâh be pleased with him, the Prophet ﷺ said:

«مَنْ غَسَلَ مُسْلِمًا فَكَتَمَ عَلَيْهِ غَفَرَ اللهُ لَهُ أَرْبَعِينَ مَرَّةً»

Whoever washes a (dead) Muslim and then keeps to himself (what he saw of the body), Allâh forgives him forty times.

In another narration, the *Hadith* ends:

«خَرَجَ مِنْ ذُنُوبِهِ كَيَوْمَ وَلَدَتْهُ أُمُّهُ»

He will be freed from sins, so that he will be like he was on the day his mother gave him birth.

In yet another narration, instead of forty times, the *Hadith* ends:

«أَرْبَعِينَ كَبِيرَةً»

He will be forgiven for forty great sins.

«وَمَنْ كَفَّنَهُ كَسَاهُ اللهُ يَوْمَ الْقِيَامَةِ مِنْ سُنْدُسٍ وَإِسْتَبْرَقِ الْجَنَّةِ، وَمَنْ حَفَرَ لَهُ حُفْرَةً فَأَجَنَّهُ فِيهَا أَجْرَى اللهُ لَهُ أَجْرَ مَسْكَنٍ أَسْكَنَهُ إِيَّاهُ إِلَى يَوْمِ الْقِيَامَةِ»

And whoever shrouds him, Allâh will clothe him with the *Sundus* and *Istabraq* of Paradise on the Day of Judgement. And whoever digs a grave to cover him in, Allâh will reward him with a dwelling near Him on the Day or Judgement. (Recorded by Al-Hakim and Al-Baihaqi. It was also recorded by At-Tabarani in *Al-Kabir* with the wording "forty great sins" and it was graded *Sahih* by Al-Albani in *Ahkamul-Jana'iz*.)

By Fulfilling Two Conditions, The One Who Washes The Corpse Of A Muslim Receives A Great Reward:

1) He must cover the body of the corpse, making sure no one sees the corpse's private parts, and then he must not inform others about the distasteful things he saw.

2) He should seek Allâh's reward for that, not seeking any worldly reward, not even thankfulness from others: it is an established principle in the *Shari'ah* that Allâh accepts only those acts of worship that are done purely for Him.

What is the Sunnah in regards to washing the deceased? Umm 'Atiyyah, may Allâh be pleased with her, related that as she and others were washing the body of the Prophet's daughter, Zainab, the

Prophet ﷺ entered and said:

«اغْسِلْنَهَا ثَلَاثًا أَوْ خَمْسًا أَوْ سَبْعًا أَوْ أَكْثَرَ مِنْ ذَلِكَ إِذَا رَأَيْتُنَّ ذَلِكَ بِمَاءٍ وَسِدْرٍ»

"Wash her three times, or five, or seven, or more if you deem that that should be done; wash her with water and *Sidr*."

Umm 'Atiyyah then asked, "An odd number." He ﷺ said,

«نَعَمْ وَاجْعَلْنَ فِي الآخِرَةِ كَافُورًا أَوْ شَيْئًا مِنَ الْكَافُورِ. فَإِذَا فَرَغْتُنَّ فَآذِنَّنِي»

"Yes, and in the last washing use camphor or something from camphor. Then when you are finished, inform me."

Umm 'Atiyyah later said, "When we finished, he gave us a loincloth and said:

«أَشْعِرْنَهَا إِيَّاهُ»

"Make her wear it."

And we combed her hair into three braids (in one narration: 'we undid her hair and washed it'). So we divided her hair into three sections: two braids and her forelocks, which we arranged behind her. And the Messenger of Allâh ﷺ said to us:

«ابْدَأْنَ بِمَيَامِنِهَا وَمَوَاضِعِ الْوُضُوءِ مِنْهَا»

"Begin with the right side and with the areas of ablution."
(Recorded by Al-Bukhari and Muslim)

We should be careful who we choose to wash our dead, for Ibn 'Umar, may Allâh be pleased with them, said, "Let only the trustworthy ones wash your dead." (See *Irwa'ul-Ghalil* by Al-Albani) The trustworthy one is he who is steadfast in performing his five compulsory prayers in congregation, who is known for his honor, manners, trust, and good dealings. (*Al-Wajazah* 53-54)

How To Wash The Dead[1]

- Who should wash the dead body of a Muslim? The Muslim may write in his testimony that he wants a specific person to wash him; otherwise, his father or grandfather and his son or

---

[1] Taken from *Al-Wajazah*, p. 59 and what is after that, with some revisions.

grandchildren should wash him. In case that the dead person did not assign someone to wash him, his family should choose an honest, trustworthy man to do the job; and a similar ruling applies to a woman.

- The place of the washing should be covered on all sides with a roof.

- The one responsible for washing the dead (i.e., who has made intention to wash the corpse) may choose two people from those who attend the funeral to witness the washing. First, he should choose someone who shows signs of being a righteous man, so that he may teach him the Sunnah in regards to washing. Next, he should choose someone who has signs of sinning on his face, so that he can see the state of the dead, in the hope that it will serve as an admonition, in the hope that he will return to the way of Allâh (and enough of an admonition is death itself!).

- When the one in charge of washing is actually washing the corpse, no one should be allowed to enter the room, except for those whom he needs — such as the two we mentioned above; it is disliked for others to be present.

What May The One Who Is Washing Use?

- He may wear a surgical mask, to protect his nose and mouth from foul odors.

- He may wear some form of plastic covering over his clothes to prevent filth or even any *Sidr* or camphor from staining his clothes.

- He may wear gloves: first to avoid direct contact with the corpse and second to prevent filth from reaching his hands.

- And he may wear protective covering over his shoes to prevent filth from getting to them.

Preparing The Water And The *Sidr* In A Washing Container:

- The container should be filled with an amount of water that is proportionate to the size of the corpse.

- Then the *Sidr* (the leaves of a special plant that are crushed and then used for cleaning) should be brought.

- For every coffee-size cup of *Sidr*, 4 liters of water should be used.

So the small-sized person should have 4 liters of water used along with a coffee-sized cup of *Sidr*. Someone bigger than him may have 8 liters of water along with 2 coffee-sized cup of *Sidr*. More may be used in the same proportion if the size of the corpse is greater, and less may be used in the same proportion if the size of the corpse is smaller.

Preparing The Camphor And The Water:

For every four liters of water, 2 cubes of camphor (a special chemical with an aromatic smell) should be used; this is the amount used for the small body. So the above-average-sized body may need eight liters of water and four cubes of camphor. The greater the size of the body the more water and camphor should be used, but in the same proportion, and the smaller the size of the body the less water and camphor should be used, but also in the same proportion.

Note: There are two kinds of camphor: it either comes soft so that it can be ground with one's hands or it comes hard, so that a special instrument is needed to crush it, so that in the end, it becomes like particles of sugar.

Before Washing The Body:

1) A large cloth should be used to cover the *'Awrah* of the body, which is the area from one's navel to one's knees.

2) The clothes should be removed:

   i) If the body and its joints are still loose and pliant enough that the clothes can easily be removed, they should be removed and washed so that one in need may benefit from them.

   ii) If the body is hard — perhaps it wasn't softened after death or perhaps because of a long stay in a freezer — the clothes should be removed using scissors. The cutting should begin at the right cuff until the neck, then the left cuff until the neck. Then the pockets should be cut until the end of the garment; care should be taken so that when the clothes are removed, the cloth above the body remains steady, so that no private area of the corpse becomes exposed. If the corpse is wearing pants, then the cutting can take place either from the right or the left of the protective cloth above. The body can then be turned over to the left and to the right so that the pieces of clothing are removed, but again, it must be made sure that the cloth above always covers the *'Awrah* of the body.

iii) If the fingernails or toenails are long, the one who is cleaning the body may clip them; he may also shave the armpit hair if it is dense; if it is short, he may pluck that hair, and he may also trim the moustache of the deceased.

iv) The nose and mouth of the deceased should be cleaned and then blocked off with cotton, only to be removed after the body is washed completely.

v) If the body is so dirty that water and *Sidr* cannot remove the filth, then the following mixture can be used:

    a) Two spoons of grated soap.

    b) Two spoons of shampoo.

    c) Two spoons of disinfectant.

    d) Three large glasses of water.

All of the above should be mixed together and then used to clean the body with a sponge. The one who is washing should begin with the head, continue to the face; thereafter, he should turn the body on its left side, so that he can scrub the right side of the body that is facing up; then he does the same on the other side. When washing the private parts, he should insert his hands from underneath the covering, always making sure that the cloth continues to cover the *'Awrah* of the corpse. Now that the mixture has been scrubbed all over, water should be brought and again, the one who is washing should begin with the head, then the face, then turning the body on its left side, washing the right side, and then the opposite. In this way, both the mixture and the filth are removed.

Note: The mixture should be increased and decreased in proportion to the size of the body. After cleaning the body, or if the body is already clean, we may begin with the following:

1) If the body is pliant, it should be placed in a semi-seated position; then someone should squeeze the stomach gently three times, so that any waste matter that is about to come out may come out; the one who is washing the body should wrap a rag around his hand, and from underneath the cloth, clean both the front and

rear private parts, removing any waste. While he is doing that, someone else should continually pour water over his hands from above.

If, however, the body is hard — because it was not made pliant or because it came from the freezer — it is enough to simply open the legs; after that is accomplished, the one who is washing should insert his hands from underneath the cloth and clean the private areas, both in the front and the rear. If he sees that the waste continues to come out of the orifices, he should wash them for a second and a third time; but if waste still continues after that, then he may use a piece of cloth to block up the orifice, and then he can keep the cloth in place by using a bandage.

2) The one who is washing should then join the deceased's hands together, saying "*Bismillah* (In the Name of Allâh)." Then he should:

- Wash the hands of the deceased three times.
- Wipe over the mouth and nose three times each.
- Wash the face three times.
- Wash the right forearm three times and then the left forearm three times.
- With wet hands, wipe over the head, going back and forth, and then over the ears, as in the Islamic ablution.
- Then he should wash the right foot three times, followed by the left foot three times.

3) Then he should bring *Sidr*, washing the head and face, lathering them with the *Sidr*; thereafter, he should rub the *Sidr* all over the body, beginning with the right side, from the shoulders until he reaches the feet; and then the same with the left side. On both sides, when he is rubbing the private areas, he should do so by inserting his hands underneath the cloth. Then he should repeat the washing a second time with water and *Sidr*.

4) This time, camphor should be used in washing the head, face, right side of the body (beginning with the shoulders until he reaches the feet), and left side of the body. And again, when dealing with the private areas, to apply the camphor, he should insert his hands from under the cloth. It should be known that

camphor is a kind of perfume: though it hardens the body and makes it cold, it is poisonous to insects.

5) Another towel should be brought: every part of the body that is visible should be dried with it, such as the face, hands, shoulders, chest, back, and calves. Then this wet towel should be placed over the cloth that covers the private areas of the body: if the former is applied gently, it absorbs much that is wet underneath, and thus the body is ready for shrouding.

Some Important Points To Consider

1) When dealing with a body that has been mutilated or injured in some way or another, the afflicted area should be cleaned and then wrapped with cotton, which should be covered with a covering that is made of the following mixture: water, *Sidr*, and camphor.

2) The ruling for washing is the same for males and females above the age of seven, except that the hair of females should be tied in three braids. Children under the age of seven have no *'Awrah*, so a male may wash a female and vice versa, washing the body three times without making the Islamic ablution. The condition, however, is that if a male is washing the corpse of a female under the age of seven or vice versa, the one who is washing must be a *Mahram* (i.e., one who the deceased could never marry while alive) of the deceased.

Men may not wash women other than their wives and women may not wash men other than their husbands. The Messenger of Allâh ﷺ once said to 'Aishah,

«مَايَضُرُّكِ لَوْمُتَّ قَبْلِي فَغَسَلْتُكِ وَكَفَنْتُكِ ثُمَّ صَلَّيْتَ عَلَيْكِ وَدَفَنْتُكِ»

"It will not harm you that you should die before me, that I should wash you, then enshroud you, then pray over you, and then bury you." (Recorded by Ahmad in *Al-Musnad*).

After the Prophet ﷺ died, 'Aishah said:

«لَوِ اسْتَقْبَلْتُ مِنْ أَمْرِي مَا اسْتَدْبَرْتُ مَا غَسَلَ رَسُولَ اللهِ ﷺ إِلَّا نِسَاؤُهُ»

"If I would now face the matter that is now behind me, no one would have washed the Messenger of Allâh ﷺ except for his wives." (Recorded by Ahmad in *Al-Musnad*)

3) The miscarried fetus that dies before it reaches four months is neither washed nor enshrouded nor prayed over; rather a hole is simply dug for it, and it is buried. But the miscarried fetus that is older than four months is a human being because the *Ruh* (soul) has been blown into it; therefore it takes the ruling of the child that is under seven years of age: it is washed, named, and the *'Aqiqah* is performed for it.

4) When washing the body, one should use water that is suitable to the weather, just as is done for people who are alive: in the summer, hot water should not be used, and in the winter, cold water should not be used.

5) If in its mouth there is a gold tooth that is embedded, the body should not be harmed: the tooth should not be removed; however, if the tooth is not embedded, but is easily removable, it should be removed. That is if the mouth is open; if it is closed, it should not be disturbed in any of the two above-mentioned situations.

It should also be known that were the one washing the body to simply pour water over every part of the corpse, then that would be sufficient.

The Shaikh said that a special kind of clay might be needed to block the orifices, referring to clay that has no sand in it.

If more than three times is required to clean the body, then that is permissible; also care should be taken to clean the hidden areas, such as behind one's knees, in one's armpits and navel. Based on what is related from Ibn 'Umar, these areas should be perfumed.

To give special status to the body parts that touch the floor during prostration, the one washing the body may apply perfume to those areas. It would even be a good thing to apply perfume over the entire body, which is what was done to Anas and Ibn'Umar, may Allâh be pleased with them. One can also use steam aromas for the body; the Prophet ﷺ said:

«إِذَا جَمَرْتُمُ الْمَيِّتَ فَأَحْمِرُوهُ ثَلَاثًا»

If you are going to use perfumed incense for the dead body, then use it three times. (Recorded by Ibn Abi Shaibah).

When A Body Cannot Be Washed, *Tayammum* Should Be Performed

If water is not available for washing the corpse, or if a man dies among a group of women or vice versa, *Tayammum* should be performed on the corpse; it should then be enshrouded, prayed upon, and then buried. Just as the *Junub* (one in a major state of impurity) performs *Tayammum* when water is not available, so too should *Tayammum* be performed on the corpse when water is not available or cannot be used. The Prophet ﷺ said:

«إِذَا مَاتَتِ الْمَرْأَةُ مَعَ رِجَالٍ لَيْسَ مَعَهُمُ امْرَأَةٌ غَيْرُهَا، وَالرَّجُلُ مَعَ نِسَاءٍ لَيْسَ مَعَهُنَّ رَجُلٌ غَيْرُهُ، فَإِنَّهُمَا يُيَمَّمَانِ وَيُدْفَنَانِ»

If a woman who lives among men dies and there is no other woman with them, and when a man dies among women and there is no other man among them, *Tayammum* is performed on them and then they are buried. (Recorded by Abu Dawud in his book *Al-Marasil* and Al-Baihaqi)

The people referred to in this *Hadith* are of the same status of he who finds no water.

Fifth: The best way to enshroud a male body is to enshroud it in three white sheets, using neither shirt nor turban. And as the Prophet ﷺ did, the sheets should be wrapped around the body. However, there is no harm in wrapping the body in a shirt, a loincloth, and a wrapping.

A woman is enshrouded in five garments: a shirt, veil, loincloth, and two wrappings. A male child may be enshrouded in one or three garments, and a female child is enshrouded in a shirt and two wrappings.

All that is mentioned above is recommended. In terms of what is compulsory for males and females, children and adults, they must be wrapped in at least one garment that covers the entire body. However, if the deceased was in a state of *Ihram*, meaning that he was in the inviolable state of a pilgrim, then he should simply be washed with water and *Sidr*, and enshrouded in the dress of the pilgrim (one lower garment and one upper garment) or in some other dress. Neither his head nor his face should be covered, and no perfume is to be used on him, because he will be raised (in the same state of *Ihram*) on the Day of Judgement, speaking the famous phrase (*Labbaik...*) of the pilgrim. That the pilgrim is an exception is related in an authentic *Hadith*. If the one who died in a state of *Ihram* is a woman, then she is enshrouded like anyone else, except for the following rulings: no perfume is to be used, and though her face and hands are not to be covered with the veil and gloves, they are to be covered with the sheets that are used for her shrouding, the same sheets that we mentioned when we described the enshrouding of a woman.

Sixth: The most deserving person to wash the body, to pray over it, and to bury it is the person who was chosen for the task by the deceased. If no one was chosen by the deceased, the next worthy person for the task is the father, followed by the grandfather, followed by the closest male relatives — that is, if the deceased is a male.

The most deserving person to wash the female is also the person who was chosen by the deceased. The next deserving person is the mother, then the grandmother, followed in succession by her closest female relatives. A husband may wash his wife and vice versa, because Abu Bakr washed his wife and because 'Ali also washed his wife, Fatimah, may Allâh be pleased with them all.

The Ruling On Enshrouding The Dead And How To Go About It

When the deceased Muslim is washed, it is compulsory to enshroud it, with a garment that covers the entire body. Mus'ab bin 'Umair, may Allâh be pleased with him, one of the martyrs in the battle of Uhud, was enshrouded in a garment that was short in length, so the Prophet ﷺ ordered his Companions to cover his head and upper body with the garment and to cover his legs with lemon grass. (Recorded by Al-Bukhari)

This indicates that it is compulsory to cover the entire body. The lemon grass was used because no other garment made of cloth was available to them.

How To Enshroud The Deceased

The majority of scholars agree that the garment used should be thick enough that it doesn't reveal the contours or the color of the body, a ruling that applies to men and women, the exception being for the one who is in a state of *Ihram*. The best cloth that one can be enshrouded in is mentioned in a *Hadith* related by 'Aishah, may Allâh be pleased with her, recorded by Al-Bukhari and Muslim, and in the following *Hadith*:

«أَحْسَنُ مَا زُرْتُمُ اللَّهَ بِهِ فِي قُبُورِكُمْ وَمَسَاجِدِكُمُ الْبَيَاضُ . . . الحديث»

The best thing to visit Allâh with in your graves and in your *Masjids* is with white... (Recorded by Ibn Majah)

First Step: Measurements of the Shroud

1) We must take into consideration the size of the deceased. If, in width, he measures 30 cm, then 90 cm of cloth is used; if, in width, he measures 40 cm, then 120 cm of cloth is needed; and if his width is 50 cm, 150 cm of cloth is needed.

2) Next, we may take into consideration the height of the deceased. If he is 180 cm tall, we will need to add 60 cm of cloth; if he is 150 cm tall, we will need to add 50 cm of cloth; if he is 120 cm tall, we will need to add 40 cm of cloth. The additional cloth is needed to tie the shroud above the head and below the feet.

Second Step: Enshrouding the Body

1) How to enshhroud a man:

Based on the *Hadith* of 'Aishah, may Allâh be pleased with her, a man is enshrouded in three garments; she said, "The Messenger of Allâh ﷺ was shrouded in three white garments made from cotton; neither shirt nor turban was used; he was placed inside of the garments and was then wrapped." (Recorded in the Six Books, also by Ibn Jarud and Al-Baihaqi)

i) The straps used to tie the shroud are taken from the width of the shroud itself, so if the body's width measure 60 cm, for example, the width of the shroud should measure 180 cm, and the straps used to tie the corpse can be taken from that width; the number of straps should be odd — 7, for example.

ii) If the body is 180 cm tall, we add 60 cm, and the shroud becomes 240 cm in length. The three shrouds should be placed one on top of the other on the bier (frame used for carrying the corpse), and the longest of the shrouds is to be placed beside the head.

Note: The measurements for the shrouds and the belts are known from experience; otherwise, there are no specific measurements mentioned in the *Shari'ah*.

iii) A *Tubban* (a garment that covers the lower body, but is one piece only and has no legs) is cut from cloth, and it measures 100 cm in length by 25 cm in width. It should be placed on top of the shrouds, underneath the buttocks of the body. A piece of cotton is placed on the *Tubban*, as well as a mixture of perfume and camphor; the mixture should also be applied to the shroud that is on top: two cups of musk and four cubes of camphor (the quantity should be reduced if the body is smaller).

iv) The body should then be placed on top of the shrouds, still with a cloth on top to cover the private areas. Then any kind of perfume stick should be applied on the places of prostration, honoring prostration to Allâh Then the perfume should be applied to the rest of the body, followed by areas that are difficult to reach, such as behind the knees. Then the arms of the deceased should be placed parallel to its sides. The *Tubban* is then tied on the body to prevent any impurities that may continue to discharge, protecting the shrouds and making sure that the purity of the deceased continues until it is buried.

v) Next, the head and legs should be placed and wrapped in the right side of the first shroud, followed by the left side, at which point the covering over the body is removed. The same procedure should then be carried out using the second and the third shrouds.

vi) The first belt is used to tie the head, and whatever is extra from the shrouds should be returned to the face. Then the legs are tied. The remaining seven belts are then evenly distributed over the body; they should be tied on the left side, making it easy to loosen the knots when the body is placed on his right side in the grave.

2) How to enshroud a woman:

It is recommended to use five pieces for a woman: 2 wrappings, a shirt, a loincloth, and a veil. If she measures 50 cm in width and 150 cm in length, the width of the wrappings should be 150 cm, from which the belts are taken, and again, the straps should be in odd number — seven, for example. Since she is 150 cm tall, 200 cm of cloth should be used. The straps are placed on the bier first, and then the shrouds. The length and width of the shrouds follows the same principles as those outlined for men.

i) The cutting of the shirt: The shirt is measured two times the length from the shoulders to the end of the ankles. An opening is cut in the middle, from which the head enters. The upper part is of a width of 90 cm.

ii) The loincloth should be 90 cm in width and 150 cm in length.

iii) The veil is 90 square centimeters.

iv) The *Tubban* should measure 25 cm by 90 cm. It is placed on top of the loincloth, so that it is directly underneath the buttocks of the deceased. A small amount of cotton is placed on it, as well as a mixture of perfume and camphor, and the same mixture is spread over the loincloth and shirt. For all female corpses, the length of the shirt, loincloth, and veil is 90 cm.

v)   The corpse is then carried and placed on top of the shrouds with the body covering still in place. The *Tubban* is the first to be tied, to prevent any waste from discharging onto the shrouds. The right part of the loincloth is tied and then the left side. The body is rolled inside, until the body covering is no longer needed and is discarded. The head is then placed inside of the shirt, after which it is placed on the rest of the body, with the sides of the garment being placed underneath the body. Next, the veil is brought: the head, its hair, and the face are veiled.

vi)   The wrappings (shrouds): The head is placed on top and then is rolled inside of the right side of the first wrapping, followed by her legs. Then her head and legs are placed and rolled into the left side of the first wrapping. Next, the same is done with the second wrapping.

vii)   The straps: First the head is tied and then the feet. Whatever is left over from both ends is returned to the head and the feet, and is tied with the extra length of the strap. Next, the remaining five straps are tied evenly over the body, with the knots on the left side, making it easy to loosen them when the body is placed on its right side inside of the grave.

Note:

1)   A young boy under the age of seven is enshrouded with one sheet that is big enough to cover his entire body, or with three sheets.

2)   A young girl under the age of seven is enshrouded with a shirt and two wrappings.

3)   Musk should be applied between the shrouds used for the deceased. Abu Sa‘id Al-Khudri, may Allâh be pleased with him, related that the Prophet ﷺ said:

«أَطْيَبُ الطِّيبِ، أوِ المِسْكُ»

The best perfume is musk. (Recorded by Muslim)

Ibn Al-Munthir said, "The majority of the scholars we know are of the view that a woman should be enshrouded in seven sheets...that is preferred because while she was alive, a woman's *'Awrah* is larger than the area of a man's *'Awrah*. While she was alive and in a state of *Ihram*, the best state to be in, she wore stitched clothing, so she may wear stitched clothing after her death. On the other hand, when alive, a man in a state of *Ihram* is not allowed to wear stitched clothing. Therefore because men and women differ in their clothing while they are living, they also differ after they are dead." (*Al-Mughni* 3:391).

A man may wash the body of his wife and vice versa. 'Aishah, may Allâh be pleased with her, said, "If I were to face now that which is behind me, no one would have washed the Prophet ﷺ except for his wives." (Recorded by Abu Dawud and Ibn Majah). In another *Hadith*, she said, "The Prophet ﷺ once returned to me after a funeral in Al-Baqi' (famous graveyard in Al-Madinah), and I had such a great headache that I was saying, "Oh, my head." He ﷺ said:

«بَلْ أَنَا وَارَأْسَاهُ مَا ضَرَّكِ لَوْ مِتَّ قَبْلِي فَغَسَلْتُكِ وَكَفَنْتُكِ ثُمَّ صَلَّيْتُ عَلَيْكِ وَدَفَنْتُكِ»

Rather me (as well), Oh, my head. It would not hurt you were you to die before me, and then I washed you, enshrouded you, prayed over you, and buried you. (Recorded by Ahmad and Ad-Daraqutni)

The Shaikh mentioned that Abu Bakr, may Allâh be pleased with him, washed the body of his wife; he was referring to Asma' bint 'Umais Al-Kath'amiyyah, may Allâh be pleased with her, who accepted Islam in the early days of Makkah. She emigrated with Ja'far, may Allâh be pleased with him, her husband at the time. When Ja'far was martyred, Abu Bakr married her, and when he died, 'Ali, may Allâh be pleased with her, married her.

 ❖ ❖ ❖

Seventh: How to pray over the dead: "Saying *Takbir* four times; after the first time, one should recite *Al-Fatihah*, and it is also good to recite a short *Surah* after that, or even one verse or two — a practice that is based on an authentic *Hadith* related by Ibn 'Abbas, may Allâh be pleased with them.

After the second *Takbir*, one should send blessings upon the Prophet ﷺ just as one does so in the seated position of the prayer. Then he should say the *Takbir* for a third time, and say:

"O Allâh, forgive our living and our dead, those present and those absent, our young and our old, our males and our females. O Allâh, whom among us You keep alive, then let such a life be upon Islam, and whom among us You take unto Yourself, then let such a death be upon faith. O Allâh, forgive and have mercy upon him, excuse him and pardon him, and make honorable his reception. Expand his entry, and cleanse him with water, snow, and ice, and purify him of sin as a white robe is purified of filth. Exchange his home for a better home, and his family for a better family, and his spouse for a better spouse. Admit him into Paradise, protect him from the punishment of the grave and the torment of the Fire; make spacious for him his grave and illuminate it for him. O Allâh, do not deprive us of his reward and do not let us stray after him."

Then one should make the fourth *Takbir*, after which one says one *Taslim* to the right.

With each *Takbir*, it is recommended to raise one's hands. And of course, the pronouns change according to who it is that died: if it is a female: "O Allâh, forgive her"; if it is more than one person that died, "O Allâh, forgive them." And if two people died, the Arabic languages accommodates the dual as well, so that one says, "the two of them."

If the deceased is a child who has not yet reached the age of puberty, rather than supplicating for his forgiveness one should say, "O Allâh, make him a preceding reward and a stored treasure for his parents, and an answered intercessor. O Allâh, through him, make heavy their Scales and magnify their reward. Unite him with the righteous believers, place him under the care of Ibrahim, and protect him by Your mercy from the torment of Hell."

The Sunnah is for the *Imam* to stand parallel to the head of the deceased male, and parallel to the middle of the deceased female. If the funeral prayer is for more than one person, the male body should be placed closest to the *Imam*. If there are children as well, then the male children are placed before the female adults, who are to be placed before the female children. The head of the male child should be parallel to the head of the male adult, and the middle part of the woman's body should be parallel to the head of the male adult. The same applies to the female child: her head is parallel to the head of the female adult, and the middle part of her body is parallel to the head of the male adult. Those praying with the *Imam* should all stand behind him, unless there remains one who finds no place behind him; he may stand to the *Imam*'s right.

❖ ❖ ❖

"**How to pray over the dead...**": It is *Fardh Kifayah* (communal obligation) to participate in a Muslim's funeral: if some of the Muslims perform it, the rest are absolved from the obligation. Indeed, the Prophet ﷺ used to pray over deceased Muslims. But when a Muslim died, leaving outstanding debts without making provision to have them repaid, the Prophet ﷺ wouldn't pray over that person; instead, he would say to his Companions,

«صَلُّوا عَلَى صَاحِبِكُمْ»

Pray over your companion. (Recorded by Al-Bukhari)

The Conditions of Praying Over The Dead

The same conditions that apply to a regular prayer apply to the funeral prayer; for example, then, one must be in a state of purity, one must cover one's *'Awrah*, and one must face the *Qiblah*. Because the Prophet ﷺ called the funeral prayer a prayer when he said:

$$\text{«صَلُّوا عَلَى صَاحِبِكُمْ»}$$

Pray over your companion.

It is given all of the rulings of any other regular prayer.

Elements That Are Compulsory To The Funeral Prayer

1) To stand, but only for one who is able.

2) Intention, for the Prophet ﷺ said:

$$\text{«إِنَّمَا الْأَعْمَالُ بِالنِّيَّاتِ»}$$

Indeed, deeds are only by their intentions.

3) Recitation of *Al-Fatihah* or praising Allâh.

4) Sending blessings and peace upon the Prophet ﷺ.

5) The four *Takbirs*.

6) Supplication.

7) The final *Taslim*.

How To Perform The Funeral Prayer

1) The bodies are placed in the direction of the *Qiblah*.

2) As the *Imam* stands for the prayer, his followers should stand behind him in three or more rows, for the Prophet ﷺ said:

$$\text{«مَنْ صَلَّى عَلَيْهِ ثَلَاثُ صُفُوفٍ فَقَدْ أَوْجَبَتْ»}$$

Whoever has three rows pray over him, then it becomes necessary (i.e., Paradise). (Recorded by At-Tirmithi who graded it *Hasan*)

4) The worshipper should raise his hands, intending to pray over the one who has died, or if they are more than one, those who died, saying, "*Allâhu Akbar* (Allâh is the Most Great)."

5) The Shaikh said that he should read *Al-Fatihah* and then a short

Surah. Here, the Shaikh is alluding to a *Hadith* related by Talhah bin 'Abdullah bin 'Awf, who said, "I prayed behind Ibn 'Abbas, may Allâh be pleased with them, over a funeral; he recited the Opening of the Book (*Al-Fatihah*) and then another *Surah* at such a voice that he made us hear what he was reciting. When the prayer ended, I took his hand, asked him about what he did, and he answered, 'I only read out loud for you to learn that it is Sunnah and right (to do so).'" (Recorded by Al-Bukhari and Muslim)

6) Then he should say the *Takbir* and send blessings and peace upon the Prophet ﷺ.

7) Then he should say the *Takbir* and supplicate for the dead.

8) Then he should say the final *Takbir*.

9) At this point, if he wishes, he may supplicate and then say the *Taslim* to end the prayer, or he may (after the fourth *Takbir*) end the prayer immediately, in both cases by saying the *Taslim* once. From the Sunnah, we know that the funeral prayer commences when the *Imam* says the *Takbir*; he then recites *Al-Fatihah* silently. Next, he sends blessings upon the Prophet ﷺ after which he supplicates for the dead. And then he ends the prayer by saying the *Taslim*.

The Wording Of The Supplication To Be Used During The Funeral Prayer

There are many different wordings related from the Prophet ﷺ regarding the funeral prayer; any one of them is sufficient; the Shaikh mentioned one wording and here is another:

"O Allâh, so-and-so is under Your care and protection, so protect him from the trial of the grave and from the torment of the Fire. Indeed You are faithful and truthful. Forgive and have mercy upon him, surely You are the Oft-Forgiving, The Most Merciful. O Allâh, forgive our living and our dead, those present and those absent, our young and our old, our males and our females. O Allâh, whom among us You keep alive, then let such a life be upon Islam, and whom among us You take unto Yourself, then let such a death be upon faith. O Allâh, do not deprive us of his reward and do not let us stray after him."

If the deceased is a child, then one should supplicate:

"O Allâh, make him a stored treasure, and a preceding reward for his parents. O Allâh, through him, make heavy their Scales and magnify their reward. Do not deprive us and them of his reward, and do not put us or them to trial after him. O Allâh, unite him with the righteous believers from before, place him under the care of Ibrahim, and exchange his home for a better home, his family for a better family. O Allâh, keep him safe from the trials of the grave and from the torment of the Fire."

Both of the above-mentioned supplications are authentic; the supplication that the Shaikh mentioned is found in a *Hadith* narrated by Abu Hurairah, which is related by Muslim and others.

"The Sunnah is for the *Imam* to stand...": Abu Ghalib Al-Khayyat related that he witnessed Anas bin Malik pray over the body of a man; during the prayer, Anas stood parallel to the head of the body. When the body was carried off, the body of a woman from the Quraish was brought. After Abu Hamzah (Anas) was told who she was, he prayed over her, but this time, he stood parallel to the middle of her body. Abu Ghalib said, "Among us on that day was Al-'Ala' bin Ziyad Al-'Adwi; when Al-'Ala' noticed the difference between the way Anas stood over the man and over the woman, he said, 'O Abu Hamzah, did the Prophet ﷺ stand the same way that you stood in relation to the man and in relation to the woman.' He said, 'Yes.' Al-'Ala' turned to us and said, 'Memorize (this Sunnah).'" (Recorded by Abu Dawud, At-Tirmithi, and Ibn Majah)

In one narration, Nafi' reported that Ibn 'Umar prayed over nine deceased Muslims at one time. He placed them right after the *Imam* and the women after the *Qiblah*. He lined the women up in one row, and he placed the corpse of Umm Kulthum, the daughter of 'Ali, and wife of 'Umar bin Al-Khattab with her son, Zaid, together. The *Imam* at that time was Sa'id bin Al-'As, and among the followers were Ibn 'Abbas, Abu Hurairah, Abu Sa'id, and Abu Qatadah. When the young boy's body was placed beside the *Imam* (and before the women), one of the men present complained and later related, "I argued against that, and as I looked at Ibn 'Abbas, Abu Hurairah, Abu Sa'id, and Abu Qatadah, I said, 'What is this!' And they said, 'This is the Sunnah.'" (Recorded by 'Abdur-Razzaq, An-Nasa'i and Ibn Jarud)

Following The Funeral Procession

It is Sunnah to follow the funeral procession until the body is buried, for the Prophet ﷺ said:

«عُودُوا الْمَرِيضَ وَامْشُوا مَعَ الْجَنَائِزِ تُذَكِّرُكُمُ الآخِرَةَ»

Visit the sick and walk with funerals: they will remind you of the Hereafter. (Recorded by Muslim)

It is recommended to walk in a fast pace when carrying the body to the grave, for the Prophet ﷺ said:

«أَسْرِعُوا فَإِنْ تَكُنْ صَالِحَةً فَخَيْرٌ تُقَدِّمُونَهُ إِلَيْهِ»

Be quick, for if the soul is righteous, then it is good that you are taking him to.

It is recommended to walk in front of the body, for that was the practice of the Prophet ﷺ, Abu Bakr, and ʿUmar. (Recorded by Abu Dawud, An-Nasaʾi and others)

As for the virtues of walking with a funeral, the Prophet ﷺ said:

«مَنِ اتَّبَعَ جَنَازَةَ مُسْلِمٍ إِيمَانًا وَاحْتِسَابًا، وَكَانَ مَعَهَا حَتَّى يُصَلَّى عَلَيْهَا
وَيُفْرَغَ مِنْ دَفْنِهَا، فَإِنَّهُ يَرْجِعُ مِنَ الأَجْرِ بِقِيرَاطَيْنِ، كُلُّ قِيرَاطٍ مِثْلُ أُحُدٍ
(وَهُوَ جَبَلٌ عَظِيمٌ قُرْبَ الْمَدِينَةِ)، وَمَنْ صَلَّى عَلَيْهَا ثُمَّ رَجَعَ قَبْلَ أَنْ تُدْفَنَ
فَإِنَّهُ يَرْجِعُ بِقِيرَاطٍ»

When one follows the funeral of a Muslim, having faith and seeking his reward with Allâh, and when one stays with the funeral until the body is prayed over and its burial is completed, then he returns with two *Qirats* (a large measurement) of reward, each *Qirat* is the size of Uhud. When one prays over it, but returns before it is buried, then he returns with one *Qirat*. (Recorded by Al-Bukhari)

Eighth: How to bury the dead: It is legislated for the grave to be dug to a depth equal to have the size of the man being buried. Inside of the grave, there should also be a hole dug (this hole is called a *Lahd*) on the side that is in the direction of the *Qiblah*. The body should then be placed on his right side in the *Lahd*. The knot of the shroud should be loosened; after it is loosened, it should not be removed, but left alone. The face of the deceased should not be exposed, regardless whether the body is female or male. Then bricks should be placed on the *Lahd* and plastered, so that the body is protected from dirt. If bricks are not available, then tablets or stones or wood may be used: anything to protect the body from dirt. Next, dirt is poured down, and it is recommended to say, "*Bismillah wa 'Ala Millati Rasoolillah.* (In the Name of Allâh, and upon the way of the Messenger of Allâh)." The ground of the grave should be raised to a level equal to the span of a hand. If possible, pebbles should be placed above the grave and it should be sprinkled with water.

It is legislated for those who participated in the burial to stand beside the grave (after the burial) and supplicate for the deceased. When the Prophet ﷺ would finish burying a body, he would stand by the grave and say:

«اسْتَغْفِرُوا لأَخِيكُمْ، وَاسْأَلُوا لَهُ التَّثْبِيتَ، فَإِنَّهُ الآنَ يُسْأَلُ»

Ask forgiveness for your brother, and ask (Allâh) to make him firm, for indeed, he is being asked right now.

❖ ❖ ❖

The Burial

To bury the dead, which means to hide the body completely underneath the dirt of the ground, is *Fardh Kifayah* (a communal obligation: at least some of the Muslims must perform it). Allâh Almighty says:

﴿ ثُمَّ أَمَاتَهُ فَأَقْبَرَهُ ﴾ (٢١)

Then He causes Him to die, and puts him in his grave.[1]

There are certain rulings regarding the Islamic burial:

1) The grave should be deep enough to prevent predators and birds from reaching the body and to prevent the odor of the body from harming those above the ground. The Prophet ﷺ said:

«احْفِرُوا وَأَعْمِقُوا وَأَحْسِنُوا وَأَدْفِنُوا الاثْنَيْنِ وَالثَّلَاثَةَ فِي قَبْرٍ وَاحِدٍ»

"Dig, dig deep, do it well, and bury two or three in one grave."

His Companions asked, "Who should we place first, O Messenger of Allâh ﷺ?" He said:

«قَدِّمُوا أَكْثَرَهُمْ قُرْآنًا»

"Give precedence to whoever from them had more of the Qur'an with him." (Recorded by At-Tirmithi who graded it *Sahih*)

No more than one body should be buried in a single grave except when necessary, such as when there are a lot of bodies (which happens very often after battles).

2) A hole in the side of the grave should be dug, though a hole in the middle of the grave is permitted; the latter is called a *Lahd*, while the former is called a *Shaqq*. The Prophet ﷺ said:

«اللَّحْدُ لَنَا وَالشَّقُّ لِغَيْرِنَا»

The *Lahd* is for us while the *Shaqq* is for others.

Recorded by Ahmad, Abu Dawud, and At-Tirmithi. In its chain is a disparaged narrator but some of the people of knowledge consider it *Sahih*.

3) Each person who is present for the burial should pour down dirt three times with his hands; he should throw the dirt into the grave from the side where the head of the deceased is, for that is what the Prophet ﷺ is described as having done as recorded by Ibn Majah with a chain that there is no harm in.

---

[1] (*Abasa* 80:21)

4) The corpse should be placed in the grave from the back, if possible; then he should be directed to face the *Qiblah* and placed on his right side. The knot of his shroud should be loosened, but his face should not be exposed. The person placing the corpse down says, "In the Name of Allâh, upon the way of the Messenger of Allâh ﷺ," for that is what the Prophet ﷺ said. (Recorded by Abu Dawud and Al-Hakim who graded it *Sahih*)

5) The woman's grave should be covered with some kind of a cloth while she is being placed in the grave and in the *Lahd*. Our pious predecessors would do that for women, but not for men.

Ninth: If one has not prayed over the deceased before the burial, it is legislated for him to pray over it after the burial, because the Prophet ﷺ did that; however, it must be performed within the period of a month. If the period is longer than that, then it is not legislated to pray over the grave, because it has not been reported that the Prophet ﷺ prayed over a grave when more than one month expired after the burial.

Tenth: It is not permissible for the relatives of the deceased to prepare food for others: the noble Companion, Jarir bin 'Abdullah Al-Bajali, may Allâh be pleased with him, said, "We used to consider gathering at the place of the deceased's relatives and the preparation of food after the burial as being a form of *Niyahah* (wailing)." (Recorded by Imam Ahmad with a *Hasan* chain)

While it is forbidden for the relatives of the deceased to prepare food for others, others may prepare food for them, especially in the case of relatives and neighbors, because it then becomes recommended. When the Prophet ﷺ heard about the death of Ja'far bin Abi Talib, may Allâh be pleased with him, in Syria, he ordered his family to prepare food for the family of Ja'far; he said:

«إِنَّهُ أَتَاهُمْ مَا يُشْغِلُهُمْ»

A matter has come to them that preoccupies them.

It is not wrong for the relatives of the deceased to invite neighbors or others to partake in the food that was given to them; we know of no time limit for that in the *Shari'ah*.

Eleventh: A woman is not allowed to mourn over the deceased for more than three days unless the deceased is her husband, in which case she must mourn for four months and ten days; but if she is pregnant, her mourning continues only until she delivers her baby. Both these rulings are based on the authentic Sunnah.

As for a man, he is not allowed to mourn at all, not for his relatives and not for anyone else.

Twelfth: It is legislated for men to visit graves every now and then, to supplicate for the deceased, to ask Allâh to have mercy on them, and to remember death and what comes after it. The Prophet ﷺ said:

«زُورُوا الْقُبُورَ فَإِنَّهَا تُذَكِّرُكُمُ الْآخِرَةَ»

Visit graves, for verily, doing so will remind you of the Hereafter. (Recorded by Imam Muslim in his *Sahih*)

The Prophet ﷺ taught his Companions to say when they visit the graves:

«السَّلَامُ عَلَيْكُمْ أَهْلَ الدِّيَارِ مِنَ الْمُؤْمِنِينَ وَالْمُسْلِمِينَ، وَإِنَّا إِنْ شَاءَ اللهُ بِكُمْ لَاحِقُونَ، نَسْأَلُ اللهَ لَنَا وَلَكُمُ الْعَافِيَةَ، يَرْحَمُ اللهُ الْمُسْتَقْدِمِينَ مِنَّا وَالْمُسْتَأْخِرِينَ»

Peace be upon you all, O inhabitants of the graves, among the believers and the Muslims. Verily we will, Allâh willing, be united with you, we ask Allâh for well-being for us and you. May Allâh have mercy on those that parted early from us and those that parted late.

As for women, it is not for them to visit graves, for the Prophet ﷺ cursed females who visit graves. Also, it is feared that by their visits, trials may result, not to mention their lack of patience. Similarly, they may not follow the funeral procession to the graveyard because the Prophet ﷺ forbade them from doing so. The funeral prayer, however, whether it is performed in the *Masjid* or anywhere else, is legislated for both men and women.

This is the last of what has been compiled here.

O Allâh, send prayers and salutations on Muhammad, his family, and his Companions.

 ❖ ❖ ❖

Study Questions

To make the book more beneficial and to allow for the material to sink into the minds of students, we have put together these questions, which may be used for competitions regarding the understanding of this book — if Allâh wills:

1) What should one do if, when as a youngster, he missed out on the opportunity of learning? And what is your obligation to those of your relatives and elders who missed that opportunity? How should you deal with them when you are teaching them, and who is your example in that regard?

2) What is the ruling for learning that which Allâh has made obligatory upon every Muslim, and how should one go about learning those matters?

3) Using a minimum of words, Rab'i bin 'Amir explained the task of the Messenger's mission and the duty for the Muslims after him. Discuss what Rab'i said to Rustum of Persia.

4) Islam is the final religion and it came to put matters in their proper place. Discuss this statement, clarifying the importance of the Messenger's mission.

5) Despite the merciless attack upon Islam, one sees that people are entering the fold of Islam in flocks. What is the reason for this phenomenon?

6) The questions regarding the *Tafseer* of the chapters studied follow one pattern:

    i) Read *Surah* [....]; recite it correctly, applying the rules of *Tajwid* (rules of reciting the Qur'an). Why is *Surah* [...] thus called? How does it relate to the chapter before it? What is its subject matter? Explain the meaning of the following words found in it: ...., ..., ..., ..., ...? And in what context or for what reason was the chapter revealed?

    ii) Without exceeding three lines, discuss its overall meaning. Then enumerate those benefits that we can derive from it?

7) What is the ruling regarding the *Isti'athah* and the *Basmalah* for the one who is praying? When does he read them? And what is the meaning of *Isti'athah*? Explain the meaning of Ar-Rahman and Ar-Rahim, clarifying the difference between the two. And

what is the wisdom behind the *Isti'athab?*

8) Enumerate the pillars of Islam, explaining the pillar "*Laa Ilaba Illallab*," its conditions, and its meaning.

9) What are the virtues of the two testimonies, and what is their status?

10) Define prayer. What is its ruling and what is the ruling regarding one who abandons it?

11) Discuss the significance of *Zakat*, fasting Ramadhan, and *Hajj* for the Muslim.

12) Define *Iman*, both according to its meaning in the Arabic language and its meaning in the *Shari'ab.*

13) Do deeds come under the heading of *Iman?* Support your answer with proof.

14) What are the false implications that result from taking deeds outside of the term *Iman?*

15) Our pious predecessors gave certain proofs which show that *Iman* increases and decreases — mention some of those proofs.

16) How do we infer from the following proofs the fact that *Iman* both increases and decreases:

i) The Prophet ﷺ said:

«الإِيمَانُ بِضْعٌ وَسَبْعُونَ شُعْبَةً أَعْلَاهَا قَوْلُ لَا إِلَهَ إِلَّا اللهُ وَأَدْنَاهَا إِمَاطَةُ الْأَذَى عَنِ الطَّرِيقِ وَالْحَيَاءُ شُعْبَةٌ مِنَ الْإِيمَانِ»

Iman consists of more then seventy branches; the highest of them is the saying, "*Laa Ilaba Illallah*" and the lowest of them is removing something harmful from the path; and modesty (*Haya'*) is one of the branches of *Iman.*

ii) The Prophet ﷺ said:

«مَنْ رَأَى مِنْكُمْ مُنْكَرًا فَلْيُغَيِّرْهُ بِيَدِهِ . . . الحديث»

Whoever from you sees an evil, let him change it with his hand...

17) In what matter does the religion come together? Support your answer with proof.

18) What is the meaning of Islam? Support your answer with proof.

19) When do "*Iman*" and "Islam" have one meaning? And when are their meanings different from one another?

20) What is the meaning of *Iman*? Support your answer with proof.

21) Can we designate the term *Iman* for outwardly performed deeds, and how so?

22) When does one complete the *Iman* and Islam that are obligatory upon him?

23) What do we mean by the "branches" in "the branches of *Iman*"? What is the difference between the branches of *Iman* and its pillars?

24) Are the pillars of *Iman* and its branches at one level in terms of belief and action?

25) Can the qualities of *Iman* and hypocrisy be combined in one person?

26) Give one proof to show that rejecting *Ar-Rububiyyah* negates one's faith?

27) What is the difference between rejecting *Ar-Rububiyyah* and rejecting the fact that Allâh deserves worship?

28) What is the ruling regarding taking intermediaries or intercessors in the worship of Allâh?

29) Is it correct to seek judgement from other than Allâh's *Shari'ah*? Support your answer with proof.

30) Clarify the ruling regarding the following matters, supporting your answer with proof.

    i) Mocking Allâh, the Qur'an, or His Messenger — even if one does so in a joking manner.

    ii) Believing that a specific person may go outside of the boundaries of Muhammad's guidance.

    iii) Believing that some people are exempt from all or some religious duties.

31) Give examples of those deeds that nullify *Iman*.

32) Define both the major and the minor sin, giving an example for each. And support your answer with proof.

33) What is the view of the People of Sunnah regarding one who

perpetrates a major sin?

34) What is a sin? And when does a sin cause one to exit from the religion?

35) What effect does a sin have on one's faith?

36) Why did the wife of Fir'awn disdain those worldly pleasures she had? And why did she invoke Allâh to save her from Fir'awn and his deeds?

37) In what way does faith in the Unseen cause love to flourish in society?

38) What are the implications of having faith in Allâh?

39) What does *Tawhid Ar-Rububiyyah* mean? And how does it differ from *Tawhid Al-Uluhiyyah*?

40) Has anyone from previous nations rejected *Tawhid Ar-Rububiyyah*? Clarify.

41) What does it mean to have *Iman* in Allâh's Names and Attributes?

42) What are the angels? What was the belief of the people of ignorance regarding them?

43) What is the ruling regarding belief in the angels? Support your answer with proof.

44) *Iman* in the angels comprises of certain matters — mention them.

45) Mention some of the tasks of specific angels — giving one proof for each task.

46) What is the relation of angels with:
   i) Mankind.
   ii) The believers.
   iii) The disbelievers.

47) There are many fruits that are reaped by having *Iman* in the angels; mention some of them.

48) What is the meaning of *Kutub* in the Arabic language? And as a term in the *Shari'ah*?

49) What is the ruling regarding *Iman* in the Books that Allâh sent down to His Messengers? Support your answer by giving one

proof.

50) What are the matters that come under *Iman* in the Books?

51) Mention a few proofs that point to the distortion that occurred in the Tawrah and the Injil?

52) The Books that the Jews and Christians possess today cannot be correctly ascribed to Allâh. Mention those proofs that confirm this statement. One of those proofs is a clear verse from the Qur'an.

53) What is the meaning of Qur'an in the Arabic language? And in the *Shari'ah*? What does it mean to have *Iman* in the Qur'an?

54) What do we mean when we say that the Qur'an is Allâh's Speech? Support your answer with proof.

55) Why did Allâh guarantee to preserve the Noble Qur'an as opposed to the previously revealed Books? And what do we mean when we say that Allâh guarantees to preserve the Qur'an?

56) Define *Nabi* (Prophet) according to its meaning in the Arabic language, and why is a Prophet called a *Nabi*?

57) What is the difference between a *Nabi* (Prophet) and a *Rasul* (Messenger)?

58) Is the status of Prophethood achieved through human efforts? What do we mean when we say that Prophethood is a divine gift from Allâh? Support your answer with proof.

59) Discuss some qualities of the Messengers, supporting your answer with proof.

60) What is the ruling on one having *Iman* in only some of the Messengers? And who is the best of the Messengers?

61) Is it obligatory to have *Iman* in those Prophets that weren't mentioned in the Qur'an?

62) What are the implications of having *Iman* in Muhammad ﷺ?

63) Mention proofs that point to the finality of Prophethood, and that Muhammad ﷺ is the final Prophet and Messenger.

64) What does *Iman* in the Hereafter signify?

65) The Messenger of Allâh ﷺ informed us of some events that will take place after death — mention some of them.

66) Explain how we affirm *Iman* in the Last Day in light of the following proofs:

a) The Statement of Allâh:

﴿إِنَّ ٱلَّذِينَ ءَامَنُوا۟ وَٱلَّذِينَ هَادُوا۟ وَٱلنَّصَٰرَىٰ وَٱلصَّٰبِـِٔينَ مَنْ ءَامَنَ بِٱللَّهِ وَٱلْيَوْمِ ٱلْءَاخِرِ وَعَمِلَ صَٰلِحًا فَلَهُمْ أَجْرُهُمْ عِندَ رَبِّهِمْ﴾

Verily, those who believe and those who are Christians and Jews, and Sabians, whoever believes in Allâh and the last Day and do righteous good deeds shall have their reward with their Lord.[1]

b) And:

﴿لَّيْسَ ٱلْبِرَّ أَن تُوَلُّوا۟ وُجُوهَكُمْ قِبَلَ ٱلْمَشْرِقِ وَٱلْمَغْرِبِ وَلَٰكِنَّ ٱلْبِرَّ مَنْ ءَامَنَ بِٱللَّهِ وَٱلْيَوْمِ ٱلْءَاخِرِ وَٱلْمَلَٰٓئِكَةِ وَٱلْكِتَٰبِ وَٱلنَّبِيِّۦنَ وَءَاتَى ٱلْمَالَ عَلَىٰ حُبِّهِۦ ذَوِى ٱلْقُرْبَىٰ وَٱلْيَتَٰمَىٰ وَٱلْمَسَٰكِينَ وَٱبْنَ ٱلسَّبِيلِ وَٱلسَّآئِلِينَ وَفِى ٱلرِّقَابِ﴾

It is not *Al-Birr* (piety, righteousness, and each and every act of obedience to Allâh, etc.) that you turn your faces towards east and (or) west (in prayers); but *Al-Birr* is (the quality of) the one who believes in Allâh, the Last Day, the Angels, the Book, the Prophets and gives his wealth, in spite of love for it, to the kinsfolk, to the orphans, and to *Al-Masakin* (the poor), and to the wayfarer, and to those who ask, and to set slaves free...[2]

c) And:

﴿ثُمَّ إِنَّكُمْ يَوْمَ ٱلْقِيَٰمَةِ تُبْعَثُونَ ۝﴾

Then (again), surely, you will be resurrected on the Day of Resurrection.[3]

d) When the Prophet ﷺ was asked about *Iman*, he ﷺ said:

«أَنْ تُؤْمِنَ بِاللهِ وَمَلَائِكَتِهِ وَكُتُبِهِ وَرُسُلِهِ وَالْيَوْمِ الْآخِرِ وَتُؤْمِنَ بِالْقَدَرِ خَيْرِهِ وَشَرِّهِ»

---

[1] (*Al-Baqarah* 2:62)
[2] (*Al-Baqarah* 2:177)
[3] (*Al-Mu'minun* 23:16)

To believe in Allâh, in His Angels, in His Books, in the Last Day, and to believe in Divine Preordainment (*Al-Qadar*), both the good and bad of it.

67) What is the ruling regarding *Iman* in the questioning of the two angels, and in the bliss and punishment of the grave? Mention proofs along with your answer.

68) What are the proofs that establish the coming of the Hour? Does anyone know when the Hour will come? Support your answer with proofs.

69) What is the difference between the greater signs of the Day of Judgement and the smaller signs? Give an example for each.

70) What does the Trumpet refer to? What are the results that will occur when it is blown into?

71) What does the Resurrection mean? What is the ruling for having *Iman* in it? Give proofs to support your answer.

72) What stance do the polytheists take regarding *Iman* in the Resurrection?

73) Refute those who reject the Resurrection, giving proof from the *Shari'ah*, as well as material and rational proof. Explain how those proofs refute their belief?

74) What is the *Hawdh*? What are the proofs that establish it?

75) Mention some of the qualities of the *Hawdh*.

76) Define the *Mizan* (Scale of deeds). Is it real? Support your answer with proof.

77) What is the *Sirat*? Does anyone enter Paradise without having to cross over it? Support your answer with proof.

78) Mention certain proofs that establish the *Sirat* and its qualities.

79) What is the *Shafa'ah*? What are its conditions? What prevents it from occurring?

80) Can people seek intercession from other than Allâh? Support your answer with proof.

81) What are the different kinds of *Shafa'ah*? What kind is specific to the Prophet ﷺ?

82) What is meant by Paradise and Hell? Are they created? Support your answer with proof.

83) Where are Paradise and Hell located? Will they cease to exist one day? Support your answer with proof.

84) Who are the dwellers of Paradise, and who are dwellers of the Hellfire?

85) What does *Al-Qadar* mean? What does *Iman* in *Al-Qadar* mean? What is your proof?

86) What do we mean when we say that evil is not ascribed to Allâh Almighty?

87) How many levels of *Iman* in *Al-Qadar* are there? List the levels, giving proof for each.

88) What benefit lies in the prohibition of delving into the topic of *Al-Qadar*?

89) What is the belief of our pious predecessors regarding Divine Preordainment? Support your answer with proof.

90) Some may use *Al-Qadar* to argue that it is okay to leave Allâh's Commands and Orders. What is the ruling regarding this view? Support your answer with proof.

91) Some people refer to *Al-Qadar* when they are afflicted with a hardship. What is the ruling regarding this practice and why? And what is your proof?

92) How does man differ from all other animals?

93) What is the purpose behind man being created? And what path has been laid out for him?

94) How is *Iman* considered to be life for the heart?

95) Why does *Iman* lead to peace and tranquility?

96) What effects does *Iman* in *Al-Qadar* and in recompense have on the individual and society?

97) Mention some of the effects of *Iman* in the life of the individual and society.

98) Discuss the different kinds of *Shirk* that the author mentioned, and clarify the ruling on the following:

   i) Magic

   ii) *Ar-Ruqya* and *At-Tama'im*

   iii) *Ar-Riya'*

99) How many conditions are there for the prayer? Clarify the pillars and obligatory components of the prayer.

100) List some of the Sunnah actions and sayings of prayer.

101) Briefly outline those actions that render one's prayer void.

102) Clarify the obligatory actions of ablution, mentioning a proof for each action. And list the different ways in which one's ablution is nullified.

103) List the seven grave (or deadly) sins that the Prophet ﷺ mentioned in a well-known *Hadith*.

104) List some of the manners and characteristics that Islam legislated for the Muslim. Discuss how a Muslim must apply those characteristics.

105) Discuss the funeral prayer, considering the following points:

i) What one should do when visiting a sick person who is going through the pangs of death?

ii) The ruling of writing a final testament for a sick person.

iii) How to wash the dead.

iv) How to enshroud the dead, both when the deceased is male or female.

v) The ruling of praying over the deceased and how to perform the prayer.

vi) Who should wash the dead? What if the deceased is male and dies among a group comprised purely of females, and what about the opposite?

vii) What is the ruling for the *Lahd*? How should one supplicate for the dead?

❖ ❖ ❖